Catholicism and the Roots of Nazism

CATHOLICISM *and the* ROOTS *of* NAZISM

Religious Identity and National Socialism

Derek Hastings

OXFORD
UNIVERSITY PRESS

2010

OXFORD
UNIVERSITY PRESS

Oxford University Press, Inc., publishes works that further
Oxford University's objective of excellence
in research, scholarship, and education.

Oxford   New York
Auckland   Cape Town   Dar es Salaam   Hong Kong   Karachi
Kuala Lumpur   Madrid   Melbourne   Mexico City   Nairobi
New Delhi   Shanghai   Taipei   Toronto

With offices in

Argentina   Austria   Brazil   Chile   Czech Republic   France   Greece
Guatemala   Hungary   Italy   Japan   Poland   Portugal   Singapore
South Korea   Switzerland   Thailand   Turkey   Ukraine   Vietnam

Published by Oxford University Press, Inc.
198 Madison Avenue, New York, New York 10016

www.oup.com

Oxford is a registered trademark of Oxford University Press.

Library of Congress Cataloging-in-Publication Data
Hastings, Derek (Derek Keith)
Catholicism and the roots of Nazism : religious identity and national socialism /
Derek Hastings.
p. cm.
Includes bibliographical references and index.
ISBN 978-0-19-539024-7
1. National socialism—Religious aspects.   2. National socialism and religion.
3. Catholic Church—Germany—History—20th century.   4. Christianity and
politics—Germany—History—20th century.   5. Germany—History—1918–1933.
I. Title.
DD256.5.H3253 2009
335.60943'09042—dc22   2009018926

1 3 5 7 9 8 6 4 2
Printed in the United States of America
on acid-free paper

For Kris, Erica, and Sara

Acknowledgments

This book could not have been written without the support of numerous individuals and institutions. My mentors at the University of Chicago—particularly John W. Boyer, Michael Geyer, and Leora Auslander—provided both inspiration and guidance, and I owe them a tremendous debt of gratitude. As an undergraduate student at Stony Brook University, I benefited greatly from the advice of Young-Sun Hong, Paul Chase, and Richard Kuisel. Numerous scholars have provided insightful comments and suggestions at various stages of this project's development, including drafts presented at conferences and workshops, and I am pleased to acknowledge their invaluable assistance here (in alphabetical order): Jim Bjork, Suzanne Brown-Fleming, Roger Chickering, John Conway, John Deak, Geoff Eley, David Ellis, Thomas Forstner, Martin Geyer, Beth Griech-Polelle, Michael Gross, Jonathan Gumz, Dagmar Herzog, Robert Hogg, Larry Eugene Jones, Hartmut Lehmann, Reinhold Lenski, Wolfgang Löhr, Sean Moran, Michael Phayer, Ronald Ross, Mark Ruff, Jonathan Sperber, Kevin Spicer, Richard Steigmann-Gall, Anthony Steinhoff, Raymond Sun, Dirk van Laak, Till van Rahden, Christoph Weber, Siegfried Weichlein, Richard Weikart, Manfred Weitlauff, Jeff Zalar, and Lisa (Swartout) Zwicker. At Oxford University Press, Susan Ferber and Jane Slusser have been absolutely wonderful to work with. I appreciate not only their editorial skill and efficiency, but also their support and enthusiasm for this project. My thanks also go to the anonymous reviewers at Oxford for their helpful and timely feedback.

I am grateful for the research aid provided by staff members of the University of Chicago's Regenstein Library (interlibrary loan), Oakland University's Kresge Library (interlibrary loan), the University of Michigan's Hatcher Graduate Library, and the National Archives and Records

Administration in College Park, Maryland. I am also appreciative of the assistance given by staff at the following institutions in Germany: Bayerische Staatsbibliothek, Institut für Zeitgeschichte, Bayerisches Hauptstaatsarchiv, Staatsarchiv München, Stadtarchiv München, Archiv des Erzbistums München und Freising, Universitätsarchiv München, Abtei Königsmünster, St. Anna-Archiv (Munich), Archiv des Bistums Augsburg, Stadtarchiv Augsburg, Archiv des Erzbistums Regensburg (CV-Archiv), Stadtarchiv Bobingen, Stadtarchiv Passau, Stadtarchiv Mönchengladbach (KV-Archiv), and the Institut für Hochschulkunde in Würzburg.

My colleagues and friends in the Department of History at Oakland University have provided encouragement and a stimulating intellectual environment. Special thanks go to my current and past department chairs, Karen Miller and Carl Osthaus, for their support. I also gratefully acknowledge the generous financial assistance this project received from the Deutsche Akademische Austauschdienst, the German Historical Institute, the University of Chicago, and the Oakland University Faculty Research Committee.

Finally, I owe an immeasurable debt to my family. My love of books and learning began at a very early age thanks to my parents, Sam and Judy Hastings, and I am sincerely grateful for their encouragement over the years, as well as that given by my sister, Paula, and brother, Ryan. Most important, my wife, Kris, and our daughters, Erica and Sara, have enriched my life in ways I still find difficult to express fully. This book is dedicated to them with deepest appreciation for the constant inspiration and joy they've given me.

Contents

Abbreviations

ABA	Archiv des Bistums Augsburg
AEMF	Archiv des Erzbistums München und Freising
AGD	*Auf gut deutsch*
AHR	*American Historical Review*
AK	Abtei Königsmünster
APZ	*Augsburger Postzeitung*
AR	*Allgemeine Rundschau*
ASTA	Allgemeine Studentenausschuss
AUR	Antiultramontaner Reichsverband
AVM	Antisemitische Volkspartei München
AZ	*Allgemeine Zeitung*
BAK	*Beiträge zur altbayerischen Kirchengeschichte*
BAVP	Bayerische antisemitische Volkspartei
BBKL	*Biographisch-bibliographisches Kirchenlexikon*
BdB	Bund der Beobachterfreunde
BDC	Berlin Document Center
BHSA	Bayerisches Hauptstaats-Archiv
BHZ	*Bayerische Hochschulzeitung*
BK	*Bayerischer Kurier*
BKB	*Bayerischer Königsbote*
BKP	Bayerische Königspartei
BSB	Bayerische Staatsbibliothek
BTB	Brieftagebuch
BV	*Das Bayerische Vaterland*
BVC	*Bayerische Volkspartei Correspondenz*
BVP	Bayerische Volkspartei
BVZ	*Bayerische Volkszeitung*
CEH	*Central European History*
CHR	*Catholic Historical Review*
CSV	Christlich-Sozialer Verein
CSU	Christian Social Union

CV	Cartellverband der katholischen deutschen Studentenverbindungen
DAP	Deutsche Arbeiterpartei
DG	*Der Deutsche Geist*
DHF	*Das Heilige Feuer*
DKZ	*Deutsche Katholikenzeitung*
DNVP	Deutschnationale Volkspartei
DSAP	Deutsch-Soziale antisemitische Partei
DSP	Deutsch-Sozialistische Partei
DSV	Deutsch-Sozialer Verein
DV	*Deutsches Volksblatt*
DVST	Deutsch-völkischer Schutz- und Trutzbund
EHQ	*European History Quarterly*
EHR	*English Historical Review*
GG	*Geschichte und Gesellschaft*
GH	*Gelbe Hefte*
GSR	*German Studies Review*
GZ	*Grossdeutsche Zeitung*
HDA	Hochschulring deutscher Art
HGS	*Holocaust and Genocide Studies*
HJ	*Historisches Jahrbuch*
HPB	*Historisch-politische Blätter*
HV	Hochland-Verband
HZ	*Historische Zeitschrift*
IDR	*Im Deutschen Reich*
JCH	*Journal of Contemporary History*
JMH	*Journal of Modern History*
KG	Krausgesellschaft
KV	Kartellverband katholischer deutscher Studentenvereine
KVZ	*Kölnische Volkszeitung*
LA	*Legauer Anzeiger*
LZ	*Landshuter Zeitung*
MA	*Miesbacher Anzeiger*
MAA	*Münchener-Augsburger Abendzeitung*
MAZ	*Münchener Allgemeine Zeitung*
MB	*Münchener Beobachter*
MCSZ	*Münchener christlich-soziale Zeitung*
MFP	*Münchener Freie Presse*
MKK	*Münchener Katholische Kirchenzeitung*
MNN	*Münchener Neueste Nachrichten*
MP	*Münchener Post*
MZ	*Münchener Zeitung*
NBZ	*Neue Bayerische Zeitung*
NJ	*Das Neue Jahrhundert*
NL	Nachlass

NMT	*Neues Münchener Tagblatt*
NS	*Der Nationalsozialist*
NSDAP	Nationalsozialistische Deutsche Arbeiterpartei
PD	Polizeidirektion
PNP	*Passauer Neue Presse*
Ren	*Renaissance*
SA	Sturmabteilung
SAM	Staatsarchiv München
SdZ	*Stimmen der Zeit*
SM	*Süddeutsche Monatshefte*
SPD	Sozialdemokratische Partei Deutschlands
SS	Schutzstaffel
StAP	Stadtarchiv Passau
StK	Staatskanzlei
SZ	*Süddeutsche Zeitung*
SZM	Sozialstudentische Zentrale München
TMPR	*Totalitarian Movements and Political Religions*
TQ	*Theologische Quartalschrift*
TTB	*Traunsteiner Tagblatt*
UAM	Universitätsarchiv, München
UV	*Unser Vaterland*
VB	*Völkischer Beobachter*
VfZ	*Vierteljahrshefte für Zeitgeschichte*
ZBL	*Zeitschrift für bayerische Landesgeschichte*
ZHDS	*Zeitschrift des Hilfsvereins für Deutschböhmen und die Sudetenländer*
20Jh	*Das zwanzigste Jahrhundert*

Note on Translation and Usage

The term *völkisch,* which connotes a radical nationalist and racist orientation, has no effective equivalent in English and has been left in the German original throughout. I have translated the term *Volk* as "people" or "race," depending on the context; when *Volk* is used alongside the more straightforward term *Rasse* ("race"), I have typically provided both German terms for clarity's sake. When discussing the Nazis' primary organ, I usually make reference to the *Beobachter,* rather than to the more complete *Münchener Beobachter* (the paper's name through December 1919) or *Völkischer Beobachter* (the name adopted in January 1920 and continued after the paper became the official and exclusive organ of the NSDAP in December 1920). Similarly, when discussing one of the central Reform Catholic publications in prewar Munich, I typically refer to the *Jahrhundert,* rather than to the more complete titles *Das 20. Jahrhundert* (in use 1902–1908) and *Das Neue Jahrhundert* (used from 1909 on). The term *Kampfchristentum,* which literally means "battle Christianity," has been translated in several cases as "warrior Christianity" for the sake of clarity, and I have chosen to render ther term *christliche Nächstenliebe* as "Christian charity" in most contexts. Finally, when translating the term *Pfarrer,* I refer most often to Catholic clergy as "priests" and to Protestant clergy as "pastors." In certain cases where the translation or usage seems either unclear or idiosyncratic, the German original is provided.

Catholicism and the Roots of Nazism

Introduction

It is certain that a belief is greatly strengthened when . . . it appears in a form that veils its origins from the eye.

—Novalis, *Das allgemeine Brouillon* (1799)

In the fall of 1933, a cheaply printed book bearing a rather singular inscription arrived at Nazi party headquarters in Munich, where it lay unceremoniously buried until eventually making its way into the Third Reich Collection housed in the Library of Congress in Washington, D.C. The book, *Das kommende Reich* (The Coming Reich), had been hastily reissued earlier that year by an obscure publisher in the Bavarian village of Niederalteich, but had originally appeared, to considerably greater fanfare, during the November 1918 revolution in Munich. Its author, the popular Bavarian Catholic writer Franz Schrönghamer-Heimdal, laid out a programmatic blueprint for the ecumenical yet distinctly Catholic-oriented spiritual rebuilding of Germany, and he contrasted the purity of Christ and his "true" followers with the perceived immorality of the "Jewish-capitalistic" spirit in tones full of bombast and revivalistic urgency. The coming Germanic reich—which Schrönghamer believed would rise triumphantly from the rubble of the decimated Kaiserreich—was to be built upon the unwavering rule of God's "divine justice," the purified product of an epic apocalyptic struggle between the two most powerful world forces, between "Christ and Antichrist, between the eternal German and the eternal Jew." Every aspect of the economy and society was to be radically refashioned to reflect the nobility of productive labor and the unhealthiness of modern capitalism, with the Catholic Church's medieval prohibition on charging interest being revived and coordinated with a wide-ranging nationalization of German agriculture and heavy industry. While Schrönghamer made no secret of his deeply held Catholic convictions, the coming Reich he envisioned was to be explicitly interconfessional, a reiteration of the unforgettable yet ulti-mately fleeting unity of the summer of 1914 in which Germans of both

Christian confessions would be forever bonded together in a harmonious "racial community [*Volksgemeinschaft*] of the same blood, the same law, and the same morals," a community of fate that would be maintained through "race-based eugenic measures" and the "most energetic elimination of all non-Aryan influences" (*strengster Ausschluss aller nichtarischen Einflüsse*).[1] The radicalism and all-encompassing scope of Schrönghamer's religio-racial vision was impressive indeed, particularly in its original 1918 context.

Schrönghamer's inscription in the copy sent to Nazi party headquarters in 1933 was perhaps even more striking than the book's contents. Claiming that his work not only had played an indispensable role in the founding and early history of the Nazi movement but had also fundamentally shaped the formulation of the Nazi party program, including its advocacy of the principle of Positive Christianity, Schrönghamer wrote:

> This book, which first appeared during the 1918 revolution, inspired the birth of the *völkisch* movement and the NSDAP [*stand Pate an der Wiege der völkischen Bewegung und der NSDAP*]. It contained already, in its entirety, the program of the NSDAP that was made public two years later and, for this reason, was publicized within party membership circles as one of the works "every National Socialist had to know."[2]

With countless nationalistic Germans having jumped on the Nazi bandwagon since the Reichstag elections in March 1933, one is tempted to dismiss Schrönghamer's claims as merely the ravings of a delusional opportunist. If Schrönghamer had actually been such a central figure in the early Nazi movement, why would he be forced to remind the party leadership of that fact in such a nakedly self-serving manner more than a decade later? Why was such an allegedly significant book reissued so inauspiciously by such an obscure publisher? And why was it subsequently held in such low esteem as to be completely ignored by the party leadership not only in 1933 but throughout the duration of the Third Reich? On the other hand, if this was merely a clumsy and exaggerated attempt at self-aggrandizement and nothing more, why would Schrönghamer choose to make such baseless claims directly to the offices of the Nazi leadership, where they could easily be checked for veracity and dismissed?

As it turns out, there was at the very least a kernel of truth in Schrönghamer's inscription, however overblown his ego undoubtedly was. Schrönghamer had in fact joined the Nazi party officially on 4 February 1920—when it was still known as the Deutsche Arbeiterpartei and its entire membership could still be accommodated in the small side room of a Munich beerhall—as the party's 222nd member, only a few months after Hitler (who was the 55th member) and less than three weeks before the famous unveiling of the party program known as the 25 Points.[3] Perhaps more important, by February 1920 Schrönghamer was without question the single most visible figure in the pages of the *Völkischer Beobachter* and had been so throughout much of the previous year, when the paper served as the unofficial organ of the young *völkisch*-Nazi movement (it became the official and exclusive organ of the Nazi party in late 1920). In addition to the dozens of major *Beobachter* articles written by Schrönghamer, both in his own name and under pseudonyms such as Widar Wälsung, the original edition of *Das kommende Reich* was marketed endlessly in the pages of the paper throughout 1919 and 1920, with Dietrich Eckart, a close friend of Schrönghamer who served also as an early intellectual father figure to Hitler, providing gushing praise for the book. Additionally, two of Schrönghamer's other flamingly anti-Semitic writings—*Vom Antichrist* and *Judas, der Weltfeind,* published in late 1918 and mid-1919, respectively—were clearly among the most significant and widely discussed works in Munich at the outset of the Nazi movement. Schrönghamer also exercised a powerful influence over a large number of racist Catholic activists who themselves played important, if subsequently overlooked, roles in the early development and spread of the movement in and around Munich. What happened to make Schrönghamer and his work so thoroughly marginalized among the Nazi leadership by 1933 and so completely forgotten thereafter?

The unceremonious burial of Schrönghamer's programmatic *völkisch*-Catholic vision was due, perhaps more than anything else, to the sharp discrepancy that exists between the nature of the Nazi regime in power in the 1930s and 1940s and that of the early Nazi movement in Munich in the immediate aftermath of the First World War. Despite the occasional maintenance of a conciliatory facade, there is little question that the Nazi party exhibited a broad antipathy toward the Catholic Church—and, in many ways, toward Christianity more generally—for most of the duration of the Third Reich.[4] Numerous historians have argued compellingly that Nazism after 1933 should best be interpreted as a type of political religion, as an all-encompassing rival form of secular devotion that strove to supplant, and was therefore largely incompatible with, more "authentic" forms of Catholic or Christian identity. In 1933 and in the years that followed, then, it is perhaps not surprising that the Nazi regime was interested in peddling its own highly idealized version of the party's earliest years, which excluded not only Schrönghamer, who was by then the editor of a small Catholic Sunday paper near Passau, but also most of the other Catholic racist activists who had, in fact, done much to shape the young movement's identity more than a decade earlier. As indicated in the quote from Novalis that opened this chapter, ideological movements often enhance their power by veiling their origins, and this unquestionably applies to the actions of the Nazi party in representing its own past.[5]

This book strives to demonstrate that the totalizing secular messianism and pseudo-sacral pageantry that characterized the Nazi aesthetic during the Third Reich had an important and colorful prehistory that the Nazis felt compelled to efface once in power. Between 1919 and late 1923, believing Catholics and their ideals played a central, and hitherto overlooked, role in the development of the Nazi movement in and around Munich, before events associated with the 1923 Beerhall Putsch and its chaotic aftermath dramatically changed the movement's nature and composition. This early Catholic orientation—informal yet palpable—was central to the party's ability to transcend its initial structure as a semi-secretive discussion club and to establish a broader appeal and an early political foothold in the overwhelmingly Catholic context of Munich. This enabled the movement to survive its infancy by differentiating itself from other *völkisch* entities with visibly divergent orientations, whether Protestant-inflected or occult-based. This book also delineates the processes whereby the Nazi movement, after its refounding in early 1925, embarked on a vastly different trajectory that ultimately culminated in the highly stylized form of political religion, with its secular-liturgical symbolism and powerful participatory aesthetic, that so strikingly characterized the Third Reich and at the same time left so little room for the simpler and more straightforward Catholic orientation at the heart of the early Nazi movement.

Seen in retrospect, Schrönghamer's striking Catholic-*völkisch* activism in the aftermath of the First World War was but the proverbial tip of an iceberg that was itself ultimately submerged beneath the waves of the all-encompassing messianic party mythology cultivated by the Nazi regime once in power. After 1945, figures like Schrönghamer had rather obvious reasons for downplaying their *völkisch*-Nazi activities in the early 1920s, further ensuring that this aspect of early Nazi history would remain largely submerged.[6] Subsequent scholars have tended to interpret the religious identity of the early movement through the lens of the undeniably oppressive nature of Nazi religious policies toward the Catholic

Church after 1933, assuming that the early Nazi movement must have been equally anti-Catholic from the outset. An examination of the young movement's earliest years, when its ideology was still fairly fluid and its constituency was limited primarily to Munich and its upper Bavarian environs, reveals a significantly different story.

Numerous important studies have been devoted to illuminating the so-called roots of National Socialism, primarily within the realm of broader intellectual and cultural currents. During the life of the Third Reich, such historians as Hans Kohn and Rohan Butler attempted to locate the longer-term roots of Nazism in a potent mixture of nihilism and fuzzy mysticism, whereas the classic studies of George Mosse and Fritz Stern have sketched the contours of a disastrous "German ideology" whose murky origins were located in equal measure in romanticized racism and widespread cultural pessimism.[7] Other less iconic approaches to the intellectual origins of Nazism have focused on a variety of perspectives ranging from the spread of Darwinian ideas to the impact of esoteric occult theories.[8] Over the decades, a long line of social scientists, many of them illustrious scholars, have attempted to lend sociological insight and theoretical nuance to the question of the social and structural origins of National Socialism.[9] Despite the obvious significance of the broader question of Nazi origins, there is a relative lack of monographic studies on the immediate and specifically local roots of the Nazi movement itself.

In contrast to the veritable mountain of scholarly literature on virtually every aspect of the Third Reich, its leadership, and its murderous policies, the earliest years of the Nazi movement in Munich have received startlingly little direct treatment. The most thorough studies of the period between the party's initial founding in January 1919 and its reconstitution in the mid-1920s are now themselves nearly historical artifacts.[10] The standard histories of Nazism and the Nazi party contain chapters encapsulating the party's origins and earliest years, but even in the best of these accounts the early material is typically treated as a mere prelude to the more significant developments that unfolded after 1933.[11] The classic biographical treatments of Hitler have shed important light on the Munich-based environment surrounding the Nazi leader in his early political career but have done so primarily through the lens of Hitler's person, experiences, and acquaintances, which illuminate significant aspects of the party's early leadership and propagandistic appeal but obfuscate a variety of other issues related to the movement's immediate social and cultural context.[12] There are also a number of effective narrower studies that have examined individual organizations associated with the early Nazi movement and the Nazi organizational structure itself.[13] Interestingly, while regional studies on the rise of Nazism have provided a variety of important insights into the Nazis' mobilization strategies and their ability to infiltrate existing local structures elsewhere in Germany, much of the material related to the earliest (pre-1923) years of the movement in its birthplace, Munich, remains distinctly under-illuminated.[14]

The paucity of scholarly investigations into the religious identity of the early Nazi movement and its members stems in part from the lack of a straightforward and easily quantifiable source base. While several surviving membership lists from the party's earliest years—containing members' names, addresses, ages, and occupations—have shed light on the social and demographic composition of the early Nazi movement, none of the surviving lists provides data on religious affiliation.[15] The rich holdings on the NSDAP membership contained in the microfilmed materials of the Berlin Document Center (BDC) also do not fully illuminate the confessional identities of members in the early movement. There are a number of early records in the BDC files for members who went on to become major Nazi figures after 1933, and the present work makes as much use of these files as possible, but there are virtually no such records for the large and important group of pre-1923 members, such as Franz Schrönghamer-Heimdal, who chose not to join the refounded party in 1925.[16] As a result, it is unlikely that a thorough quantitative or statistically based account of the movement's early confessional makeup will ever emerge. Even if it were possible to establish an exact percentage of early Nazi members at a specific date who came from Catholic backgrounds, that in itself would not shed much light on the gradations of individual religious identity in practice, which could range from indifference to fervor. Of necessity, then, the approach of this book is more qualitative than quantitative, and I utilize a variety of archival and printed sources to explore the ways in which the young Nazi movement specifically framed itself as, and was widely perceived to be, intricately intertwined with Catholic identity in Munich. It is not so much an examination of Catholicism per se, or of the Catholic Church as an institution, but of the role played by individual Catholics—both clergy and laity—within the Nazi movement in its earliest years.

Due to a tendency to project backward onto the early 1920s the undeniable antagonism that existed between the Catholic Church and the Nazi regime in power in the 1930s and 1940s, scholars have typically assumed that the early Nazi movement must have been composed of bitter apostates and opponents of Christianity or that its support must have been drawn from Munich's small but vocal (and, in any case, largely secularized) Protestant minority. According to Guenter Lewy, for instance, "in the early twenties the Hitler movement was small in numbers and Catholic membership within it smaller still."[17] Björn Mensing has noted quite simply that "it seems that the majority of Hitler's early supporters in Munich were Protestant."[18] While not attempting to overturn completely the basic image of Catholic-Nazi antagonism—which is accurate in many ways for the 1930s and 1940s—the present work strives to demonstrate that this antipathy was neither universal nor inevitable.

From the earliest stages of the Third Reich, the seemingly clear-cut oppression of the so-called church struggle (*Kirchenkampf*) dominated accounts written by émigré theologians and, especially, American and British commentators, with Hitler playing the demonic starring role and party theoretician Alfred Rosenberg supplying the satanic ideological script from behind the scenes.[19] In the immediate aftermath of the Nazi collapse, Catholic figures in Germany were especially quick to establish the image of a fundamental and unequivocal opposition between Catholic and Nazi identities. Church officials such as Johannes Neuhäusler, auxiliary bishop of the archdiocese of Munich-Freising, and Konrad Preysing, bishop of Berlin, contributed greatly to the sense that the Catholic Church not only had been a central victim of the Nazi regime but had also been fundamentally and consistently opposed to Nazi anti-Semitism.[20] Beginning in the 1960s, this image was strengthened by the increased activism of a large and energetic Catholic scholarly community in Germany, whose works have continued to stress the heroic oppositional stance and victimhood of the Catholic Church during the Third Reich.[21] The 1960s and 1970s also witnessed the beginning of a critical dialogue regarding the relationship between Catholicism and Nazism, as scholars subjected to greater scrutiny the behavior and specific responses of Catholic opinion leaders, the German episcopate, and the Vatican toward the Nazi regime.[22] By the 1980s and 1990s, individual German scholars like Georg Denzler and Richard Faber were raising deeply troubling questions about the actions of individual Catholics and church leaders during the Third Reich, but in a general sense, at least, the image of a basic and fundamental opposition between Catholicism and Nazism remained essentially intact.[23]

In recent years, the veritable explosion of works, particularly in English, on the relationship between the Catholic Church and Nazi Germany has been dominated in large part by the question of Holocaust guilt, often in highly sensationalized form. Daniel

Goldhagen's inflammatory and heavily publicized work linking the Holocaust to perceived Catholic complicity and the long trajectory of Catholic anti-Judaism is part of the broader literature connected to the so-called Pius Wars over the actions and attitudes of Pius XII and the church hierarchy during the Holocaust.[24] More nuanced studies by such scholars as Beth Griech-Polelle and Kevin Spicer have illuminated important aspects of the complex and conflicted choices that faced individual German bishops, priests, and theologians during the Third Reich.[25] Spicer in particular has sketched out the theological and mental universe inhabited by the "brown priests" who broke with the norm during the 1930s and openly embraced various aspects of Nazi ideology.[26] This book provides part of the backdrop against which the activism of these pro-Nazi priests, who were embattled and isolated throughout the course of the Third Reich, later unfolded.

Richard Steigmann-Gall's *The Holy Reich* examines Nazi attitudes toward Christianity, primarily in the 1930s and 1940s, and concludes that Nazism can ultimately best be characterized from the time of its founding in 1919 as an essentially Christian phenomenon, albeit one typically skeptical of traditional piety and doctrine. In his view, the Nazi ideal of Positive Christianity was an indirect and rather fuzzy descendant of the liberal Protestant trajectory of both nondogmatic ecumenicism and higher biblical criticism. Despite the preponderance of Catholics among the party's earliest leadership, Steigmann-Gall sees the Nazis' Christianity as being both essentially anti-Catholic and primarily Protestant-inflected—at least up until the more overtly anti-Christian turn taken by party leaders around 1937 or so. Building on the ideas of prewar *Kulturprotestanten,* he argues, major Nazi figures not only "Aryanized" the figure of Jesus but also laid claim to Luther as a model of heroic German Christian identity.[27] In a slightly different trajectory, valuable work has also been done by the Israeli scholar Oded Heilbronner, who has examined the rise of Nazism in the Black Forest region beginning in the late 1920s and early 1930s. Heilbronner argues persuasively that the Nazi successes in the heavily Catholic *Schwarzwald* in the early 1930s were inextricably linked to the collapse of the Catholic milieu on the local level, which allowed the Nazis to effectively step into the vacuum.[28] One of the more notable approaches in the recent literature has been to interpret Nazism as a form of "political religion," reviving an older paradigm associated with the philosopher Eric Voegelin.[29] In this analysis, Nazism is seen as fundamentally incompatible with Christianity (and Catholicism in particular), since it operated essentially as a replacement or substitute for revealed religion and constituted an ersatz form of secular devotion that sacralized the political sphere through highly aestheticized pageantry, symbolic-liturgical language, and a powerful participatory appeal.[30] At present, however, the insights opened up by the renewed political-religion perspective in regard to the period between 1933 and 1945 have not been accompanied by a sufficient exploration either of the processes by which the Nazis' striking political-aesthetic cult was initially pioneered or of the early Catholic-oriented background against which this new secular religiosity originally unfolded.

The analysis in this book fuses certain aspects of these existing approaches while ultimately drawing conclusions that differ markedly from each. A close examination of the earliest years of the Nazi movement reveals a more immediate connection to the prewar phenomenon in Munich known as Reform Catholicism than to prewar *Kulturprotestantismus* elsewhere. I see the early Nazis' success in mobilizing in Munich after the First World War as the partial result of their ability both to step into the vacuum left by the demise of prewar Catholic movements in Munich and to build skillfully upon the discursive legacy those movements left behind. And while Nazi articulations of a broadly Christian identity during the Third Reich often took on an essentially Protestant-oriented veneer, this book attempts to trace the early stages of the process whereby that vague Protestant orientation, however superficial it may ultimately have been, first came to supplant the earlier Catholic orientation of the Nazi movement. Finally, while I believe that there is much merit in approaching Nazism during the Third Reich as a form of (essentially anti-Christian) political religion, it is inaccurate to see that quality in static or unchanging terms, projecting it back onto the earliest years of the Nazi movement. The sacralized political aesthetic of the Third Reich, with its powerful ritual-liturgical appeal, was itself the result of a broader transformation that altered the Nazi movement's early identity and ultimately left little or no room for more "authentic" Catholic (or Christian) substance by the time the Nazis came to power. Ultimately, the goal of *Catholicism and the Roots of Nazism* is to shed new light not only on the broadly Catholic orientation of the movement before the 1923 putsch, but also on the transformative process whereby that early orientation was lost and never entirely regained.

One of the central reasons that the story of Catholic activism in the early Nazi movement has in many ways remained lost is that the type of Catholic who was drawn most powerfully to the early Nazi movement in and around Munich does not fit neatly into the so-called Catholic milieu paradigm. Much of the literature on German Catholicism has relied heavily on the concept of the "social-moral milieu," stemming from the work of M. Rainer Lepsius, who posited the existence of four essentially antagonistic milieus within German society: conservative, bourgeois-liberal, socialist, and Catholic.[31] The Catholic milieu in the late nineteenth and early twentieth centuries has often been portrayed as a nearly monolithic block within German society, which unified Catholics across geographic distances by common patterns of ultramontane piety and predisposed them to express this unity publicly in overwhelming support for political Catholicism.[32] While the most recent work has been more nuanced, the image of a fairly hermetic Catholic subculture separated from other social groups by the tenacious walls of the milieu has continued to persist.[33] However, Catholicism in and around Munich exhibited a number of distinctive characteristics that set it apart in significant ways from the patterns of the broader Catholic milieu in Germany, including an energetic and open tradition among many believing Catholics of opposition to ultramontanism and, especially, to political Catholicism.

This relative distinctiveness is borne out clearly in the electoral behavior of Catholics in and around Munich, where Catholics made up between 80 and 90 percent of the population.[34] Support for political Catholicism specifically among Catholics was lower in Munich and in the surrounding region of upper Bavaria than in any other Catholic area in Germany beginning in the late 1890s. Whereas the overwhelmingly Catholic Center Party received a fairly impressive 80.1 percent of the Catholic vote (76.8 percent of the total) in upper Bavaria in the 1874 Reichstag elections, this figure dropped to only 45.3 percent among Catholics by 1898 and remained the lowest of any German Catholic area well into the 1920s.[35] By 1919, only 38.7 percent of Catholic voters in upper Bavaria voted for the Bavarian successor to the Center Party, the Bayerische Volkspartei (BVP); after spiking somewhat in 1920, Catholic support for the BVP then stabilized at around 42 percent in both the May and December 1924 elections—an improvement over earlier numbers but still a dramatically lower level than in other Catholic regions.[36] The election returns from the city of Munich itself were more striking still. In a city whose population was more than 80 percent Catholic, the Center Party received only 15.9 percent of the total vote in the key Reichstag election of 1912; following the war, the BVP vote in Munich initially peaked at 31.7 percent in 1920, having briefly drawn an influx of Catholics who had previously opposed the Center Party, but dropped back to 21.9 percent by May 1924.[37] At that point, as in 1912, nearly four out of every five *Münchener* were voting against the forces of traditional political Catholicism.

In the chapters that follow, these figures have important implications for understanding Catholic involvement in the early NSDAP after the First World War, as the perceived "immunizing" effect exercised against Nazi radicalism by allegiance to political Catholicism was largely absent in and around Munich.[38] Before the war, this widespread Catholic dissatisfaction with political Catholicism manifested itself in a rather remarkable openness toward Social Democracy on the part of believing Catholics, an openness that was not nearly as visible after the war. In contrast to the standard image of overwhelming mutual antipathy between the socialist and Catholic milieus throughout imperial Germany, it was actually quite possible in the "mild political climate" of prewar Munich to be both a good Social Democrat and a loyal Catholic at the same time—in other words, to transgress boundaries thought to be impenetrable elsewhere.[39] A spirit of mutual cooperation and understanding characterized the behavior not only of reform-oriented Marxist leaders in Munich but also of some local Catholic clergy, and in at least one interesting case socialist candidates ran openly (specifically as socialists) for seats on a local parish administrative board and were elected.[40] While this phenomenon has been seen essentially as a *Sonderfall* (exceptional case) that was likely due to a general weakness of religious identity and practice in Munich, the statistical evidence does not at all indicate that Catholic religious practice was weaker in and around Munich than elsewhere in Germany.[41] One study designed to measure the percentage of "religiously practicing" Catholics throughout Germany, based on communion statistics from each diocese, found that the level of religious practice in the archdiocese of Munich-Freising was markedly higher than the average for other Catholic areas, surpassing even the numbers for Cologne, which was widely regarded as a model of the religious practice that underpinned the Catholic milieu.[42]

The archdiocese of Munich-Freising itself, which encompassed the city of Munich and much of its environs, had been created through the elevation and expansion of the former *Fürstbistum* (prince-bishopric) of Freising in 1818, at a time when the population of Munich itself numbered slightly more than 50,000.[43] Over the next century or so, the growth of Munich was striking—exceeding 600,000 in the immediate aftermath of the First World War—and with it, the archdiocese and its structures were forced to expand.[44] The regular diocesan clergy, which numbered some 1,500 in the early twentieth century, was responsible for the approximately 1.1 million Catholics living within the boundaries of the archdiocese, which was itself divided into 36 deaneries (*Dekanate*) and more than 400 parishes.[45] Despite the historical importance of the ecclesiastical center of Freising, just north of Munich, the archdiocesan administrative complex was located in the heart of Munich in the shadow of the city's landmark cathedral, the Frauenkirche, where Michael von Faulhaber presided as archbishop from 1917 until his death in 1952.[46] In addition to the traditional clerical seminary that continued to operate in Freising, the archdiocese maintained both its official theological faculty and the Georgianum, the residential college for candidates for the priesthood, at the University of Munich, which dominated the intellectual life of the city.[47] The university was also home to a rich community of Catholic university fraternities, which were organized in several overarching fraternity federations such as the Cartellverband (CV), the Kartellverband (KV), Rhaetia, and the Hochland-Verband (HV), all of which thrived until they were forcibly dissolved by the Nazi regime in the mid-1930s.[48] The flavor of the local Catholic environment was also influenced strongly by the distinctive nature of Catholic lay organizations in Munich, which often exhibited a local or regional identity that differed from similar Catholic organizations in the Rhineland and in northern Germany.[49] The so-called Catholic press in and around Munich was quite diverse, ranging from large daily newspapers like the *Bayerischer Kurier,* which served as the organ of the Bavarian Center Party and, after the First World War, of the BVP; to widely read Catholic intellectual and cultural journals, such as *Hochland* and the *Allgemeine Rundschau;* to devotional weeklies like the official diocesan *Münchener Katholische Kirchenzeitung.*[50]

Many works on the archdiocese of Munich-Freising specifically during the Third Reich have tended to emphasize the heroic victimhood of individual Catholics and oppositional organizations within the archdiocese.[51] Although much of this apologetic literature is, in my view, justified in regard to the period after 1933, one goal of this book is to demonstrate that, in earlier years, the divisions between Catholic and Nazi identities were anything but hermetic and airtight.

The distinctiveness of Munich's Catholic tradition provides the point of departure for chapter 1, which examines important prewar Catholic trends—particularly the Christian Social and Reform Catholic movements—that energetically opposed the twin "evils" of ultramontanism and political Catholicism. One of the most notable products of this trajectory was the formulation of a rabidly nationalistic brand of so-called religious Catholicism, which was envisioned as a powerful antidote to the perceived hypocrisy of political ultramontanism, particularly that of Center Party politicians who, it was claimed, called themselves Catholic but were all too willing to make immoral compromises with the Jews and "atheistic" socialists for political gain, thereby sullying the nobility of the Catholic faith. In addition to the concept of religious Catholicism, the related ideal of Positive Christianity—technically interconfessional but strongly Catholic-oriented in practice—was picked up and developed further to great gain by members of the early Nazi movement, who fashioned it into a central component of the movement's local appeal.

Chapter 2 begins by examining the apocalyptic nature of the aftermath of the First World War in Munich and charts the interplay between the anti-Semitic responses to chaotic political developments that characterized official and semi-official Catholic circles in 1919 and 1920, on the one hand, and those of Catholic elements within the embryonic Nazi movement, on the other. Rabidly anti-Semitic figures like Franz Schrönghamer-Heimdal, who emerged from Munich's prewar Reform Catholic movement, served as important conduits between such mainstream Catholic publications as the official diocesan weekly *Münchener Katholische Kirchenzeitung* and the *Allgemeine Rundschau,* for which Schrönghamer wrote numerous front-page articles beginning in the summer of 1919, and the nascent *völkisch*-Nazi movement gathering around the *Beobachter,* in which Schrönghamer published dozens of major articles in 1919 and 1920. After initially embracing the radical anti-Semitism of Schrönghamer and others, Catholic figures associated with the BVP, which claimed semi-officially to represent Catholic interests in Bavaria, increasingly turned to more moderate and "respectable" forms of anti-Jewish critique—continuing to attack brutally the alleged immorality, greed, and godlessness of the Jews while stopping short of the radicalism of Nazi anti-Semitism. This strategy often had the unintended effect of reinforcing the Nazis' claim that their uncompromising stance made them the most principled and resolute defenders of Catholic Christianity in and around Munich, in stark contrast to the perceived weakness and hypocritical opportunism of the BVP's approach to the Jews. This complicated trajectory of Catholic apocalypticism and anti-Semitism constitutes an important, and hitherto largely overlooked, part of the immediate context within which the Nazi party platform—and, with it, the principle of Positive Christianity—was unveiled publicly in February 1920.

The next two chapters trace the evolution of an unofficial, yet palpable, Catholic-Nazi synthesis that developed within the movement between 1920 and 1923. Although the central principle of Positive Christianity remained explicitly interconfessional, it was envisioned and implemented first and foremost within a local context that was overwhelmingly Catholic. Chapter 3 traces that early implementation process by examining the propagation of the concept of religious Catholicism by a variety of Catholic students, publicists, and other opinion leaders, many of whom not only were influential early Nazis but also had important connections with the prewar Reform Catholic movement in Munich. It was partly in response to the effectiveness of the Nazis' contrast between the purity of religious Catholicism and the hypocrisy of ultramontane political Catholicism that the BVP launched a campaign in late 1922 to enlighten Bavarian Catholics about the religious dangers of the radical anti-Semitism and anti-ultramontanism espoused by Catholic Nazis, who were increasingly characterized by BVP figures as heretical apostates. Chapter 4 explores the corresponding response of the Nazi movement to the BVP campaign, focusing most notably on a lengthy Nazi membership drive that targeted believing Catholics, a drive characterized throughout the spring and summer of 1923 by energetic appeals in the *Beobachter* for attendance at mass (including a detailed schedule of local masses in every Sunday edition), by the publication of striking devotional prayers and poems to enhance Nazi members' personal piety, and by the staging of a series of massive Catholic-oriented demonstrations and militaristic field sermons in and around Munich. The membership drive also mobilized numerous Catholic priests throughout Bavaria who stepped forward to publicly and energetically support the Nazi movement, blunting the force of BVP criticisms, emphasizing the superiority of religious Catholicism, and ultimately providing the young Nazi movement's advocacy of Positive Christianity with an important measure of religious legitimacy in the eyes of nationalist Catholics seeking a political home beyond the confines of political Catholicism. At the same time, however, the later stages of the Catholic-oriented membership drive also witnessed the initial growth of the forces that would ultimately undermine the nascent Catholic-Nazi synthesis.

Chapter 5 addresses the developments that ultimately set the Nazi movement on a markedly different trajectory, dramatically altering both its orientation and constituency. Hitler had been deeply impacted by Mussolini's dramatic seizure of power in Italy, and in September 1923 he made the fateful decision to abandon his previous insistence on strict organizational independence and linked the Nazi movement, which was largely Catholic-oriented, with other radical right-wing organizations under the leadership of the staunchly anti-Catholic Erich Ludendorff to form the Kampfbund, a broader *völkisch* coalition that Hitler believed would be in a better position than the Nazi party alone to launch a successful coup. Relations between Catholics and anti-Catholics within the Kampfbund were tense even before the infamous failure of the so-called Beerhall Putsch in November 1923, but relations deteriorated even more rapidly in its aftermath. Following the bloody shootout that killed sixteen Kampfbund members and sealed the fate of the coup attempt, disillusioned participants (most notably the anti-Catholic followers of Ludendorff) blamed Catholics in Munich for having betrayed the entire enterprise, unleashing a flood of anti-Catholic venom. Whereas earlier rhetoric had praised religious Catholicism as a noble alternative to ultramontanism and political Catholicism, in the aftermath of the putsch the Catholic faith itself was often condemned, which put Catholic members of the movement in an increasingly difficult position. As a result, by late 1924, when Hitler was released from the prison term to which he had been sentenced for his role in the putsch, the formerly robust movement had been almost irreparably shattered and the vast majority of believing Catholics had been driven out. Many of the early Catholic Nazis who chose to remain in the movement after 1924 did so largely at the expense of their Catholic identities, often becoming—as in the case of Heinrich Himmler—staunch opponents of Christianity more generally.

Chapter 5 also explores two important consequences of the failed putsch and its aftermath. First, when the NSDAP was refounded in early 1925, it was unable to regain a foothold in primarily Catholic Munich, and the party's organizational center of power shifted to northern Bavaria, to the primarily Protestant regions of upper and middle Franconia. The clergymen who presided at Nazi events following the refounding were almost exclusively Protestant—whereas before the putsch not a single Protestant pastor in Munich had emerged to join the numerous Catholic priests who publicly supported the Nazis—and from the mid-1920s on, Nazi appeals to Positive Christianity became increasingly Protestant-inflected, albeit in a manner that remained rather superficial. Second, the refounded movement underwent a striking broader transformation in terms of its propagandistic aesthetic, shifting from a fairly straightforward Catholic-Christian framework before the putsch to an increasingly secularized, all-encompassing political religion. This dramatic shift helps to make both recognizable and more understandable the striking pseudo-sacral aesthetic of the Third Reich, which can be seen in many ways as a sort of hollow residue of the liturgical performativity of the earlier Catholic orientation. There were, of course, brief attempts in the early 1930s to revive the initial Catholic-Nazi synthesis, but these invariably ended in failure and disillusion, raising the broader question of whether there could ever have been, under any circumstances, genuine and lasting harmony between the Nazi and Catholic world views. This issue is addressed in the conclusion, which attempts briefly to take stock of the religious identity of the early Nazi movement and to assess its significance in broader terms.

It was in the midst of an attempt to resuscitate the early Catholic-Nazi symbiosis that Schrönghamer's *Das kommende Reich* arrived at Nazi party headquarters in the fall of 1933, at which point its striking inscription served as little more than a distant, unwanted echo of an earlier era. The self-interested Schrönghamer believed, it seems, that the influence he had wielded within the young *völkisch*-Nazi movement more than a decade earlier could be parlayed into some career gain, although it is doubtful that he had any illusions regarding the Nazis' altered religious orientation. Ultimately, what the unceremonious burial of Schrönghamer's striking vision reveals is the dramatic extent to which the Nazi regime in power differed from the small protean movement that had been born in chaos and had struggled so colorfully in its infancy to forge a viable identity in a predominantly Catholic city after the First World War.

CHAPTER I

Ultramontanism and Its Discontents

The "Peculiarities" of Munich's Prewar
Catholic Tradition

In August 1922, Munich hosted Germany's annual Catholic congress (Katholikentag) for the first time in more than twenty-five years. As thousands of Catholic visitors from all parts of the country streamed into Munich's main train station, many of them for the first time, they were greeted by a vast array of publicity materials assembled by the local welcoming committee, including tourist guides, museum pamphlets, and brochures advertising many of the city's best restaurants and hotels. Standing out amid the various commercialized displays of civic boosterism was a special issue of the Munich-based cultural journal *Hochland*, which featured an essay by local journalist Philipp Funk designed to introduce Catholics from elsewhere in Germany to the relative distinctiveness of Munich's Catholic tradition—or, as Funk put it, to "Munich's Catholic peculiarity" (*Münchener katholischen Eigensein*). In surveying the previous few decades, Funk praised the "naturalness and self-assuredness" of Munich Catholicism and the tradition of openness cultivated there under the long and benevolent rule of the Catholic Wittelsbach dynasty, while criticizing the defensive insularity of German Catholicism elsewhere, particularly in the embattled north, which he claimed was characterized by a "confessional nervousness" that manifested itself in "anxious feelings of inferiority" and in a "combative party-consciousness" fueled by "resentment of 'the other.'" Munich was, according to Funk, simply different. Admitting that Catholicism in Munich perhaps lacked some of the "refined purity of catacomb Christianity" and the "unity, solidarity, and sacrificiality of the north German diaspora," Funk nonetheless stated that Munich's distinctive openness toward interconfessional cooperation could and should serve as a "significant stimulus to all of Catholic Germany."[1]

Not content with vague generalities, Funk proceeded to confront visitors to Munich with specific criticisms of two of the central hallmarks of German Catholicism that had coalesced over the preceding decades. First, he took aim at the density and all-encompassing nature of Catholic associational life, which was a source of pride among Prussian Catholics in particular; he referred to the confessional exclusivity of organizations like the massive Volksverein as a "sickness" that was "not naturally at home in Munich, where the west and north German organizational mania [*Organisierwut*] and over-exaggerated hustling is lacking." The other target of Funk's scorn was the "divisive" exclusivity of political Catholicism, which Funk viewed as an unhealthy outgrowth of the combative atmosphere of the Prussian *Kulturkampf* that had been imported into Bavaria in the form of both the Bavarian Center Party during the Kaiserreich and its successor after the war, the Bavarian People's Party (Bayerische Volkspartei, or BVP).[2] For Funk, Munich had remained over the decades a refreshing oasis of freedom within a larger Catholic culture that often forcibly equated religious sincerity with support for political Catholicism:

The spiritual essence of Munich's Catholic character was never besmirched by politics. Here there were always believing Catholics who did not subscribe to the policies of the Bavarian Center Party ... and there are still today earnestly believing Catholics [*ernsthafte gläubige Katholiken*] who cannot go along with the successor of the Bavarian Center Party [the BVP], which seems to be guided much less by Catholic principles than by concern for the mood of the voters and by unrefined popular instincts based in part upon resentment.

Funk ultimately advocated the principle of strict confesional neutrality in political matters, stating that a "free and neutral stance" should replace the assertion elsewhere in Germany that all good Catholics, by definition, supported political Catholicism.[3] In retrospect, Funk's criticisms of the Center Party and BVP foreshadowed the rancor and controversy for which the 1922 Katholikentag would ultimately come to be remembered.[4]

Although Funk's essay was framed in deliberately provocative terms, his characterization of Munich's Catholic distinctiveness—religiously loyal but broadly skeptical of political Catholicism—clearly resonated with his contemporaries.[5] Studies of German Catholicism have often tended to conflate religious identity and support for political Catholicism to such an extent that one wonders just how the Munich

Catholics praised by Funk could oppose political Catholicism and still in good conscience be considered "earnestly believing Catholics."[6] What was it that fueled their opposition? In the two decades or so leading up to the 1922 Katholikentag, local commentators like Funk had not only chronicled the widely recognized "peculiar complexion [*eigenartiges Kolorit*] of Catholic life in the Bavarian capital," but had focused intense critical attention on the common element perceived as underpinning the support for the Center Party and BVP: the allegedly unhealthy role played by ultramontanism within German Catholicism.[7]

The ultramontane movement had initially taken shape in the late eighteenth and early nineteenth centuries as Catholics throughout Europe looked increasingly to the pope, who resided *ultra montes* ("over the mountains" to the south, in Rome), as the guarantor of church freedom from the intrusions of modernizing state bureaucracies into religious affairs.[8] The ultramontane orientation spread throughout the German lands in conjunction with the so-called devotional revolution of the middle decades of the nineteenth century, an energetic revival of emotive popular piety that ultimately helped to solidify the Center Party's constituency in the earliest years of the Kaiserreich.[9] Some historians have perceived a healthy democratic impulse within ultramontane popular piety, while others have interpreted it as an irrational and obsessive—even proto-fundamentalist—devotion to the papacy, which was venerated not only as a defense against state incursions but also as a backward-looking bulwark against the perceived evils of the "modern" world, a trajectory embodied perhaps most notably in the pronounced anti-intellectualism of the 1864 Syllabus of Errors and the 1870 proclamation of papal infallibility.[10] Although a distaste for ultramontanism and political Catholicism was visible among middle-class Catholics in various parts of Germany, such as the Rhineland and Black Forest regions, Munich was home to perhaps the most energetic and vehement forms of Catholic anti-ultramontanism in all of Germany.[11] Indeed, for many nationalistic Catholics in Munich, ultramontanism and Catholicism were not to be equated; rather, the former was seen both as a potential threat to the religious purity of the latter and as a dangerously divisive element within the German national community more generally.[12]

By the time Funk wrote his 1922 retrospective essay, the "peculiar complexion" of Munich Catholicism was already a contributing factor to the rise of the Nazi movement, which had begun to mobilize energetically among Catholic critics of ultramontanism and political

Catholicism.[13] This chapter explores the extent to which Munich's relative distinctiveness in the prewar era contributed to the local environment within which the Nazi movement was born after the First World War, focusing in particular on political and cultural movements that developed outside the framework of—and explicitly in opposition to—"ultramontane" political Catholicism, despite being distinctly Catholic-oriented in both their internal self-perception and external publicity. This broader tradition of Catholic opposition to political ultramontanism helped to pioneer a vocabulary with which the early Nazi movement could appeal to disillusioned Catholics in Munich in the immediate aftermath of the First World War.

The Tradition of Catholic Opposition to Ultramontanism and Political Catholicism in Munich

The organizational history of political Catholicism in Bavaria did not begin ex nihilo with the formation of the Bayerische Patriotenpartei in 1868. Its most significant early roots lay in the emergence in the 1830s of the Munich-based ultramontane movement associated with such figures as Joseph von Görres and Franz von Baader and the short-lived journal *Eos*, which helped to cement in the minds of many an inextricable link between ultramontanism and political Catholicism.[14] The ultramontane movement received a significant boost at midcentury from the emotive "devotional revolution" that spread through German-speaking Catholic territories, including much of the rural Bavarian countryside.[15] By the 1860s, however, the ultramontane movement had spawned its most articulate and perhaps most formidable early opponent in Ignaz von Döllinger, the famed Munich theologian who began his career as a leading advocate of ultramontanism but came eventually to view the movement as both anti-German and almost pathologically destructive (see fig. 1.1).[16]

The anti-ultramontane chauvinism that Döllinger increasingly embraced was unmistakable in the controversial speech he delivered to a gathering of scholars at Munich's St. Boniface Abbey in the fall of 1863, when he was without question among the most influential Catholic scholar-priests in Europe.[17] Distressed by what he viewed as the rising reactionary spirit associated with both the ultramontane revival in Germany and the continued dominance of neoscholastic orthodoxy within Catholic intellectual and theological circles, Döllinger claimed that God had given Germans in particular the world historical task of reinterpreting Catholic theology for the dawning modern age, and he

Figure 1.1. Ignaz von Döllinger (1860s).

called on German Catholics to shed the yoke of ultramontanism and to assume their predestined role as "teachers of all the nations."[18] While such chauvinistic convictions were far from uncommon among university-trained Catholics throughout the German territories, Döllinger chose to frame his broader discussion of the malignant influence of neoscholastic orthodoxy specifically in terms of its ultramontane-Roman roots, assuming as self-evident not only the "superior skill" of the German "national spirit" but also the contrasting and allegedly inescapable mediocrity of southern European (Roman) culture and its various ultramontane emanations.[19] Döllinger, who frequently linked ultramontanism to femininity in a pejorative sense, went on to employ an unmistakably phallic metaphor in ridiculing the "impotent" nature of his ultramontane neoscholastic opponents, whose "Roman" theological conservatism stood in contrast to the noble German theological trajectory:

[Theology must] carry within itself a life seed [*Lebenskeim*] that is energetic through and through. It can, however, in the hands of an intellectual vulgarity that passes itself off as conservative theology, shrink and become withered to the point that it shrivels up like an elderly body and in its impotence loses the power to beget life and light. Since dogmas, in the form of the Church's definitions, are in themselves only words, however rich and carefully chosen they may be, they continually require spiritual impregnation by theology and teaching.[20]

Both the image of German theology as a sort of potent spiritual phallus and the analogy between ultramontane conservatism and the physical impotence of a "shriveled" body were crude and perhaps a bit grotesque; they were certainly perceived that way by Döllinger's ultramontane opponents at the time. But Döllinger was never one for moderation, and herein lay the roots of both his popular influence among Catholic nationalists and his ultimate marginalization within the broader church.

Following his opposition to both the 1864 Syllabus of Errors and the 1870 proclamation of the doctrine of papal infallibility, Döllinger was officially excommunicated in 1871, becoming a somewhat unwilling heroic figure for the schismatic Old Catholic Church (Altkatholische Kirche) despite his principled refusal to join that movement.[21] Until his death in 1890, Döllinger continued to attend traditional Catholic mass in Munich's Theatinerkirche, and in the decades after his death he continued to influence Munich Catholicism—particularly the influential *Hofklerus* surrounding Prince Regent Luitpold and other educated nationalists who remained deeply skeptical of ultramontanism.[22] Among these pious yet non-ultramontane figures was Gebhard Himmler, a deeply religious Catholic who served as the personal tutor to the Wittelsbach family beginning in the 1890s and who, in the 1920s, became rector of Munich's Wittelsbach-Gymnasium, where his piety and rigidity would later be immortalized by his former student Alfred Andersch in a story entitled "The Father of a Murderer." The murderer in Andersch's title, Himmler's son Heinrich, was born into this milieu in 1900 and raised as a deeply pious Catholic, remaining so at the time he joined the early Nazi movement in the summer of 1923. Gebhard Himmler also managed to use his personal connections to arrange the 1908 appointment of his nephew the priest and future Nazi Wilhelm August Patin to the prestigious position of *Hofstiftsvikar* at Munich's St. Kajetan.[23]

One of the principal lessons drawn from Döllinger's life and career by later Catholic anti-ultramontanes and opponents of political Catholicism was that a nationalistic reform of the church could best be brought about by remaining explicitly inside the church; they learned from Döllinger's excesses and would attempt to avoid excommunication at all costs.[24]

By the time of Döllinger's death, the Patriotenpartei had ceased to exist, having been supplanted in 1887 by the newly founded Bavarian Center Party as the primary regional incarnation of the ultramontane political Catholicism so scorned by Döllinger and his supporters.[25] Throughout much of the 1890s, the Bavarian Catholic countryside was convulsed by the emergence of the Bauernbund movement, which had been founded in 1893 not only as an alternative to the strongly Protestant-oriented Bund der Landwirte that was at the time spreading rapidly through agrarian Prussian territories but also as the expression of a rural Catholic-peasant identity that viewed itself as fiercely independent from the tradition of Bavarian political Catholicism.[26] Among the more visible characteristics of the Bauernbund's harsh opposition to political Catholicism was a tendency toward Catholic anti-ultramontanism with a pronounced anticlerical inflection—a tendency that was confrontational and controversial, to be sure, but one that must be viewed as separate from outright anti-Catholicism.[27] Whereas the Bauernbund offered a distinct challenge to the Bavarian Center Party among peasants and farmers in rural areas, it was above all the emergence of the anti-Semitic Christian Social movement based in Munich—but eventually with important ties to Vienna—that drew increasing numbers of Catholic artisans, workers, and members of the urban *Mittelstand* away from their previous support for traditional political Catholicism. The key figure in this movement was the cartographer Ludwig Wenng, who not only did much to shape Christian Social anti-Semitism in prewar Munich but later lived to see his own anti-Semitic legacy carried on in the energetic support given by numerous members of his family to the early Nazi movement.

The early development of the Christian Social movement in Munich was both colorful and convoluted. Following the 1891 founding of Munich's first organized anti-Semitic club, the Deutsch-Sozialer Verein (DSV), Ludwig Wenng emerged from his cartographic studio to assume the editorship of the DSV's weekly, *Deutsches Volksblatt*.[28] In November 1892, members of the DSV, which had initially pitched its anti-Semitic message largely in economic terms to both express and appeal to the frustrations of the lower *Mittelstand*, formed an official party, the Deutsch-Soziale antisemitische Partei (DSAP). The DSAP supplemented the DSV's economic appeal with a heightened emphasis on racial anti-Semitism and found an increasingly receptive response within the context of the increased emigration of *Ostjuden* to the Bavarian capital in the early 1890s.[29] By the spring of 1893, the DSV and DSAP merged to form the Antisemitische Volkspartei München (AVM), which was initially connected to the broader movement led by Otto Böckel on the national level.[30] The first mass meeting held by the AVM in Munich on 11 April 1893 featured both Böckel and the local AVM leader Gustav Geisler as speakers, and the official police report noted the conspicuous presence of large numbers of anti-Semitic Catholic university students among the 700 attendees.[31] The very visible public support stirred by the AVM initially moved its political rival, the Bavarian Center Party, to seek official cooperation for certain Munich seats in the June 1893 Reichstag elections.[32] This cooperation was extremely short-lived. On 13 August 1893, the AVM split officially from Böckel's movement on the national level—and from any connection to the Bavarian Center Party on the local level—to form the Bayerische antisemitische Volkspartei (BAVP), with Geisler and Ludwig Wenng as co-chairs and Wenng's *Deutsches Volksblatt* as the BAVP's official organ.[33] In October 1893, the BAVP organized Munich's first mass "Christian" boycott of Jewish-owned businesses, with Wenng trumpeting the refrain "Don't Buy from Jews" in the *Deutsches Volksblatt* while providing readers with a list of Jewish-owned stores throughout the city.[34]

As Wenng's influence continued to eclipse that of Geisler within local anti-Semitic circles, the BAVP sought closer contact with the Christian Social movement of Karl Lueger in Vienna, which was technically interconfessional and exhibited mild anticlerical traits on occasion but was explicitly Catholic-oriented, receiving important support from a growing number of anti-Semitic Catholic priests in and around Vienna.[35] At the time of his most widely publicized visit to Munich, in August 1896, Lueger had already been elected lord mayor of Vienna in three separate municipal elections, although his election would not be confirmed by the reluctant Franz Josef until the spring of 1897.[36] The wild popularity of the charismatic Christian Social leader among Catholic anti-Semites was already undeniable, and Lueger's 10 August 1896 appearance on behalf of Ludwig Wenng and the BAVP proved to be one of the most controversial and widely discussed events of the year in Munich.[37] Advance publicity for the Lueger event emphasized the explicitly Christian nature of the BAVP, while both distancing the party from traditional political Catholicism and identifying its anti-Semitic mission in nascent *völkisch* terms.[38] Lueger's speech itself, which drew a remarkable crowd of more than 5,000 to Munich's Kindlkeller, was touted as a resounding success—one official police report emphasized the adulation showered on Lueger when he made his triumphal entrance, during which he was "greeted by endless jubilation"—and was interpreted as evidence of the growing strength of the anti-Semitic groundswell surrounding Wenng and the BAVP.[39] This groundswell continued to grow over the next several years. In March 1900, Munich's Demokratischer Verein invited Lucian Brunner, a Jewish politician from Vienna who was one of the harshest critics of Lueger and the Christian Socials, to speak in Munich's Kreuzbräu beerhall.[40] In response, the city was once again convulsed by an outbreak of anti-Semitic Lueger fever, fanned into flames by Wenng and hundreds of Catholic anti-Semites. They broke up Brunner's speech with endless shouts of "Hail Lueger" and posted a striking placard outside the Kreuzbräu entrance that stated "Due to a shortage of coal, Jews will be burned here."[41]

The next month, in April 1900, Wenng dissolved the BAVP and founded the Christlich-Sozialer Verein für Bayern, headquartered in Munich but with explicit connections to Lueger's Christian Social movement in Vienna. Under the leadership of Wenng and other leading figures like Andreas Wagner, a glass worker, and local Catholic priest Heinrich Schnepper, the Christlich-Sozialer Verein (CSV) became a visible, if ultimately fleeting, force in Munich politics in the first decade of the twentieth century.[42] By 1905, the Christian Socials could celebrate the election of Andreas Wagner to the Munich Gemeindekollegium, even as greater collaboration was being cultivated with anti-Semitic elements within the anti–Center Party Bauernbund movement, particularly the Bauernbund's Munich organ, *Das Bayerische Vaterland*, which had been founded by J. B. Sigl.[43] Ultimately, however, Christian Social fortunes waned, in part due to internal rivalries and frequent clashes of incompatible egos; their supporters numbered only 3.6 percent of the vote in the 1908 Munich municipal elections and only 2.7 percent in the 1911 elections.[44] By the eve of the First World War, the movement had come to a veritable standstill, at least in an organizational sense, as Christian Social anti-Semitism ultimately proved incapable of politically mobilizing Munich's urban *Mittelstand* in anything more than a temporary situational sense. Nonetheless, Ludwig Wenng and the broader Christian Social movement were central in helping to shape the discourse of Catholic-oriented anti-Semitism in Munich in several significant ways.

One of Wenng's leading partners at the time of the founding of the CSV in 1900, the Catholic priest Heinrich Schnepper, was also centrally involved in the early stages of the Reform Catholic movement that came to prominence in Munich in the years leading up to the First World War.[45] On 10 March 1900, only four days after the demonstrative display of anti-Semitic venom by Wenng's supporters during the Lucian Brunner affair—which produced the placard about burning Jews rather than coal—the founding meeting of the first Reform Catholic organization, the Katholischer Reformverein München, was held in the same venue, Munich's Kreuzbräu beerhall.[46] Although several other priests were visible at the inaugural Reformverein meeting, with Schnepper being one of the most vocal participants, the moving force behind the new organization was Josef Müller, an eccentric priest-scholar who venerated Döllinger, maintained close contact with the Christian Social movement, and increasingly exhibited a virtual obsession with Nordic-Aryan *völkisch* identity.[47] Müller had coined the phrase "Reform Catholicism" two years earlier in what became his most influential work—a sweeping vision of a nationalistic, non-ultramontane, and irenic Catholic identity that would, Müller predicted, help to overcome the tragic confessional division within the German *Volk* and serve as the "religion of the future for the educated of all confessions."[48] The broader Reform Catholic movement inspired by this work has received a fair amount of attention from theologians and ecclesiastical historians, due in large part to its connections to the controversial phenomenon of theological modernism and, eventually, to the sweeping changes of the Second Vatican Council.[49]

Although the organizational history of Reform Catholicism in Munich can be said to have begun with the founding of the Katholischer Reformverein München in March 1900, Josef Müller had in fact taken an important preliminary step two months earlier in founding the Munich-based cultural monthly *Renaissance*, which drew energetic praise for its nationalistic opposition to ultramontanism and political Catholicism.[50] Müller's *Renaissance* built a loyal readership among Catholic academics and students in Munich, and counted several influential supporters in Munich among the *Hofklerus* who had been especially close to Döllinger.[51] Additional Reform Catholic publications were begun in Munich over the ensuing years, including most notably *Das 20. Jahrhundert*, founded in 1902 by reform-oriented priests Franz Klasen and Johannes Bumüller; *Hochland*, a cultural monthly founded in 1903 by the publicist Karl Muth; and the *Allgemeine Rundschau*, founded in 1904 by Armin Kausen.[52] The year 1904 also witnessed the founding of two other Reform Catholic organizations in Munich: the Verein Renaissance, founded by Josef Müller as a successor to his earlier Reformverein, and the Krausgesellschaft (KG), which became the most influential Reform Catholic group in Munich.[53]

The roots of the KG lay most notably in a meeting in Munich's famous Isarlust banquet hall in October 1902 headlined by the Würzburg theologian Herman Schell, whom historian Thomas Nipperdey has characterized aptly as "the [Hans] Küng of the *Jahrhundertwende*."[54] At the time, Schell, who served as the intellectual father figure to Josef Müller, was perhaps the most influential (and controversial) German Catholic thinker since Döllinger; he was the author of the bestselling *Catholicism as the Principle of Progress* (1897), which called for a radical opening up of the Catholic Church to modern scholarship and culture and which preached the superiority of German identity over the detrimental "Roman" influence associated with ultramontanism and, especially, the Jesuit order.[55] In criticizing the perceived anti-intellectualism of the ultramontane movement, Schell echoed the phallic-impotency imagery of Döllinger decades earlier, advocating a nationalistic, masculine-oriented Catholic identity and arguing that Christ had called his followers to be "vigorous intellects, not intellectual eunuchs [*geistige Eunuchen*]."[56] The explicit purpose of Schell's Isarlust speech was to build support for the nascent publication *Das 20. Jahrhundert.*[57] Ultimately, when the decision was made two years later to give the *Jahrhundert* an organizational arm in Munich, the KG was born, taking its name from the liberal-nationalist Catholic priest and historian Franz Xaver Kraus, who had died in 1901, and drawing into its radically nationalistic ranks a variety of local reform-oriented Catholic students, academics, and professionals.[58]

The leading figures in the KG included priests like Otto Sickenberger, who had been a central participant at the founding of Josef Müller's Reformverein in 1900; theologians such as Joseph Schnitzer and Hugo Koch; lay Catholic cultural leaders such as art critic Alexander Heilmeyer and publicist Philipp Funk; and Catholic professionals like businessman Wilhelm Briemann, architect Paul Fuchs, and engineer Karl Böhm.[59] Although the KG's organizational center remained in Munich, its ideas also spread to nearby Rosenheim through the energetic activism of the reform-oriented Catholic businessmen Hans Huber and Johann Stegmaier on the eve of the First World War.[60] While each of these KG figures, with the lone exception of Philipp Funk, would come to be involved in the early Nazi movement in some capacity after the war, the most notable was Joseph Schnitzer.[61]

Schnitzer had been ordained in the diocese of Augsburg in 1884 and engaged in pastoral work for several years before obtaining his doctorate and habilitation from the University of Munich, which enabled him to launch his theological teaching career at the state lyceum in Dillingen in 1892.[62] After his appointment to the theological faculty of the University of Munich in January 1902, Schnitzer quickly became a popular mentor for Catholic theology students; years later, in a glowing Nazi tribute to Schnitzer, one of his earliest theology students described his initial impact on the Catholic student body as a "fresh March wind blowing through the musty lecture halls."[63] Schnitzer, who embodied much of the bombastic nationalism, anti-ultramontanism, and irenic openness of the broader Reform Catholic movement, participated centrally in the Isarlust meeting of October 1902 and collaborated with Müller in the pages of *Renaissance* before becoming a central figure in the founding of the KG in 1904.[64] During the modernist controversy that swirled around the publication of the papal encyclical *Pascendi* in 1907, Schnitzer was suspended from the priesthood and forced to transfer to the philosophical faculty, while continuing, alongside Otto Sickenberger, as a central figure within the KG.[65] As both a teacher and a reform-oriented activist, Schnitzer atracted a growing circle of young nationalistic Catholic students in Munich. His influence extended after the First World War to leading Catholic students within the early Nazi movement, such as Alfred Miller, one of Schnitzer's most devoted disciples.

Radically nationalistic university students were an indispensable component of the Reform Catholic movement in Munich throughout the prewar years. At the Isarlust gathering in October 1902, Catholic fraternity students from the CV, the Kartellverband katholischer deutscher Studentenvereine (KV), and Rhaetia were among the most energetic participants.[66] Among them was Lorenz Pieper, a member of the CV who had been ordained into the priesthood in the Paderborn diocese and had moved to the University of Munich as a doctoral student of Lujo Brentano in the summer of 1902.[67] His contact with Herman Schell at the Isarlust event led to Pieper's passionate devotion to nationalistic (anti-ultramontane) Catholicism, which was perhaps matched only by Pieper's almost obsessive idealization of Ignaz von Döllinger and Franz Xaver Kraus.[68] After completing his doctorate and returning to Westphalia in 1903, Pieper would maintain a close relationship with the Reform Catholic movement in Munich before returning to Munich in 1923 as one of the most visible Catholic priest propagandists for the young Nazi movement.[69]

Similarly, when Josef Müller founded his Reformverein in March 1900, Catholic university students were perhaps the most conspicuous attendees. Müller's fatherly support of literary stirrings among the Catholic student body in Munich won him an increasing number of devoted disciples.[70] Two students who were deeply impacted by Müller—Ernst

Figure 1.2. Franz Schrönghamer (1901).

Thrasolt and Franz Schrönghamer—would embark on notable *völkisch*-oriented literary careers, collaborating closely with radical Catholic racists like Dietrich Eckart after the First World War. Schrönghamer, by far the most influential of Müller's student disciples, was born in Passau in 1881 and entered the seminary of the diocese of Passau in 1900, initially unsure about his priestly calling but determined that his Catholic faith should shape his future career (see fig. 1.2).[71] By 1902, the young seminarian had decided that his calling could best be fulfilled outside the priesthood, and he moved to Munich to study architecture and became an energetic member of the Catholic student fraternity Rhaetia.[72] In 1903, Schrönghamer was centrally involved in the fledgling literary enterprise organized by Reform Catholic students in Munich known as the *Musenalmanach katholischer Studenten*, which was enthusiastically supported by Josef Müller in the pages of *Renaissance*.[73] When Müller founded the Verein Renaissance in 1904, Schrönghamer was elected alongside Müller to the local leadership committee and served as the group's first treasurer.[74] Ultimately, when Schrönghamer decided to embark on a literary career after finishing his architectural studies in 1905, it was Müller's connections that helped him to land a position in the editorial offices of Munich's satirical *Fliegende Blätter*, which Schrönghamer went on to edit from 1907 through 1912.[75]

In addition to drawing its most ardent support from the ranks of Catholic students, academics, and young professionals in Munich, the Reform Catholic movement remained in close contact with important Christian Social elements. The leading Christian Social priest Schnepper had been involved alongside Müller in the founding of the Katholischer Reformverein München in 1900, and influential Viennese Christian Social priests such as Joseph Scheicher and Franz Schindler worked closely with Reform Catholic figures on numerous occasions.[76] Although both the Christian Social and Reform Catholic movements contributed in open and direct ways to the membership of the early NSDAP— whether in the form of Ludwig Wenng's family or central members of the KG—their most significant impact on the early Nazi movement was achieved more subtly and indirectly.

A Discursive Legacy? Prewar Tropes and the Postwar *Völkisch* Movement

In his brilliant study on the connection between religious motifs and political activism, the cultural anthropologist Victor Turner pioneered the concept of "root paradigms" in an attempt to understand the ways in which the ideational universe of political actors can be constructed and underpinned, typically in indirect fashion, by broader religious-oriented metaphors and tropes.[77] Although Turner's classic essay focused on the discursive fields that helped to structure the self-sacrificial behavior of the twelfth-century martyr Thomas Becket, his insights have subsequently been applied much more broadly by scholars. They can also be useful in attempting to understand some of the less direct influence exercised on the early Nazi movement by the tradition in Munich of prewar Catholic anti-ultramontanism, whose central tropes and metaphors echoed fatefully in the crisis-laden atmosphere of the immediate postwar years and, in important ways, provided the early Nazi movement with a sort of vocabulary with which to appeal to disillusioned and radicalized Catholics. Three intertwined points of emphasis in particular will infuse the analysis in subsequent chapters in this volume: the contrast between religious Catholicism and ultramontane political Catholicism, the related attempt to overcome internal divisions within the German *Volk* under the aegis of Positive Christianity, and the cultivation of an irenic yet distinctly Catholic-oriented form of *völkisch* nationalism.

A common element shared by the Christian Social and Reform Catholic movements was a strong advocacy of Catholic religious faith combined with a corresponding condemnation of the intertwined "evils" of ultramontanism and political Catholicism. The explicit distinction between religious and political Catholicism stemmed most notably from the priest-historian Franz Xaver Kraus, who argued that the nobility of the Catholic faith was being sullied and blasphemed as it was dragged repeatedly into the realm of self-serving and petty politics, with the opportunistic and power-hungry clerical politicians of the Center Party representing the most lamentable aspects of the divisive ultramontane world view.[78] The contrast between the alleged depth and openness of religious Catholicism and the pathological superficiality of ultramontane political Catholicism was also emphasized in the writings of Josef Müller.[79] He attacked the confessional exclusivity of the Center Party by proclaiming bombastically that "the evolution of German Catholics into a closed political party is the most serious national catastrophe imaginable!"[80] As a priest, Müller was concerned in a pastoral sense over the divisiveness within individual parishes brought about by ambitious clerical politicians: "The priest should stand as an ambassador of peace, as a man above the parties; he should bring together on the common ground of religion those who are divided, not bring further discord into his parish by branding everyone except a certain clique [Center Party voters] as second-class or bad Catholics."[81] Herman Schell's Isarlust speech was trumpeted as the clarion call for the "religious movement within Catholicism," which was framed in stark contrast to the alleged "anti-religious" opportunism that characterized political Catholicism.[82] Similarly, when Karl Muth founded *Hochland* in October 1903, his primary goal was to foster "religious" Catholicism by remaining explicitly above the fray of party politics.[83] None of this was framed as an argument for keeping religious faith out of the public sphere. In fact, KG figures consistently argued that "faith must permeate the entire life of the individual, and it must also achieve expression in political activity in the proper place and time"; the problem, they argued, was that political Catholicism amounted to "the prostitution of religion for the political, and perhaps only financial, goals" of the Center Party and its leaders, working explicitly at cross-purposes with both the nobility of the Catholic faith and the internal unity of the German nation.[84] A passionate appeal from the KG in December 1911 summed up the broader Reform Catholic position: "The poisoning of our political life through the misuse of religion must be overcome! Religion itself needs to be kept pure from political exploitation!"[85]

Building on imagery reminiscent of Döllinger, a strident critique of ultramontanism was consistently folded into the contrast between religious and political Catholicism, separating the perceived evils of the (southern European) ultramontane world view in the political sphere from the virtues of (Germanic) religious Catholicism in the spiritual realm. In a programmatic definition of ultramontanism, Johannes Bumüller, the Reform Catholic priest who co-founded the *Jahrhundert*, focused on the obsessive ultramontane "mixing of religion and politics," in addition to its characteristic "lack of truthfulness" and its "excessive elevation of [external] church structures over religion."[86] Joseph Schnitzer's encapsulation of anti-religious ultramontane superficiality, with its various southern European manifestations, required only one word: "frivolity."[87] Perhaps not surprisingly, the Jesuit order was attacked as the most subversive manifestation of the ultramontane world view, and KG leader Hugo Koch provided perhaps the most influential critique of the differences between religious Catholicism and the anti-German superficiality fostered by "Jesuitism."[88]

Beyond negative attacks on political Catholicism and ultramontanism, Reform Catholics were careful to emphasize the perceived virtues associated with religious Catholicism. Far from being an agent of religious indifference, Josef Müller saw the battle against ultramontanism and political Catholicism as a form of religious revivalism that would lead to the "renewal and deepening of religious life" among German Catholics "who are loyally devoted to their Church," while also fostering broader unity in the name of the "German national spirit."[89] Similarly, the KG framed its religious purpose in terms of encouraging "deeper" faith among German Catholics.[90] By shifting the emphasis away from opportunistic activism in the political sphere, Reform Catholic leaders urged the clergy to devote more time to improving religious education, religious practice, and morality within their parishes, which would help to stem the rising tide of secularism within the church and within German society more generally.[91] Most important, Reform Catholic leaders drew a key lesson from the fate of Döllinger, insisting that the movement remain firmly and loyally within the Catholic Church and emphasizing the primacy of religious faith over politics while avoiding excommunication at all costs.[92] Toward this end, the KG issued several programmatic statements on the imperative to combine nationalistic anti-ultramontanism in political and scholarly terms with an unshakable religious loyalty to the Catholic Church both as an institution and as a broader spiritual community spanning the centuries.[93] The Old Catholic Church in particular was identified explicitly by Reform Catholic leaders as a schismatic and disastrous "heresy," while organizations like the Antiultramontaner Reichsverband (AUR), which shared some of the goals of the Reform Catholic movement, were ultimately rejected as too Protestant-oriented and potentially damaging to the cause of religious Catholicism.[94] Joseph Schnitzer likewise condemned the attempt of the 1840s Deutschkatholiken to establish a German national church, advocating instead a religiously loyal form of "nationalistic, German Catholicism—not in the sense of a German *Nationalkirche*, but in the sense of a Catholicism that has understanding of and a heart for the German essence and German nature."[95] Similarly, the Christian Social movement, while avoiding the appearance of dogmatism or confessional exclusivity, pitched its anti-Semitic message in explicitly Catholic-oriented terms, differentiating itself starkly from anti-Semitic elements within Protestant-nationalist circles in Munich, which remained on a separate trajectory even after the young Nazi movement had been formed.[96]

In sum, a new form of religious identity was sought that would be characterized by loyalty to the Catholic Church and its hierarchy in a spiritual sense but would also be open to a radically nationalistic political and cultural course. For many Catholic opponents of ultramontanism in Munich, the search for religious Catholicism would ultimately end in an embrace of the Positive Christianity advocated by the early Nazi movement.

The phrase "Positive Christianity" itself, representing an interconfessional ideal that became central to the Nazi program of February 1920, was so commonplace in prewar Reform Catholic circles as to require little explication at the time and no special conceptual differentiation from other powerful, yet ultimately vague, formulations like "religious Catholicism." When the *Jahrhundert* attempted to link its ideals to a popular book series to which several Reform Catholic authors contributed, it pointed self-evidently to the "standpoint of Positive Christianity [*positiven Christentums*] and warm-hearted German conviction" advocated by the series.[97] When the KG wanted to protect itself from ultramontane criticisms, it often clothed itself not only in the rhetoric of religious Catholicism but also with the mantle of a "positive" irenic Christianity.[98] Similarly, when Karl Muth founded the monthly *Hochland* in October 1903, one of his central goals was to emphasize common ground between Reform Catholics and nationalistic Protestants under the rubric of Positive Christianity, engaging energetically and confidently with leading currents in modern German scholarship and culture.[99] Muth's leading advisor in founding the journal—and the one who suggested its name—was the ecumenical Protestant-nationalist poet Friedrich Lienhard, who was one of Muth's closest friends and was an extremely influential force in the developing *völkisch* movement.[100] Although Muth pledged his unwavering loyalty to the ecumenical ideal of "our healthy German and Christian nationality" and to the goal of overcoming Catholic "alienation from the *Volksgemeinschaft*," the extent to which his perspective remained explicitly Catholic-oriented is indicated by his frequent use of the hybrid formulation "Positive-Christian-Catholic" (*positiv-christlich-katholisch*), which was used interchangeably with the term "Catholic-Christian" (*katholisch-christlich*).[101] The Christian Social movement was also eager to frame itself in broadly interconfessional terms—Wenng's BAVP pledged to "recognize Christianity as the most important foundation of our *völkisch* development, while rejecting any interference with the religious convictions of the individual"—even as it emphasized its own "Christian-Catholic" (*christ-katholisch*) basis.[102]

A corollary to the emphasis on interconfessional cooperation was the desire to overcome class divisions within the German *Volk*, with the broader ideal of Positive Christianity serving as a rallying cry to help wean workers away from the "godlessness" and internationalism of Social Democracy, and to cultivate a broader interconfessional nationalistic identity that would transcend class lines while remaining within a broader Catholic-oriented paradigm.[103] In a strategy that would later be utilized to great effect by the early Nazi movement, the electoral collaboration between the Center Party and the Social Democrats (SPD), particularly in 1907, was used as a wedge issue to further demonstrate to practicing Catholics that the lack of principle and the shameful opportunism of political Catholicism was diametrically opposed to the purity of the Catholic faith itself. Karl Gebert, a spokesman for the KG, noted that the unprincipled cooperation between the Center Party and SPD, a party that had "atheism at its core," demonstrated better than anything else the "fundamental deficiency in the intellectual life of [political] Catholicism."[104] Josef Müller viciously attacked Marxist social-ism for its godlessness and its embrace of revolutionary upheaval, while calling openly for an ecumenical yet Catholic-oriented form of "national socialism" (*Nationalsozialismus*) that would strengthen ties among work-ers, their nation, and their Christian religious faith.[105]

Perhaps the most effective vehicle for overcoming confessional and class divisions in Munich under the rubrics of religious Catholicism and Positive Christianity was a striking brand of social-moral activism fueled by a near-missionary zeal. Reform Catholic students at the University of Munich were central in pioneering the Sozialstudentische Bewegung (social student movement), which championed the cause of eradicating social divisions between university students and young workers within a nationalistic and interconfessional, yet strongly Catholic-tinged, framework.[106] The key early figure in the Sozialstudentische Zentrale München (SZM) was Karl Nischler, who founded it in 1912 and then died tragically the following year.[107] Nischler's social activism—both as a student and, after graduation, as a young trainee in the Bavarian civil service—focused on the establishment of workers' instruction courses in which his reform-oriented Catholic student colleagues would give free lectures and instruction to local factory workers, particularly in Munich's Neuhausen section.[108] In founding the SZM, Nischler's goal was to combine deep Catholic piety with a socially oriented *völkisch* nationalism, all in the interest of overcoming social divisions and helping Catholic students to "establish the closest possible relationships with our *Volks-genossen* who are not academically trained."[109] As Nischler put it, the two hallmarks of a true "Catholic-Christian" lifestyle among students were the energetic "cultivation of a nationalistic orientation" and the battle against "the danger of social division and the spirit of class hatred."[110] Nischler's eventual successor as head of the SZM, the Catholic student Martin Weigl, would come to believe that the best avenue through which to achieve these goals was participation in the young Nazi movement. The prewar Christian Social movement also attempted, albeit in a rather rudimentary manner, to bridge divisions between local university stu-dents and young artisans and workers with the goal of creating an overarching Christian–anti-Semitic *Volksbewegung*—an ideal later fos-tered successfully by the early Nazi movement.[111]

In addition to the attempt to overcome class divisions through social-student activism, Reform Catholic figures were deeply involved in the attempt to transcend confessional divisions through the public morality campaign spearheaded by the Munich-based cultural journal *Allgemeine Rundschau*. The *Rundschau* served as the official organ of the Münchener

Männerverein zur Bekämpfung der öffentlichen Unsittlichkeit (Munich Men's League for Combating Public Immorality), which was established by Armin Kausen in 1906 and drew together a remarkably broad coalition of Reform Catholic activists, ecumenically minded Protestant nationalists, and members of the right wing of the Bavarian Center Party under the banner of Positive Christianity and moral purity.[112] The provisional leadership committee of the Männerverein included, in addition to Kausen, influential members of Munich's reform-oriented *Hofklerus* like Jakob von Türk; nationalistic Protestants such as the pastor Hermann Lembert and the secondary school teacher Ludwig Kemmer; and Catholic intellectuals like Hermann Sickenberger, the brother of KG chairman Otto Sickenberger.[113] One of the Männerverein's most notable characteristics was its radical nationalism, which carried a nascent *völkisch*-eugenic tinge, as demonstrated by the central involvement of the Munich racial hygienist Max Gruber.[114] Across the board, the Männerverein insisted that the battle against moral excess was indispensable to the protection and enhancement of German "fighting strength" (*Wehrkraft*).[115] Perhaps not surprisingly, the most notable agents and purveyors of this moral excess were typically identified as Jews.[116]

The nascent eugenics focus of the moral purity campaign and the broader attempt to overcome class and confessional divisions were both manifestations of a broader *völkisch* orientation that began to emerge especially within the Reform Catholic movement in Munich in the decade or so before the First World War.[117] In criticizing ultramontanism, Johannes Bumüller not only lambasted the "senile Romanism" it represented, but went much further and constructed an explicitly race-based appeal, openly predicting the future "supremacy of the German race [*Herrschaft der germanischen Rasse*] within the Catholic Church" and proclaiming:

When we [Reform Catholics] advocate a joining together of the Catholic religion and German culture, we do so in the conviction that the religion of a people [*Volk*] or of a race [*Rasse*] must stand and live in harmony with its culture or be cast off to the side. . . . The Catholic Church must now reckon above all with the principle of race and nationality [*Rassen- und Völkerprinzip*].[118]

Along the same lines, Josef Müller came to exhibit a marked fascination with racial-eugenic thought and a near-obsession with Nordic-Aryan identity. When Müller introduced a striking new cover illustration for his journal *Renaissance* in April 1902, it featured an almost grotesquely

Figure 1.3. Josef Müller's *Renaissance* (1903).
Source: *Renaissance* 4:12 (Dec 1903).

muscular nude male titan, bearing a torch with an eternal flame, on the side of a cliff—a sort of Arno Breker figure *avant la lettre*—which Müller claimed was taken explicitly from an "ancient Aryan cultic legend" (see fig. 1.3).[119] One cannot but notice the blending of Nordic-Aryan imagery and explicitly Catholic visual references, including the liturgical stole that flows conspicuously from the stem of the titan's torch. This imagery undoubtedly had a deep impact on the idealistic students whom Müller gathered around himself in Munich, including Franz Schrönghamer. Years later, when he was a leading figure in the early Nazi movement, his fascination with this mixing of Nordic-Aryan and Catholic identities remained, alongside his rabid anti-Semitism, as perhaps the most striking aspect of Schrönghamer's thought.

The *Renaissance* cover also visually reinforced the primacy of the New Testament, which is illuminated specifically by the torch of the titan, over the (Jewish) Old Testament, which is pushed far to the margins of the image. The tablets of the Ten Commandments are on the verge of toppling out of view and into the void of insignificance. The Old Testament would become a rather vexing problem for early Nazi Catholics with Reform Catholic roots, such as Franz Schrönghamer and Lorenz Pieper. Josef Müller, for his part, cultivated important contacts with leading Catholic anti-Semites, including perhaps most notably his famed collaborator in the pages of *Renaissance*, the theologian August Rohling, whose infamous manifesto *Der Talmudjude* had been a central landmark in the development of German anti-Semitism in the 1870s and whose work would have a profound impact on the anti-Semitic development of Schrönghamer in particular.[120] Rohling's work had also resonated throughout Christian Social circles in Munich since the 1890s, when Ludwig Wenng's *Volksblatt* had launched a series of bombastic Catholic-oriented campaigns against the Talmud, using Rohling's *Talmudjude* as a springboard and pushing for the expulsion of all eastern Jews who had emigrated to Munich since the 1880s.[121] The latter issue—which was at the heart of four mass meetings organized by Wenng in the fall of 1899 that produced resolutions urging Bavarian state authorities to undertake a systematic review of "morally offensive" passages from the Talmud and, on the basis of that review, to expel all *Ostjuden* who had emigrated to Munich in the preceding decade—would be revived in almost identical (Catholic-oriented) terms by the Nazi movement in the early 1920s, spearheaded in the pages of the *Beobachter* by Catholic students and leading early Nazis Hansjörg Maurer and Alfred Miller.[122] Josef Müller was intent on reaching beyond the confines of the Catholic anti-Semitism represented by Rohling, and he energetically publicized the ideas of the flaming racial anti-Semite Theodor Fritsch, frequently reprinting in *Renaissance* entire articles from Fritsch's infamous Leipzig-based journal *Hammer*.[123] Müller also expressed fawning admiration for the "downright stupendous erudition" (*geradezu stupender Gelehrsamkeit*) of the self-loathing anti-Semitism and nervous misogyny of Otto Weininger and publicized the eccentric works of Jörg Lanz von Liebenfels, the racist former Catholic monk who has been labeled famously by Wilfried Daim, in a clear overstatement, as "the man who gave Hitler his ideas."[124]

Throughout Munich's prewar Reform Catholic community, a steady yet dramatic escalation of *völkisch* and eugenics rhetoric is visible in the years leading up to the First World War. One of Joseph Schnitzer's most devoted students within the Krausgesellschaft, Leonhard Fendt, virtually apotheosized Germanic racial identity in a striking 1907 article attacking (yet again) the evils of ultramontanism. Fendt argued: "The whole of Catholicism is more Roman today than ever. We are Germans . . . and it must be admitted from the bottom of our hearts that, if we were free to decide between Roman and German Catholicism, we Germans would be religious traitors to opt for the Roman type."[125] But rather than envisioning a vague Germanic-Christian amalgamation without any doctrinal rigor, Fendt argued explicitly against any notion that Reform Catholics should leave the Catholic Church, asking rhetorically: "So should we then become a new branch of Protestantism?" In answering his own question firmly in the negative, Fendt proclaimed: "We would not be Christians if we wanted to abandon our [Catholic] brothers."[126] Instead, Fendt envisioned a future of national glory fueled by political cooperation between *völkisch*-oriented Protestants and Catholics who, while respecting the distinctiveness of the other's religious convictions, would "come together in generosity, richer and stronger than before all [confessional] division."[127]

The thought of major racial theorists like Houston Stewart Chamberlain and Arthur de Gobineau was also circulated energetically among Munich's Reform Catholic community, with Gobineau being praised all the more emphatically because, despite his French nationality, he had been both pro-German and Catholic.[128] Schell wrote a major lead article in Muth's *Hochland* on the religious thought of Chamberlain in particular, which brought about heavy criticism from conservatives and ultramontanes who attacked Muth for allowing Schell to present a far too uncritical portrait of Chamberlain's ideas.[129] Gobineau was lauded in *Hochland* for the "heroism of his view of life," which was based in part on the conviction that "the white race, in comparison to the black and the yellow, is the only race truly equipped with the elevated qualities, with creative power and organizational capabilities. . . . In comparison, the other [races] are dull and wretched. Their ruler is the Aryan family, whose crowning glory are the Germans."[130] In another gushing tribute to Gobineau, a frequent *Hochland* contributor proposed Gobineau's pro-German racial thought as a potential solution for Germany's perpetual internal struggles and divisions.[131] Similarly, in a programmatic article entitled "Aryan World View," an unnamed KG activist praised Gobineau in the highest terms, citing his work to argue that "the German race is destined to spread its hegemony across the earth, as a result of its higher intellectual ability." The same activist then went on to interpret for Reform Catholic readers in Munich the "loftiness" of Chamberlain's construction of the ancient Aryan racial identity, which was based on a sweeping rejection of all things Jewish:

Unique in the whole of Indo-European history, *altindisch* thought and literature is free from all contact with the Semitic spirit, and is therefore pure, undefiled, genuine, and distinctive. What is pronounced in these words [of Chamberlain] should not be considered anti-Semitism. The Semitic spirit, however, which is characterized to an exceedingly great extent by the lack of individual creative power, is the enemy of our own existence [*der Feind unseres eigenen Daseins*].[132]

An even more striking article enlisted Chamberlain's thought in support of a broader appeal to purge all non-German elements from the noble Aryan-Germanic world view represented by *völkisch*-oriented Reform Catholics, condemning racial egalitarianism as un-Christian and honoring instead what were perceived as the God-ordained differences among the races. The unnamed KG activist concluded by simulating God's message to the movement, giving its racist orientation the urgency of missionary zeal: "Set your strength in motion, work and be faithful unto death, and I will give you the Crown of Life. Such is the honorable, German, efficacious *Weltanschauung*."[133] Not surprisingly, the KG also publicized the ideas of the flaming anti-Semite Theodor Fritsch.[134] While typically avoiding what he regarded as unsophisticated *Radau-Antisemitismus*, Karl Muth was not above publishing in *Hochland* anti-Semitic articles, such as a vehement 1914 diatribe by the Catholic statistician Hans Rost that sweepingly labeled the Jews as "the ultimate carriers of the symptoms of degeneration of our times," a theme that Rost would later revive in the apocalyptic aftermath of the First World War in Munich.[135]

The broader implications of this nascent *völkisch*-racist world view can be probed by examining the overarching eugenic vision of which it was a part. Müller, for example, came heavily under the sway of the eugenic ideas of Max Gruber, who had been affiliated with the inter-confessional moral purity movement and thus opposed the institution of mandatory clerical celibacy as "a perpetual debasement of the [German] race" because it deprived racially healthy priests from contributing to the national gene pool at a crucial point in the demographic development of the German *Volk*.[136] Citing Gruber as an authority, Müller insisted that "the breeding and maintenance of a healthy and noble race is incomparably more important than the passing on of the highest *Kulturgüter*, which will be nothing more than worthless rubble in the hands of degenerate offspring."[137] Muth's close friend and collaborator Josef Grassl, a Catholic eugenicist and expert on racial hygiene (he was a founding member of the Deutsche Gesellschaft für Rassenhygiene), published a number of radically *völkisch*-oriented articles in *Hochland*.[138] Ernst Thrasolt, the priest-publicist who had worked with Schrönghamer and Müller on the *Musenalmanach* project, continued to emphasize *völkisch* ideals as editor of the Catholic youth magazine *Efeuranken* between 1909 and 1912.[139] In the fall of 1913, Thrasolt, who was at the time serving in a small parish in Haag, founded the reform-oriented and radically *völkisch* Catholic journal *Das Heilige Feuer*, through which he maintained close connections to *völkisch* elements in Munich.[140] Among the Reform Catholic contributors to *Das Heilige Feuer* were Müller, Schrönghamer, and Christoph Flaskamp (who served as chair of the KG and was on Muth's editorial team at *Hochland*), in addition to the flaming Protestant anti-Semite Philipp Stauff, who provided a connection between *völkisch* Reform Catholic circles and the murky occult-oriented circles surrounding Guido von List and Lanz von Liebenfels.[141] According to Thrasolt, *Das Heilige Feuer* was to serve as the advance guard of an openly irenic but specifically Catholic-oriented movement for racial hygiene (*Rassenhygiene*), which not only would ensure the "purity of the race" but would also prevent the imminent threat of "racial degeneration."[142]

August Hallermeyer, a member of the KG's leadership committee, offered an even more expansive eugenic-*völkisch* vision, lamenting that German racial power (*Rassenkraft*) was being threatened by a "slow but certain degeneration," a process that was significantly worsened by allowing "racially inferior elements" to reproduce at alarming rates.[143] Identifying this trend as "racial suicide" (*Rassenselbstmord*), Hallermeyer insisted that "[i]t is not the indiscriminate propagation of the race, but only the effective cultivation of the better racial elements that can provide the basis for a rational population policy," and he went on to call for Reform Catholic nationalists to commit themselves to a wide-ranging and radical eugenics program in the interest of protecting the God-given racial superiority of the German *Volk*. For Hallermeyer and many of his Reform Catholic colleagues, maintaining "racial fitness" (*Rassentüchtigkeit*) was an almost religious duty to which German Catholics were called by God. In pursuit of this objective, Hallermeyer proposed, "The next step would be to demand obligatory health certificates at the time of marriage. The foundations would thereby be laid for the mandatory sterilization of racially inferior elements."[144] Foreshadowing policies that were to emerge in the not-so-distant future within the Nazi movement, Hallermeyer noted that it might take some time for these ideas to find broader acceptance: "These policies can only be the beginning of greater and more fundamental reforms, for which the times are not yet ripe. Public opinion must first be transformed in favor of a racially based ethic before a renewal from the ground up can be conceived."[145] As it happened, of course, it did take a number of years before a fundamental racial reform of this sort was effected under the Nazis. But the fact that such an elaborate *völkisch*-eugenics model was already laid out among Reform Catholic nationalists in Munich in 1914 is significant.[146]

The outbreak of the First World War ignited a groundswell of chauvinistic enthusiasm in Munich and throughout Germany.[147] As Ellen Lovell Evans has remarked more generally, in the early stages of the war, German Catholics "shared in the national upsurge of patriotic feeling and, as the war continued, came to believe that its requirements would bring opportunities for the full integration of Catholics into German society."[148] The seeming erasure of social divisions that accompanied the so-called *Burgfrieden* declared by Wilhelm II in the opening days of the war appeared to many in Munich as the culmination of the integrative nationalism advocated by the Reform Catholic movement.[149] The KG called for its supporters to commit fully to the interconfessional Christian-oriented nationalist unity that the group had been preaching for years:

> Now is no longer the time for the representation of our ideals on paper. The time for action has now come. Now we no longer need merely to preach to our Catholic co-religionists to join in the cultural work of our nation: the need of the hour now presses us all together, stronger than all admonitions of the word. German sentiment [*das deutsche Gefühl*] has now once again become a moral imperative.[150]

Within a few weeks, the leaders of the KG felt their integrative mission to be so nearly accomplished that they voluntarily suspended publication of the *Jahrhundert*, along with most of the activities of the society itself, so that members could devote their full attention to the all-encompassing war effort.[151] Karl Muth gushed about the nationalistic zeal called forth by the war, and he pledged to use the pages of *Hochland* both to foster commitment to the great world historical "mission" now facing the German *Volk* and to help create an unprecedented internal German unity that was to replace once and for all "the bitter discord that has so often divided the *Volk* in political, social, and religious conflicts."[152]

The fascination with *völkisch* and racial thought that was evident before the war became more pronounced after the outbreak of hostilities.

In a programmatic *Hochland* article on Catholic-oriented racial hygiene during the first month of the war, Josef Grassl proclaimed that the conflict would serve to "blow away all that is sickly and superficial" and would enable the "German *Volk* to rise to new heights from this challenge." Grassl also laid out his vision of the three main racial identities that had shaped world history—primary, secondary, and "parasitical" races—and praised the war as an opportunity to demonstrate once and for all the "vitality" of the German *Volk* and its superiority over all parasitical races, including most notably the Jews.[153] Other *Hochland* contributors, such as Julius Wolf, reinforced the idea that the war was essentially God's way of perfecting the potency and fighting strength of the German race.[154] Konrad Guenther argued that the German race, which was characterized by "courage," "industriousness," and "efficiency," was completely separate from the Jewish race, claiming more generally that "the Semites stand in complete contrast to the Indo-Europeans."[155] Albrecht Wirth, the radically racist history professor at the Technische Hochschule in Munich, also became closely aligned with Reform Catholic circles after the outbreak of the war, publishing numerous articles in *Hochland*.[156] Precisely at the time Muth energetically sought Wirth's collaboration, Wirth was beginning to gain national attention as a result of his *völkisch* manifesto *Rasse und Volk;* between 1921 and 1923, he became both the leading figure in the small Nazi group in Burghausen, a town near Altötting in southeastern Bavaria, where he had a second home, and a major contributor to the *Beobachter* in Munich.[157] Similarly, in the early months of the war, Thrasolt laid out a programmatic vision of a future Catholic-oriented racial movement, as yet undefined but identified as explicitly "*deutsch-völkisch.*" In Thrasolt's vision, this movement would renew Germany not only spiritually, but also specifically in terms of race and blood—through an insistence on flushing all "races of foreign blood" (*fremdblütige Rassen*) out of the German national bloodstream. Thrasolt portrayed the nature of Jewish influence within German culture in brutally graphic terms as "cultural excrement" (*Kulturexkrementen*) that was the direct result of racial and genetic characteristics. This Jewish presence within the German *Volkskörper* was so damaging and so pervasive that the only hope might be to remove it through a type of surgical excision, which Thrasolt hoped would be one of the major achievements of the war on the home front: "When a nationality [*Volkstum*] is already so weakened that [it is] no longer able to expel [*ausscheiden*] the foreign element from its body, then it is finished—unless an operation [*Operation*] helps. Will the 'operation' of war be a success? That is what we want to bring about!" Thrasolt closed with a clarion call to *völkisch* Catholics to maintain racial and cultural purity: "Let German blood and German character reign on German soil!"[158] The progression from the racial-eugenics vision of the KG's August Hallermeyer, which called for the "mandatory sterilization of all racially inferior elements," to Thrasolt's call for the surgical excision of the Jewish racial presence within the German *Volkskörper* is important to note, especially in light of the radical *völkisch* ideas that would soon be circulated in Munich by the early Nazi movement.

Given the virulence of this broader racial world view, it is perhaps not surprising that, by the end of the war, Ernst Thrasolt and Franz Schrönghamer emerged among the earliest contributors to a new and radically racist enterprise: the monthly journal *Auf gut deutsch*, which was founded in Munich by the Catholic-*völkisch* poet and playwright Dietrich Eckart in December 1918.[159] Whereas Thrasolt eventually settled in Berlin and increasingly embraced pacifism, ultimately disavowing his early *völkisch* activism and becoming a principled opponent of the Nazis, both Schrönghamer and Eckart became central figures in the *völkisch*-Nazi milieu that flourished in postwar Munich. Ultimately, however, the Reform Catholic movement that had given Schrönghamer his start failed to reconstitute itself after the First World War, suffering the fate of other so-called progressive movements across Germany in the face of the harsh realities of the postwar world.[160] The secretary of the KG, Josef Giliard, attempted to revive the organization but was forced to confide dejectedly to a friend in early 1919: "I feel so lonely now in the Krausgesellschaft, and if our forces do not gradually pull themselves together again, then Reform Catholicism can soon be put into the books as a movement that died a quiet death."[161] Although it remained in the Munich municipal registry until 1926, the KG was in fact dissolved for all intents and purposes by early 1920.[162] And the broader Reform Catholic movement did indeed recede from public view almost completely between the 1920s and the 1950s, only to be revived and rehabilitated—cleansed almost miraculously from its problematic association with both theological modernism and radical nationalism—as a forerunner to the spirit of ecumenical openness and scholarly engagement that suffused the deliberations of the Second Vatican Council.[163]

Ultimately, the demise of the distinctive tradition of Catholic anti-ultramontanism in prewar Munich left a complex legacy. Of the publications connected to the prewar Reform Catholic movement in Munich, only *Hochland* and the *Allgemeine Rundschau* continued into the postwar period, with *Hochland* embracing an increasingly apolitical conservative position and the *Rundschau*, under new leadership, placing itself energetically in the service of the newly founded BVP. With both *Renaissance* and the *Jahrhundert* defunct, the primary printed medium for Catholic opposition to ultramontanism and political Catholicism in Munich after the war became the *Beobachter* of the young *völkisch*-Nazi movement. Before tracing the resonance of central prewar tropes in the pages of the *Beobachter* and early Nazi circles more generally, the chapter that follows will illuminate the immediate postwar atmosphere of apocalyptic chaos and disillusion within which the Nazi movement was born.

CHAPTER 2

The Path toward Positive Christianity

Religious Identity and the Earliest Stages of the Nazi Movement, 1919–1920

At the time of the Nazi movement's founding in January 1919, its religious identity was in many ways vague and undefined. Shaped initially by a variety of competing influences, the young movement struggled to define a coherent ideological orientation, with religious ideals coexisting and intersecting with the often more pressing discourses of economy and race. By February 1920, after its fitful first year of existence, the movement's search for a recognizable religious identity found expression most famously in the principle of Positive Christianity, the centerpiece of point 24 of the party's program:

> We demand freedom for all religious confessions within the state, insofar as they do not threaten its existence or conflict with the ethical and moral sentiments of the German race. The party as such represents the principle of Positive Christianity, without binding itself to a particular confession. It combats the Jewish-materialistic spirit within and without us and is convinced that a lasting recovery of our *Volk* can only proceed from within, based on the principle: common interest before personal interest [*Gemeinnutz vor Eigennutz*].[1]

The vagueness of this formulation has been interpreted most frequently as evidence of the Nazi art of cynical obfuscation, appealing to Christianity publicly while in reality pursuing from the very beginning goals that were deliberately inimical to the Christian faith.[2] Not surprisingly, existing interpretive approaches have largely overlooked the overwhelmingly Catholic context within which the principle of

Positive Christianity was initially formulated and publicized as the official Nazi antidote to the "Jewish-materialistic spirit."

This chapter explores the background to the Nazi articulation of the ideal of Positive Christianity in early 1920. Beginning with the apocalyptic aftermath of the First World War, it examines the extent to which radical forms of anti-Semitism championed by Catholic figures like Franz Schrönghamer-Heimdal increasingly permeated throughout 1919 and early 1920 the Catholic press in Munich, including not only the official diocesan weekly *Münchener Katholische Kirchenzeitung* but also the local organs of the BVP, which claimed semi-officially to represent the political interests of the Catholic Church in Bavaria. When such mainstream and pro-BVP Catholic media eventually began turning away from their initial embrace of radical anti-Semitism toward more restrained and "respectable" forms of anti-Jewish critique, Catholic publicists like Schrönghamer and his close friend Dietrich Eckart became increasingly alienated from the BVP, which both had energetically supported initially.

This chapter will then proceed to examine the simultaneous development of the young *völkisch*-Nazi movement, whose uncompromising and radical anti-Semitism often appeared principled and decisive in contrast to the perceived opportunism, weakness, and hypocrisy of pro-BVP Catholics. Special emphasis will be placed on the young movement's leading organ, the *Beobachter,* and on the important roles played within the movement by Schrönghamer, Eckart, and other radical Catholics, many of whom were strongly influenced by the anti-ultramontane ideas of the prewar Reform Catholic movement. The intertwining of these two trajectories—Catholic and *völkisch*—helped to provide much of the immediate framework within which the Nazi party program was promulgated and, with it, the ideal of Positive Christianity.

Postwar Chaos, Apocalypticism, and Anti-Semitism in Catholic Munich

Whatever else it might have been, the Nazi movement was above all a child of the atmosphere of extreme crisis that engulfed Munich after the First World War, where the revolution that toppled the Wittelsbach monarchy and brought the socialist theater critic Kurt Eisner to power in November 1918 was succeeded in the spring of 1919 by two progressively radical attempts to erect a Soviet dictatorship in the Bavarian capital. This brief but brutal Soviet experiment in Munich, in which Russian Jewish émigrés played an important part, did much to accelerate and radicalize anti-Semitic and anti-Marxist attitudes among Munich's overwhelmingly Catholic population. The perceived linkages between Bolshevism, atheism, and the Jews were given a much more sinister edge by the Soviet regime's infamous authorization of the murder of a group of right-wing hostages in Munich's Luitpoldgymnasium in late April 1919. The ensuing "liberation" of the city from Red forces by counterrevolutionary military and paramilitary troops in early May was brutally violent as well, characterized not only by spontaneous executions of known Soviet activists but also by widespread arbitrary shootings, such as the killing of more than twenty members of a Catholic Gesellenverein mistakenly identified as communists. Following the ultimate defeat of the Soviet republic, Munich and Bavaria more generally continued to be wracked by economic turmoil and swirling social and political unrest—an environment characterized fittingly by Martin Geyer as a *verkehrte Welt,* a world turned literally upside down.[3] By March 1920, with the installation of the ultraconservative Gustav von Kahr as minister-president in the aftermath of the Kapp Putsch, the political pendulum had completed a dramatic swing, and Bavaria was well on its way to earning its reputation as a refuge for right-wing radicals from across Germany. It was within this fluid climate of crisis and uncertainty between early 1919 and early 1920 that the Nazi movement took its first steps, as one initially insignificant group in an expanding sea of radical political organizations in Munich.

The broader circumstances of military defeat and revolution, along with the intense psychological convolutions they spawned, were interpreted not only within a general spiritual framework but also in distinctly apocalyptic terms by many Catholics in Munich.[4] In November 1918, Archbishop Michael von Faulhaber encapsulated much of the existential confusion and despair felt throughout his diocese, launching into an impassioned discourse on the four horsemen of the apocalypse—with each "apocalyptic rider" corresponding directly to specific aspects of the immediate crisis in Munich—and invoking as preferable the fate of those who had been lucky enough to die on the battlefield.[5] Faulhaber, who had been among the most outspoken and energetic supporters of the war effort within the German episcopate, now became perhaps the most articulate prophet of disillusion and desperation.[6] As brutal as the humiliation of the war's conclusion undoubtedly was, for many Catholics the most pressing danger was the threat of the new socialist government in Munich, which was being driven forward by a perceived cabal of Jews and atheists surrounding Kurt Eisner, who, it seemed, had destroyed the existing God-given order and were ushering in a period of apocalyptic and perhaps irreparable devastation, creating an "expanse of ruins more monumental than the ruins of the Tower of Babel."[7] The immediate focal point of much of Faulhaber's rage was the issue of religious education, in particular a government proposal of 25 January 1919 to declare religious instruction optional rather than mandatory in Bavarian schools.[8] Reviving imagery of the Prussian *Kulturkampf* of the 1870s, Faulhaber called for Catholics to mobilize in oppositon to socialist educational policies in an all-out crusade fueled by "flaming indignation," with the issue of religious education serving as the sharpened tip of a broader counterrevolutionary blade.[9] The eight major protest rallies organized by the archdiocese in the first week of February 1919 were framed as a tangible expression of justified Catholic outrage.[10]

The overarching conclusion drawn in the aftermath of defeat and revolution was that the Jews above all were behind these machinations and were simultaneously in the process of launching a broader apocalyptic conspiracy, a coordinated international assault on Christian values.[11] The brutal sentiments expressed by the influential Catholic priest Anton Braun in a well-publicized sermon in December 1918—that Eisner was nothing more than a "sleazy Jew" and his administration a dishonorable "pack of unbelieving Jews"—were increasingly pervasive throughout Bavaria.[12] Attempting to come to grips with the broader dimensions of the radical changes since the revolution began, the *Münchener Katholische Kirchenzeitung* ran a conspiratorial feature article on the sinister role of international Freemasonry, praising the most recent work of the raving Austrian anti-Semite Friedrich Wichtl for its "astonishing thoroughness" and noting with special emphasis Wichtl's tirades against the role played by Jewish politicians in the secret Masonic-Jewish conspiracy to dominate the world.[13] Similarly, the pro-BVP press in Munich, especially the cultural weekly *Allgemeine Rundschau,* which had placed itself energetically in the service of the new BVP, publicized Wichtl's racist ramblings as an indispensable aid in interpeting rapidly changing world events and expressed hope that the book would "be read in circles to which books from Catholic authors and presses usually do not have access."[14]

The BVP itself had been formed initially in mid-November 1918 as a rightist Bavarian offshoot of the Center Party, which BVP organizers initially portrayed as unprincipled and opportunistic for accommodating itself too quickly to the new revolutionary order, being tainted further by the collaboration of Center Party politicians like Matthias Erzberger with socialist leaders in the latter stages of the war.[15] The BVP claimed at its founding to be much more than an exclusively Catholic entity, pitching itself instead as a truly interconfessional *Volkspartei* that would "bear the true Bavarian spirit, uniting all segments of the *Volk*."[16] The earliest in-house history of the BVP, published in 1920, also emphasized the importance of this explicitly interconfessional ideal, identifying the party as an "overarching, Christian *Sammlungspartei*" that was to remain "free from any confessional barrier" while serving as a "crystallization point . . . for all *Volksgenossen* who espouse a positive nonsocialist orientation."[17] This stance initially drew to the party an influx of Catholics who had previously opposed political Catholicism, including elements from the former Reform Catholic and Christian Social movements. In campaigning for the January 1919 elections, the BVP issued broad interconfessional appeals addressed to the "Christian *Volk*" of Bavaria as a monolithic entity and attempted to position the party as the only true defender of Christian ideals and institutions in Munich against the anti-Christian machinations of the communist Spartakusbund, then engaged in bloody turmoil on the streets of Berlin.[18] Even in its earliest propagandistic rhetoric, however, the BVP betrayed the limits of its self-professed interconfessionalism. The party's official language spoke of the protection of Christianity more generally, to be sure, but it was no accident that Munich's Frauenkirche rather than the Protestant Markuskirche was emblazoned throughout the BVP's propagandistic imagery. In reality, the BVP strove quite self-consciously to position itself as the quasi-official representative of the political interests of the Catholic Church in Bavaria—a message hammered home through the party's leading organs in Munich, the daily *Bayerischer Kurier* and the *Allgemeine Rundschau*—while the BVP eventually set to work explicitly, albeit occasionally with some tension, as the sister party of the Reich-level Center Party.[19]

The BVP leaders in Munich were particularly intent on weaving together anti-republican sentiment with strong doses of local Catholic-oriented anti-Semitism, famously directing hostility at Berlin not only as the seat of the new republican government but, especially, as the city of "Jews and asphalt" in one of its earliest propaganda pamphlets.[20] Throughout the first several months of 1919—stretching from the initial heated debates over the removal of mandatory religious education to the aftermath of the *Räterepublik*—the pages of the *Rundschau* were dominated by a major multipart series on the deleterious influence of the Jews that was written by the Catholic statistician Hans Rost, a major proponent of the BVP who had been a regular contributor to *Hochland* before the war. With the memory of decaying bodies on the battlefield still fresh in the public consciousness, Rost's first installment morbidly associated the impact of the Jews with the rotting of "the body of the German nation" (*Volkskörper*).[21] In a later installment, Rost thundered against the dangers to the German race presented by the alleged physical degeneration and biological-racial inferiority of the Jews—attempting to provide statistical evidence of disproportionately high rates of genetically induced alcoholism, sexually transmitted diseases, mental illness, and blindness—while stopping short of embracing full-fledged racial anti-Semitism. Ultimately, however, Rost warned that, although the Jews made up only a tiny percentage of the population, Germans could not afford to remain apathetic regarding the "corrosive" threat they comprised, a threat that could ultimately result in the apocalyptic "downfall of our German culture."[22] The *Historisch-politische Blätter,* the Munich-based Catholic intellectual journal that also strongly backed the BVP, albeit from a more traditionally conservative position than the *Rundschau,* offered similarly brutal assessments of the political and cultural impact of the Jews, attacking the immorality of the "Jewish and Christian-Jewish traffickers" who sought profit above all else and were destroying the nobility of German culture.[23]

The experience of the Munich *Räterepublik* in April 1919 greatly accelerated these initial apocalyptic trends in pro-BVP circles.[24] Immediately following the brutal "liberation" of the city in early May, the *Kirchenzeitung* published a striking appeal to Munich Catholics, calling for expressions of gratitude for the troops that had freed them from the Soviet regime's Jewish ringleaders (identified euphemistically as "foreign elements") and explicitly justifying, even idealizing, the deadly arbitrary violence carried out by Freikorps forces:

> That here and there mistakes may have been made is of course clear. But of what significance are these in comparison to the terrorism under which we still suffered only a few days ago? And even if occasionally things were undertaken too brusquely, even if completely innocent people lost their lives—for which we feel pain—we must also keep in mind the way in which so many of the courageous soldiers who came to our rescue were murdered in cowardly fashion in recent days. We understand if, at the sight of their massacred comrades, soldiers were possessed by a rage that led occasionally to an all-too-energetic course of action.[25]

With regard to broader events, the *Kirchenzeitung* pursued an explicitly conspiratorial line of thought, perceiving a sinister hidden connection between leading Jewish elements in the Munich Soviet and their "racial comrades" like the Rothschild family, who were endangering Christian values through unfettered world plutocracy.[26] The *Historisch-politische Blätter* made similar connections regarding the broader anti-Christian objectives of the Jewish world conspiracy that had been "unmasked" during the Munich Soviet debacle.[27] In continuing to celebrate the defeat of the *Räterepublik* later in the summer, the *Rundschau* also insisted on reminding its readers of the role played by the "hustling Semites" and the "swarms of Jews and foreigners" who had nearly destroyed the Christian character of Munich that the BVP was striving so heroically to preserve.[28]

The broader implications of this trajectory can perhaps best be seen in the activism of two radical Catholic publicists—Franz Schrönghamer and Dietrich Eckart—who initially supported the BVP in early 1919 but eventually abandoned it in favor of the young Nazi movement. Schrönghamer, who added the Nordic suffix "Heimdal" to his name on the eve of the First World War, had been shaped decisively by his participation alongside Josef Müller in the prewar Reform Catholic movement, helping to found the Verein Renaissance in 1904 and coming into contact with influential Catholic nationalists and anti-Semites like August Rohling, who collaborated with Müller in publishing the journal *Renaissance* (see fig. 2.1). After completing his architectural studies in Munich, Schrönghamer assumed the editorship of the satirical magazine *Fliegende Blätter* in Munich while also beginning to write poetry and humorous short stories.[29] While never giving up his interest in humor, after the outbreak of war in 1914, Schrönghamer became a leading Catholic devotional author, focusing especially on the moral and spiritual dimensions of the war in a number of popular works published with the leading Catholic press, Herder.[30] By the later stages of the war, Schrönghamer had turned his focus increasingly to the two main fixations that would dominate his thought and political writing over the next several years: the fusion of *völkisch*-Nordic ideology with the Catholic faith, which he saw as providing the basis for a glorious Germanic empire that would dominate the future; and the eradication of what he saw as the greatest nemesis and historical archenemy of the true Christian-Germanic spirit, international Jewry.[31]

In the summer of 1918, while splitting his time between Munich and Passau, Schrönghamer published the apocalyptic *Vom Ende der Zeiten* (On the End of Days), a rambling theological and philosophical treatise. His goal was to outline a distinctly Catholic-oriented interpretation of the end times based on a mixture of Germanic, scholarly, and biblical sources—or, as Schrönghamer put it, on the powerful triumvirate of

Figure 2.1. Franz Schrönghamer-Heimdal (1926).

"legend, science, and revealed faith"—within which the revealed truth of Catholic faith (*Glaubensoffenbarung*) would, it was claimed, always take precedence.[32] Schrönghamer argued that Catholic revelation and Nordic legend were in perfect God-ordained harmony, with the full-blown heroism of the Christ of the New Testament having been foreshadowed dimly yet valiantly by the figures of the *Edda,* the ancient Nordic saga that spoke of the son of God as "Widar." And since Jesus himself had railed against the Jews, calling them "children of Satan" in the Gospel of John, Schrönghamer believed that it was incumbent on German Catholics to recognize the possibility that the *Edda* might also contain divine inspiration as a form of "pre-Christianity," at least to the extent that the allegedly inferior "Jewish" Old Testament was accepted as divinely inspired by traditional Catholic theology.[33] Schrönghamer's book appeared with the imprimatur of the vicar general of Augsburg, Magnus Niedermair, who noted explicitly that it "contains nothing contrary to Catholic faith and morals," thus providing the author with a crucial measure of legitimacy in the eyes of his Catholic readers even as he began to press the limits of Catholic theological orthodoxy.[34]

Schrönghamer quickly published the second installment of his sweeping 1918 apocalyptic vision, *Vom Antichrist,* a venomous missive identifying the "eternal Jew" as the archenemy of the biblical end days. Elaborating his claim regarding the harmony between the *Edda* and Christian revelation, he thundered against the alleged materialism and atheism of international Jewry, whose activities constituted a global conspiracy equivalent to the apocalyptic "great whore" of Babylon from the book of Revelation.[35] The influence of August Rohling, with whom the young Schrönghamer had collaborated in the prewar circle surrounding Josef Müller's *Renaissance,* was particularly evident throughout the book, which made frequent reference to the *Talmud-Juden* as the "sworn enemies of Christianity." Following Rohling, Schrönghamer stated flatly that the "eternal Jew is the born Antichrist; the two are the same thing."[36]

Schrönghamer's apocalyptic ravings in 1918 culminated with the publication of the programmatic manifesto *Das kommende Reich,* which was written during the upheaval of October and November and appeared in print shortly thereafter. Building on the ideas of his two preceeding works, Schrönghamer portrayed himself as the prophet of a new world historical epoch in which the German *Volk* would fulfill its God-given mission as the agent of God's justice and would establish a new Germanic Reich, a Third Reich that would be more glorious and lasting than the Holy Roman Empire or Bismarck's Second Reich. Schrönghamer argued that the experience of war had chastised and hardened the German *Volk* and that the nascent revolution, while godless and unjust in itself, could serve unwittingly as the agent of God's providence, tearing down the decayed ruins of the hopelessly outdated Kaiserreich and ushering in a new era in which the forces of Christian-Germanic "justice" would prevail over the forces of "Jewish materialism and greed."[37] The anti-Semitism that had permeated his previous works emerged in sharpened form here, with the Jews being condemned as "hereditarily tainted" and as "interest-earning parasites and extortionary blood suckers."[38] Schrönghamer argued that the Jews were a biologically inferior race that must not be allowed to mix with Aryan Germanic blood under any circumstances:

> Race equals purity, above all purity of conscience. And in this sense racial and hereditary cultivation [*Rassen- und Sippenpflege*] must be practiced in the coming Germanic Reich.... A goal-oriented racial community [*Volksgemeinschaft*] cannot do without determined leadership, and this includes the expulsion of all [racial] forces that work against the German essence.[39]

In equating racially pure Germanic identity with revealed Christian doctrine, Schrönghamer also displayed a strange fascination with word-play, attempting to connect disparate ideas through perceived common etymological roots. In one extended discourse, he made the claim that the German "essence" was built upon the God-given command to engage in productive work, which was inimical to the usurious identity of the Jews: the Germanic concept of work (*Arbeit*) was, according to Schrönghamer, the revealed "light" and "law" of God (*Arbot*), which the Germans' ancient Nordic forebears were in reality worshipping when they appeared outwardly to be worshipping the pagan concept of the sun (*Sonnengebot*).[40] Somewhat surprisingly, this convoluted and seemingly childish word-play was one of the aspects of Schrönghamer's work that resonated most powerfully in Munich.[41] Finally, the devotional reflections that ran throughout the book were steeped in the Reform Catholic idea of counterbalancing the "unhealthiness" of political Catholicism with the nobility of religious Catholicism.[42] In the months after its appearance, *Das kommende Reich* became one of the most widely discussed books in Munich.[43]

Throughout 1919, Schrönghamer continued his frenetic publishing pace, producing four more political monographs on specialized aspects of his broader vision. The first installment, which identified itself as a "guide through the collapse of the world," focused on the resurrection of Nordic-Germanic greatness from the ruins of the revolution, fueled by a crusading Christian zeal.[44] The second appealed to the eternal "spirit of love" and preached that the secret to rebuilding German greatness was the creation of a unified (and racially pure) *Volksgemeinschaft* based on the practice of Christian charity embodied most nobly in the Sermon on the Mount.[45] The third focused on the overcoming of "Jewish-inspired" capitalism through the abolition of all income not earned through productive labor.[46] The fourth, by far the most radical, was a manifesto that claimed to lay out both the nature of the "Jewish problem" and its painful, yet necessary, solution: "The salvation of the world can only come through the extermination [*Vernichtung*] of the world poison [*Weltgift*] whose destructive capacities we recognize in the intellectual foundations of Jewry."[47] Remarkably, during this period, Schrönghamer also found time to continue writing novels and humorous short stories.[48] In the summer of 1919, however, Schrönghamer began a period of especially intense journalistic activity in Munich focused initially on the official and semi-official Catholic press, especially the pro-BVP *Rundschau,* both reflecting and helping to shape broader apocalyptic and anti-Semitic trends within Munich Catholicism in the aftermath of the *Räterepublik.*

In August 1919, under the title "Collapse of the World," the *Rundschau* published Schrönghamer's programmatic interpretation of the tumultuous events of the previous several months, which he identified, in typically apocalyptic fashion, as the early stages of the "final struggle [*Endkampf*] between two world forces, between Christ and the Antichrist . . . between the eternal German and the eternal Jew."[49] Turning to the issue of religious education, which was still burning in Catholic circles in Munich, Schrönghamer built further upon his earlier apocalyptic end-of-days imagery and, with the flourish of a revivalist preacher, concluded by calling Munich Catholics to join in the coming epic battle between the Catholic-Christian forces of light and the Jewish-Marxist forces of darkness and evil:

> Today the Jews continue to attack and persecute Jesus Christ [through] the de-Christianization of the schools, the separation of church and state, and the rooting out of all Christian ideas from civic and public life. . . . Do you not see that the Antichrist is at work here, that this is part of the *Endkampf?* Where will you stand, dear Christian, when the battle cry in the spiritual struggle sounds forth: Here Christian, here Antichrist?[50]

In the midst of his diatribes against Jews and Marxists, Schrönghamer was not afraid to tread openly on shaky theological ground by insisting that Christ was not Jewish but in fact a Galilean Aryan from Nazareth whose racial identity stood in stark contrast to the racially inferior Jews of Jerusalem: "Was Jesus a Jew? We know that it is the spirit that bestows life. Jesus-spirit and Jew-spirit—is any greater contradiction imaginable? That is why the Jews attacked, persecuted, and drove to a shameful death the savior of the world, the Galilean. They never counted Jesus as one of their own, because he was not a Jew, neither in spirit nor in body." Although he would go on to expand on these ideas in greater depth in a multipart series entitled "Was Jesus a Jew?" in the *Beobachter* shortly after officially joining the Nazi party some six months later, Schrönghamer's repudiation of the Jewish identity of Jesus was already remarkably sweeping.[51]

Schrönghamer's views were apparently deemed acceptable within pro-BVP Catholic circles, at least initially, and were likely not idiosyncratic. Rather than censuring him for his unquestionably unorthodox theological position—or even publishing a short editorial caveat—the *Rundschau* instead ran another major anti-Semitic feature article by Schrönghamer in the next issue, which linked international capitalism and Bolshevism through the agency of world Jewry (*Alljuda*) in an overarching apocalyptic conspiracy to "subjugate and enslave the Christian world." A central component of this conspiracy was, according to Schrönghamer, the Jews' ability to manipulate capitalist markets to keep Christian peoples in a perpetual state of "interest slavery." In contrast to the ideas of Gottfried Feder, with whom the concept of "interest slavery" ultimately came to be most closely identified, for Schrönghamer and other Catholic anti-Semites this condition was seen in large part as the tragic by-product of the earlier abandonment of the Catholic Church's laudable and long-standing prohibition during the Middle Ages against charging interest.[52] In spite of their radical anti-Semitism and seemingly problematic theological content, Schrönghamer's works continued to appear in the *Rundschau* with great regularity throughout late 1919 and early 1920.[53] In the swirling confusion, chaos, and disillusionment of the immediate postwar years, it was often the mere ability to lay plausible claim to "authentic" Catholic identity—bolstered perhaps by a diocesan imprimatur—that was of greater significance than the technical orthodoxy of one's theological views.

By the fall of 1919, leading elements within the BVP felt the need to distance themselves from this type of radical anti-Semitism—not because of theological concerns over Schrönghamer's Aryanization of Jesus, which was left entirely uncontested, but at least in part for political reasons connected to the BVP's position within the current Bavarian governing coalition.[54] The general secretary of the BVP, Anton Pfeiffer, began to single out individual Jews who were "highly respectable" in speeches that otherwise continued to attack the Jews with great vehemence.[55] Similarly, in a series of articles beginning in November 1919, the editor of the *Rundschau,* Joseph Kausen, began arguing for a more moderate and respectable form of Catholic anti-Jewish critique.[56] Responding in particular to the brutality of Schrönghamer's utilization of Rohling's *Talmudjude,* Kausen argued that the Talmud should not be used as a weapon to attack the entire Jewish population and noted, moreover, that one could cite numerous Christian writings that contained unfortunate and morally problematic excesses. After providing this laudable caveat, Kausen embarked on a deeply problematic and potentially contradictory discourse with the apparent intent of not alienating readers who supported Schrönghamer's radical anti-Semitism. Emphasizing the importance of continuing to identify and battle against what he viewed as the undeniably unhealthy influence of the Jews—citing the "Golden International," "international freemasonry," and "war profiteers, revolutionaries, price-gougers, and usurers" as characteristically Jewish manifestations—Kausen attempted somewhat meekly to differentiate "honest" Jews from "immoral" ones and claimed that this distinction would allow Catholic anti-Semites to continue to attack the Jews while still practicing "Christian charity."[57] Kausen's article was followed in the same issue by a learned exposition on the difficulties of laymen and non-Jews being able to accurately interpret passages of the Talmud, making it wiser to keep the Talmud out of the realm of political propaganda and to leave its interpretation to qualified scholars.[58] Kausen continued a few weeks later with another rather muddled article that attempted to demonstrate the justness of energetic critiques of demonstrable Jewish immorality, which was rooted explicitly in the "detrimental characteristics of the Jewish race," while hypocritically condemning racial anti-Semitism as an offense against Christian charity.[59] At the same time, the *Rundschau* insisted on continuing the political fight against the forces of Marxism by mercilessly attacking the Jewish identity of many of its leading figures, consistently using race as a clear dividing point and continually pointing to the "disgusting characteristics of the Semitic race," while claiming to decry racial anti-Semitism as un-Christian.[60] A similar shift was visible starting in late 1919 in other pro-BVP organs in Munich, such as the *Historisch-politische Blätter,* which emphasized the moral imperative to battle energetically against the Jews, often identified in explicitly racial terms, while it attempted to maintain a fine distinction between full-fledged racial hatred and and Christian charity.[61] This "distinction," which characterized the BVP position more generally but often appeared simply confusing and contradictory in practice, was a major contributing factor to the bitter defection of Schrönghamer and other radical Catholic anti-Semites from the BVP in late 1919 and early 1920.[62]

In addition to his apocalyptic attacks on the Talmud and the Jews, Schrönghamer's *Rundschau* contributions in 1919 had also given open

Figure 2.2. Dietrich Eckart (early 1920s).
Source: Sesselmann and Hoffmann, *Deutschlands Erwachen.*

support and publicity to the works of his friend Dietrich Eckart, whose rabid anti-Semitism and unorthodox Catholic identity would come to exercise a significant influence on the young Nazi movement (see fig. 2.2).[63] Eckart was born and raised in the Catholic Bavarian *Oberpfalz* and had initially embarked on a career in medicine, but he was forced to abandon his medical studies either as the result of a nervous disorder or, perhaps more likely, following the first of many bouts with morphine addiction. After receiving a sizable inheritance upon the death of his father in 1895, Eckart strove to establish himself as a playwright and literary translator in Regensburg, Leipzig, and Berlin, eventually achieving some measure of publishing success which provided him access to fairly elevated social circles.[64] After cultivating initial connections with Reform Catholic cultural figures in Munich before the First World War, Eckart moved permanently to Munich in 1915.[65] Circulating during the war years in Catholic-nationalist circles in Munich, Eckart exhibited a growing fixation with the allegedly superficial Jewish materialism prevalent in Schwabing, which he claimed was in danger of destroying the Christian-Germanic soul. Eckart honed an increasingly apocalyptic racist message in numerous journalistic forays, typically from a bombastic self-professed Christian-Catholic perspective, and he often broke with other *völkisch* thinkers by mercilessly attacking the anti-Christian ideas of Nietzsche, whom Eckart labeled "that lunatic despiser of our religious foundations."[66] After participating in the surge of Catholic support for the Vaterlandspartei in 1917, Eckart became an increasingly visible public figure in Munich and continued to publish widely in a variety of local papers and journals.[67]

Following the military collapse and the initial establishment of the Eisner regime, Eckart founded a new radical right-wing weekly entitled *Auf gut deutsch: Wochenschrift für Ordnung and Recht* (*In Plain German: Weekly Journal of Law and Order*), which he funded largely with his own money and which gained a varied readership throughout Germany—especially among nationalistic Catholics, including several notable priests.[68] Eckart initially placed his journalistic energies strongly in the service of the newly founded BVP, attempting to steer the party away from the excessive internationalism and ultramontanism of the Center Party to create a true Christian *Volkspartei* capable of battling the revolutionary and atheistic policies of the Jews and Marxists. While the struggle against the Jews was and would remain his first priority, Eckart echoed the Reform Catholic critique of political ultramontanism as a disastrous influence on both the Catholic faith and the German nation. The first issue of *Auf gut deutsch* trumpeted Eckart's Catholic identity ("I am a Catholic from the *Oberpfalz*") and featured a programmatic diagnosis of the potential "blemishes" within the BVP that might limit the party's effectiveness, focusing especially on the role of ultramontane cleric-politicians and the initially clumsy BVP attempts to appeal to newly enfranchised Catholic women.[69] At the same time, appropriating a central catchphrase from his friend Schrönghamer, Eckart proclaimed in no uncertain terms that the BVP was, despite its imperfections, the only viable political option in the apocalyptic battle of "Christian versus Antichrist," with the most pressing threat being the issue that so consumed Faulhaber and others, the Jewish-socialist separation of church and state and the impending removal of mandatory religious instruction from Bavarian schools. Defending himself from ultramontane forces offended by his criticisms of excessive clerical electioneering, Eckart went on to insist unequivocally that political support for the BVP in the January 1919 election was a holy duty for Catholics, a moral imperative to stand up for "the only party that places itself wholeheartedly upon the foundation of Christianity" in the face of the apocalyptic machinations of the Jews.[70]

Over the course of 1919, however, Eckart abandoned his initial support for the BVP and, feeling that the party had betrayed its Christian identity by collaborating increasingly with a fatal mixture of pro-republican Center Party figures, Jews, and Marxists, eventually became, along with Schrönghamer, one of the BVP's most vocal opponents in Munich.[71] Opening the pages of *Auf gut deutsch* to a number of energetic Catholic racists and nationalists who were similarly critical of the Center Party and BVP—including Catholic priests like Ernst Thrasolt and Anton Fischer—Eckart attempted to stake out a Catholic position that was non-ultramontane yet religiously observant, uncompromising in opposition to the Jews yet advocating selfless sacrifice toward fellow Christians, and open to interconfessional cooperation.[72] Furthermore, as a corollary to his very vocal emphasis on his Catholic identity, Eckart's ideas moved onto shaky theological ground to an even greater extent than did the ideas of Schrönghamer—not only questioning but personally rejecting the validity of the Old Testament, for instance—and ultimately he gave his BVP opponents a rather easy target to attack over the next several years.[73] Had Eckart somehow remained politically supportive of the BVP throughout this period, it is unlikely that he would have been singled out for his convoluted racial and religious ideas; there were undoubtedly "good" Catholic laypeople within the BVP who personally held unorthodox theological views, in addition to Protestant BVP members, whose religious views were often diametrically opposed to official Catholic teaching. In any event, theological nuances were frequently beyond the grasp (or interest) of disillusioned Catholics in Munich swept up in a period of chaos and confusion. As was the case with Schrönghamer, Eckart's public plausibility as a believing Catholic provided cover for other Catholic racists to follow in his steps without seeming to come into conflict with the essence of their Catholic faith. This plausibility was, in turn, enhanced by the numerous Catholic priests who stepped forward to campaign on behalf of the Nazis over the next few years.

To cite one example, in the wake of the early wave of activism by Schrönghamer and Eckart, the weekly diocesan *Kirchenzeitung* adopted in early 1920 a similarly rabid anti-Semitic line under the editorship of the local priest Franz Xaver Meisl, who simultaneously occupied the influential position of secretary of the diocesan Pressverein.[74] Rather than embrace the shift toward more moderate anti-Semitism, Meisl's paper accelerated the battle against the ever-present dangers of internationalism and Jewish-sponsored Freemasonry, pointing back to the nobility of the medieval Catholic persecution of the Jews and going beyond basic cultural and economic anti-Semitism to construct a muddled pseudo-racial definition of international Jewry based on "nationality" and "blood."[75] Meisl continued this line of thought in publishing a series of sensationalistic articles on the role of the Jews in anti-Christian activities in eastern Europe, thundering against the "communist *Ostjuden*" who "represent a great threat to the Catholic Church in Austria,"[76] and viewing with cynicism and open contempt the questionable sincerity of several thousand Jewish converts to Catholicism in the wake of the overthrow of the Bela Kun regime in Hungary.[77] Clearly caught up in broader apocalyptic currents, Meisl went on to fully embrace the most radical of anti-Semitic world-conspiracy theories, the *Protocols of the Elders of Zion,* providing his diocesan readers with the address in Berlin-Charlottenburg from which they could obtain the latest German translation and echoing the claim of the *Elders* text that the First World War had unquestionably been manufactured by the Jews as an attack on Christianity and as the first step toward a future Jewish world dictatorship of apocalyptic proportions.[78] After several additional racist missives, Meisl reached a fevered pitch in what turned out to be his final anti-Semitic assault in the *Kirchenzeitung,* sounding the call to Munich Catholics to launch an all-out war against the Jews and claiming justification in the fact that the Jews had themselves already "declared war on Catholicism." After characterizing this campaign alternately as a religious revival and a "new Reformation," Meisl closed with the demand that the "usurious spirit" of the Jews be "exterminated" (*ausgerottet*).[79] Although envisioning this type of extermination is far different from calling for the physical extinction of the Jews, the message from the editorial offices of the *Kirchenzeitung* had been sent only too clearly.

Meisl had attempted to cover himself with a fig leaf of legality—calling first for an end to the legal immigration of *Ostjuden*—but the extremism of this string of articles ultimately cost him his position at the *Kirchenzeitung.* Only a week or so after his last anti-Semitic diatribe, Meisl's superior within the Catholic Pressverein in Munich, the pro-BVP priest Ludwig Müller, made a much-publicized appearance at a major gathering of the local Jewish community (Israelitische Kultusge-meinde München) in the lavish Hotel Bayerischer Hof to disavow this type of harsh anti-Semitic activism and to claim publicly that radical anti-Semitism, particularly of the racial variety, was incompatible with true Catholic Christianity.[80] Meisl had anticipated these sorts of criticisms, arguing that radical Catholic anti-Semitism was not to be seen merely as an expression of backward and vulgar hatred but rather as justified self-defense; true Catholics, he claimed, had a religious and moral responsibility to fight explicitly against the Jews—including the outlawing of Jewish-Christian intermarriage—not in contradiction to their Catholic faith but as a clear expression of it.[81] In the end, however, Müller's declaration to the Kultusgemeinde was accompanied by the simultaneous demotion of Meisl, who was allowed to remain, apparently chastised, on the *Kirchenzeitung* staff for another few months but was stripped of his title as secretary of the diocesan Press-verein and transferred to another post.[82] Interestingly, Meisl's person-nel file in the Munich archdiocesan archive does not contain any disciplinary notes regarding this transfer; in fact, all of his yearly performance reviews from before the incident are missing entirely, and they begin again only after the transfer. The overwhelmingly positive nature of these later reviews, from February 1921 and Janu-ary 1922, likely stems from the fact that they were written by his new superior, Johann Widmann, the flamingly nationalistic parish priest (*Stadtpfarrer*) in Munich-Haidhausen who would later become one of the growing number of Catholic clergymen performing *völkisch* and Nazi-oriented masses in the summer of 1923.[83] Ultimately, how-ever, in place of the brutal anti-Semitism pursued previously by the *Kirchenzeitung*, a more restrained anti-Jewish stance mirroring that of the *Rundschau* prevailed.

The shift within pro-BVP circles, and especially the changes at the *Kirchenzeitung*, drew the ire of an increasing number of Catholic anti-Semites in Munich. The impassioned sentiments expressed in the *Beobachter* some three weeks after Ludwig Müller's Kultusgemeinde remarks, condemning Müller by name and idealizing the heroic courage of anti-Semitic Catholic "warriors," grew more and more widespread.[84] By that time, large numbers of Catholic anti-Semites had already begun to gravitate toward the young *völkisch*-Nazi movement, using the *Beobachter* as a sort of counterweight to compensate for the effective declawing of Catholic anti-Semitism in organs like the *Kirchenzeitung* and the *Rundschau*.

"A Strike Force against All Racially Foreign Machinations": Catholic-*Völkisch* Activism, the *Beobachter,* and the Deutsche Arbeiterpartei

In the midst of the broader turmoil in Munich in the aftermath of the war, exacerbated by growing economic misery, the Nazi movement began its organizational life in January 1919 with the founding of the German Workers' Party (Deutsche Arbeiterpartei, or DAP).[85] The party's primary founder, Anton Drexler, was born and raised in Munich and had begun his political activism during the First World War, most notably at the central workshop of the Bavarian state railway in the Neuhausen section of Munich, where he had worked since 1902. In 1917, Drexler joined the Munich branch of the Vaterlandspartei and, in March 1918, founded the short-lived Freie Arbeiterausschuss für einen guten Frieden (Free Workers' Committee for a Good Peace), through which he hoped to spread the annexationist ideals of the Vaterlandspartei to Munich's working classes. In late 1918, in the context of military defeat and nascent revolution, Drexler then established the Politischer Arbei-terzirkel (Political Workers' Circle), through which he propagated a distinctly anti-Marxist and anti-Semitic message, capitalizing on rampant frustrations associated with the new Eisner regime. In January 1919, the DAP grew directly out of the Politischer Arbeiterzirkel.[86]

While the religious identity of the DAP at its inception remains somewhat shrouded, almost all of the original founding members came from broadly Catholic working-class backgrounds.[87] Drexler claimed in his 1919 memoir, which Hitler later credited with attracting him to the party, to have found his inspiration directly in the heroism of Jesus Christ, and he pledged that his nascent political activism would proceed explicitly "in the spirit of Christ, the most magnificent figure in the history of the world."[88] Although the young DAP exhibited connections to the Catholic-oriented anti-Semitism of the prewar Christian Social movement led by Ludwig Wenng—who was by then too old and ill to be politically active but who witnessed two of his sons, a daughter-in-law, and a nephew become energetic early members—a much more significant characteristic of the movement was the overrepresentation of distinctly *bürgerlich* elements, ranging from decommissioned officers to university students to young professionals who had been radicalized and galvanized by the disillusion and chaos of the immediate postwar period. By the time the DAP began its public emergence in early 1920, these elements in particular would contribute greatly to the embodiment of the ideal of Positive Christianity advocated by the newly publicized party program. In the first year or so of the party's existence, its ideas emerged most prominently in the pages of the *Beobachter,* which became the official and exclusive organ of the Nazi Party in late 1920 but served before that as a central mouthpiece of the broader *völkisch* milieu within which the young DAP strove increasingly to distinguish itself.[89]

One of the early DAP leaders, Karl Harrer, was also a member of the Thule-Gesellschaft, a semi-secretive mystical club with vaguely occult overtones that was devoted to Germanic racial purity and the revival and study of ancient Nordic legends. The Thule-Gesellschaft has been characterized almost unfailingly as the most important organizational entity in the prehistory of the Nazi movement and has generated a substantial literature somewhat out of proportion to its modest size.[90] It had initially been founded in Munich in August 1918 by Rudolf von Sebottendorff, Walter Nauhaus, and Johannes Hering as an offshoot of the north German racist Germanenorden.[91] The club soon gained an important foothold among wealthy Protestant nationalists in Munich, particularly through the agency of the lawyer (and leading National Liberal politician) Hanns Dahn and the publisher Julius Friedrich Lehmann, who was a leading figure in the Munich branch of the Pan-German League. Because of the wealth of its influential backers, the organization's offices were located in one of Munich's most lavish hotels, the Vier Jahreszeiten, and Sebottendorff was able to acquire a small newspaper, the *Münchener Beobachter,* which served as the group's official mouthpiece beginning in August 1918.[92]

From the summer of 1918 until the spring of 1919, Sebottendorff, who had been raised Protestant but had abandoned his faith completely, served as editor of the *Beobachter* and pursued not only a distinctly anti-Catholic editorial line but exhibited a deep contempt for Christianity more generally. In this sense, the Thule-Gesellschaft under Sebottendorff constituted much more of a contrast than a role model for the religious identity of the early Nazi movement. When discussing the significance of the early Christianization of the Germanic regions, for instance, Sebottendorff lamented bitterly that the "Germanic god [*Allvater*] was dethroned and in the place of our hereditary faith a new [Christian] faith emerged, one whose forms and customs were in contradiction to our Germanic religious sensibilities."[93] In stark contrast to the early Nazis' clear advocacy of the protection and maintenance of religious education in Bavarian schools, Sebottendorff called for the removal of mandatory religious instruction as a step toward dismantling the broader Catholic dominance he found so distasteful.[94] In the aftermath of the November 1918 revolution, in contradistinction to Dietrich Eckart in particular, Sebottendorff campaigned energetically against the newly founded BVP, which he viewed as irreparably Catholic-oriented despite its initial claims of interconfessionality, in favor of secular Protestant nationalists running as candidates for the National Liberal Party, especially his fellow Thule activist Hanns Dahn.[95] Overall, the contrast between Sebottendorff's religious views and those of the early Nazi movement were summed up pithily in a programmatic editorial statement outlining his personal goals for the *Beobachter:* "Religion is a matter of complete indifference to us."[96]

Sebottendorff was forced to leave Munich under somewhat murky and potentially embarrassing circumstances in the spring of 1919, ushering in a significant shift.[97] From that point on, Sebottendorff exercised no direct influence over the Thule-Gesellschaft (aside from an attempt to refound it much later, in 1933), and a noticeably different editorial line was pursued in the pages of the *Beobachter* as contributions from local Catholic figures like Schrönghamer and Eckart became increasingly prevalent. Although there were clearly elements within the Thule-Gesellschaft that agreed with Sebottendorff's aversion to Catholicism and to Christianity more generally, including Ludwig Nenner and Johannes Hering, in May 1919 the editorial duties at the *Beobachter* were taken up by two professing Catholics, Max Sesselmann and Hanns Georg Müller, whose ideas contrasted starkly with those of Sebottendorff.[98] As Catholics, both Sesselmann and Müller would also emerge—unlike Sebottendorff, Nenner, Hering or any of the other leading anti-Christian figures within the Thule-Gesellschaft—as major early Nazi publicists in their own right, with Sesselmann playing a particularly visible propagandistic role in tandem with the Catholic priest Lorenz Pieper in the summer of 1923.[99] Succeeding the departed Sebottendorff as business manager of the Eher Verlag was the local Catholic publicist Franz Xaver Eder.[100] Starting in the early summer of 1919, under the leadership of Sesselmann, Müller, and Eder, the *Beobachter* placed itself increasingly at the forefront of a distinctly Catholic-inflected anti-Semitic crusade.

The opening salvo of this campaign was launched in the pages of the *Beobachter* with significant fanfare in early June 1919 by an anonymous Catholic priest. In a programmatic front-page article entitled "Can a Catholic Be an Anti-Semite?" the anonymous priest attempted to demonstrate not only that anti-Semitism was not in conflict with Christian charity but that it was in fact a Catholic duty to engage in radical anti-Semitic activism, particularly against the "immorality" of the Talmud.[101] The article's pronouncements were given greater weight by the author's emphatic reference to the "highest teaching authority of the church" and his insistence that the growing ranks of the anti-Semitic movement included not only "many pious Catholics" but also "a great number of bishops and popes" from the past and present of the church. Dietrich Eckart, who already had important connections to the DAP but had not yet broken permanently with BVP circles, was quick to realize the significance of the article, rapidly reprinting it in its entirety in *Auf gut deutsch* with an editorial preface praising the "manly" courage of the *Beobachter* for publishing the much-needed article in the first place.[102] Momentum began to build quickly behind the Catholic-inflected anti-Semitic campaign. The next issue of the *Beobachter* contained another lengthy discourse from a different Catholic priest, also anonymous, who praised the previous article in the strongest terms and reiterated its emphasis on the anti-Semitism of the popes and the need for a distinctly Catholic-oriented crusade to counter the "abominable offensive, the artillery barrage against Christian ideals" being launched by the Jews.[103] While the identity of the priest who authored the initial programmatic article remains uncertain, the author of the latter submission was the Catholic priest and journalist Bernhard Stempfle, who would become one of the most frequent contributors to the *Beobachter* in the ensuing months.[104]

Stempfle had been born in 1882 in Munich and, after entering the priesthood in 1904, joined the Hieronymite (San Girolamo) order in Italy and immersed himself in journalistic activity initially in Rome, writing for the *Corriere della Sera* and a variety of German and Italian papers in the years leading up to the First World War. After the outbreak of war, he returned to Munich and engaged in pastoral work at the university, attempting to bridge divisions between Catholic university students and workers, while also cultivating close relationships with Reform Catholic elements in Munich, especially the nationalistic *Hofklerus* at St. Kajetan.[105] In 1919, when he first began publishing in the *Beobachter,* Stempfle was listed among the official clergy of the archdiocese of Munich-Freising, although there is no surviving record of any official ecclesiastical transfer (*Inkardination*) into the archdiocese upon his return from Italy.[106] In his articles in the *Beobachter* Stempfle returned consistently to the same common themes: the destructive influence of Jewish atheism, particularly in the Jewish press; the moral acceptability and necessity of ruthless persecutions of the Jews—even, potentially, pogroms—waged in defense of the faith and institutions of the Catholic Church; and the noble example set throughout the years by "courageous" anti-Semitic leaders within the Catholic Church's hierarchy.[107] In early 1920, Stempfle became increasingly involved in radical right-wing paramilitary activites throughout the upper Bavarian hinterland, particularly as a central leader of the secretive anti-republican Organisation Kanzler (Orka), and for this reason his official involvement with the Nazi movement after its purchase of the *Beobachter* remained rather sporadic.[108] By early 1923, when he was chief editor of the anti-Semitic daily *Miesbacher Anzeiger,* headquartered some thirty-five miles southeast of Munich, Stempfle would reemerge not only as a leading journalistic figure within the broader *völkisch*–anti-Semitic movement in Bavaria but also as a regular confidant of Hitler.[109]

In virtual simultaneity with Stempfle's activism and in the midst of the broader Catholic-oriented anti-Semitic campaign in the summer of 1919, Josef Roth, a young Catholic theology student (and future priest) with connections to the prewar Reform Catholic movement, emerged prominently in the pages of the *Beobachter* for the first time. Roth was born in 1897 in Ottobeuren and raised in Munich. His deeply religious parents, three of whose sons entered the Catholic priesthood, were extremely close to Archbishop Faulhaber.[110] A decorated war veteran, Roth enrolled as a philosophy student at the University of Munich in February 1919; later that year, after fighting with the Freikorps Oberland during the brutal liberation of Munich from the *Räterepublik,* Roth switched officially to the study of theology to begin preparation for the Catholic priesthood.[111] Roth quickly emerged as one of the central student leaders of the Munich branch of the racist Deutschvölkischer Schutz- und Trutzbund (DVST), which would funnel countless members into the young Nazi movement. The DVST had been founded in northern Germany several months earlier as perhaps the most aggressive of all of the initial anti-Semitic groups established after the First World War and spread throughout virtually all major cities in Germany, particularly those with large university student populations.[112] While the DVST tended toward a nondogmatic and generally Protestant-oriented form of racist Christianity elsewhere, the Munich branch had much more of a Catholic inflection at its inception, with Dietrich Eckart serving as the featured speaker at the inaugural DVST gathering in Munich in May 1919.[113] While Eckart was busy forging ties between the new DVST group and a variety of smaller right-wing organizations in Munich, such as the Deutsche Bürgervereinigung he had founded weeks earlier, plans were set in motion to establish an official DVST student section at the University of Munich that summer.[114]

In July 1919, Josef Roth, the future priest, wrote the DVST's first official public appeal to Munich students in the pages of the *Beobachter*.[115] Noting that the DVST had already established student groups in other university cities, Roth's impassioned call to arms focused on the pressing need for such an organization to "cultivate national honor and the *völkisch* mentality" among the "healthy student body" in Munich; he identified the Jews as the most dangerous threat to German identity and prescribed membership in the DVST as the first step toward reestablishing German greatness.[116] Two weeks later, Roth followed this appeal with a programmatic manifesto in the *Beobachter* written specifically on behalf of *völkisch* Catholics in Munich. Drawing heavily on the ideas of the prewar Reform Catholic movement, Roth displayed a deeply critical attitude toward ultramontanism, invoking the "cultural mission" of prewar religious Catholicism and excoriating the confessional exclusivity of political Catholicism, while also demonstrating a radical unwillingness to compromise in the battle against the Jews, even to the point of justifying full-blown racial anti-Semitism. After arguing initially that "Catholicism is the born enemy of Jewry," Roth staked out the contours of his race-based position clearly and decisively: "The individual German Catholic must, as a German, recognize and fight against Jewry as a foreign race [*fremde Rasse*], as the enemy of the German culture and nation. . . . The Jewish race cannot be allowed to merge with the German race. It must therefore be expelled [*ausgestossen*]." Ever the master of the memorable phrase, Roth recalled the prewar Reform Catholic emphasis on interconfessional nationalism and closed by issuing a flaming appeal for Munich Catholics to form the backbone of a broader Christian "strike force [*Stosstrupp*] against all racially foreign machinations."[117] Not surprisingly, the article created a stir in Munich and initiated further discussion in the pages of the *Beobachter* over the importance of remaining religiously loyal to the Catholic faith while cooperating with Protestants. One notable response, whose author made sure to note that he came "from a family that has produced a remarkably large number of priests over the centuries and is himself a convinced Catholic," called for linking the *völkisch* anti-Semitic campaign to a ruthless attack against one of the principal targets of prewar Reform Catholic critics of ultramontanism, the Jesuit order. The missive concluded by claiming legitimacy for the ideal of religious Catholicism at the heart of the *Beobachter* crusade, noting that "the author raises these accusations [against Jews and Jesuits] not as a fallen son of the church, but rather as a soldier for the truth of Christianity, and in this he is certain of the support of many Catholic priests."[118]

Although Roth himself was clearly too young to have been directly involved in the prewar Reform Catholic movement, he was likely influenced during his first semester at the University of Munich by Joseph Schnitzer, the prewar Reform Catholic nationalist and leading critic of ultramontane political Catholicism.[119] Perhaps more important, Roth was impacted deeply by the ideas of Franz Schröngha-mer-Heimdal.[120] Like Schrönghamer, Roth was a member of the small and close-knit Catholic fraternity Rhaetia during his student years, living in the Rhaetia house in 1919 before moving into the Georgianum as a candidate for the priesthood; since Schrönghamer remained active in the fraternity's local alumni association (Philisterium), it is likely that this is how the two initially came into contact.[121] Not coincidentally, the same *Beobachter* issue that contained Roth's striking Catholic-*völkisch* manifesto also featured two separate and very lengthy articles from Schrönghamer.[122]

Between the summer of 1919 and the following spring, Schrönghamer was without question the most visible figure in the pages of the *Beobachter,* dwarfing the output of all other contributors to the paper.[123] Schrönghamer's emergence represented not only the beginning of his own contact with the DAP, which he joined officially several months later, but also concided with Dietrich Eckart's first appearance at a DAP event.[124] A few weeks later, on 12 September 1919, Adolf Hitler attended his first DAP gathering and was granted permission by his military superiors to join the tiny group as member number 55.[125] Hitler soon emerged as the dominant figure within the party, which culminated in his inner-party *Machtergreifung* in the summer of 1921.[126] Throughout the fall of 1919, however, Hitler was still overshadowed by more prominent and more established *völkisch* figures like Eckart, Drexler, Schrönghamer, and even Gottfried Feder.[127]

Schrönghamer's early *Beobachter* articles reflected the same basic preoccupations of his simultaneous activity in the *Rundschau,* both of which were characterized by a ruthless form of radical anti-Semitism with somewhat muddled racial overtones, as he blamed the Jews for both the war and the ensuing revolution as part of a broader apocalyptic conspiracy.[128] His brief monograph *Judas, der Weltfeind,* published in October 1919 by the leading *völkisch* publisher in Munich, was trumpeted and publicized almost obsessively in the pages of the *Beobachter.*[129] Advertised as an indispensable "spiritual weapon," the book was remarkably brutal in its attacks on the Jews, claiming that they had committed a crime that could "only be redeemed through death" and identifying the influence of the Jews as "poison" whose only remedy was "extermination" (*Vernichtung*).[130] Beyond Schrönghamer's trade-mark anti-Semitism, these *Beobachter* contributions are marked by his emphasis on combating "interest slavery" as part of a broader attack on Jewish-inspired world capitalism. Although the concept of interest slavery is rightfully associated most centrally with the works of Feder, it is interesting to note that Schrönghamer's ideas were formulated either concurrently with, or possibly slightly earlier than, Feder's and appeared in the pages of the *Beobachter* before the first such contribution from Feder.[131]

Schrönghamer's articles in the fall and winter of 1919 were aimed primarily at framing the *Beobachter*'s ongoing anti-Semitic crusade as a form of Catholic-Christian revivalism, clearly in line with the Reform Catholic emphasis on religious Catholicism. One such feature, essentially a revivalist sermon entitled "Awake, You Sleepers! A Call to Return to the Living God," appeared in the context of the BVP's move away from radical anti-Semitism. Schrönghamer specifically targeted the self-professed "good Catholics" within the BVP (using that phrase at least six times) and urged them to awaken from their hypocritical complacency and to embrace a genuinely religious form of Catholic revivalism based on action, particularly battling the Jews and helping to meet the needs of their poor fellow Christians. Thundering against the perceived hypocrisy of many BVP supporters in Munich, who acted like Catholics on Sundays but did little to practice their religion during the week, Schrönghamer railed: "They have certainly been baptized, they certainly go to church—in short, they preserve a Christian facade—but their faith is dead."[132] In writing the *Beobachter*'s main devotional reflection for Christmas 1919, Schrönghamer argued for the necessity of maintaining German folk traditions during the holidays, but not as a pagan-oriented replacement for traditional Catholic Christian identity. Rather, he argued that it was only through the person of Christ that the Germanic spirit, foreshadowed imperfectly in pre-Christian times by the heathen Germanic tribes, could find its fullest expression. The secret to understanding the complex relationship between "nature and super-nature" was only offered through Christianity: "In Christ, the greatest in the world, the unity is achieved—the God-man forever united heaven and earth. In him we are sons of the Father, who won for us the eternal victory." The devotional piece then closed with a revivalistic appeal to join in the *völkisch*-Catholic anti-Semitic crusade: "Becoming a fellow soldier is the meaning and purpose of the spiritual experience of the Christmas season."[133] In all of his writings, the centerpiece of Schrönghamer's imagery remained the figure of Christ, whose uncompromising pursuit of truth made him the best example of the type of leader Germany so desperately needed, one who could unite "true Christians" in the *völkisch* crusade against the Jews. The proper Christian spirit was, according to Schrönghamer, summed up in a central theme that echoed frequently throughout his writings: "Common good before individual interest."[134]

Schrönghamer continued to serve throughout early 1920 as the spokesman and most visible representative of the Catholic-inflected anti-Semitic crusade waged in the pages of the *Beobachter*. The campaign at first had not been associated exclusively with the (still tiny) DAP, but had been aimed at more diffuse *völkisch* and rightist circles in Munich, including the pro-BVP readers targeted by Schrönghamer in his *Rundschau* pieces. As the BVP turned increasingly away from radical anti-Semitism, however, a distinct Catholic-*völkisch* orientation began to coalesce around the DAP, with *Beobachter* leaders Sesselmann and Müller officially joining the party in December 1919 and Schrönghamer following suit less than two months later. Eckart cut all ties with the BVP and increasingly became a sort of fatherly poet-prophet figure for the DAP and for Hitler in particular. More generally, the influence of young elites (students, officers, professionals) continued to grow within the party, as Anton Drexler's colleagues at the railway workshop increasingly receded into the background. By February 1920, Schrönghamer's central formulation, "Common good before individual interest," would be reflected, virtually unaltered, in point 24 of the party's program as part of the principle of Positive Christianity that the young DAP pledged to champion.

Going Public: The First DAP Mass Meeting and the Unveiling of the Party Program

The party's program was unveiled publicly at the DAP's first mass meeting in Munich's Hofbräukeller on the night of 24 February 1920.[135] Over the previous several weeks, the DAP had been embroiled in a dispute over the nature and purpose of the party, with Karl Harrer advocating the maintenance of a small discussion club identity as a sort of semi-secret lodge (along the lines of the Thule-Gesellschaft) and Hitler, who had just begun to emerge as an effective party speaker, eager to forge the tiny group into a movement with a broad mass appeal, which would bring with it important consequences in an overwhelmingly Catholic city like Munich.[136] Anton Drexler, the DAP founder, sided with Hitler, leading to the marginalization of Harrer and his ultimate expulsion from the party in January 1920, as the DAP laid plans for both a pithy encapsulation of the party's central ideas and a large public gathering at which to unveil them.[137] The provenance of the party platform itself, which has gone down in history as the 25 Points, is somewhat unclear. Hitler and Drexler have been most centrally credited with its formulation, with Gottfried Feder often cited because of the reference in point 11 to the concept of interest slavery.[138] In early 1941, the Nazi Party Hauptarchiv attempted to gather official statements about the origins of the party's program and was ultimately unable to establish an uncontested account, although the most reliable version is likely the one presented by Drexler. While not completely dismissing the involvement of Hitler, Drexler's correspondence with Hauptarchiv director Erich Uetrecht cited as the primary influences on the program Drexler's own memoir *Mein politisches Erwachen* and certain "program drafts" he had personally written and which he believed must be present somewhere in Uetrecht's vast archive.[139] There is, in fact, such a draft in the Hauptarchiv files, undated and titled simply "Deutsche Arbeiterpartei: Grundsätze" (Basic Principles), among the papers of Ferdinand Wiegand, who served as a sort of secretary for the early DAP and whose office and typewriter were useful to a party lacking sufficient resources to purchase its own supplies and office space. The "Grundsätze," almost certainly written by Drexler, were first presented at a key DAP meeting on 5 February 1920 in the restaurant Zum deutschen Reich in the Neuhausen section of Munich, at which Dietrich Eckart was the main speaker.[140] Claiming to represent the "origins, purpose, and goals of the Deutsche Arbeiterpartei" and created for the purpose of being "printed and distributed to bring into the DAP numerous and committed new members," the "Grundsätze" emphasized the role of religion, stating that whereas politics was concerned with the relation of people to the state, religion dealt with the all-important relationship between individuals and God, and for that reason religion could never be subordinated to politics or the state.[141] In pursuit of the centrality of a personal Christian faith, Drexler identified the ultimate goal of the party to be the establishment of a new holy "world order" built on the maxim "idealism rather than materialism!"[142] In addition to Drexler's presentation of the "Grundsätze" and the speech by Eckart, the 5 February 1920 meeting in Neuhausen was also significant because of the presence of the DAP's most widely published new member, who had trumpeted such a holy world order in the *Beobachter* for months. At the behest of Drexler, Franz Schrönghamer-Heimdal had officially joined the DAP the night before.[143] The Catholic-oriented influence of Schrönghamer and Eckart far outweighed that of the anti-Christian sentiments stemming from the Thule-Gesellschaft and other minor *völkisch* entities.

Regardless of whatever informal influence he may have had on Drexler or the DAP's "Grundsätze," Schrönghamer's 1933 claim to have directly influenced the 25 Points is undoubtedly overblown, at least in the immediate sense of having acted as an intellectual "godfather" to the program itself, as Schrönghamer put it. To call him in any way the originator of the Nazis' brand of Positive Christianity, which is how the egotistical Schrönghamer envisioned himself, would be a stretch, especially since the phrase itself had been so commonly used in the prewar Reform Catholic community.[144] However, one of the earliest external histories of the origins of the NSDAP, written in 1931 by Ulrich von Hasselbach, made the important but often overlooked observation that the bombastic Catholic-oriented religious identity associated with Schrönghamer (and, to an extent, Eckart) was of indispensable importance to the DAP's growing appeal in Catholic Munich, differentiating the young party explicitly from anti-Catholic *völkisch* organizations like the Thule-Gesellschaft:

> Positive Christianity was represented emphatically by the party. The reason for this special emphasis was to be found in the fact that at that time not only anti-Catholic but also explicitly anti-Christian currents were making themselves noticeable in the *völkisch* movement.... Against this tendency, represented primarily by the Thule-Gesellschaft, one wanted to and had to draw a sharp line of differentiation. The National Socialists were united in their embrace of Christian ideals.[145]

This broader objective—framing the Nazi movement as the lone explicitly Catholic-Christian option within Munich's *völkisch* milieu—was clearly the common thread running through Schrönghamer's works at the time, although any more direct influence he may have had on the principle of Positive Christianity must remain in the realm of speculation.

There are, of course, instances of clear overlap between Schrönghamer's work, especially his 1918 *Das kommende Reich,* and a variety of other individual points of the party platform.[146] The problem, however, is that the significance of this broader overlap is impossible to determine reliably, especially since similar points of convergence can be established with parts of the 1919 program of the Deutsch-Sozialistische Partei as well.[147] Although the phrase "common good before individual interest" can be connected to Schrönghamer, virtually all of the ideas represented in the Nazi program were circulating and cross-fertilizing in countless beerhalls and cafes throughout Munich. However, one issue that can be established with some reliability is the resonance of Schrönghamer's ideas at the 24 February 1920 meeting in the Hofbräukeller at which the 25 Points were unveiled.

Although Hitler was fond of recalling (and exaggerating) his own role in the gathering in the Hofbräukeller, he was still a fairly minor figure unable to draw a sufficiently large crowd on his own, with most of his DAP speeches drawing between several dozen and a few hundred in attendance.[148] It is true that Hitler had managed to attract significant attention outside Munich as a result of a well-attended speech he gave in Passau on 19 February 1920—a speech perhaps arranged in part through the agency of Schrönghamer, who split his time between Munich and Passau and who became a founding member of the Passau Ortsgruppe a few months later—but the DAP leaders were afraid that a disappointing turnout in Munich might irreparably damage the young fragile party.[149] As a result, Drexler and Hitler settled on Johannes Dingfelder, a better-known *völkisch* speaker in Munich, as the headliner who could give the event sufficient exposure.[150] Dingfelder was a practicing physician in Munich and had gotten his start in political activism in the 1890s as a leading figure in the anti-ultramontane Bavarian Bauernbund movement, eventually establishing contact with Catholic *völkisch* figures like Eckart and Schrönghamer in the aftermath of the First World War.[151] Dingfelder's speech at the Hofbräukeller, entitled "Was uns not tut" (What We Need to Do), touched on a variety of religious and cultural themes, but emphasized several that were inextricably intertwined with the well-known thought of Schrönghamer.[152] That Dingfelder never felt the need to mention Schrönghamer by name is perhaps further evidence of the pervasiveness of the latter's thought, as there was no one—not even Eckart and certainly not Hitler—among the 200–300 party members whose *Beobachter* output at the time could even remotely approach that of Schrönghamer.[153] Dingfelder's central discussion of the need to return to the "true religion" of Christianity utilized generic formulations that could be found in countless contemporary sources, to be sure, but his explicit repetition of key talking points and phrases—"God's sovereignty over the world" (*göttliche Weltführung*) and the "divine law of order" (*göttliche Gesetz der Ordnung*)—bear a striking likeness to the phrasing in Schrönghamer's chapter "Das Reich des Rechtes" in *Das kommende Reich*.[154] Much more explicit, however, was Dingfelder's usage of Schrönghamer's eccentric formulation of the centrality of work (*Arbeit*) to the God-given spiritual nobility of the German soul, as he replicated verbatim Schrönghamer's distinctive *völkisch* word-play from *Das kommende Reich* that established the linkage among *Arbeit, Arbot,* and *Sonnengebot.*[155] The explicit association of Schrönghamer with this equation was certainly enhanced by the fact that Eckart had given his friend's famous passage increased publicity in its own right by reprinting it as a stand-alone article in *Auf gut deutsch* a few months earlier.[156] Although the *Beobachter* coverage provided only brief direct quotes from Dingfelder's speech, Schrönghamer's distinctive formulation was among the few sections reprinted word for word.[157]

Schrönghamer's influence in helping to shape the atmosphere within which the party program was promulgated is further demonstrated by the topic that dominated religious-oriented conversations within the movement beginning on the evening of 24 February 1920 and that shaped perceptions of the principle of Positive Christianity at the very moment of its public articulation. The next day's issue of the *Beobachter,* already available at the mass meeting that night, unveiled the first programmatic religious statement from a Nazi member following the announcement of Positive Christianity: the opening installment of a much-anticipated and highly publicized five-part series by Schrönghamer that further fleshed out his earlier arguments in the *Rundschau* on the divinity of Jesus and the "impossibility" of the Savior having been Jewish. Schrönghamer wrote under what he undoubtedly saw as the clever pseudonym of Widar Wälsung, a name that both reflected his famous fascination with Nordic-Aryan imagery and did essentially nothing to conceal his identity.[158]

That series was the first step in a broader campaign led by Schrönghamer and others, several of whom also had important Reform Catholic connections, to broaden the base of Catholic-*völkisch* activism both within and beyond the confines of the young (NS)DAP and to further differentiate the Nazi movement from anti-Catholic or anti-Christian *völkisch* entities. While the principle of Positive Christianity continued to point toward the ideal of interconfessional cooperation, its deployment and perceived meaning within a local and regional context that was overwhelmingly Catholic would give the young Nazi movement an even more distinctive Catholic inflection that would grow increasingly unmistakable in the eyes of local contemporaries over the ensuing years.

CHAPTER 3

Embodying Positive Christianity in Catholic Munich

The Ideal of Religious Catholicism and Early Nazi Growth, 1920–1922

In December 1921, the Social Democratic daily *Donauwacht* featured a humorous interpretation of Bavarian political developments since the collapse of the socialist government of Johannes Hoffmann in the spring of 1920.[1] In the form of a satirical encyclopedia entry entitled "Bavaria," the article documented with a mixture of dismissive scorn and growing alarm the existence of an increasingly undeniable synthesis of Nazi-oriented racism and vigorous Catholic piety emanating from Munich. Mocking the flag of the new Bavaria as a religious "battle standard" featuring the combination of "a *Stahlhelm* and a rosary," the entry continued: "The climate of the region is Catholic and, particularly on Sundays and at military ceremonies, especially humid. The local industry produces primarily prayer books, steel helmets, rosaries, and rubber truncheons." Noting derisively that the nearby town of Miesbach sported the area's most notable sightseeing attraction, a "giant swastika to which thousands of pilgrims stream throughout the year," the author poked fun at the anti-Semitic daily *Miesbacher Anzeiger,* the *Beobachter*'s leading publicistic ally, whose editorial offices, he claimed, were located, fittingly, in a "giant outhouse." The entry concluded by stating that Munich had clearly lost its earlier position as a leading artistic and cultural center and was now known primarily as the home of the Nazi party, characterized memorably as a "Christian-nationalist anti-Semitic sect that...calls for a new Crusade against the Jews."[2] While the *Donauwacht* account was clearly intended as satire, relying on polemical caricature rather than journalistic objectivity, it nonetheless communicates a sense of how easily Catholic and Nazi identities could be fused at the time, both in reality and in popular perception, undergirding and at the same time making tangible the otherwise vague notion of Positive Christianity.

The ideal of Positive Christianity, articulated officially in point 24 of the party's program, was explicitly interconfessional and a central component of the overarching goal of forging a true *Volksgemeinschaft* that would overcome political, class, and confessional divisions. What has been largely overlooked, however, is the fact that this ideal did not exist in some abstract disembodied realm, but rather had to be put into practice first and foremost in the overwhelmingly Catholic context of Munich and its immediate environs. Once the decision had been made to fashion the (NS)DAP into a mass movement rather than a small discussion club, the principle of Positive Christianity brought with it, of necessity, the imperative to appeal to large numbers of believing Catholics in and around Munich. It is also important to note that an extensive commentary on the individual components of the Nazi party program did not appear until 1923, at which point the religious elements of the program were given a problematic and deeply idiosyncratic definition by Alfred Rosenberg, and his views went on to color subsequent interpretations.[3] The less formal early indications of what the principle of Positive Christianity might look like in practice were embodied in tangible form in the religious-oriented activism of individual figures within the Nazi movement.

This chapter focuses on a central aspect of this early embodiment: the emphasis on religious Catholicism, which had been one of the central root paradigms of the prewar Reform Catholic movement in Munich and which continued after the war as one of the Nazis' most effective discursive weapons in the battle against the perceived hypocrisy and superficiality of ultramontanism and political Catholicism. Just as prewar Reform Catholic nationalists and critics of ultramontanism—ranging from Josef Müller and his Verein Renaissance to Joseph Schnitzer and the Krausgesellschaft—had insisted on remaining inside the Catholic Church even as they were labeled as heretical and religiously dangerous by their opponents, the early Nazi movement strove to position itself as the champion of religious Catholicism in the face of vigorous attacks from the BVP and its journalistic allies throughout Bavaria.

Modest Beginnings: The Subtle Linkage of Positive Christianity and Religious Catholicism

> Political Catholicism is to be sharply differentiated from religious Catholicism, which we have always welcomed as our comrade in arms against decadence.
>
> —Alfred Miller, *Völkischer Beobachter,* October 1921

In early 1920, following the announcement of the party platform, the 25 Points, the interconfessional idea of Positive Christianity remained essentially undefined and open, at least potentially, to a variety of inter-pretations. By 1923, however, that principle would be largely subsumed in a membership drive designed explicitly to draw believing Catholics into the NSDAP, with numerous Catholic priests serving as official Nazi spokesmen and local Protestant pastors being almost completely uninvolved. Indeed, on the eve of the caesura ushered in by the Beerhall Putsch, the public face of the Nazi movement would come to be strik-ingly Catholic-oriented, as the party positioned itself as the most natural political home for *völkisch* Catholics in Munich and contrasted itself explicitly to Protestant-oriented (and anti-Christian) *völkisch* entities despite the party's continued professions of interconfessionality. The path toward the ostentatious Catholic-Nazi synthesis mocked by the *Donauwacht* satire began rather modestly, as the concept of Positive Christianity was given informal embodiment and at least partial defini-tion through the early activism of prominent *völkisch*-Catholic figures who helped to link Nazi identity with the expression of religious Catholicism in subtle yet important ways.

The most significant early figure in this regard was Franz Schrön-ghamer-Heimdal. His bombastic five-part series entitled "Was Jesus a Jew?" written under the pseudonym Widar Wälsung, dominated the pages of the *Beobachter* and discussions within the DAP more generally beginning on the night of the party's first mass meeting. Schrönghamer's manifesto built on the principle of Positive Christianity—technically interconfessional but strongly Catholic-inflected—and preached its vir-tues to a *völkisch* readership that he believed was potentially in danger of developing in anti-Christian directions, as had been the case with the Thule-Gesellschaft.[4] In addition to claiming that the denial of Jesus' Jewish identity should be fully acceptable to Catholics, Schrönghamer's goal was explicitly evangelistic: to spread the message within broader *völkisch* circles that Jesus Christ was "not simply a unique prophet," as claimed by non-Christian *völkisch* writers, but rather the divine Savior figure at the heart of the Catholic faith, "the express Son of God, of the same essence as the Father and the Holy Spirit." Since the Jews had persecuted Jesus, revealing their "true" nature as minions of the satanic forces of the Antichrist, Schrönghamer argued not only that Jesus, hailing from Nazareth in Galilee, was Aryan and not related racially to the Jews of Jerusalem but that his spiritual message of "eternal light" was the complete and utter antithesis of the this-worldly materialism of the Jews.[5] The importance of Schrönghamer's attention-grabbing missive—the first programmatic religious statement from a Nazi member following the articulation of Positive Christianity—should not be overlooked.

At the same time that he was preaching the divinity of the "Aryan" Christ to the *völkisch* movement, Schrönghamer launched, with almost equal missionary zeal, several attempts to spread the Nazi anti-Semitic gospel of Positive Christianity to religiously loyal Catholics who had not yet heard it. In early February 1920, Schrönghamer began intensive journalistic activity in the pages of the *Deutsche Katholikenzeitung,* a small Munich-based weekly envisioned as an "organ of religion" rather than as a tool of political Catholicism, which he briefly co-edited alongside the anti-Semitic Catholic priest Sebastian Wieser.[6] One of Schrönghamer's most bombastic *Katholikenzeitung* articles, which rehashed the ideas of August Rohling to condemn the alleged immorality of the Talmud, appeared during the publication of his *Beobachter* series on the racial identity of Jesus and sparked widespread discussion.[7] In response, the Munich Catholic lawyer Anton von Pestalozza, one of the few truly principled Catholic defenders of the Jews, wrote an open letter to Wieser in early March, appealing to Wieser's pastoral scruples, condemning the "utter depravity" of Schrönghamer's radical anti-Semitism, and suggesting that it would make better sense for the *Katholikenzeitung* to simply "merge itself with the *Völkischer Beobachter.*" As a result of Pestalozza's condemnation and the publicity it generated, both Schrönghamer and Wieser were removed from the editorial leadership of the *Katholikenzeitung* in early March.[8] When the *Katholikenzeitung* was forced out of business permanently the following year, religiously practicing Nazi Catholics like Alfred Miller, a disciple of both Schrönghamer and Joseph Schnitzer, would decry the fact that the political press of the Center Party was so well funded while the apolitical *Katholikenzeitung,* which "strove only for religious deepening [*religiösen Vertiefung*]," had suffered through constant struggles for financial survival.[9]

Almost immediately after his dismissal from the *Katholikenzeitung,* the ever-energetic Schrönghamer, eager to continue to spread the Nazi idea of Positive Christianity throughout broader Catholic circles, managed to get himself hired as the founding editor of the *Bayerischer Königsbote,* the new publication of the leading Catholic-oriented monarchist society in Bavaria, the Bayerische Königspartei (BKP). The BKP, which was essentially a single-issue pressure group rather than an actual political party, had been founded in November 1919 in Munich as an expression of broader dissatisfaction among those on the far right of the BVP.[10] Upon officially registering with the Munich authorities in January 1920, the BKP named as its first chair Josef Mayer-Koy, one of the central leaders of the Bavarian Einwohnerwehr movement, who in turn hired Schrönghamer as the founding editor of the *Königsbote* because of the "esteem" Schrönghamer enjoyed "throughout all levels of the *Volk.*"[11] Schrönghamer's inaugural editorial claimed explicitly that the *Königsbote* "would not engage in party politics," but his own membership in the Nazi party offered a clear signal regarding the editorial line he would follow.[12] In offering his programmatic vision for the paper, Schrönghamer strove to build bridges between local Catholic monarchists loyal to the Wittelsbach dynasty and his fellow Nazi members, most of whom were decidedly nonmonarchist. Attempting to rework the monarchist idea into a form potentially acceptable to *völkisch* nonmonarchists, Schrönghamer differentiated the BKP from traditional prewar monarchism and spoke instead of a metaphorical monarchy of the "Germanic spirit."[13] He fleshed out this idea by returning in greater depth to the central hallmarks of his earlier apocalyptic publications, combining a revivalist emphasis on religious Catholicism with a stinging critique of political Catholicism and an obsession with *völkisch*-Nazi anti-Semitism.

As editor, Schrönghamer succeeded in drawing to the *Königsbote* an eclectic mixture of activists, ranging from well-known *völkisch* leaders like Johannes Dingfelder to local cultural figures who shared Schrönghamer's ties to prewar Reform Catholicism.[14] The radicalism of his Nazi-oriented program, however, ensured that Schrönghamer's tenure as the *Königsbote*'s editor would be short-lived. Already in the second issue of the paper, his friend Philipp Haeuser—a Catholic priest in Strassberg, near Augsburg, who would eventually emerge as a major pro-Nazi spokesman in his own right—was forced to write a supplemental programmatic statement to "clarify" Schrönghamer's original program, which had "already become distorted through hate" in the hands of critics, primarily those among the ranks of more traditional monarchists.[15] Despite Haeuser's efforts to make Schrönghamer's ideas more palatable, it was ultimately not possible to build a lasting bridge between Catholic monarchists and Nazi circles in Munich; had the *Königsbote* proceeded along the lines laid out by its inaugural editor, it would have lost its raison d'être and the BKP itself would likely have been swallowed by more aggressive organizational entities like the young Nazi movement, which may in fact have been Schrönghamer's original intent.[16] While he continued to be a dominant force in the *Königsbote* throughout much of the spring of 1920, Schrönghamer was quietly replaced as editor by Josef Mayer-Koy, who quickly reasserted a more traditional (literal) interpretation of monarchism, and by the summer Schrönghamer had stopped contributing to the *Königsbote* entirely. His attempt to forge a union between Catholic monarchism and *völkisch* racism was ultimately overturned completely, with Mayer-Koy also steering the BKP away from radical anti-Semitism and toward a much more moderate stance toward the Jews.[17] Eventually, Mayer-Koy would join with the Nazis' opponents in the BVP in labeling Schrönghamer's ideas dangerous to the Catholic faith, condemning in particular his "close relations with Mr. Dietrich Eckart" and his role in spreading Catholic anti-ultramontanism in the pages of the *Beobachter*.[18]

At the same time that Schrönghamer was launching his attempt both to evangelize *völkisch* circles and to Nazify Catholic monarchist circles, the *Beobachter* began publicizing a new *völkisch*-oriented cultural monthly with clear religious overtones, *Der Deutsche Geist,* edited by local Catholic priest Alfons Heilmann. Beginning the week after the announcement of the party's program and in the midst of Schrönghamer's *Beobachter* series on Jesus, this brief publication initially helped to further define the nature of Positive Christianity as officially interconfessional but strongly Catholic-oriented in practice.[19] Like Schrönghamer, Heilmann's roots lay in the prewar Reform Catholic movement. Heilmann had begun as a candidate for the priesthood alongside his best friend, the future Krausgesellschaft spokesman Philipp Funk, and like Funk, Heilmann was centrally impacted by Josef Müller and his journal, *Renaissance.*[20] After briefly leaving the seminary at the height of the modernist controversy in 1908 due to the radicalism of his reform-oriented ideas, Heilmann returned and was ordained into the Catholic priesthood the following year.[21] In 1914, he moved to Munich in part to be closer to the Krausgesellschaft, especially to Funk and Joseph Schnitzer, and to assume the editorship of the Catholic illustrated magazine *Sonntag ist's.*[22] By early 1920, Heilmann had forged a particularly close relationship with local painter Edmund Steppes, who had been raised Catholic but had experienced a crisis of faith and left the church in 1912. Largely through the pastoral influence of Heilmann, Steppes returned to his Catholic faith after the First World War, became a central figure in Munich's Gesellschaft für christliche Kunst, contributed to Heilmann's weekly *Sonntag ist's,* and collaborated closely with Dietrich Eckart in the pages of *Auf gut deutsch.*[23] When the publicity for *Der Deutsche Geist* was announced in the *Beobachter,* Heilmann and Steppes were spearheading the enterprise collaboratively, with Heilmann as editor of the journal and Steppes as chairman of the corresponding religio-cultural organization, the Verein "Der Deutsche Geist," which planned to use Heilmann's journal as its official organ.[24]

The stated goals of both the journal and the new organization were explicitly *völkisch*-oriented: to repair the wounded "soul of the German *Volk*" which had been "poisoned and made seriously ill" by internal enemies.[25] Heilmann claimed that his and Steppes' efforts were being undertaken specifically in response to idealistic students and "German-feeling youths" in Munich who were hungry for *völkisch* spiritual leadership. The resulting partnership was designed to work in concert with other *völkisch* entities like the Nazi party rather than competing with them—"we will keep our distance from all forms of party politics"—and its stated religious ideal was in complete harmony with the interconfessional yet Catholic-oriented framing of Positive Christianity. *Der Deutsche Geist* pledged explicitly to "respect all Christian confessions" while at the same time it was led by a well-known Catholic priest.[26] In addition to Steppes, who became a leading Nazi art critic before eventually distancing himself from the movement in the aftermath of the Beerhall Putsch, Heilmann also brought together a wide variety of *völkisch* figures, ranging from Fritz Doerfler, a Catholic gymnasium teacher in Munich, to Wilhelm Kotzde, an influential racist writer, to Alexander Heilmayer, the Reform Catholic sculptor and art expert who had been a leading member of the Krausgesellschaft and had served on the editorial committee of *Hochland* before the war.[27] Despite the publicity it received in the *Beobachter* and in Eckart's *Auf gut deutsch,* Heilmann's journal ultimately failed to get off the ground, as did the related club chaired by Steppes, but both were important in helping to provide an initial sense of what the idea of Positive Christianity might look like in practice.[28] Some five years later, when the Nazi movement attempted to reestablish a foothold in Catholic Munich following its 1925 refounding, Heilmann's works were once again energetically publicized in the pages of the *Beobachter.*[29] But by that time, Heilmann, like so many other Catholic priests who initially sympathized with the *völkisch*-Nazi movement before the Beerhall Putsch, had begun to distance himself permanently from the NSDAP, eventually becoming a vocal critic who was himself persecuted by the Nazi regime.[30]

More successful than the short-lived *völkisch* endeavor of Heilmann and Steppes was the early Nazi activism of Hans Huber, a Reform Catholic activist and businessman in Rosenheim, some forty miles southeast of Munich. Huber had received his degree in architecture in Munich before settling in Rosenheim and eventually joining the Krausgesellschaft in January 1912, helping the organization to expand beyond its base in Munich.[31] Back in Munich after the war, Huber had joined the Deutsch-völkischer Schutz- und Trutzbund (DVST) and was drawn to the DAP around the time of the February 1920 mass meeting in the Hofbräukeller.[32] At the time that Schrönghamer was missionizing among disparate Catholic-oriented circles in Munich in the spring of 1920, Huber was similarly intent on spreading the Nazi gospel to Rosenheim. In April 1920, alongside the Catholic railway inspector Theodor Lauböck, Huber helped to found the NSDAP Ortsgruppe Rosenheim, which was not only the earliest Nazi party branch outside of Munich but also the fastest growing.[33] Huber's emphatic embrace of religious Catholicism, which was combined with a corresponding abhorrence of political Catholicism, was perhaps his most notable characteristic, and it continued to dominate his later (problematic) relationship with the NSDAP even into the 1940s.[34] Joining Huber as a key early member of the Ortsgruppe Rosenheim—and further reinforcing the initial association with religious Catholicism—was his fellow KG activist Johann Stegmaier.[35] The linkage with religious Catholicism was furthered by several other Krausgesellschaft figures who joined the NSDAP in Munich in 1920, including the architect Paul Fuchs, the engineer Karl Böhm, and the businessman Wilhelm Briemann.[36] Briemann had been involved in the Krausgesellschaft campaign to raise funds for Catholic priests who opposed the infamous antimodernist oath; he eventually rose to become the top secretary for the early NSDAP, a central leadership position he held from January 1923 through the dismantling of the party in the aftermath of the Beerhall Putsch.[37] Several other leading Krausgesellschaft figures—including priests Otto Sickenberger, Hugo Koch, and Johann Baptist Müller—also eventually aligned themselves with the NSDAP.[38]

Finally, in a rather different sense, the informal association of Catholic and Nazi identities was furthered by the striking *völkisch* activism of the Catholic *Ordensschwester* known as Sister Pia, who was born Eleonore Baur in 1885 and became one of the most visible Nazi figures in Munich in the spring of 1920. Her mother died when she was very young, and she moved with her father and stepmother from Bad Aibling to Munich at the age of five, attending *Volksschule* until the age of fourteen, when she began work as an informal assistant to a local midwife. After enduring deeply troubled teenage years, which included an arrest for "public immorality" and the birth of an illegitimate son named Wilhelm, Eleonore moved to Egypt, where she worked as a nurse's assistant at the German hospital in Cairo.[39] By the time she returned to Munich in 1907, she had almost completely remade herself, announcing a newfound religious and charitable purpose in her life and working under the name "Sister Pia" in conjunction with the Catholic charitable order Gelbes Kreuz.[40] After serving as a nurse during the First World War, Sister Pia became a near-legendary figure within Catholic-*völkisch* circles in Munich for her alleged fearlessness in accompanying the Freikorps Oberland troops through intense street fighting during the "liberation" of Munich from the Soviet regime in May 1919.[41] She further reinforced her folk hero status by providing assistance to the Free Corps forces on a Baltic campaign later in 1919, before returning to Munich and joining the Nazi party in February 1920.[42] In the immediate aftermath of the Nazis' first mass meeting that month, Sister Pia was one of the most visible Nazi members on the streets of Munich, wearing her trademark uniform and its conspicuous crucifix in public and serving as a veritable walking advertisement for the activist spirit of religious Catholicism in contrast to the alleged complacency and hypocrisy of political Catholicism. Her notoriety grew when she was arrested on 11 March 1920 following a women's rally on Munich's Theresienwiese at which she had launched into a violent tirade against the Jews and was charged with disturbing the peace. Her case became a virtual cause célèbre within the Nazi movement.[43] Following her acquittal, the *Beobachter* trumpeted the triumph of the "German-blooded" Sister Pia over the Jewish "forces of darkness," who were given a resounding "moral boxing of the ears" in their attempt to silence the righteous Nazi *Ordensschwester*.[44] Sister Pia remained in the spotlight on frequent occasions throughout the remainder of 1920, making numerous (albeit typically more subdued) public speeches and organizing Nazi-based charitable events, such as a striking *Allerheiligen* fundraiser commemorating the *völkisch* heroes who had "given their lives" in resisting the 1919 Soviet republic and pledging financial support for their still-grieving families.[45]

Among those who worked most closely with Sister Pia in the *Allerheiligen* fundraiser were Johannes Heldwein, who had been a central member of the Krausgesellschaft before the First World War, and several *völkisch*-Catholic students at the University of Munich, including Johann Prechtl and Hansjörg Maurer.[46] It was in fact idealistic *völkisch* students like them, claimed by Alfons Heilmann to be so desperate for spiritual leadership in the aftermath of the war, who emerged most notably within the Nazi movement in 1920 as champions of religious Catholicism at the University of Munich.

Catholic University Students and the NSDAP

Despite its self-identification as a workers' party, the NSDAP grew especially quickly among university students and other *bürgerlich* elements, with actual factory laborers being statistically underrepresented within its ranks.[47] Catholic students contributed centrally to this early growth. Building on the earlier *völkisch* activism of Josef Roth, two students in particular—Alfred Miller and Hansjörg Maurer—emerged in 1920 as primary purveyors of the ideal of religious Catholicism among students at the University of Munich and in the pages of the *Beobachter*.

Miller was born in Ulm in 1897 and became active in the Catholic Quickborn youth movement as a teenager on the eve of the First World War.[48] After his discharge from military service, Miller matriculated at the University of Munich in February 1919 and quickly espoused a flamingly nationalistic and distinctly non-ultramontane Catholic identity shaped decisively by the legacy of the Krausgesellschaft.[49] Perhaps his most significant mentor at the university was the former KG chair Joseph Schnitzer, whose seminars on the history of religion and on church and state Miller took in 1919 and 1920.[50] Miller would consider himself a deeply devoted disciple of Schnitzer for the rest of his life, and even in the 1930s—by which time Miller, like so many other early Nazi Catholics who chose to stay in the movement after the Beerhall Putsch, had turned completely against Catholicism and Christianity more generally—he maintained a striking admiration for his "highly esteemed teacher and fatherly friend."[51]

As an outgrowth of his involvement with the Catholic youth movement, Miller joined the fraternity officially related to Quickborn at the University of Munich, the Hochland-Verband (HV), whose goal was to foster and maintain the ideals of the Catholic youth movement in a university setting.[52] An interesting glimpse into the nature of the HV at the time Miller was a member is provided by the influential church historian Hubert Jedin, who had joined the group around the same time. According to Jedin's memoirs, the Munich HV was literally teeming with radical nationalists and *völkisch* activists in 1920, and it was in the Hochland fraternity house in Munich that, Jedin claimed, he was introduced to Catholic-oriented *völkisch* and racist ideas.[53] The leading role in this regard was played by Ottmar Weinzierl, a medical student whom Jedin surmised may have been a Nazi member and Hitler follower already in 1920, but Jedin also noted the energetic participation of numerous other Hochland members in *völkisch* and radical paramilitary activities, including the March 1920 Kapp Putsch.[54] Given the depth of their *völkisch* activism, which included the obsessive Nordic-Aryan fascination typical of Schrönghamer's works, local HV members felt compelled to continually assure diocesan authorities of their uncompromising commitment to the Catholic faith. Interestingly, though, when the sibling leadership duo of Ludwig and Klara Schätz wrote to Archbishop Faulhaber, they identified themselves in ostentatiously *völkisch* terms, as the "Gauleiter" and "Gauleiterin" of the Munich HV branch, and insisted on following *völkisch* precedent in using the ancient Germanic names for months rather than the standard Latin.[55] Faulhaber, for his part, claimed to have no qualms about the religious sincerity of HV members, despite their *völkisch* fixations.[56] In any case, in addition to partaking of the *völkisch* atmosphere within his own fraternity, Alfred Miller maintained close ties to a variety of other Catholic-*völkisch* fraternity students in Munich, including his good friend Josef Roth.

Miller's first *Beobachter* contributions appeared in early 1920, at the height of his involvment in the HV. Between then and the spring of 1922, when he completed his studies at the University of Munich and moved to Breslau, Miller was without question the leading Nazi commentator on religious issues in the pages of the *Beobachter,* publishing dozens and dozens of individual articles and eclipsing the early output of Alfred Rosenberg, who only later assumed the role of leading Nazi religious commentator in Miller's absence.[57] Claiming to write on behalf of "we national-oriented Catholics for whom nationalism is the driving force behind true religiosity," Miller aligned himself fully with the emphasis on religious Catholicism and the apocalyptic anti-Semitism characteristic of Schrönghamer.[58] Returning regularly to themes that had been preached by the prewar Reform Catholic movement, Miller insisted that anti-ultramontane Catholics should remain inside the Catholic Church, working from within to demonstrate the contrast between the alleged hypocrisy of political Catholicism and the nobility of an explicitly "religious Catholicism," which Miller claimed ostentatiously was the Nazis' "comrade in arms against decadence."[59] Miller also frequently idealized the religious Catholicism of prewar Reform Catholic heroes like Reinhold Baumstark and Heinrich Hansjakob, who had been staunch critics of ultramontanism and political Catholicism.[60] In emphasizing the virtues of this religious Catholicism, Miller was careful to stress the importance of interconfessional cooperation and, in pursuit of the ideal of Positive Christianity, the overcoming of ultramontane "confessional egoism."[61] This fundamental emphasis on religious Catholicism is consistent throughout Miller's early writings.[62]

Beginning in mid-1920, Alfred Miller's chief collaborator in spreading the idea of religious Catholicism in the pages of the *Beobachter* was his fellow student Hansjörg Maurer. Maurer was born and raised in lower Bavaria, attended a Benedictine gymnasium, and, like Alfred Miller, participated in the nascent Catholic youth movement before the First World War.[63] After four years of military service, Maurer studied briefly at the University of Berlin before transferring to the University of Munich in early 1920 to study veterinary medicine. After being drawn initially into *völkisch* student circles connected to Josef Roth and the university branch of the DVST, Maurer demonstrated an increasingly strong interest in *völkisch*-oriented journalism. His first *Beobachter* contribution appeared in May 1920 and then, in a somewhat surprising development given his lack of journalistic experience, Maurer was rapidly promoted to editor in chief in mid-July, a position he held while continuing his studies.[64]

Maurer quickly emerged as a central figure in a new *völkisch* organizational entity known as the Bund der Beobachterfreunde (Union of Friends of the Beobachter; BdB), which was first announced in late May 1920 as an umbrella organization to help consolidate the energies of the diffuse racist and nationalist groups that made up Munich's *völkisch* milieu and to help shore up the *Beobachter*'s struggling finances.[65] Maurer served as the secretary of the BdB alongside the Catholic publicist Franz Xaver Eder—who was business manager of the Eher Verlag, in addition to serving both as Maurer's immediate predecessor as *Beobachter* editor and as the first chair of the BdB—and together the two demonstrated how great a distance the *Beobachter* had traveled since the departure of the anti-Catholic Rudolf von Sebottendorff the previous year. Rather than meeting in the Thule-Gesellschaft offices in the elegant Hotel Vier Jahreszeiten, the BdB chose as its official meeting place the assembly room of the Catholic Society House (Katholisches Gesellschaftshaus) on Munich's Brunnstrasse.[66] The BdB's official inaugural meeting, held on 28 July 1920, was attended by a variety of Catholic-*völkisch* figures, most from within the Nazi movement, with Hitler speaking publicly to urge the BdB to clarify its rather hazy aims and to focus more exclusively on political party building behind the leadership of the NSDAP.[67] Under the leadership of Maurer and Eder, the BdB was able to raise sufficient funds to keep the *Beobachter* operational until it was purchased officially by the NSDAP in December 1920.[68]

Although he waited until late 1920 to make his membership in the NSDAP official, beginning in June 1920 Maurer was personally responsible for the publicity and coverage of Nazi events in and around Munich.[69] In October 1920, his father, Georg Maurer, co-founded the NSDAP Ortsgruppe in Landshut, north of Munich, and he was able the next year to bring the family's parish priest from Deggendorf, Rupert Kölbl, into the small Nazi cell group in Landshut as a member.[70] Demonstrating the influence of other *völkisch*-Catholic activists like Schrönghamer, the younger Maurer made several speeches at Nazi gatherings throughout the summer and fall on the Talmud and the Jews, including a well-publicized speech on the "immorality" of Jewish profiteers and price gougers before the NSDAP Ortsgruppe Landshut on 9 November 1920.[71] As chief editor of the *Beobachter,* Maurer helped to lay the groundwork for the official Nazi acquisition of the paper.[72]

Maurer's leading colleague on the *Beobachter* staff was clearly Alfred Miller, but he maintained a broader circle of *völkisch*-Catholic collaborators that included Schrönghamer, Max Sesselmann, and, importantly, an unnamed Catholic priest whom Maurer brought onto the editorial staff in September 1920 to be officially responsible for issues pertaining to the *Judenfrage*.[73] This priest's identity was never made public, but it was almost certainly Christian Huber, a flamingly anti-Semitic young priest who had been been decisively shaped by the prewar Reform Catholic movement in Munich. Born in 1888 in Freising, just north of Munich, Huber had studied philosophy at the University of Munich and came under the influence of Joseph Schnitzer. After making the decision to enter the Catholic priesthood, Huber briefly left the seminary in 1912 over the issue that caused so much trouble for reform-oriented priests: the infamous antimodernist oath, which Huber claimed he could not swear "without vile hypocrisy" and against which the Krausgesellschaft had campaigned so energetically.[74] Following his ordination in 1915, Huber was posted to the Maria Himmelfahrt Church in Miesbach after the First World War, where he began engaging in explicitly *völkisch*-oriented anti-Semitic agitation. On 5 October 1919, Huber preached a particularly striking anti-Semitic sermon that was covered widely in the press—especially in the racist *Miesbacher Anzeiger.*[75] Then, in November 1919, when the BVP began its shift away from radical anti-Semitism and toward more "respectable" criticisms of the Jews, Huber was abruptly transferred out of his parish in Miesbach, sent back to Munich, and placed briefly in a sort of limbo that diocesan records delicately characterized as a "leave for health reasons,"[76] but was more likely a disciplinary measure. By the summer of 1920, as the young Nazi party was mobilizing increasingly in Catholic circles, Huber managed to gain appointment to a midlevel position in the diocesan Gesellenverein, which allowed him to work closely with both young working-class men and students. Although diocesan officials would later recall that Huber attempted to "turn the Gesellenverein into a Nazi formation," Huber was quite cautious at first, joining Maurer's editorial staff at the *Beobachter* in September 1920 in an anonymous capacity only.[77] In his initial *Beobachter* contributions, Huber lambasted the Jews for attempting to "strangle" Germany and argued forcefully that the Christian imperative to love one's neighbor, which the BVP claimed necessitated a milder form of anti-Semitism, was not incompatible with radical and uncompromising Nazi anti-Semitism.[78] Although Huber's *völkisch* activities remained anonymous at this point in 1920, he would emerge openly as an energetic pro-Nazi activist in the summer of 1923.

While Alfred Miller remained the chief commentator on religious issues more generally, Hansjörg Maurer's own *Beobachter* contributions frequently appealed to the spirit of religious Catholicism, and, in his role as editor, he eagerly publicized religious events designed to strengthen and deepen Catholic piety, such as the revivalistic outdoor passion play staged in Munich's Herzogpark in July 1920, while he condemned the weakness and hypocrisy of political Catholicism.[79] Maurer also opened the pages of the *Beobachter* to the lay-oriented pastoral and devotional activities of the newly founded (and strictly apolitical) Katholische Heimatmission, which provided the quintessential embodiment of the spirit of religious Catholicism. The stated goal of the Heimatmission was to gather devoted Catholic laypeople in Munich "to support on a volunteer basis the pastoral activities of the parish clergy in religious and charitable fields." Maurer urged engagement in the Heimatmission as both a spiritual and a patriotic duty, concluding: "Anyone who takes to heart the spiritual needs of our suffering Fatherland should support this organization."[80] From the time of its founding in August 1920, the Heimatmission was chaired by Andreas Stoeckle, a prominent lay activist in Munich who was head of the state comptroller's office (*Oberrechnungshof*) and who had, as a leading member of the Bavarian Beamtentum, key connections with the prewar Reform Catholic movement, particularly the nationalistic *Hofklerus* at St. Kajetan.[81]

At the time he was publicizing Andreas Stoeckle's Catholic Heimat-mission in the pages of the *Beobachter,* Hansjörg Maurer also made the decision, together with Stoeckle's son Edmund, to join the Catholic university fraternity Aenania, which was part of the broader Cartellver-band (CV) association.[82] Also among those initiated into Aenania in the summer semester of 1920 was the future pro-Nazi priest Karl Hofmann.[83] Edmund Stoeckle in particular, an ambitious and athletic young war veteran, would soon emerge as a leading figure not only within the CV but also within broader student circles in Munich, furthering the proliferation of *völkisch*-Nazi ideas begun by pioneering Catholic student activists like Roth, Miller, and Maurer.

Edmund Stoeckle had been born in 1899 into an elite Catholic family whose prominence in Munich was not only based on the stellar bureau-cratic career of Andreas Stoeckle and his forebears but was also enhanced by the influential position attained by Edmund's older brother Hermann within the ecclesiastical hierarchy of the archdiocese.[84] By the time he enrolled at the University of Munich in the fall of 1919, Edmund Stoeckle had been decisively shaped by the battle action he saw both on the western front in 1917–1918 and on the streets of Munich as a member of the Freikorps Epp in the spring of 1919.[85] Rather than joining one of the more prestigious non-Catholic fraternities, such as the Korps or Burschenschaft, Stoeckle followed his father and three brothers in joining Aenania, which was explicitly Catholic, like Alfred Miller's Hochland-Verband, but was more socially prestigious.[86] In November 1918, the Münchener CV, an amalgam consisting of the seven local CV fraternities, including Aenania, had initially taken the lead in the forma-tion of the new organization of the student body at the University of Munich, which would give students much more power in terms of university governance than they had exercised during the Kaiserreich.[87] The student leader of the Munich CV at the time, Franz Xaver Hecht, a pro–Center Party priest who had returned to the university to study law, had worked with democratically oriented students at the university—most notably Immanuel Birnbaum, a leading progressive-left democrat who was also Jewish—to establish the new Munich Allgemeine Studen-tenausschuss (ASTA) in the common room of the Aenania fraternity house.[88] In light of his willingness to cooperate with Jewish and demo-cratic circles surrounding Birnbaum, it is not surprising that Hecht was extremely cool toward the early *völkisch* stirrings among the Munich student body, particularly among his fellow CV students. Already in his mid-thirties at the time and somewhat out of step with the more radical attitudes of younger students, many of whom were veterans, Hecht stepped down from his position in the Munich CV in late 1919; leadership was eventually exercised by the ambitious Stoeckle, who forged connections between university students and young workers in Munich while also striving to embody the *völkisch*-militaristic ideal of heroic physical prowess and charismatic leadership.[89]

Under the influence of Stoeckle, the Munich CV increasingly embraced both the principle of religious Catholicism and an unmistakably *völkisch* orientation, joining the interconfessional and radically racist Hochschulring deutscher Art (HDA) in the fall of 1920.[90] This move was initially criticized by traditional conservatives within CV alumni circles in Munich who supported the BVP and opposed interconfessional cooperation between Catholic and non-Catholic fraternities. In response, Stoeckle's Aenania brother Felix Brandl published an energetic defense of *völkisch* interconfessionality in the CV's official journal, mirroring the Nazi ideal of Positive Christianity to argue that the spirit of unity forged in the trenches of war had demonstrated the possibility of maintaining a religiously loyal Catholic identity while working closely with *völkisch* non-Catholics.[91] Three central Munich CV members—Franz Pfeiffer representing Aenania, Josef Diehl representing Moenania, and Karl Hugo Siegert representing Tuiskonia—served as key figures within the regional Bavarian leadership of the HDA, with Pfeiffer ascending further to a position on the national HDA leadership committee.[92] Throughout the early 1920s, the HDA was consistently publicized and praised by the early Nazi movement as its most important ally at the university, working in common pursuit of the goal of "cleansing the *Hochschulen* in Munich of Jewish students and professors."[93]

It was this overarching goal that was at the heart of the November 1920 decision by the Munich CV, under the influence of Stoeckle, to radically reverse Hecht's tolerant stance toward the Jews and to expel all CV members with Jewish blood in their backgrounds—a move celebrated by Maurer in the *Beobachter* as a "joyous provision" and as an indication of the CV's important position in the growing *völkisch*-Nazi movement.[94] By that point, several of Maurer's and Stoeckle's CV brothers had officially joined the NSDAP. One of the earliest to do so was Robert Liebel, a nineteen-year-old engineering student and member of Vindelicia who joined the party on 4 March 1920, in the midst of Schrönghamer's *Beobachter* series on the racial identity of Jesus.[95] Over the ensuing few months, members from a variety of individual Munich CV fraternities—including Hans Vianden of Burgundia, Josef Mayer of Langobardia, and Karl Schreiber of Rheno-Franconia—joined the NSDAP, as did alumni such as Josef Brücklmayr of Aenania, a prominent lawyer employed in the Munich police head-quarters.[96] The same could undoubtedly be said of numerous students from the Catholic KV (Kartellverband) fraternities in Munich, plus Catholic *Freistudenten,* and members of both Alfred Miller's Hochland-Verband and Josef Roth's Rhaetia. In late 1920, there were somewhere between 100 and 150 members of the NSDAP who were students—not some faceless mass, but rather a circumscribed community whose members knew each other—and it is important to keep in mind that individual *völkisch*-Catholic students were not simply insignificant cogs in a giant organization at this point.[97] Additionally, the fact that the CV, KV, HV, and Rhaetia later, to their credit, produced principled and honorable opponents of the Nazis in the 1930s should not blind one to the fact that in the fluid aftermath of the First World War, when the young NSDAP was a far cry from the totalitarian anti-Catholic entity it would become once in power, Catholic students played a central role in helping the Nazi movement get on its feet initially.

Perhaps most notably, Edmund Stoeckle's *völkisch*-oriented activities at the university were widely publicized in the *Beobachter,* especially following the official Nazi acquisition of the paper in December 1920; one laudatory article featured a major university speech given by Stoeckle in January 1921, which combined the anniversary celebration of the founding of the German nation-state with a gushing tribute to German youth who had fallen in battle during the First World War.[98] Stoeckle's primary goal in this programmatic speech—and throughout his activism more generally—was to forge unity between *völkisch* university students and young members of the working class, drawing explicitly on the ideals of the social-student activism of the prewar Reform Catholic movement, which had been deepened by the brother-hood of blood and sacrifice experienced by students and workers in the trenches.[99] Not coincidentally, in the early months of 1921 the NSDAP embarked upon a simultaneous propagandistic push aimed at overcom-ing the distance between students and workers, as exemplified in a widely publicized mass meeting headlined by Hitler in the main hall of the Hofbräuhaus on 12 February 1921. In describing this "unforgetta-ble" event, the *Beobachter* observer (likely, Hansjörg Maurer) claimed that Hitler had created an atmosphere of patriotic fervor so powerful that all social barriers at the "fully packed" meeting hall fell away in a veritable orgy of *völkisch* unity:

Hitler possesses the youth, possesses the academic youth of our *Hochschulen,* possesses those who wish to sacrifice themselves to the last breath for Germany's *völkisch* recovery. Hitler has thus built a bridge between intellectual and manual laborers. . . . I looked around me and saw glowing eyes, and images of life on the battlefield emerged—we were together like this once before, German workers and students. For us the same heart pulsed beneath the field-gray uniform, and it shall be that way once again![100]

The student-worker relationship was to remain one of the most consistent themes of the party's propagandistic appeal in Munich, with huge numbers being drawn to similar mass meetings.[101] While the Nazis' appeal in later years would become remarkably broad in social terms, functioning in the 1930s as the first genuine *Volkspartei* in German history, the earliest growth of the movement in Munich was driven overwhelmingly by the party's ability to appeal simultaneously to young workers and to university students, both of which had been hardened by the common experience of war.[102] It is also important to note that non-Catholic workers and students in Munich—whether Marxist laborers or democratically oriented young intellectuals—were often decidedly resistant to the initial Nazi mobilization, making the party's broadly Catholic appeal an even more central factor in its early growth.

In addition to Hitler's speeches and mass meetings, the early Nazi appeal was often forged on a much more mundane level. The spirit of *völkisch* social unity was expressed perhaps most explicitly in the activism of the local Catholic social-student movement (Sozialstudentische Bewegung), which had its roots in Munich's prewar Reform Catholic movement; the social-student movement found itself severely out of step with the staunchly conservative-agrarian BVP and continued to focus instead on the virtues of religious Catholicism and practical Christianity in opposition to political Catholicism.[103] The official student leader of the Catholic Sozialstudentische Zentrale München (SZM), Martin Weigl, had joined the NSDAP in the spring of 1920 and ultimately brought along with him a number of other socially minded Catholic students, such as the future literary scholar Karl Debus.[104] Members of the SZM emphasized the movement's roots in prewar Reform Catholicism and characterized, with thinly veiled anti-Semitic overtones, the group's goal to constitute a "storm troop in the battle against materialism and mammonism."[105] Among Catholic university fraternities in Munich, the SZM had the closest ties with the egalitarian Hochland-Verband, with HV member Fritz Beck taking the lead alongside Weigl in organizing a massive social-student conference in Munich

in November 1920 that was publicized in the *Beobachter.*[106] Both
the HV and the SZM saw as one of the chief impediments to their
Catholic-*völkisch* goals the remnants of elitism that still clung to more
socially prestigious fraternities—including not only the non-Catholic
Burschenschaften and Korps but also some elements within the CV.[107]
This anti-elitism clearly resonated within the early Nazi movement.
When an egregiously elitist CV student from Cologne published
a short book in the fall of 1921 advising CV members throughout
Germany not to mingle with the working classes—and, as evidence of
proper breeding, to refuse even to eat with university students of lower
social standing—Beck's HV brother Alfred Miller waged a campaign in
the *Beobachter* against this "poisonous" ideology, which he viewed as a
threat not only to the *völkisch* ideal of harmony between students and
workers but also to the principles of the Christian faith and the "holy
mission" to be fulfilled by socially minded Catholic students.[108] Völkisch-
oriented members of the Munich CV—most notably Karl Hugo Siegert
of Tuiskonia—also sharply condemned the elitist pamphlet and declared
it a clear violation of the CV's Positive Christian mission to "bridge social
divisions and overcome social misery."[109]

Overall, perhaps the most thoughtful and reflective articulation of the
ideal of religious Catholicism within the context of *völkisch* social-student
activism was provided by Munich CV member Willy Glasebock in an
appeal to Catholic students written officially on behalf of the
Hochschulring. Reiterating the central differentiation between religious
and political Catholicism, Glasebock claimed that *völkisch* Catholic students had a "religious duty" to oppose ultramontane internationalism
and political Catholicism while at the same time maintaining the purity
of both their Catholic faith and their German nationality:

> For us Catholics, the highest and greatest value is our religion, our
> faith in a supernatural God. The values given [to] us by our religion
> are to be cultivated first and foremost. Yet for us, *völkisch* identity is
> also something for which we are accountable to God. We therefore
> have the moral and religious duty to protect the *völkisch* distinctiveness
> given [to] us by God.... For this reason we must also lead the battle
> with all our strength against internationalism of every variety.

Most important for Glasebock was that Catholic students should hold
firmly to their religious ideals in the midst of the healthy interconfessional activism associated with Positive Christianity. Condemning the
often anti-Catholic "nationalistic pantheists" in various branches of the

völkisch movement who "elevate nationality to the position of religion," Glasebock insisted that a true *völkisch* mass movement could only exist if believing Catholics were allowed to maintain and celebrate their Catholic religious identity while striving to purify Germany from the evils of political Catholicism. Glasebock closed with an appeal for continued Catholic support of the interconfessional Hochschulring in particular, portraying it as the "pioneer of the path toward confessional reconciliation."[110] It was precisely this type of religious appeal—self-consciously interconfessional but fundamentally Catholic-oriented—that made the Nazis' brand of Positive Christianity especially attractive to young Munich Catholics in the early 1920s, in contrast to secular, occult-based, and often anti-Catholic *völkisch* elements elsewhere.

The emphasis on cross-class and interconfessional social unity was complemented by the flamingly anti-Semitic "public morality" campaign spearheaded by Alfred Miller and Hansjörg Maurer in the *Beobachter* throughout 1920 and 1921. The campaign was designed in part to demonstrate the activist piety of religious Catholicism in contrast to the complacent hypocrisy attributed to the forces of ultramontane political Catholicism. Throughout the month of October 1920, there was tremendous publicity over an upcoming lecture on human sexuality to be given by Ferdinand von Reitzenstein, a researcher at the Institut für Sexualwissenschaft in Berlin and a close colleague of the institute's Jewish founder, the homosexual rights advocate Magnus Hirschfeld.[111] The Nazi movement and its allies were quick to set themselves up as the leading defenders of Christian-Catholic morality in Munich in the face of the Jewish sexual "perversity" represented by Reitzenstein and Hirschfeld. Two days before Reitzenstein's speech, Hitler held a major mass meeting in the Kindlkeller decrying the "deliberate Jewish corruption of the *Volk*" initiated by Hirschfeld and his allies.[112] On the day of the Reitzenstein speech, the *Beobachter* ran a series of bombastic articles by Alfred Miller laying explicit claim to the Catholic-Christian nature of Munich—in the name not only of Positive Christianity but also of the "priestly lackeys and knights of the swastika" (*Pfaffenfreunde und Hakenkreuzritter*), who had been recently ridiculed by Hirschfeld supporters in the local left-wing press—and announcing that "there is no room for such [homosexual] perversities in Munich."[113] Following Reitzenstein's speech, which was entitled "Love and Sexual Abstinence" and dealt explicitly with heterosexual relations, Miller railed against Reitzenstein's assertion that "men over twenty-one years of age can no longer remain sexually abstinent," condemning the "poisonous" moral implications of this assertion and appealing to "Catholic leaders" in Munich to speak out in outrage.[114] Maurer then issued an impassioned plea to the local diocesan authorities—referring directly to a recent pronouncement on public immorality by the bishops' conference—to launch a broad-based offensive strike against the "immorality" of the Jews as represented by the Reitzenstein lecture, with Catholic clergy offering essential "practical leadership":

> The German bishops addressed the issue of public immorality on All Saints Day and gave the summons for an across-the-board battle. An across-the-board battle is difficult if, in cases like the speech of Reitzenstein on "Love and Sexual Abstinence," not a single Catholic publication takes a stand.... Why don't the German bishops act in concert against the Jews, the secret and at the same time public bearers of morally contaminating toxins in literature, art, and theater? I hear the objection that this battle against the Jews contradicts Christian *Nächstenliebe*. But what if the Christian world view slowly but surely goes to the devil? It is truly time for the clergy to pursue things to their roots.... It is easy to threaten sinners with the punishment of hell. It is difficult to provide practical leadership, but that is the only path upward.[115]

Over the ensuing year, Maurer and Miller continued to position themselves as the self-appointed moral conscience of Catholic Munich, preaching with revivalist zeal against the evils of sexual immorality— especially homosexuality, which was the subject of a major propagandistic pamphlet written by Maurer and publicized throughout Munich in 1921.[116]

Such explicit appeals to Catholic-Christian morality, pitched in terms of religious rather than political Catholicism and appealing directly to the Nazi ideal of Positive Christianity, transcended Catholic student circles and found resonance among local anti-Semitic priests such as Alois Hecker, who had spent most of his lengthy pastoral career in Füstenfeldbruck, on the western outskirts of the city of Munich.[117] Finding inspiration in Maurer's energetic call to arms on the part of Catholic clergy, in early 1921 Hecker answered by launching his own brutally anti-Semitic missive, which opened by reprinting the entirety of Maurer's *Beobachter* plea for Catholic leadership.[118] In attacking Jewish "immorality" throughout nearly 200 pages of rambling text, Hecker's central goal was to prove that "when the believing Catholic becomes an anti-Semite, he is simply following the spirit of Jesus."[119]

If judged in terms of a coherent pursuit of this thesis, Hecker's book must be considered a dismal failure; in his confused ruminations, he alternately swings between fairly traditional Catholic anti-Jewish dia-tribes and lengthy digressions fusing racial pseudo-science and explicit calls for the "extermination of the Jews" (*Ausrottung der Juden*) without any consistency or sustained clarity of thought.[120] Importantly, Hecker not only cited richly from the pages of the *Beobachter*—including lengthy verbatim passages from essays by Schrönghamer, Miller, and Maurer—but went further to reprint the entirety of the Nazis' 25 Points, word for word, trumpeting the phrase "Positive Christianity" in bold type and idealizing the NSDAP as the ultimate "model" (*Vorbild*) for anyone who hoped to "achieve the elevated goals" Hecker himself had laid out in his treatise.[121] Hecker's unqualified praise for the religious orientation of the NSDAP contrasted sharply with his brutal criticisms of political Cathol-icism, particularly Center Party leader Matthias Erzberger, whom Hecker attacked as a tool of international Jewry.[122] The Nazis were more than happy to return the praise in the *Beobachter,* giving publicity to Hecker's book and idealizing the "brave priest" whose participation in the movement would, it was hoped, inspire numerous followers from within the Bavarian Catholic clergy.[123] There were, in fact, growing numbers of *völkisch*-oriented priests who began to support the Nazi movement between 1920 and 1922; Alfred Miller was not incorrect in claiming of the *Beobachter*'s anti-Semitic crusade that "especially here in Bavaria there are numerous Catholic priests who have placed themselves in the service of this holy cause."[124] In stark contrast to the high point of open Catholic-Nazi activism achieved in 1923, however, most still chose at this point to work anonymously and behind the scenes.[125] Despite the covert nature of much of the earliest pro-Nazi activism of Catholic priests, one is struck in contrast by the complete and utter absence of corresponding activism among Protestant clergy in and around Munich; they were completely and utterly uninvolved in the early Nazi movement and instead gravitated overwhelmingly toward rival *völkisch* groupings that were more openly Protestant-oriented.[126]

Finally, connected to the Nazi public morality campaign—and fur-ther fleshing out the ideal of religious Catholicism in practice—was a bombastic campaign against the alleged immorality of the Talmud led, once again, by the Catholic-Nazi student duo of Miller and Maurer. Building on the broader anti-Talmud criticisms common to the *völkisch* movement throughout Germany and, more specifically, on the Munich-based works of Schrönghamer, beginning in the fall of 1920 Miller and Maurer launched a campaign designed to test the legal protection offered to the Talmud by paragraph 166 of the German *Strafgesetzbuch,* which covered "offenses against religion." In an outlandish exposé in the *Beobachter,* Miller went beyond stereotypical accusations of Jewish involvement in female trafficking to connect specific Jewish figures, whose names were provided, to the prostitution trade and, more important, to claim that they operated with the explicit approval of Jewish religious leaders, whose interpretation of the Talmud established the trade in Gentile women, viewed as "human cattle," as a religiously justified endeavor sanctioned by God.[127] As expected, a legal case was initiated against Maurer (as *Beobachter* editor) and Miller (as author of the offending article) by the Munich branch of the Zentralverein deutscher Staatsbürger jüdischen Glaubens. The trial, which began on 17 April 1921 and ended with the exoneration of Maurer and Miller on 8 June 1921, provided the two activists with a forum through which to whip up religious indignation and disgust with the local Jewish community among Munich Catholics. In a series of *Beobachter* articles, Maurer reprinted bizarre passages from the Talmud and "related texts" (such as the *Toldoth Jeschu*) in an attempt to demonstrate Jewish mockery and blasphemy of the Virgin Mary and Jesus.[128] After launching a fundraising drive to help cover potential court costs, Maurer revealed that the goal of the entire endeavor was "to achieve clarity through this trial on whether or not the Talmud is legally protected under 'religion'" and supplied readers with a form letter they could sign and send to authorities demanding that the Talmud be declared "anti-religious" and banned within Germany's borders in the name of "Christian religion and morality."[129] Following the announcement of their acquittal, a jubilant Maurer announced that "thousands of signatures" had been collected in the petition drive, and he reprinted in the *Beobachter* both the original Alfred Miller article that had started the process and the entire text of the judgment from the sympathetic court, claiming that it set the legal precedent he had been looking for and that the Talmud was in fact not covered by German laws protecting religion.[130] Maurer next announced plans to launch a broader campaign throughout Germany to get the Talmud banned, sharply differentiating his "religiously sincere" efforts from those of *völkisch* forces elsewhere that strove to condemn not just the Talmud but the Bible entirely.[131]

After losing its court case against Maurer and Miller, the Zentralverein successfully lobbied the Munich police authorities to take legal action against the *Beobachter* on grounds of breaching the peace and potentially inciting violence, and the paper was banned completely in Munich for a month. During that time, Maurer vowed to carry on his religious crusade against the Talmud in the Nazis' temporary replacement paper, *Der Nationalsozialist,* continuing to emphasize the basic Catholic-moral motivation for condemning the Talmud.[132] By the time the *Beobachter* reappeared in print, however, Maurer's campaign was over-shadowed by the massive power struggle within the NSDAP which brought Hitler to sole power within the party and brought the *Beobachter* into the hands of Dietrich Eckart, who took over as editor and led the paper into an increasingly bitter political battle with the BVP in competition for the support of Catholics in Munich.

War of Words: Religious Catholicism and the Political Battle against the BVP

I am a Catholic, Dr. Wirth, and precisely for this reason I refuse most decisively to allow you, in your un-Catholic shallowness, to abuse the name of Catholic.

—Dietrich Eckart to Center Party leader Joseph Wirth,
September 1921

In May 1921, in the midst of their Catholic-oriented campaign against the Talmud, Alfred Miller and Hansjörg Maurer had co-authored a programmatic statement that encapsulated one of the central strategies employed in the political machinations of the early Nazi movement against the BVP, based again on the distinction between religious and political Catholicism. Noting the fundamental importance of the Catholic faith and pledging respect specifically for the "religious authority of the pope," Miller and Maurer launched into a broadside against the BVP and the Center Party explicitly on religious grounds—for betraying the Catholic faith by exploiting it politically at election time and then, by proceeding to engage in self-interested political cooperation with "Jews and atheists" in the Social Democratic Party, ultimately failing miserably to defend the religious interests of the Catholics they claimed to repre-sent.[133] This central argument was hammered home repeatedly and quite effectively throughout 1921 and 1922, as the *Beobachter* portrayed the NSDAP as the only true and uncompromising defender of Positive Christianity (and religious Catholicism more specifically), in contrast to the allegedly destructive and hypocritical exploitation of the Catholic faith by the BVP and Center Party.

This tactic was especially clear in the journalistic labors of Dietrich Eckart, who took over as chief editor of the *Beobachter* in August 1921, in the aftermath of the famous power struggle that gave Hitler dictatorial control of the NSDAP. Eckart had accompanied Hitler, to whom he had become a sort of father figure and etiquette trainer, on a fundraising trip to Berlin in June. While they were away, a crisis developed back in Munich as some elements within the NSDAP, eager to increase their own power, pushed for a merger with the rival *völkisch* movement of Otto Dickel.[134] Hitler was intent on maintaining the organizational independence of the Nazi party at all costs and, upon returning from Berlin, responded to the power play by angrily resigning from the NSDAP in July 1921, cognizant of the fact that the party could not afford to lose its star attraction and most effective propagandistic speaker. Following the intervention of Eckart, Hitler agreed to rejoin the NSDAP and was given as a result sole power within the party; he undertook a major restructuring that included, among other things, the installation of his mentor Eckart at the *Beobachter*.[135] For the duration of his tenure as editor, Eckart waged a brutal political campaign against the ultramontane forces of political Catholicism, attempting first and foremost to link the BVP in the minds of Munich Catholics with major figures on the left wing of the Center Party, such as Matthias Erzberger and Joseph Wirth, who were deeply unpopular in the Bavarian capital.

In his first front-page statement as editor, Eckart attacked the Center Party for betraying Catholic principles and working with Marxist Jews and atheists "in the most perfect harmony," ostentatiously trumpeting his identity as a professing Catholic and signing his editorial "Dietrich Eckart, Catholic."[136] After the assassination of Erzberger in late August 1921, a sanctimonious Eckart claimed in a scathing obituary that Erzberger's willingness to sacrifice religious convictions for political gain disqualified him from any posthumous celebration as a Catholic hero.[137] Similarly, in criticizing Center Party leader Joseph Wirth (then in his first term as chancellor) for joining with Jewish and Marxist politicians in praising Erzberger as a martyr, Eckart insisted that his commitment to unmasking the evils of political Catholicism was in complete harmony with the depth and profundity of the Catholic faith, in contrast to the "un-Catholic superficiality" that was characteristic of Wirth.[138] Alfred Miller and Hansjörg Maurer continued as two of the most visible *Beobachter* contributors under Eckart and pursued the same strategy of attempting to decouple political Catholicism and ultramontanism from individual Catholic religious conviction. Miller lambasted the alleged duplicity of Wirth and other Center Party leaders who "go around cloaked in the hypocritical mantle of Christianity in order to grab people by their religious convictions" only to make them "bow willingly under the Jewish authority of Berlin," and he closed by asking: "Is there anyone who doesn't gag over this type of 'Christianity'?"[139] Similarly, in mockery of the Center Party's election slogan "Back to God's Holy Law," Maurer proclaimed: "A party that makes political 'business' with God and Christianity, like the Center Party has done especially in recent years, now appeals to God! The Center Party has sold its convictions to the Marxist enemies of religion! . . . And this party now wants to take the name of God in its mouth and so blaspheme Him?"[140] However contrived it may seem in retrospect, this sense of righteous indignation, which had also fueled much of the student socio-moral activism of Miller and Maurer, remained an especially effective political weapon in the Nazis' early arsenal.

When the main BVP daily in Munich, the *Bayerischer Kurier,* began criticizing the left wing of the Center Party and launched its own brief attack on *Germania,* the Center Party's leading organ in Berlin, Eckart's *Beobachter* followed the conflict with undisguised glee.[141] Upon the September 1920 formation of a new Bavarian coalition government under the BVP's Hugo Max von Lerchenfeld, however, the Nazis perceived an opportunity to focus more explicitly on the BVP itself, portraying the moderation and reflectiveness of Lerchenfeld as evidence of hypocrisy and weakness.[142] It was Maurer who took the lead initially in attacking the new minister-president, and the radicalism of his criticisms promptly resulted in a ten-day ban on the *Beobachter.*[143] Over the next several months, Nazi attacks on Lerchenfeld became increasingly brutal, including unseemly allegations about his wife and the "immoral" Jews with whom she allegedly consorted; she was ultimately portrayed as an unfit model of Catholic femininity.[144] When Lerchenfeld began responding indignantly to the radicalism of the attacks against him, the Nazis were quick to cry foul, asking why Lerchenfeld was unwilling to criticize the Center Party's "atheistic" Jewish and socialist partners with similar fervor.[145] In response, Lerchenfeld delivered what has become perhaps his most famous speech, a diatribe before the Bavarian Landtag in early April 1922 that attacked the "machinations of the so-called National Socialists" and closed with the categorical statement that his personal convictions "as a man and as a Christian" forced him to oppose anti-Semitism.[146] It was this speech by Lerchenfeld that provoked one of the most striking pronouncements on Catholic religious faith—and, with it, on the religious identity of the early movement—ever made by Adolf Hitler.

In a widely publicized mass meeting in the Bürgerbräukeller on 12 April 1922, Hitler spoke at length about the impact of his own personal Catholic faith on his political activism, noting that it was his religious convictions in particular that compelled him to be a ruthless anti-Semite. Referring directly to Lerchenfeld's speech, Hitler proclaimed:

> [Lerchenfeld] stated in the last Landtag session that his sentiment "as a man and as a Christian" prevents him from being an anti-Semite. I say: my Christian sentiment points me toward my Lord and Savior as a warrior. It points me to the man who at one time, lonely and surrounded by only a few followers, recognized the Jews and called for the battle against them, and who—God be true!—was the greatest not as a sufferer but rather as a warrior! In boundless love as a Christian and as a man I read through the passage which tells us how the Lord at last rose up and seized the whip to drive out of the temple the brood of vipers and serpents. With deepest emotion I recognize today, after two thousand years, his monumental struggle against the Jewish poison, and I am moved most powerfully by the fact that it was for this that he had to shed his blood on the cross.[147]

This speech is significant on at least two levels. First, it pledges Hitler's personal devotion to his "Lord and Savior" in no uncertain terms and embodies the type of activist warrior Christianity that the Nazi movement would utilize to great effect over the course of the following year. At this point, Christianity was not merely being tolerated publicly in the interest of social harmony—as would be the case later in Hitler's *Mein Kampf*—but was being embraced and preached with equal measures of apparent sincerity and revivalist fervor. Second, the speech was not an atypical lapse nor an unscripted digression by Hitler, but rather a well-planned programmatic statement intended to embody the movement's early religious identity and to demonstrate its genuine commitment to Positive Christianity. This is made unmistakably clear by the fact that the speech was reprinted and distributed in mass quantities throughout Munich in the spring of 1922 as the first Nazi propagandistic pamphlet of its kind, claiming to officially represent "the basic principles and goals of our movement" and thereby serving as an authoritative pronouncement of party doctrine.[148] None of Hitler's other speeches to that point—whether on the Treaty of Versailles, the perfidy of the Jews, or any other topic—had ever received that type of official approbation or widespread distribution by the NSDAP.[149]

Building on Hitler's striking profession of faith and the publicity it engendered, the Nazis continued to accentuate the contrast between religious and political Catholicism when the national Katholikentag convened in Munich in the summer of 1922. They trumpeted strictly religious events—such as a major concert mass at the Frauenkirche which "promises to be an exceptional pleasure"—while in the same *Beobachter* issue berating the Center Party for, again, selling out Catholic principles through cooperation with atheistic Jews and socialists.[150] The *Beobachter* seized especially eagerly on Cardinal Faulhaber's infamous opening speech at the Katholikentag, which condemned the Weimar Republic and the revolution that brought it into existence as "perjury and high treason, remaining throughout history hereditarily tainted and cursed with the mark of Cain."[151] Even greater emphasis, however, was placed on Faulhaber's anti-Semitic comments targeting the "Jewish press in Berlin" and appealing explicitly to "racially pure Catholics."[152] The Katholikentag and Faulhaber's statements, in particular, were used consistently over the coming weeks and months to reinforce the claim that the Nazis' uncompromising brand of anti-Semitism was in full accord with the Catholic religious faith as expressed by Faulhaber, in contrast to the hypocritical political opportunism of the BVP and Center Party.[153] Anyone looking for an official public denunciation of Nazi anti-Semitism from Faulhaber would have to wait more than a year—until early November 1923, on the eve of the Beerhall Putsch—at which point the NSDAP had already succeeded in mobilizing thousands and thousands of Catholics in and around Munich.

The BVP seems to have been somewhat unsure as to how best to respond to the political attacks of the NSDAP initially. For some time, the *Bayerischer Kurier* virtually ignored the upstart party, which was still comparatively insignificant—in the early fall of 1922, the NSDAP still numbered just 3,000 members—and could only benefit from the increased publicity that would be generated by a direct confrontation with the pro-BVP press.[154] As a result of the successes of the Nazi emphasis on religious Catholicism, however, and apparently feeling it unwise to continue a policy of non-engagement, the BVP passed a resolution at its annual party congress in late October 1922 to initiate for the first time an official publicity campaign to "enlighten" Bavarian Catholics about the dangers posed by the NSDAP, specifically on religious grounds.[155] Just as the *Beobachter* had gone to great lengths to tie the BVP to the left wing of the Center Party and its alleged betrayal of Catholic principles, the BVP and its allies in the press attempted to label the Nazi movement in Munich as religiously dangerous to Catholics by linking it to the anti-Catholic or overtly anti-Christian sentiments of *völkisch* organizations elsewhere that were either loosely affiliated with or sympathetic toward the NSDAP—most typically, the Bohemian National Socialist Party under Rudolf Jung, whose political identity continued to be shaped by the virulent anti-Catholicism of the Los-von-Rom movement, and the north German racist movements associated with Theodor Fritsch and Artur Dinter, which openly espoused replacing traditional Christianity with some vague form of pagan or Germanic religiosity.

Already in December 1920, the Jesuit Augustin Bea had pioneered this strategy, publishing a major article in the Jesuits' Munich-based organ linking the radical anti-Semitism of the local *völkisch* milieu, including the NSDAP, to the Germanic racial and religious ideas of both Fritsch and Dinter through the common condemnation of the Talmud and Old Testament.[156] In response, the *Beobachter* was quick to defend the NSDAP against such connections and, in doing so, made sure to distance the movement in Munich from overtly anti-Christian *völkisch* ideologies elsewhere. A programmatic article from mid-January 1921, clearly written from a Catholic perspective, energetically defended the Christian faith from its admittedly numerous detractors within the larger *völkisch* movement: "I consider it unjust and, from a purely Aryan standpoint, reprehensible when the attempt is made, as I have unfortunately witnessed frequently in *völkisch* circles, to portray the Christian religion as something inferior which must be combatted because it is saturated with a Semitic spirit." Clearly distancing himself (and the NSDAP) from the anti-Christian Germanic religious ideologies with which the Nazis were being linked, the author urged *völkisch* Catholics to stay faithful to the Catholic "faith of their fathers" with the explicit plea "Let us not fabricate any surrogate [religions]."[157]

In its late 1922 "enlightenment" campaign, however, the BVP expanded on the linkage pioneered by Bea. In November, the BVP's Franz Schweyer, who served as interior minister in the Lerchenfeld cabinet, went before the Landtag several times to speak on the National Socialist danger, "which has been given too little attention to this point," characterizing the movement as an anti-Christian pathology and an unhealthy "symptom of these sick, unsettled times."[158] Official BVP statements throughout December 1922 and January 1923 focused overwhelmingly on the "duty to enlighten the Bavarian population, with word and pen, about the dangers of [the Nazi] movement . . . especially the lack of understanding for Catholic feeling and thought."[159] The centerpiece of the BVP enlightenment campaign was provided by the activism of Wilhelm Vielberth, a Catholic priest and outspoken BVP deputy who wrote an influential series of articles in December 1922 claiming that it was time to penetrate the deliberate opacity of the Nazis' religious facade to reveal the party's true anti-Catholic and anti-Christian nature.[160] Vielberth criticized both the vagueness of the Nazi version of Positive Christianity and its alleged potential for reducing all substantive Christianity (of both the Catholic and Protestant varieties) into a nondescript and religiously meaningless Germanic amalgamation.[161] Vielberth also condemned the extreme anti-Semitism of the movement, which he saw as anti-Christian for both its tendency to deny the validity of the Old Testament and its violation of the decree to love one's neighbors, and he vigorously attacked the anti-Christian "pantheism" he perceived throughout *völkisch* rhetoric.[162]

Unfortunately Vielberth's analysis was undermined by the fact that drew all of his anti-Christian examples from the recent work of the Bohemian National Socialist Rudolf Jung, prompting even the anti-Nazi priest Erhard Schlund, of Munich's St. Anna cloister, to concede that Vielberth had essentially missed the boat with regard to the Munich NSDAP, which "would not be willing to identify itself with [the anti-Catholic ideas of] Jung."[163] Despite the central weakness of Vielberth's approach and Schlund's accurate assessment of it, Vielberth's project was to that point the most detailed and potentially most damaging critical reframing of an issue the Nazis had hoped to continue to frame on their own terms.

The BVP's broader enlightenment campaign reflects at least in part the concern created by the initial effectiveness of the Nazis' embodiment of Positive Christianity within a Catholic context. It also seems to have prompted the NSDAP to make its religious stance more tangible and explicit than ever before. Over the course of the following year, the party's discourse would become considerably more overt in its appeal to Catholic-Christian identity—with numerous Catholic priests, for instance, dropping their earlier anonymity to emerge openly as pro-Nazi spokesmen. By the summer of 1923, both the public face of the movement and its stated ideal of Positive Christianity would become increasingly Catholic-oriented.

CHAPTER 4

A "Catholic-Oriented Movement"?

The Zenith of Catholic-Nazi Activism, 1922–1923

On 5 July 1923, a Thursday afternoon, the St. Rupertuskirche on Munich's Kiliansplatz hosted an event that drew but scant attention from neighboring residents at the time. Following a perfunctory civil ceremony performed earlier in the day, two of St. Rupert's young parishioners were joined in marriage in a traditional Catholic mass, accompanied by a small group of supporters. Although the bride, Therese Deininger, was joined in celebration by several friends and family members, the young groom, just three weeks shy of his twenty-third birthday, was accompanied merely by two unobtrusive groomsmen who distinguished themselves from the others in attendance perhaps only because they sported, as did the groom, distinctive "toothbrush" moustaches. The shortest and perhaps quirkiest of the half-mustachioed men, who had become something of a local political celebrity in Munich over the previous few years, congratulated the newlyweds in fatherly tones although he was barely more than a decade older than the groom. He would also deliver brief but apparently memorable congratulatory words at a private celebration later that night. That groomsman was Adolf Hitler, the other was Anton Drexler, and the young groom was Hermann Esser, whose traditional Catholic wedding ceremony was announced tastefully the following day in the *Beobachter* (see fig. 4.1).[1] The Deininger family may not yet have been in a position to fully appreciate the significance of the political ideology that bound together their daughter's new husband and his two attendants. It is, however, almost certain that the parish priest who performed the ceremony was fully aware of the nature of the movement they led; by the summer of 1923, the NSDAP had become a steady topic of public

Figure 4.1. Hermann Esser (1923).
Source: Sesselmann and Hoffmann, *Deutschlands Erwachen.*

discussion and was growing dramatically—particularly among Catholics—in and around Munich.

Less than a week after the Deininger-Esser wedding at St. Rupert's, an unrelated front-page feature article appeared in the leading Social Democratic daily, *Vorwärts,* documenting one of the most striking and, from the paper's perspective, deeply troubling recent developments in Bavarian politics: the energetic and open propagandistic agitation of Catholic priests on behalf of the rapidly expanding Nazi movement. Whereas socialist critics of the NSDAP had, over the past few years, frequently poked fun at the increasingly visible combination of Nazi radicalism and Catholic piety forged in and around Munich, by the summer of 1923 the attitude of detached bemusement had become one of deep concern. Stating that "it is no secret that a significant portion of the Bavarian clergy has committed itself heart and soul to swastika-ism," the article noted the unmistakable boost given to the Nazi movement by its numerous priestly propagandists: "Today in Bavaria there is no nationalistic event without a Catholic priest giving his 'blessing' to it.... It seems now to have become the fashion for Catholic priests to provide leadership services to the National Socialists." After appealing directly to the Vatican and the German episcopate to try to stem the growing flow of Catholic clergy and laity into the Nazi movement, the article concluded by lamenting the oft-cited uniqueness of Bavarian Catholicism: "Catholic priests as Nazi storm-troop preachers—such a thing is only possible in the Bavarian 'cell of order.'"[2]

This concern over Catholic Nazi "storm-troop preachers" was not unique to the Nazis' socialist opponents. A few months later, the parliamentary leader of the BVP, Heinrich Held, wrote a particularly impassioned appeal to Cardinal Faulhaber in response to the massive numbers of Bavarian Catholics who were helping to fuel the dramatic growth experienced by the NSDAP throughout 1923, when the party's membership nearly tripled. While Held claimed that the leadership of the movement consisted "almost exclusively of Protestants" (a claim that was true of the broader *völkisch* movement but certainly not of the Nazi party itself), he was forced to concede implicitly that the rank and file was made up largely of Catholics, and he referred to the movement as a "great falling-away from the Catholic faith and from the Church." Unwilling to admit that a true Catholic would willingly join the Nazis' radical racial and political crusade, Held asserted that many Catholics were simply naïve and were blindly allowing themselves to be misled: "many Catholics are going along with the crowd, infatuated by catchy phrases and not knowing the end to which they are being misused." The brunt of Held's anger was thus focused on the role played by Catholic opinion leaders, most notably priests, in propagandizing against the BVP: "Even priests are being caught up in National Socialist ideas and are allowing themselves to be shamefully misused as [Nazi] agitators.... Under the guise of paramilitary field sermons the Catholic populace, especially the Catholic youth, is being duped about the true intentions of the leaders of the movement. It is a shame and a disgrace." Held concluded by pleading for Faulhaber publicly to condemn the Nazi movement and to offer an "open, forceful word of warning and repudiation to the Catholic populace," a warning that would have, not

coincidentally, strongly benefited Held's BVP in its fierce local competition with the NSDAP.[3] Despite frequent attempts to establish an
image of incompatibility between Catholicism and Nazism, in the summer of 1923 even staunch opponents such as Erhard Schlund were forced
to admit that the Munich-based NSDAP had managed to become, in
contrast to anti-Catholic *völkisch* movements elsewhere in Germany, a
"Catholic-oriented movement."[4]

It was partly in response to the "enlightenment" campaign launched
by the BVP against the allegedly problematic religious identity of the
NSDAP that the *Beobachter* had begun boasting in early 1923 about
the participation of large numbers of "outspokenly Catholic men and
women" in the movement, including not only laypeople but also, significantly, Catholic priests.[5] Throughout much of 1923, the party's Catholic
orientation, earlier embodied informally under the broader rubric
of Positive Christianity, would be emphasized to an unprecedented
degree in a membership drive featuring a striking emphasis on religious
imagery and the energetic activism of numerous Catholic priests
and prominent laypeople. Importantly, just as the BVP was initially
launching its anti-Nazi enlightenment campaign in the fall of 1922, a
simultaneous development in Italy emerged that would deeply impact
the nature of the Nazi movement and Hitler's self-perception: the
"march on Rome" that brought Benito Mussolini to power. Even as
the Catholic-oriented membership drive was making dramatic gains
for the Nazis throughout Bavaria, Hitler and other Nazi leaders became
obsessed with the possibility of following Mussolini's example, dreaming
of forcing their way into power first in Munich and then staging a
dramatic march on Berlin to replace the entire democratic system with a
nationalistic dictatorship. Massing the strength necessary to achieve this
goal would require Hitler to reverse his previous insistence on maintaining
the strict independence of the NSDAP; as a result, he would allow himself
to be placed at the head of a broader *völkisch* coalition whose religious
identity—especially with respect to the followers of Erich Ludendorff—
was markedly different from that cultivated previously by the Nazis
themselves. At the same time, the prospect of attaining dictatorial power
by force tapped into Hitler's already massive ego and unleashed a powerful
form of political messianism that would not only come to destroy much
of the Catholic-Nazi synthesis forged so sucessfully up to 1923 but
would ultimately leave little or no room in the Nazi movement—certainly
among its leadership—for any genuine claim to Catholic identity.

The Nazi Ideal of "Warrior Christianity" and the Catholic-Oriented Membership Drive

The enlightenment campaign launched by the BVP in the fall of 1922, especially the detailed and specific criticisms offered by Wilhelm Vielberth, seemed to exploit a potential chink in the Nazis' armor and threatened to frame the political battle for Catholic Munich on the BVP's terms and to establish a fundamental correlation in the popular Catholic imagination between the NSDAP and anti-Christian *völkisch* movements elsewhere in Germany.[6] The Nazi movement responded energetically to the allegations of the BVP, publishing several programmatic statements on the religious identity of the NSDAP and accentuating the movement's continually growing Catholic orientation. An early statement from December 1922 not only decried the BVP criticisms as laughable but claimed that the Nazis answered to a much higher Catholic authority: "The battle, which according to Catholic teaching takes place before the judgment seat of God, between Christianity and anti-Christianity, between idealism and materialism—this is the battle we National Socialists want to wage."[7]

Perhaps the most notable response to Vielberth was written by Magnus Gött, a radically anti-Semitic Catholic priest in Lehenbühl, in southwestern Bavaria. Born in 1881, Gött had studied philosophy and church history both in Dillingen and at the University of Munich, coming under the influence of the Reform Catholic leader Joseph Schnitzer.[8] He was ordained in 1908 and began serving at a parish in Lehenbühl in January 1913. Almost immediately, Gött began writing a weekly column in the nearby *Legauer Anzeiger,* demonstrating both a strong sympathy for the working classes and a rabidly anti-Semitic outlook.[9] In the aftermath of the Eisner revolution in November 1918, Gött lambasted the new regime as a result of "pure political horse-trading under the flag of the Jews."[10] When Eisner was assassinated in February 1919, Gött continued to heap scorn on the "asiatic Jew" who had brought his own assassination on himself.[11] Like fellow Catholic anti-Semites Schrönghamer and Eckart, Gött had originally supported the BVP, especially during the January 1919 elections.[12] By the fall, however, he was beginning to distance himself from the BVP and by the spring of 1920 had nothing but scorn for the party's "hypocritical" leaders.[13] In the summer of 1922, after the strongly pro-Nazi priest Christian Huber was transferred from his Gesellenverein post in Munich to the parish in Kronburg, just a few miles from Lehenbühl, Gött was introduced officially by Huber to the NSDAP and its ideas.[14]

In his programmatic *Beobachter* response, Gött addressed Vielberth's accusations directly and offered a point-by-point refutation from a theological perspective, focusing especially on the charge that the racial anti-Semitism of the NSDAP was un-Christian because it denied, at least implicitly, the inspiration of the Old Testament:

> Then *Pfarrer* Vielberth condemns us for our opposition to the Jews and for disrespecting the Old Testament. The Old Testament is not mentioned in the party program—and every Christian knows in any case that it is something imperfect, provisional, and now obsolete, otherwise we would still be bound by such things as blood vengeance, polygamy, the prohibition on pork, and absolute this-worldliness. We live under the new covenant.

Gött also took issue with Vielberth's tendency to identify the anti-Christian "pantheism" of the Bohemian National Socialist Rudolf Jung as the accepted policy of the Munich-based NSDAP: "But Herr *Pfarrer,* where does anything like that appear in the party program? Herr Jung, whom you cite for evidence, is not the party and not its program."[15]

A similar approach was adopted in early 1923 by Franz Schrönghamer-Heimdal in a programmatic feature article in the *Beobachter* condemning what he called the BVP's shameful "campaign of defamation." Proclaiming that the NSDAP was perfectly compatible with the Catholic faith in both theory and practice, Schrönghamer insisted that the private statements of individual non-Catholic members could not be used to declare the Nazi movement to be anti-Catholic any more than the occasional presence within the ranks of the BVP and Center Party of Protestant pastors—who denied central aspects of Catholic doctrine publicly from the pulpit every Sunday—could be used to somehow paint those parties as problematic for Catholics. For Schrönghamer, the BVP and Center Party were of course problematic for Catholics, not for reaching out to believing Protestants but because of the "abyss of hypocrisy" created by their cooperation with Jews and socialists.[16]

In response to the BVP's "campaign of defamation," the Nazis also began to emphasize what they frequently termed "warrior Christianity" in explicit contrast to the alleged complacency, hypocrisy, and weakness of BVP supporters. At official Nazi Christmas celebrations in December 1922, Hitler and Esser emphasized the explicitly Christian combat mission of the NSDAP, with Hitler not only invoking Christ's "heroic spirit" but also admonishing his Nazi listeners in revivalist fashion: "We should not be Christians in word only, but rather Christians of the deed and of the sword."[17] It will be recalled that Hitler's first mass-circulation pamphlet, published earlier in 1922, had explicitly emphasized the "warrior" identity of his "Lord and Savior" in combatting the Jews.[18] The image of the heroic (Aryan) Christ driving the (Jewish) money-changers out of the temple was a staple of Nazi imagery more generally.[19] It was in this spirit that Hitler, in a major address on 6 April 1923, attacked the recent charges that the Nazis were anti-Christian, claiming instead that they pursued an activist form of warrior Christianity that was much more genuine than the lethargy of the weak and hypocritical BVP:

> We are characterized as anti-Christian by the party that most seriously threatens Christianity through its connection with Marxist atheism: the Center Party....We must once again raise up Christianity, but it must be warrior Christianity. Christianity is not the teaching of silent suffering and burden bearing, but rather of battle. As Christians we have the duty to fight against injustice with all the weapons Christ has given us; now is the time to fight with fist and sword.[20]

Importantly, this speech coincided with the arrival in Munich of one of the central Christian warriors who would help to lead the Nazi expansion throughout Catholic Bavaria over the ensuing months: the Catholic priest Lorenz Pieper. Hitler's speech and Pieper's arrival marked the beginning of an unprecedented propagandistic drive for new members that was saturated with Catholic-inflected religious imagery. In the face of BVP condemnations of their alleged anti-Christian nature, the Nazis chose to go on the offensive.

The initial announcement of the new membership drive explicitly echoed Schrönghamer's "campaign of defamation" imagery, albeit in reverse, calling for a "propaganda campaign against lies and defamation"[21] to be kicked off in mid-April 1923 with a series of public mass lectures by Hitler. This was followed by announcements indicating that the initial campaign was to be extended for several weeks; it aimed to achieve a "record level of propagandistic activity" and encompassed not only Munich but also the surrounding Bavarian countryside, utilizing both mass meetings and small local discussion groups to win "new warriors for our idea."[22] In early May, more specific instructions were given regarding behind-the-scenes work that strongly resembled evangelistic proselytization, with local neighborhood "discussion evenings" providing the best way to solidify and personally strengthen the convictions of new members who had been attracted to the party through the larger mass meetings. Listing each of Munich's seven neighborhood party chapters, these instructions admonished all members to invite their friends and colleagues to the neighborhood meetings and to attend themselves, at the very least, two such events each month.[23] Following a remarkably successful first few weeks, the membership drive was extended through the entire summer of 1923.[24]

As a striking corollary to the new membership drive, the Nazis began placing an unmistakable emphasis on religious piety and practice, maintaining the party's interconfessional stance but foregrounding Catholic elements explicitly. In April 1923, the *Beobachter* began, for the first time in its history, to publish extensive listings of Sunday services in Munich and admonished its readers through the summer to attend church and to scrupulously fulfill their religious obligations.[25] The new Nazi Jugendbund, the forerunner to the Hitler Youth, met on Sundays in the late morning but gave explicit instructions that "every member" had to attend mass before coming to the Jugendbund meeting.[26] Similarly, the Nazi hiking society instructed its members to attend church en masse before embarking on their Sunday outings.[27] A variety of Catholic religious services and events were publicized vigorously, encouraging the deepening of personal piety associated with religious Catholicism while continuing to condemn the evils of political Catholicism.[28]

Throughout the duration of the membership drive, the *Beobachter* also published a series of religiously tinged devotional poems, including several written by the Catholic priest Ottokar Kernstock, whose credentials were prominently publicized. The most widely circulated of these was framed as a hymn of praise to the emblem of the movement—"the swastika on a field of white, against a fire-red background"—which was venerated as the spiritual symbol of God's blessing on the young movement, inspiring the courage and conviction "to fear neither death nor devil."[29] The *Beobachter* also provided readers with the texts of numerous Catholic-*völkisch* prayers that could be recited during their daily devotions, further unifying the movement through the practice of personal piety. One such prayer, which was attached directly to the schedule of Catholic masses in Munich, focused on the person of Hitler, not as a godlike or messianic figure in his own right—those images would come to dominate later, after the party's refounding in 1925—but as an upright Catholic-Christian leader reliant on the faithful prayers of his followers:

O God, protect our Hitler,
lead him in the correct path and bless his work.
O let your light triumph on earth,
and break the proud power of the enemy!
Grant our people the order, composure, and peace of the
    German day
that follows the dismal night.[30]

Other prayers reinforced the imagery of warrior Christianity and appealed directly to Catholic piety.[31] As a further expression of the Christian warrior ideal, the movement also reinforced the image that its highest-profile leaders—most notably, Hitler and Hermann Esser—were both practicing Catholics and decisive men of action.[32]

In addition to the marked emphasis on religious practice, the propagandistic membership drive was characterized most notably by the active engagement of influential Catholic opinion leaders speaking on behalf of the NSDAP, as the movement strove to strengthen its support within Catholic circles in Munich while also expanding energetically into Catholic regions throughout Bavaria. Prominent lay Catholics who were long-time party members were centrally involved; Franz Schrönghamer-Heimdal, for example, kicked off a propagandistic tour through heavily Catholic lower Bavaria with a well-publicized mass meeting sponsored by the NSDAP's Ortsgruppe Deggendorf in April 1923.[33] But the most striking new development was without question the active and open involvement of Catholic priests.

"Catholic Priests as Nazi Storm-Troop Preachers": Forging the Catholic-Nazi Synthesis

As the Nazis attempted to penetrate further into Catholic organizational and parish life in Munich and throughout Catholic Bavaria, the participation of large numbers of priests in this process led the Social Democratic *Vorwärts* to coin a particularly memorable phrase, lamenting the increasingly visible emergence of "Catholic priests as Nazi storm-troop preachers."[34] In stark contrast to developments after the Beerhall Putsch, it should be noted that not a single Protestant pastor was involved in speaking, campaigning, or writing—either anonymously or under his own name—on behalf of the early Nazi movement at this time.[35] The officially interconfessional ideal of Positive Christianity had developed in practice, by the spring and summer of 1923, into an increasingly striking Catholic-Nazi synthesis.

Even before the announcement of the Catholic-oriented membership drive, in response to the BVP enlightenment campaign and in contrast to the anonymity maintained previously, a few Bavarian Catholic priests had begun to emerge openly in support of the NSDAP starting in late 1922. Anton Braun, an influential priest at Nürnberg's largest Catholic church, the Frauenkirche, was praised in the *Beobachter* for stating publicly in December 1922 that "when it comes down to it we, namely the Catholic part of the German *Volk* and its clergy, will not stand apart from the National Socialists."[36] In January 1923, when Magnus Gött wrote his programmatic refutation of the criticisms of Wilhelm Vielberth and the BVP, he was willing to be identified publicly.[37] Additionally, in early 1923, one of Munich's better-placed priests, Dr. Wilhelm August Patin, became involved with the NSDAP; Patin was court vicar at Munich's St. Kajetans-Hofkirche, had important Reform Catholic contacts, and was also the cousin of Heinrich Himmler.[38] More notable, however, were three priests who also began their affiliation with the Nazi movement before the beginning of the Catholic-oriented membership drive and went on to exercise important influence on the early Nazi movement: Philipp Haeuser, Alban Schachleiter, and Bernhard Stempfle.

Beginning in late 1922, Philipp Haeuser—who had previously had extensive contact with Catholic elements within the NSDAP, including Schrönghamer and Alfred Miller—drew increased attention as the result of a conflict with his ecclesiastical superiors over the vehemence of his anti-Semitic activism.[39] Haeuser had been scheduled to give a speech entitled "Jew and Christian" at a Catholic businessmen's club in Augsburg on 5 December 1922, but was prevented from doing so under threat of ecclesiastical discipline following complaints from BVP figures and a secret meeting between the bishop of Augsburg, Maximilian von Lingg, and two leaders from the city's Jewish community.[40] Sensing a valuable opportunity to contrast their commitment to the Catholic faith with the weakness of the BVP, the Nazis were quick to leap to Haeuser's defense, publishing a vehement critique written by an unnamed priest from Haeuser's diocese contrasting the allegedly Christ-like courage of Haeuser with the shameful weakness of diocesan leaders who were all too willing, at the instigation of the BVP, to compromise with "Jewish-communist" elements for political gain.[41]

Over the next few months, the Nazi movement embraced Haeuser as a key representative of the ideal of warrior Christianity—an ideal that took on increasingly masculinist and sports-oriented overtones, as seen in the Nazis' striking idealization of the fourteenth-century Archbishop Balduin of Trier, whose priestly masculinity and warrior-like athleticism was presented as a shining example for young Catholic Nazis.[42] Building on Alfred Miller's earlier praise, the *Beobachter* renewed its publicity for Haeuser's book *Wir deutschen Katholiken* in early 1923 and held him up as a paragon of manly courage, noting, "When the day of the National Socialists has finally arrived, this valiant priest will have to be remembered."[43] Similarly, when Haeuser published an expanded version of the prohibited speech "Jew and Christian" in book form in early 1923, the *Beobachter* urged Nazis of both Christian confessions to purchase the book while lamenting that those who most needed the book's message—the leaders of the Center Party and BVP—would likely prove deaf to its rebukes, leaving the courageous Haeuser a "voice calling in the wilderness."[44] Importantly, Haeuser's continued emphasis on warrior Christianity would make him an especially effective propagandist for the Nazis in the summer of 1923.[45]

In addition to Haeuser's initial emergence within the early Nazi movement, in late 1922 Alban Schachleiter, a flamingly nationalistic Benedictine monk and musicologist, first became closely associated with the NSDAP and, importantly, with Hitler personally (see fig. 4.2). Schachleiter was originally from Mainz but served as the long-time abbot of the Emmaus monastery in Prague before being forced out of that position in the wake of the establishment of the new Czechoslovak state in late 1918.[46] After brief stops at several Austrian monasteries, including St. Florian near Linz, by early 1920 Schachleiter had settled at Munich's St. Boniface Abbey. By early 1922, Schachleiter was already in contact with *völkisch* figures such as Erich Ludendorff, with whom he would share a fairly close friendship until the latter's anti-Catholic agitation led to their progressive alienation after the Beerhall Putsch.[47] By September 1922, Schachleiter was raising eyebrows due to the radicalism of his anti-Semitic agitation and his involvement with groups like the *völkisch* Bund Bayern und Reich.[48] Schachleiter also cultivated good connections with members of Munich's Catholic upper crust, including several who had been involved with the Reform Catholic movement in prewar Munich, such as Karl Alexander von Müller, professor of history at the University of Munich, and Helene Raff, a prominent high-society matron.[49] Müller records in his memoirs that he became acquainted with Schachleiter shortly after the latter's arrival in Munich and that the two met on numerous occasions to discuss politics and Schachleiter's musical fascination with Gregorian chant. It is likely that Schachleiter's musical

Figure 4.2. Alban Schachleiter.
Source: Engelhard, *Schachleiter.*

interests were what also brought him into contact with Helene Raff, whose father was the renowned composer Joachim Raff.[50] It was by way of these connections that Schachleiter first met Hitler in late 1922. Both Müller and Hitler's close friend Ernst Hanfstaengl, who was himself first introduced to Schachleiter by Helene Raff, make mention in their memoirs of the first meeting between Hitler and Schachleiter, when Hitler was invited to a luncheon at the apartment of Hanfstaengl's sister (who lived in the same building as both Müller and Raff) attended by Müller, Raff, Schachleiter, and both Hanfstaengls. Müller and Ernst Hanfstaengl both recorded that Hitler and Schachleiter engaged in a lively and very lengthy conversation and were impressed with each other, and this first meeting marked the beginning of a relationship that lasted until Schachleiter's death in 1937.[51] Most important, the meeting also opened the door for Schachleiter to play an important propagandistic role on behalf of the NSDAP in the summer of 1923.

By early that year, the priest Bernhard Stempfle was once again stepping up his engagement with the Nazi movement as it began to expand its activities throughout Catholic Bavaria. Already a major *völkisch* activist in the pages of the *Beobachter* and responsible for the anti-Semitic daily *Miesbacher Anzeiger,* Stempfle emerged as an increasingly outspoken Nazi sympathizer and was often the target of Social Democratic satire.[52] The December 1921 *Donauwacht* piece that mocked the growing Catholic-Nazi synthesis in Bavaria had lampooned Stempfle as the "anti-Semitic bishop" of Miesbach, who drew throngs of pilgrims to a "giant swastika" displayed nearby and who ran the editoral offices of the *Anzeiger* out of a giant outhouse.[53] In late 1922, in the context of the BVP's anti-Nazi enlightenment campaign, Stempfle's support for the NSDAP became unmistakably vocal and strident, and he began publishing a steady stream of articles that gushingly praised the Nazi movement—and, most notably, Hitler, who was idealized as a "real man"—while excoriating the BVP, Center Party, and their alleged Jewish backers.[54] By early 1923, according to Hitler's personal photographer, Heinrich Hoffmann, Stempfle had emerged as a "prominent member" of Hitler's inner circle, regularly making the short trip to Munich to join Hitler at his corner table at the Cafe Heck and advising him frequently on religious issues.[55]

Despite the importance of this earlier priestly activism on behalf of the NSDAP, it was as the result of striking new impulses emerging within the context of the propagandistic membership drive that the zenith of Catholic-Nazi activism was reached. The most important factor in this regard was the arrival in Munich of Lorenz Pieper on 6 April 1923, the same day that Hitler gave a major speech emphasizing warrior Christianity and only a few days before the initial announcement of the membership drive.

Pieper had been deeply influenced by prewar Reform Catholicism in Munich and maintained connections with Reform Catholic nationalists after moving back to Westphalia. The rabidly anti-Semitic Pieper, devastated by the outcome of the First World War, viewed the subsequent revolution as part of a demonic plot by atheistic Jews and socialists to destroy Germany. In 1920, he became a founding member of the radical Jungdeutscher Orden (Jungdo) in Hüsten, the Westphalian town where his parish was located, and joined the local branch of the DVST.[56] He also began to renew his anti-ultramontane and anti-Semitic Catholic contacts—most notably, Dietrich Eckart—in Munich in 1920, and he became a leading advocate of both the *Beobachter* and Stempfle's *Anzeiger,* energetically distributing and publicizing the racist rags in and around Hüsten throughout 1921 and 1922.[57] In the fall of 1922, Pieper became an official member of the NSDAP, receiving member number 9740 upon joining the fledgling Nazi Ortsgruppe in nearby Hagen following a speech there by the young Catholic Nazi firebrand Hermann Esser.[58] Immediately after joining the party, Pieper began organizing Nazi events and proselytizing among his parishioners in Hüsten, beginning with a small meeting in October 1922 and culminating with a large-scale event headlined by a Nazi speaker from Hagen in February 1923, during which Nazi leaflets and copies of the *Beobachter* were distributed throughout the town.[59] The latter event apparently stirred up tremendous unrest among Center Party supporters in his parish in Hüsten and in the surrounding area, and it was in this context that Pieper made the dramatic decision in early April to take a temporary leave from his pastoral duties and move to Munich to campaign full time on behalf of the NSDAP.

Although Pieper's arrival in Munich coincided with the large-scale event at which Hitler repeatedly invoked the importance of warrior Christianity, Pieper's earliest days in Munich were spent largely behind the scenes; he apparently lived with Hitler at least briefly and helped to plan the Nazi membership drive that commenced shortly after his arrival.[60] The Nazis soon began openly trumpeting Pieper's membership in the party, presenting him as the embodiment of the Nazi ideal of Positive Christianity and noting gleefully that "not only Dr. Pieper, but also a further succession of younger members of the Catholic clergy" had made the decision to cast their lots with the NSDAP "in the battle for the salvation of the German-Christian spirit."[61]

In the early stages of the membership drive, in April and May, increasing numbers of Catholic clergy emerged in support of the NSDAP, with Magnus Gött praising Hitler openly as a Catholic-Christian hero who would forever be remembered as "among the men of faith who have moved mountains."[62] Back in Munich, the NSDAP began publicizing and participating in the *völkisch*-oriented activities of a number of local Catholic priests who were joining in this "battle," many of whom had seen active duty in the First World War, either as soldiers or as military chaplains, and who were often idealized at least implicitly as examples of the Nazis' brand of warrior Christianity. Ludwig Attenberger, priest at Munich's St. Peter's, was especially effective in meshing Catholic imagery, fervent nationalism, and militaristic commemoration of the war dead, as was seen in a Nazi-supported memorial ceremony at St. Peter's on 15 April 1923.[63] Nazi units also participated in a massive *völkisch*-oriented flag consecration ceremony (*Fahnenweihe*) at the soldiers' memorial in the Moosach section of Munich two weeks later, which was sponsored by the local sharpshooters' association and presided over by the parish priest, Josef Knogler.[64] In early May, the Nazis came out in strong support of a striking commemorative event organized by Johann Georg Widmann, priest at St. Johann-Baptist in the Haidhausen section of Munich, on behalf of the "fallen warriors" of the First Bavarian Reserve Infantry Regiment, which featured a torchlight parade and a Saturday evening mass meeting in the Bürgerbräukeller, followed the next morning by a *völkisch*-oriented mass presided over by Widmann.[65] Perhaps not surprisingly, when Franz Lukas, a highly decorated military chaplain and recipient of both the Iron Cross, second class, and the Bavarian Military Service Cross, unveiled a plan to erect a memorial chapel to commemorate fallen warriors inside his parish church, Munich's Heilig-Geist-Kirche, he turned directly to the NSDAP for publicity and help with the fundraising.[66]

In addition to these Munich-based events, the Nazis also began using priests to target Catholic regions elsewhere in Bavaria. On Sunday, 29 April 1923, when the NSDAP Ortsgruppe Ingolstadt organized a major paramilitary ceremony, it was presided over jointly by Hitler and two local Catholic priests, Dr. Klemens Wagner and Johann Baptist Götz. Wagner, who had been appointed dean (*Dekan*) of the new Stadtdekanat Ingolstadt in 1920 and served simultaneously as Stadtpfarrer of the famous Kirche zur Schönen unserer lieben Frau, consecrated the standards of the new local Nazi Sturmabteilung (SA) group and performed what the *Beobachter* termed a "glowingly nationalistic" field sermon.[67] Götz, a militaristic Stadtpfarrer at St. Moritz in Ingolstadt who also oversaw the local garrison church, preached a sermon for the Nazi delegation that intertwined religious faith and radical nationalism— proclaiming that "true, genuine love of fatherland is rooted in faith"— and celebrated mass to the choreographed rising and falling of the SA standards.[68] Götz was well known in the Ingolstadt area for his support of *völkisch*-Nazi events; the week before the large Nazi ceremony, the local leftist press had decried Götz's support for the NSDAP and called openly for a boycott of his masses.[69] Additionally, when the Ortsgruppe Günzburg, in western Bavaria, sponsored a propagandistic meeting targeting the surrounding rural areas on 19 May 1923, organizers credited much of their success to the advocacy of an unnamed Catholic priest in the region; this was very likely Anton Fischer, the anti-Semitic priest from nearby Rieden who had published in Dietrich Eckart's *Auf gut deutsch* in 1919.[70]

As the membership drive picked up steam through the summer months, the participation of Catholic priests became even more pronounced. In early June, the *Beobachter* featured a striking series of propagandistic articles by Josef Roth, who had been ordained in Munich the previous June and was serving in a parish in nearby Indersdorf, entitled "Catholicism and Jewry." Although Roth's earlier anti-Semitic agitation in the pages of the *Beobachter* as a student in 1919 had already exhibited a radical racial fixation, calling for a "strike force against all racially foreign machinations" and the physical expulsion of Jews from Germany, his June 1923 ruminations further emphasized and radicalized these themes, as he proclaimed the need for the Jewish race to be utterly "eliminated" (*ausgeschaltet*) from German public life. The first installment differentiated between more traditional forms of anti-Semitism and an explicitly racial anti-Semitism based on modern "racial-biological principles," directly addressing the question of whether racial anti-Semitism should be considered anti-Catholic or anti-Christian more generally. Defining *race* as "the totality of internal and external characteristics that binds one person to another as a result of the homogeneity of blood"—a God-ordained condition in which "the spiritual orientation of a person is determined primarily by the blood of the body in which the spirit lives"—Roth contended that full-fledged racial anti-Semitism was, for Catholics and Christians, the only principled response to the destructive moral and cultural impact of the Jews as a result of their biological makeup:

> Certainly the Catholic Church stands above races and nations, but the Catholic idea stands first and foremost against immorality; and when immorality and race combine, then the Catholic idea stands against that race, no longer above the races. An anti-Semitism conceived on this basis is not only allowed for the Christian, but rather obligatory.... The Jewish race must be eliminated from public life because it exercises, as a result of its very nature, a demoralizing influence on our religion and our *Volk*.[71]

Remaining within the racial paradigm, the second installment attempted to overcome the common BVP objection that radical racial anti-Semitism was in conflict with the spirit of Christian charity, asserting that "the defensive battle against the Jewish influence is in no way a transgression of Christian charity; otherwise Christ himself would have acted un-Christlike when he drove the [Jewish] merchants and money-changers out of the temple." For Roth, the battle against the Jews could not be fought with the feeble weapons of traditional Catholic anti-Judaism or with the halfhearted weakness of the BVP, and he called for a radical all-encompassing crusade that would, he admitted, likely victimize even pious and apparently law-abiding Jews, since Jewish immorality was ultimately "hereditary," rooted in blood, and thus required an unflinching systematic response:

> If, in such a course of action against the Jews as a race, even individual good and harmless Jews, in whom the hereditary immorality is only latent, have to suffer along with the guilty, even that is no transgression against Christian charity—especially as long as the church acknowledges the moral justification of war, for example, in which many more "innocents" are forced to suffer along with the "guilty."[72]

In the final installment, Roth dealt with the apparent problem of Christianity's Jewish roots, claiming that the Christian religion had grown only out of the Jewish faith in God and had nothing to do with the specific characteristics of the Jewish race. Moreover, he argued, by the time of the emergence of Christianity, even the original connection with the Jewish faith had been effectively severed, becoming at most a distant historical memory.[73] In an ideational maneuver common to anti-Semitic discourse at the time, Roth cited the blistering critiques of the Old Testament prophets against the "immorality" of the Jewish people in an attempt to enlist the prophets themselves in the anti-Semitic cause; Roth went further, however, to argue that the "anti-Semitism" of the biblical prophets provided the means through which modern-day Catholic anti-Semites could be overt racists and still consider themselves in compliance with Catholic teachings on the Old Testament. Roth concluded by stating that it was not enough merely "to use the swastika as a lapel pin or a house decoration" but, with a flourish strongly reminiscent of Schrönghamer, claimed that *völkisch* Catholics had a pressing duty to join in preparing for the brutal apocalyptic battle of the "last days, when the Jews with their messiah, the Antichrist, wage a terrible war against God's church to achieve a temporary dominion that will then culminate in their eternal destruction."[74] As an indication of the effectiveness of Roth's arguments, several weeks later the Nazis' Eher Verlag issued his series in expanded form as an official NSDAP propaganda pamphlet and publicized it energetically.[75]

Roth's ideas were compelling in part because he was so successful in building upon the existing foundation of widespread Catholic anti-Semitism in and around Munich, fusing it skillfully with the racial anti-Semitism of the Nazis. The influential pro-BVP priest Erhard Schlund issued a nearly simultaneous missive that openly labeled the Jews as "racial aliens" and proclaimed that loyal BVP Catholics should be "united with the anti-Semites in distress over the increasing influence of Jewry, especially in Germany, and in the desire to see this influence restricted." In keeping with the BVP's insistence on "respectable" anti-Semitism, Schlund attempted to soften his position by distancing himself delicately from "fanatical" racism.[76] Ultimately, Roth's radical and uncompromising stance—as disingenuous and intellectually shoddy as it may appear in retrospect—seemed to many at the time to be more principled than the conditional and often inconsistent anti-Semitism of the BVP and its supporters.

In addition to the activism of Josef Roth, the Catholic-oriented membership drive also witnessed in the summer months of 1923 the continued emergence of Philipp Haeuser as a leading propagandist for the NSDAP. In a well-publicized speech to the Ortsgruppe Augsburg on 13 June 1923, Haeuser emphasized the virtues of warrior Christianity, proclaiming, "We need men of action. If only there were more men like Hitler... who would put the words of Christ into practice: 'I have not come to bring peace, but rather the sword.'"[77] Hitler's Catholic identity—and, with it, that of the movement—was also on prominent display in the Nazis' massive Deutscher Tag events in Passau on Sunday, 17 June 1923, which were structured entirely around an early morning procession of NSDAP units to the Passau cathedral, attendance at a special Catholic mass, and the consecration of the Nazi SA standards that afternoon, presided over by both Catholic clergy and Hitler himself.[78] The image of crusading Catholic Nazi warriors during the procession was especially foregrounded in the *Beobachter*, as was the pious fervor of the religious ceremony itself:

First came the mass in the magnificent cathedral, which was rebuilt after the fire of 1680 in its original form. On both sides of the street stood the densely packed residents of Passau, whose shouts of "Heil" did not want to end. Flowers rained down from the open windows, thrown by the delicate hands of women and girls. Everyone sensed the monumental historical import of this moment: here are the cadres of the German army that will lead the liberation battle of the German *Volk* against its internal and external enemies! The legions of National

Socialism will bring us once again to freedom! Then a quiet mass at the High Altar, for which the disciplined Zocher musical ensemble played a chorale. As the "Dutch Prayer of Thanksgiving" sounded and the fervent fortissimo boomed through the immense expanse, there were tears in the eyes of many: Lord! Make us free![79]

This mixing of Catholic piety and Nazi-oriented warrior imagery was also evident throughout Catholic Bavaria in June 1923 in the paramilitary masses performed by priests like Thomas Stadler, who served at Munich's St. Maximilian and was idealized by the Nazis for having served heroically during the First World War; the Carmelite Pater Theodor from the St. Magdalena monastery near Schwandorf; and Dr. Anton Foohs, a priest in the Würzburg diocese who had studied under the Reform Catholic theologian Herman Schell and whom the Nazis explicitly touted as a heroic military chaplain.[80]

In July and August 1923, the involvement of Catholic priests in Nazi-sponsored events continued to receive steady publicity, both in the *Beobachter* and, especially, among socialist critics of the growing ranks of Nazi "storm-troop preachers." Christian Huber—another former military chaplain who served as the head of Munich's diocesan Gesellenverein while also holding a pastoral post at the Bürgersaalkirche—made a tour of Nazi groups throughout Catholic Bavaria to give his standard speech on "Anti-Semitism and the National Socialist Position on Property." On 17 July 1923, Huber delivered the speech to the NSDAP Ortsgruppe Ottobeuren at the invitation of Augustin Krimm, the prior of the local Benedictine monastery, and held his listeners "captivated" despite speaking for a full three hours on the topic of the Nazi economic vision and its relation to Christian morality.[81] Krimm, for his part, further accelerated his pro-Nazi activism the next month, hosting an official NSDAP Deutscher Tag celebration at the Ottobeuren monastery on 19 August 1923 that was to feature morning mass in the massive Benedictine church and the subsequent consecration of a new set of SA standards.[82] At the last minute, however, diocesan authorities in Augsburg refused to allow an official Nazi flag consecration to take place inside the church itself—a move that, according to the subsequent *Beobachter* report, "unleashed limitless frustration among the party comrades, who are almost without exception of the Catholic faith." As it turned out, the Nazi SA units did participate in the regular Sunday mass in the huge Klosterkirche but had to hold the consecration of the standards outside in the open air, where Hermann Esser delivered a celebratory address before the "nearly two thousand National

Socialists" who had traveled to Ottobeuren from various locations throughout Bavaria.[83]

In a diary entry dated 5 June 1923, Lorenz Pieper noted how busy he had been in the early stages of the membership drive, having spoken at Nazi gatherings "almost every day" after moving to Munich in April.[84] These activities continued throughout the remainder of the summer, as Pieper emerged as one of the Nazis' busiest and most highly publicized official speakers. All of his standard stump speeches, typically delivered in priestly garb, dealt with explicitly Catholic topics and were a huge draw both in Munich and throughout the surrounding Catholic Bavarian countryside. His most popular speech, "Can a Catholic Be a National Socialist?" was often delivered in collaboration with the out-spokenly Catholic Max Sesselmann, with Pieper providing the pastoral perspective and Sesselmann that of the committed Catholic Nazi layman. The *Beobachter* typically covered these speeches in great detail; at a major Pieper-Sesselmann event on 26 June 1923 in Pfaffenhofen, north of Munich, the two speakers emphasized the consistent theme of warrior Christianity, calling for the support of believing Catholics in the "battle for the German soul." Pieper began his part of the program by focusing on the religiously based criticisms of the BVP:

> Of course we are filled with the utmost indignation that [the BVP] has attempted, hypocritically and through malicious means, to attack us on *religious grounds* by accusing us not only of being unreligious but direct opponents and destroyers of Christianity, advocates of a wishy-washy nondogmatic Christianity. This cowardly way of fighting forces us to answer the question of whether a Catholic can be a National Socialist.[85]

Pieper's resoundingly affirmative answer was structured around two central points. First, Pieper noted that the Vatican had never issued a statement endorsing the Center Party or BVP, and by nature never would do so, leaving individual Catholics completely free to determine which non-Marxist party most effectively represented their own Catholic religious beliefs. Pieper's second point was to argue, as the *Beobachter* had consistently done over the previous couple of years, that the political cooperation of the Center Party (and, by extension, the BVP) with Jews, atheists, and Marxists made these parties extremely poor, perhaps un-conscionable, political choices for truly principled Catholics, especially in contrast to the NSDAP which, unlike secular non-Marxist parties, served as the most uncompromising defender of the Christian faith both in theory and in practice. Sesselmann, in his part of the program, echoed Pieper's comments and emphasized the need for lay activism in contrast to self-satisfied religious complacency, once again characterizing the warrior mission of the NSDAP as the "battle for the soul of our *Volk*" and a "struggle for internal purity."[86]

Another of Pieper's popular speeches attempted to combine the radicalism of the Nazis' mission with the genuine religiosity of Joseph von Görres, one of the leading heroes from Munich's Catholic past, emphasizing Görres's "glowing nationalism" while completely eliding the fact that Görres had been an advocate of the ultramontanism and political Catholicism so despised by Pieper and the Nazis.[87] In giving the speech to the NSDAP group in the Neuhausen section of Munich on 3 July 1923, Pieper portrayed Görres not only as a deeply religious Catholic but also as a "warrior" who was willing to fight for his convictions and who could therefore serve as a "source of inspiration and power" for the Nazi movement's campaign to "revive the *Volk* from its slavery, from physical and spiritual subjugation."[88] Other standard Pieper speeches, such as "The Essence of National Socialism," railed continually against the flimsiness and perceived weakness of Center Party and BVP claims to represent the religious interests of believing Catholics, proclaiming instead that "it is not only permissible, but rather the duty of all Christians—and especially Catholics—to become members of our party."[89] On numerous occasions, Pieper seems to have been fully convinced, and was clearly eager to convince others, of the fundamentally loyal Catholic identity of Hitler and other Nazi leaders, portraying them as heroic Christian warriors and proclaiming, in a fairly typical formulation, "The NSDAP is not a party of Christianity-of-the-mouth but rather of pure Christianity-of-the-deed, for which the true Christian conviction of the Führer Adolf Hitler stands as a guarantee."[90]

Among Pieper's most explicit propagandistic goals was to try to remove all potential obstacles, particularly from a theological perspective, that might prevent religiously practicing Catholics from joining the Nazi movement. The most substantial stumbling blocks consisted of the twin claims, hammered home consistently in the BVP's anti-Nazi propaganda, that the racial anti-Semitism of the NSDAP was in conflict with Catholic theology and that the Nazi movement was at heart a pagan-oriented movement, secretly striving, like openly anti-Christian *völkisch* movements elsewhere in Germany, to replace the Christian cross with the pagan swastika. In regard to the latter, Pieper gave a well-publicized speech entitled "History and Meaning of the Swastika" to the local Neuhausen section on 24 July 1923, claiming, with reference to archaeological evidence, that the swastika was widely used by early Christians in the catacombs of Rome and could also be found in artwork depicting Christian knights and Catholic clergy in the Middle Ages. More important, however, Pieper argued from a theological-historical point of view, despite its various connections with sun deities and eastern fertility cults, the swastika was actually more authentically Christian than the crucifix symbol currently used throughout Christendom and was the key developmental link between the original Roman T-shaped cross on which Christ was crucified and the common form of the +-shaped crucifix eventually adopted by the church.[91] In regard to the issue of racial anti-Semitism, Pieper insisted on numerous occasions that, despite BVP claims to the contrary, the Nazis' radical racism was not theologically problematic but was drawn explicitly from the "extreme Christian point of view," based on the conviction that "race is not an arbitrary, artificially contrived impulse but is rather ordained by God."[92] In a mass meeting in Straubing on 8 August 1923, Pieper further fleshed out his vision of the full compatibility between Nazi racial anti-Semitism and the Catholic faith:

> Beneath religion comes the elevated holy ideal of Fatherland, which means the unity of all German comrades of blood, fate, and *Volk*. God himself created the separate races according to blood, essence, and nature, and therefore he desires differences based on blood, nationality, and race. He also desires that what he created should remain pure. We must attack anything that damages our racial unity. For that reason the racial standpoint of National Socialism corresponds completely with Christianity. It is therefore in the spirit of Christ that we must proceed against the Jews.[93]

Pieper made his position even clearer in a widely publicized mass meeting in Regensburg on 25 August 1923, when he insisted on the morality of keeping Jews separate from Germans and proclaimed, "Compatriots are blood comrades, and the Jews are not German blood comrades. God himself desires that there be racial differences, or he would not have created them. But since God does desire these differences, it is the duty of each race to keep itself pure from foreign pollutants. Therefore anti-Semitism is not un-Christian, but rather a command!"[94]

Overall, the unambiguous pro-Nazi propaganda presented by priests like Pieper with such conviction and in so many gatherings throughout Bavaria allowed the NSDAP to claim with plausibility that its racial program was the principled and logical conclusion of what many Catholic figures, especially in the BVP, believed but were too hypocritical (or too blinded by political opportunism) to act upon. In effect, the NSDAP was able to portray its anti-Semitic mission as the outgrowth not only of Positive Christianity but also of an essentially Catholic world view and to package it in a form that was both uncompromising and unencumbered by the "respectability" (or, put less charitably, the self-interested inconsistency) practiced by the BVP and its supporters.

As significant as the energetic activism of Pieper and other pro-Nazi priests was during the summer of 1923, the opportunity to portray perhaps the most effective human embodiment of the Nazis' Catholic-oriented ideal of warrior Christianity materialized somewhat by chance. In late May, a French firing squad executed the young German saboteur Albert Leo Schlageter near Düsseldorf for terrorist activity in opposing the French occupation of the Ruhr region.[95] As it turned out, Schlageter had been not only a decorated war veteran and seasoned Freikorps fighter, but also a deeply religious Catholic and, as a student, a member of the Cartellverband (CV) fraternity.[96] Schlageter was also a member of the NSDAP, having been in his nomadic travels one of the founding members of the small party branch in Berlin in 1922 before transferring his membership to the Munich branch in January 1923.[97] While he quickly became a heroic martyr figure in *völkisch* and ultranationalist circles throughout Germany, the Nazi leadership in Munich decided to base much of its membership drive propaganda on the foundation of Schlageter's Catholic faith, making him for a couple of months into the most visible symbol of the party itself, the harmonious physical embodiment of the heroic Catholic-Nazi synthesis (see fig. 4.3).

Undeterred by the fact that Schlageter was not originally from Munich and had spent only limited time there in late 1922 and early 1923, Nazi leaders quickly began constructing an elaborate Munich-based propagandistic cult to surround "their" fallen hero, and official party events began to be opened with a solemn moment of remembrance for Schlageter.[98] Additionally, a wide variety of commemorative keepsakes—Schlageter photos, medallions, commemorative stamps, biographical pamphlets, and even sheet music for the popular "Schlageter Song"—were produced and marketed endlessly in the *Beobachter*.[99] One of the local Munich sections of the Nazi SA even took on Schlageter's name, becoming the SA-Schlageter, and organized through the summer a series of major commemorative events, ranging from a long-distance

Figure 4.3. Albert Leo Schlageter.
Source: Brandt, *Schlageter.*

motorcycle procession to Schlageter's hometown to formal dinners in his honor.[100]

What is perhaps most striking about the Nazi cultivation of this commemorative cult is the overt emphasis on Schlageter's Catholic faith and its positive relationship to his Nazi identity. Although the brave final hours of Schlageter's life were recounted, almost step by step, in a wide variety of press accounts throughout Germany, the *Beobachter* made sure specifically to stress the religious significance of Schlageter's end, which had occurred under the most difficult of circumstances:

In the night before the execution [Schlageter's confessor] pleaded repeatedly to be allowed to honor the wishes of the condemned, to hear his confession and give him communion, but in vain. Only shortly before the departure [for the execution site] was the priest given this permission, and Schlageter was allowed a total of only fifteen minutes to give his final confession and to receive holy communion. And even then the holy observance was repeatedly interrupted by cries of "Hurry! Hurry!"[101]

Despite the brutal behavior of his French captors, Schlageter went decisively and with almost Christlike composure to his death, "refusing the offer of a stay of execution" and vowing to "die the way a German officer dies."[102] Schlageter thus provided, in his devout faith while alive and strong determination in the face of death, a model of warrior Christianity for all *völkisch* and nationalistic Catholics. The lesson to be learned from Schlageter's brief but heroic life was that his Nazi and Catholic identities were not in conflict, and his religious principles were precisely what had helped to make Schlageter a model Nazi: "On his final walk he was accompanied by two Catholic priests, and he showed here again before his death that the most passionate nationalism is not something that stands in contradiction to religious identity. . .but that on the contrary, it is in the passionate love of nation that religious sentiment finds its most genuine support."[103]

These somewhat elusive images and ideas were translated skillfully into more tangible form in the striking commemorative activities of 10 June 1923, which included a massive rally in honor of Schlageter staged by a number of *völkisch* and patriotic organizations on Munich's Königsplatz and attended by between 20,000 and 30,000 activists. Perhaps more important than this larger rally—which had a broad paramilitary orientation and not much overt religious content—was the Catholic memorial mass held immediately after the rally in the neighboring St. Boniface Abbey, which was organized exclusively by the NSDAP and presided over by Abbot Alban Schachleiter.[104] The decision to organize the St. Boniface ceremony had been made, according to Ernst Hanfstaengl, while Hitler was briefly vacationing in Berchtesgaden with Dietrich Eckart, Anton Drexler, and Hanfstaengl in late May or early June. Hitler, still somewhat despondent over his loss of face in the infamous May Day confrontation with the Bavarian authorities a few weeks earlier, was not initially planning to return to Munich to participate in the Königsplatz rally.[105] However, when Hanfstaengl sketched out the symbolic impact that a related Catholic-Nazi mass for Schlageter would have on Munich's Catholic population and suggested that their mutual friend Schachleiter not only eulogize Schlageter but also consecrate the standards of the SA, Hitler quickly agreed.[106] It is unclear whether Hanfstaengl or Hitler were initially aware of it, but the fact that Schachleiter was himself an alumnus of the CV fraternity, as was Lorenz Pieper, made him an even more appropriate choice to perform the memorial mass.[107] In any case, Schachleiter readily agreed to the suggestions of Hanfstaengl and Hitler, and plans proceeded.

The St. Boniface ceremony itself, which was attended by a broad cross-section of Munich Catholics ranging from the uniformed masses of SA men to Schlageter's CV fraternity brothers, was a resounding success for the NSDAP. Contemporary observers were struck by the stunning imagery of row after row of brighly colored SA standards being marched through the entrance to St. Boniface, where Schachleiter consecrated each flag with holy water, fashioning an impressive visual union of the most sacred of Catholic and Nazi emblems.[108] The *Beobachter* emphasized the important role played by the intricate synchronization between the SA standards and the liturgical elements of Schachleiter's mass: "The flag-bearers and standard-bearers stood at attention on both sides of the altar for the duration of the mass.... During the transubstantiation the flags and standards were lowered on both sides of the altar in obedience to the words of the priest."[109] Schachleiter's eulogistic sermon emphasized the imagery of warrior Christianity, presenting Schlageter as a powerful living union of Catholic and National Socialist identities and a "martyr for the German cause" who could now "stand before the judgment seat of God as a victim of the strictest loyalty to duty." Schlageter's life provided the evangelistic proselytizer in Schachleiter with an occasion to challenge all those in attendance also to observe a "firm and unwavering faith in God" and to recognize the "one and only way forward for the German nation out of the present-day distress and affliction. That way is the return to the true faith."[110] Observers took especially keen notice of Schachleiter's impressive personal presence and the powerful impact of his message on the listeners present that day. Hans Hinkel, one of the young SA men who attended the St. Boniface mass, later attempted to convey the unforgettable force of Schachleiter's eulogy: "At the pulpit stood the powerful personality of Abbot Alban Schachleiter, who in a fiery sermon praised Albert Leo Schlageter and the significance of his struggle and death for Germany. We youths were literally transported by Schachleiter into a holy rapture. We have never been able to forget this hour."[111]

The significance of Schachleiter's indelible performance and his portrayal of Schlageter as a heroic Catholic Nazi warrior is difficult to overestimate. While this significance is also impossible to quantify statistically within the context of the Catholic-oriented membership drive, it is likely that Schlageter's exemplary image exerted a nearly irresistible pull on large numbers of Catholic men, as evidenced by at least one very important example: the young and devoutly pious Heinrich Himmler joined the NSDAP in the wake of Schachleiter's eulogy. In particular, the powerful image of Schlageter enabled the Nazis to mobilize with even more effectiveness among Catholic students, as his membership in the CV was emphasized explicitly by the NSDAP on numerous occasions. When the Ortsgruppe Forchheim, in northern Bavaria, staged a commemorative Schlageter ceremony on 22 June 1923, one of the featured speakers was Forchheim mayor Hans Knorr who, as a proud alumnus of the CV, praised the "manly" courage of his fraternity brother and vowed to honor his memory by introducing a proposal in the local city council to name one of its major thoroughfares Schlageter-Strasse.[112] Similarly, when a Schlageter ceremony was organized at the University of Innsbruck on 27 June 1923, it was touted as a joint venture between the CV and representatives of the local Nazi organization.[113] In publicizing a student memorial for Schlageter to be held in Berlin on 5 July 1923, with an accompanying mass in Berlin's largest Catholic church, St. Hedwig, the *Beobachter* made sure to emphasize that Schlageter "was an active member of the Cartellverband der katholischen deutschen Studentenverbindungen (CV)."[114]

The CV itself, particularly its leadership in Munich, was in many ways eager to embrace the Schlageter cult, devoting the summer 1923 issue of its official journal, *Academia,* to the idealization of Schlageter as both a heroic warrior figure and a devout Catholic. The editor of *Academia,* the Munich archivist and CV alumnus Dr. Joseph Weiss, opened the issue with a flaming poetic tribute that pledged to avenge Schlageter's death and explicitly echoed Nazi imagery:

> Who was it that with resolution stared death directly in the eye?
> Who placed his faith in the German Fatherland and in the
>   Lord on high?
> Who, as a holy champion, surrounded by strangers, was
>   willing to die?
> CV! He was blood of your blood! Vengeance for Schlageter
>   is our cry![115]

Similarly, CV student Joseph Priemer apparently perceived no conflict between Schlageter's terrorist activity, his Nazi membership, and his Catholic religious faith, portraying him as the ultimate role model for CV members: "For us you are the ideal paradigm of loyalty unto death. The Cartellverband is proud to be able to name you as one of its own. The cross that adorns your grave is for us the emblem of the fact that you did not fight, defend and suffer for your fatherland alone, but also for your world view."[116]

For many moderate and anti-Nazi Catholics, however, the morally dubious nature of the activity for which Schlageter was arrested—the attempt to blow up a major train line, which would have caused significant civilian casualties—made him a problematic figure at best. When the head of a Catholic Jugendverein dormitory demanded in July 1923 that one of the adolescent residents remove the commemorative picture of Schlageter he had purchased from Nazi headquarters and placed on the wall over his bed—complete with the inscription "The National Socialist movement and the swastika fight against the world slavery of Jewish internationalism"—the *Beobachter* was quick to seize on the propagandistic value of the issue, painting Schlageter as the heroic inheritor of the radical and uncompromising spirit of Christ and contrasting Schlageter's joint membership in both the CV and the NSDAP with the halfhearted "respectability" maintained by the Center Party and BVP.[117]

Despite its morally problematic nature, Schlageter's image was also central to the Nazis' remarkable success in penetrating Catholic regions across Bavaria through the remainder of the summer, as the powerful Nazi-Catholic spectacle of the St. Boniface ceremony was replicated in various forms on countless occasions. At the founding meeting of the Ortsgruppe Unterwössen on 10 June 1923, Max Sesselmann's speech placed special emphasis on the "murdered hero" Schlageter, as did Hitler's address following the dramatic Nazi mass in the Passau cathedral on 17 June 1923.[118] From a priestly perspective, Philipp Haeuser idealized Schlageter as a central inspiration for the Nazis' continued advocacy of heroic warrior Christianity and pious self-discipline, proclaiming in a well-publicized Nazi propaganda speech: "Only hardness can save us, hardness in regard to the *Volk,* hardness in regard to our leaders, hardness in regard to ourselves.... May the example of our heroes from the world war and the example of the murdered Schlageter point us to the path on which we must proceed. We want to act the way he acted, we want to fight the way he fought!"[119] Performative events mirroring the St. Boniface mass were staged by local Nazi organizations throughout Bavaria on virtually every Sunday through the summer.[120] A particularly striking high mass (*Hochamt*) in honor of Schlageter was performed by the Capuchin monks at the Heilig-Kreuz-Kirche in Kempten on 29 June 1923, with Nazi SA flags flanking a dramatic procession to and from the church. Konrad Seufert, a leading member of the SA-Schlageter group in Munich, followed the mass with an emotional memorial address that emphasized the seamless harmony achieved by Schlageter between his deep Catholic piety and his Nazi warrior identity: "He demonstrated how a child-like and devout Christianity is fully compatible with relentless vigor and that it is in fact a deep faith that first and foremost produces uncompromising courage in the face of death."[121] A similarly dramatic, albeit significantly larger, weeknight Schlageter commemoration was staged by the NSDAP Ortsgruppe in Passau on 7 August 1923, with a "deeply moving" torchlight procession numbering "many thousands" winding its way through the streets of the city as the bells of the Catholic cathedral rang out in Schlageter's honor.[122]

On occasion, however, diocesan authorities summoned the conviction to refuse to allow official Catholic masses to be constructed around the commemoration of the criminal Schlageter. In the BVP stronghold of Regensburg, *Domkapitular* Dr. Richard Reichenberger, a central BVP supporter, refused to authorize either an official church consecration of Nazi SA standards or a commemorative mass for Schlageter, pointing to the morally reprehensible nature of Schlageter's actions and informing the Ortsgruppe Regensburg in an early August letter: "It certainly cannot be denied that Schlageter was a Catholic and a Christian, but he acted against the intent and disposition of the Holy Father when he engaged in his 'act of sabotage,' placing himself outside of the Christian world view.... For this reason permission for a mass for Schlageter must be denied." Playing up this refusal, the *Beobachter* claimed that Reichenberger threatened to order "the doors of the church to be closed" if the Nazi SA forces who had gathered to honor Schlageter decided to attend mass in formation, since this "would amount to a provocation of the rest of the populace and would disturb the meditation of the other parishioners."[123] This image—a pro-BVP church dignitary barring ostensibly pious Catholic Nazi parishioners from attending mass for what appeared to be political reasons—became a powerful weapon in the Nazi propaganda arsenal.[124]

An effective culmination to the Catholic-oriented membership drive within the NSDAP can be identified, in more than one way, in the formative events that took place in Nuremberg on 1–2 September

Deutscher Tag in Nürnberg
Anmarsch der Kampfverbände zum Festakt auf der Deutschherrnwiese

Figure 4.4. Nazi units marching toward Josef Roth's field
sermon, Nuremberg, September 1923.
Source: Sesselmann and Hoffmann, *Deutschlands Erwachen*.

1923 (see figs. 4.4 and 4.5). Having garnered significant attention
as a result of the publication of *Katholizismus und Judenfrage* as an
official Nazi propaganda pamphlet in early August, the young priest
Josef Roth traveled with the local Nazi delegation from Munich
to Nuremberg to attend the massive Deutscher Tag demonstration
organized by a broad coalition of radical right-wing and *völkisch*
forces. Roth's role in this event, which was attended by thousands,
was covered extensively in the press. The striking field sermon he
delivered amounted to a flamingly masculinist discourse on the Nazi
theme of warrior Christianity and used Jesus Christ as the supreme
example:

> Our vision of the Savior is Jesus, who did not come into this world to
> bring peace but rather a sword, to sling fire into this world. . . . This,

Ein Blick auf den Fahnenwald der Kampfverbände während des Gottesdienstes auf der Deutschherrnwiese

Figure 4.5. Nazi units during Josef Roth's field sermon,
Nuremberg, September 1923.
Source: Sesselmann and Hoffmann, *Deutschlands Erwachen.*

our view of the Savior, is much more accurate than that deformed, sweet, soft, passionless, defeatist and pacifistic image of the Savior with which many today seek deliberately to extinguish the nationalist activism of our beloved German youth. A deformed [image of Jesus], or even one that is outdated and misplaced, amounts to sin and deception.[125]

Interestingly, Roth's sermon was preceded by a ceremonial procession of flag-bearing units that originated at the Catholic hospice on Nuremberg's Tafelhofstrasse, making the entire affair a rather striking demonstration of Nazi Catholic identity in the heart of overwhelmingly Protestant Nuremberg.[126] The striking liturgical performativity of Roth's sermon, which was demonstrated in the Nazi Schlageter commemorations and various militaristic Catholic field sermons more generally, should be seen as a central precursor to the pseudo-sacral participatory aesthetic that later characterized the Third

Reich, by which point all that remained of the early Catholic content were distant and indistinct echoes. By October 1923, as the BVP's Heinrich Held was making his impassioned appeal for Faulhaber to denounce Catholic participation in the Nazi movement, Philipp Haeuser wrote an equally impassioned letter to Hitler, assuring Hitler of his continued devotion "as one who sympathizes and suffers alongside you" and claiming to speak on behalf of massive numbers of "true" Catholics in idealizing the person of Hitler as "our last, but hopefully also our strongest and most successful hope."[127]

By early September, the party was able to proclaim that the membership drive had been successful beyond all expectations, trumpeting in the *Beobachter,* "The growth of the movement over the past weeks... has been so extraordinarily great that at present we are lacking the administrative staff to thoroughly work through the new membership forms that have come in."[128] In a statistical sense, it is clear that the NSDAP nearly tripled between February 1923, when the party numbered approximately 20,000 members, and the fall of 1923, at which point membership topped 55,000.[129] While the most commonly cited explanations for the rapid growth of the NSDAP in 1923—nationalist outrage over the French occupation of the Ruhr and growing despair over the inflationary crisis—are certainly valid, they do not in themselves explain why so many in overwhelmingly Catholic regions chose the NSDAP over other radical rightist groups that were preaching similar nationalistic, economic, and anti-Semitic messages at the time.[130] The Catholic-oriented membership drive, while by no means the only relevant factor, was without question an essential component of the rapidly growing Nazi appeal in and around Munich throughout the summer of 1923. Philipp Haeuser was far from alone in viewing Hitler as the "hope" for the future.

Seeds of Discord: The Kampfbund, Political Messianism, and the Drive to the Feldherrnhalle

The massive Deutscher Tag event in Nuremberg in early September witnessed, in addition to Josef Roth's powerful Catholic-Nazi field mass, the culmination of a radically different and perhaps more important trajectory, as the NSDAP joined with several other *völkisch* groups in forming the so-called Kampfbund that would eventually launch the ill-fated Beerhall Putsch in November.[131] This was a major departure for the Nazi movement, whose independence from other *völkisch* entities had been strictly maintained by Hitler since he officially assumed dictatorial control of the party in the summer of 1921.[132] The motivation for abandoning strict independence and joining with these other groups is clear: Hitler had set his sights on seizing power, by force if necessary, and the organizational strength needed for such an undertaking could not be mustered from within the ranks of the NSDAP alone.

The model for Hitler and the Nazis was in many ways Mussolini, who had brought himself and his fascist movement to power in Italy following the so-called march on Rome in October 1922.[133] The comparison between Hitler and Mussolini should not be made too sweepingly, although the Nazis' opponents in the BVP were certainly quick to ascertain striking similarities between Mussolini's brutal tactics and those of the Nazis, who would at the very least, it was feared, be emboldened by the success of the fascists.[134] From early November 1922, the Nazis themselves also actively cultivated the image of Hitler as "Germany's Mussolini."[135] Although most scholars have dated the completion of Hitler's transformation from the self-professed "drummer" of the *völkisch* movement to near-omnipotent Führer figure to the aftermath of the putsch and Hitler's incarceration, it makes good sense to locate the beginnings of that broader transformation in the fall of 1922.[136] Although building on earlier Führer imagery stemming from Hitler's takeover of power within the NSDAP in the summer of 1921, Nazi leaders began trumpeting Hitler's leadership qualities in heroic, almost messianic, terms only in the wake of Mussolini's rise to power.[137] In early 1923, Hitler was already interpreting his recovery from being blinded in a gas attack late in the war as the miraculous result of divine intervention, through which Hitler was "delivered by an inner rapture that set him the task of becoming the Deliverer of the *Volk*."[138] During the spring of 1923, Hitler began to refer to himself alternately as the "strong man who would rescue Germany" and, in particularly striking language, as the agent of a messianic force bestowed by heaven upon the German people:

> What can save Germany is the dictatorship of the national will and national determination. The question arises: is the suitable personality at hand? Our task is not to look for such a person. He is a gift from heaven, or he is not there. Our task is to create the sword that this person will need when he is there. Our task is to give the dictator, when he comes, a people ready for him![139]

The fact that he had already come to see himself not simply as the drummer preparing the way for such a messianic figure, but as the "gift from heaven" himself, is further illustrated in Hitler's statement to the British *Daily Mail* in October 1923, only a few weeks before the putsch: "If a German Mussolini is given to Germany...people would fall down on their knees and worship him more than Mussolini has ever been worshipped."[140]

These trends were far from uncontested among the Nazi leadership; some of Hitler's close advisors and followers became increasingly alienated by what they viewed as an unhealthy messianic delusion attaching itself to Hitler. As early as May 1923, Dietrich Eckart had remarked to Ernst Hanfstaengl that Hitler had almost come to view himself literally as the modern incarnation of "Christ in the temple," and his growing ego represented "a megalomania that is halfway between a messiah complex and Neroism!"[141] In any event, it was the pursuit of this adulation and the goal of imitating Mussolini's dramatic rise—to summon the necessary organizational strength to successfully seize power, first in Bavaria and then throughout the Reich—that largely informed Hitler's willingness to abandon the independence of the NSDAP and to join with other *völkisch* groups in September 1923.

Between September and early November, then, the NSDAP technically operated as but one of the radical organizations comprising the Kampfbund.[142] One clear result of this agglomeration was the increased influence over the NSDAP of the rabidly anti-Catholic Erich Ludendorff, who had come to the Munich area in 1920 and whose military prestige made his home in the suburb of Solln a magnet for a wide variety of *völkisch* activists, but who had also for some time remained distant from the local Nazi movement.[143] Ludendorff was by far the Kampfbund's most prestigious and visible symbol on the national level, and his influence began to be seen clearly in the fall of 1923 in the pages of the *Beobachter,* which by then had come under the editorial guidance of Alfred Rosenberg. In one programmatic front-page article, Ludendorff acknowledged the existence of widespread unease in Munich and its Catholic environs over his outspokenness regarding his Prusso-Protestant identity, but he insisted that his public political confession was loyally *deutschvölkisch* and nothing else. At the same time, he did not shy away from reaffirming that he would always remain proud of his family's *protestantisch-hohenzollerisch* background and, in regard to his stance toward Bavarian Catholicism, proclaimed that "without question I declare my loyalty to the Protestant confession in which I was baptized and raised."[144]

Although elements of the Catholic-oriented membership drive continued in somewhat attenuated form—such as the Nazi-oriented field mass in honor of Schlageter performed on 9 September by Hermann Mencke, parish priest in Garmisch, or the commemorative mass performed for the NSDAP by Wilhelm Würzberger in Bamberg on 7 October 1923—a distinct change in tone was ushered in through the influence of Ludendorff and his followers after the formation of the Kampfbund.[145] Hitler himself made clear the shift away from the very public Catholic orientation of the earlier membership drive in a speech in late September, relegating religious identity explicitly to the private sphere.[146] At times, the overshadowing of Catholic-oriented elements was quite plain, as in the case of a field mass organized jointly by Bund Oberland and the NSDAP in Schliersee, which was scheduled for 30 September 1923 with Adalbert Obermayr, the parish priest in Schliersee, publicized as the main speaker.[147] By the time the ceremony itself took place, Obermayr's mass was completely drowned out by an overwhelming emphasis on the aggressive militarism of Bund Oberland and gushing heroic imagery surrounding Ludendorff, who attended at the last minute and spoke briefly.[148] For the first time, Protestant pastors from heavily Protestant areas in northern Bavaria, such as Wilhelm Heerdegen from Hof and Friedrich Leuthel from the Bayreuth area, began emerging openly as leading spokesmen for the broader Kampfbund movement.[149] Throughout the fall of 1923, the Protestant-nationalist orientation of the affiliated groups within the Kampfbund diverged markedly from the religious identity earlier cultivated by the NSDAP and created a potential conflict for the large numbers of believing Catholics who had joined the Nazi movement over the preceding months and who began to perceive increasing anti-Catholic tendencies within the broader movement. As a perceptive critic noted with reference to the fall of 1923, "the antipathy within the [Kampfbund] movement toward the Catholic Church grows to the extent that the influence of Ludendorff and other north German Protestants grows."[150]

Rising discontent among Catholic supporters of the NSDAP over the influence of Ludendorff and other *völkisch* anti-Catholics in the movement became increasingly visible through October and early November, as evidenced at least in part by the campaign waged against Ludendorff by Bernhard Stempfle in the pages of the *Anzeiger.*[151] Eckart had become almost completely estranged from the new direction taken by the movement by the fall of 1923. After being replaced at the *Beobachter* by Alfred Rosenberg earlier in the year, Eckart toyed openly in October with the idea of reviving his previous anti-Semitic journal, *Auf gut deutsch,* since he felt that his ideas were being ignored by Hitler and Ludendorff.[152]

Furthermore, in October 1923, Pieper left Munich and his Nazi propaganda activities to return to Westphalia, taking over a small parish in the town of Wehrden. Pieper later suggested that he had wanted to stay longer in Munich, but the crafty Jesuits had "discovered" his location, apparently in early October, and gave his address to his ecclesiastical superiors in Paderborn, who then ordered him to leave Munich and to resume his priestly duties under threat of suspension.[153] This account is less than convincing if for no other reason than that Pieper's activities in Munich were so visible and so widely coererd in the press over the course of several months that there was little need for him to be "discovered" by the Jesuits. It is possible that Pieper's departure may have been a sign of unhappiness with the increased Protestant orientation of the Kampfbund.

In the end, Hitler's momentous decision to accept the position of political leader of the Kampfbund in late September made clear not only that Hitler was now casting his political sights far beyond Munich and its environs but also that he had little time for, and perhaps little interest in, religious-oriented membership drives or other such organizational issues within the NSDAP itself.[154] Consumed by an increasingly messianic sense of his own political mission, Hitler focused his energies throughout the fall of 1923 almost entirely on the Kampfbund plot to overthrow both the Bavarian governmental system and the "traitorous" democratic regime in Berlin.

In the days immediately preceding the putsch, Cardinal Faulhaber began to speak out against anti-Semitism with a clarity and sense of determination not present in previous official statements on the Jews, a clarity that was certainly alien to the confusing "respectable" anti-Semitism pursued by the BVP. In his sermon of 4 November 1923, Faulhaber condemned in no uncertain terms the growing tide of racism in Munich and expressed sympathy with "our Israelite fellow citizens."[155] The Kampfbund movement, colored visibly by the influence of Ludendorff and his followers, was quick to attack the perceived hypocrisy of Faulhaber's sermon, noting derisively the contrast between his current stance and the "sharp words against the Jewish press" that Faulhaber had delivered at the Munich Katholikentag in 1922.[156] The defense of Faulhaber in the official Catholic press made sure to note the overtly anti-Catholic influence of Ludendorff and his followers.[157] As the uproar over Faulhaber's defense of the Jews made unmistakably clear, the stage was set for confessionally based divisions that would reach a boiling point within the *völkisch* movement in the aftermath of the putsch and dramatically alter the movement's nature and composition.

CHAPTER 5

The Beerhall Putsch and the Transformation of the Nazi Movement after 1923

On the night of 8 November and the morning of 9 November 1923, the NSDAP, as part of the larger *völkisch* coalition known as the Kampfbund, attempted to seize control of the Bavarian state, with the ultimate goal of organizing a march on Berlin to topple the government there and to erect a nationalist dictatorship in place of the hated republic. This attempt—known as the Beerhall Putsch, since the Kampfbund's first move was to abduct the primary leaders of the Bavarian government during a political rally in the Bürgerbräukeller—failed miserably, ending in a gun battle on Munich's Odeonsplatz that resulted in the deaths of sixteen members of the Kampfbund and four Munich police officers.[1] The NSDAP and the *Beobachter* were promptly banned, while Hitler and the other major putsch conspirators, including Erich Ludendorff, were arrested and in early 1924 were tried for treason in a genuine celebrity trial that was covered exhaustively in the press throughout Germany. Whereas Hitler accepted full responsibility and used the trial as a pulpit from which to publicize his and the movement's message to its broadest audience yet, Ludendorff attempted to shift the blame onto others and perceived the trial as an eagerly awaited opportunity to attack the Catholic Church and, more specifically, the person of Cardinal Faulhaber, whom he blamed for betraying the putsch. When the verdicts were issued in early April 1924, Ludendorff was acquitted, Hitler and the others received token prison sentences, and the ban on the NSDAP remained in effect, to be lifted in February 1925 after Hitler's release from prison.

Despite initial evidence of the continued popularity of the Nazi successor groups in the immediate aftermath of the trial, during the course of 1924 the increasingly divided movement slid into greater and greater decline, entering the period often referred to in histories of the Nazi party as the "wilderness years" that preceded the party's dramatic rise to national prominence in the early 1930s. The most frequently cited causes of this decline—organizational disunity and inept leadership in Hitler's absence combined with the increased stability of the years 1924–1929, which replaced the atmosphere of crisis on which the NSDAP thrived—are certainly applicable.[2] However, the initial demise of the Nazi movement was also due in no small part to a groundswell of vehement anti-Catholicism that swept through broader *völkisch* circles, including large segments of the former NSDAP itself. This cost the movement much of its support among believing Catholics in Munich, and there is evidence that many of the early Munich Catholics who did remain in the movement did so from then on often at the expense of their Catholic identity. By the time the party was refounded in early 1925, and even more so by the time it began its drive toward power in the early 1930s, the religious identity it cultivated was markedly different from that of the early 1920s. The striking Catholic orientation of 1923 was initially reversed and supplanted by a noticeable shift toward Protestant imagery, in keeping with the party's new and growing power base in the Protestant Franconian regions of northern Bavaria. Perhaps more important, however, the refounded NSDAP, now equipped not only with a messianic leader but also with its own set of powerful martyr figures and sacred objects of veneration drawn from the failed putsch, increasingly cultivated a striking form of secular-political religiosity. Despite continued Nazi references to the principle of Positive Christianity, from the mid-1920s on the concept became increasingly hollow and artificial.

Parting of the Ways: The Demise of the Early Catholic-Nazi Synthesis

In the wake of the failed putsch, intense disillusion and frustration were expressed in an outbreak of anti-Catholic venom that engulfed the ranks of the Kampfbund movement. The university quickly became one of the primary centers of *völkisch* unrest, and on 12 November Munich's most striking demonstration to protest the violent quashing of the putsch was staged in the main university building.[3] The student leader who convened the event was Karl von Guttenberg, a member of the Catholic fraternity Rheno-Bavaria (within the KV), who had emerged as one of the most outspoken activists within the *völkisch* Hochschulring in Munich. Writing on behalf of Nazi Catholic students and the

Hochschulring, Guttenberg had published a flaming appeal in the *Beobachter* some three weeks before the putsch, pledging the loyalty of the *völkisch* student body to Hitler and the Kampfbund movement in no uncertain terms while attempting to maintain support for Gustav von Kahr, who had been appointed Bavarian commissioner the previous month.[4] Apparently against the will of Guttenberg, the 12 November demonstration he initially summoned quickly degenerated into a morass of wild rumors and crass insults, with the most venomous accusations being leveled at Cardinal Faulhaber. It was alleged that Faulhaber, who was widely rumored to have been spearheading his own separatist plot to create a new south German "Danubian monarchy," had performed the act that decisively doomed the putsch only hours after it began, by meeting secretly with Kahr to convince him to reverse his statement of support for the new Hitler-Ludendorff dictatorship. Among the more humorous accusations made were the charges that a Jewish-Catholic conspiracy, apparently orchestrated by Faulhaber, had actually succeeded in getting Kahr to reverse himself by bribing him with "seven Persian rugs" and the promise of honorary membership in the Jesuit order. As a result, the chant that echoed throughout the university rally was "Down with Kahr and Faulhaber, the Jesuit lackeys."[5]

Accusations of treachery were further embellished and expanded over the coming weeks and months to apply at least in principle to all believing Catholics, who were frequently lumped together as potential traitors to the *völkisch* cause. The distinction between religious and political Catholicism, so often emphasized on previous occasions, was almost completely eclipsed in the flood of invective. In a widely publicized speech to Munich university students less than two weeks after the putsch, Ludendorff follower Albrecht Hoffmann went beyond simple anti-ultramontane rhetoric to define the future mission of the *völkisch* movement in terms that excluded Catholics almost by definition: "We are presently in the ultimate battle for our national existence. Bismarck's legacy and much else along with it, has already been shamefully squandered. Now the legacy of Luther, who restored to us Germans . . . our very existence from the domination of Rome is [in danger of] being destroyed." As the ultimate example of treason against the German *Volk*, Hoffmann pointed to the fateful manipulation of Kahr by sinister Catholic forces during the putsch: "It was reserved for the Protestant Kahr, in destroying the *völkisch* freedom movement, to betray Luther's accomplishments into the hands of Rome with a Judas kiss."[6] Another of Ludendorff's adherents, a Protestant-*völkisch* activist named Born, made a series of speeches throughout Bavaria in early 1924 that were explicitly designed to expose the potential treachery represented by the continued presence in the movement of believing Catholics, whose religious loyalties and national identity would, he argued, always remain irreparably divided. Not content to attack merely the perceived duplicity of Faulhaber, Born took special aim at the numerous Catholic priests who had engaged in Nazi propaganda activities throughout 1923, condemning them as agents of international Jesuitism: "Do not be deceived even if Catholic priests deliver fiery sermons at military events. Remember that there are no greater actors than these 'Jesuits.'"[7] Moving fluidly from Protestant to pagan imagery, Born further attacked what he saw as the dangerously flawed Catholic orientation of the movement throughout 1923, and he attempted in another speech to wrench even the powerful symbol of Albert Leo Schlageter away from Nazi Catholics by claiming, "Schlageter in reality went to Valhalla, which is much better than the heaven of these [Catholic] bloodsuckers."[8] A central hallmark of Born's speeches was the sweeping proclamation that, in the wake of the failed putsch, "peace with the church is as unthinkable as peace with France."[9] Importantly, *völkisch* attacks against Catholic institutions and figures, particularly the person of Cardinal Faulhaber, were not limited to words and speeches. Faulhaber's residence was physically attacked on several occasions in the weeks and months following the putsch, forcing the Bavarian minister of cultural affairs, Franz Matt, to order special police protection in early February 1924.[10] In one well-publicized attack, an unnamed "prominent lady of Munich society," who in the course of her charitable work had occasion to pay a visit to Faulhaber, was accosted and "spit upon from head to toe" by unknown *völkisch* assailants as she waited at the front entrance to the episcopal residence.[11]

Public discourse in Munich in the early months of 1924 was dominated first by preparations for the Hitler-Ludendorff trial, which began in late February, and then by the intense and incredibly detailed press coverage of the defendants' courtroom statements through the month of March. Ludendorff's famous verbal assaults against the pope, the Catholic Church, and Cardinal Faulhaber were widely perceived as the most incendiary aspect of the trial, certainly in Munich, and they dominated local headlines for several weeks.[12] Furthering the widespread theory that a secret Catholic-Jewish conspiracy was responsible for the failure of the putsch, the defense lawyer for the Protestant Friedrich Weber, Dr. Alfred Holl, charged during the trial that the Kampfbund movement had been betrayed at least in part by the attempt to establish "the hegemony of the Catholic Church, [which] could only succeed through the support of international Jewry."[13] Even after his acquittal in early April 1924, Ludendorff continued his vehement attacks on Faulhaber in particular.[14]

In the face of such imagery, however, it is important to note that Hitler's personal religious identity was largely disconnected from the broader anti-Catholic groundswell. In preparing for his client's defense in December 1923, Hitler's lawyer, Lorenz Roder, made an explicit and very public statement attesting to the religious sincerity of Hitler's Catholic identity in the face of allegations, emanating from BVP circles, that Hitler had abandoned the Catholicism of his youth and was perhaps as anti-Catholic as Ludendorff. At the heart of these allegations were rumors that Hitler had, as a child in Austria, not only sympathized with the anti-Catholic Los-von-Rom movement but, more seriously, had personally desecrated the eucharistic host on at least one occasion by spitting it out and placing it in his pocket.[15] Against the backdrop of the overarching Catholic orientation of the NSDAP in and around Munich in 1923, Roder claimed that the rumors were so implausible as to be laughable—stating that the adolescent Hitler had "never participated in the Los von Rom movement" and had "never spit out the host"—and closed with the sweeping proclamation, "Herr Hitler is still today a convinced Catholic."[16] The tremendous disparity between Hitler's perceived Catholic sincerity and the rabid anti-Catholic sentiment sweeping through the former Kampfbund movement was furthered by widespread reports that Hitler had launched the putsch in the first place only after receiving a dramatic religious vision of the Virgin Mary, reviving images of Constantine's pious vision before the Milvian Bridge.[17] There is no question that, in stark contrast to Hitler's religious identity after 1933, the image of Hitler as a loyal Catholic still possessed a striking plausibility in Munich in the aftermath of the putsch. This plausibility, while never entirely uncontested, was also evident in the early 1924 attempt to defend the embattled Faulhaber and to fashion him into a unifying figure who could potentially transcend and heal political divisions and bring together a wide variety of Munich Catholics, including especially Catholic Hitler supporters from the former NSDAP.

In the aftermath of the putsch, an ad hoc entity calling itself the Zentralkomitee der Münchener Katholiken was set in motion by local engineer Johann Rauch to organize the defense of both Cardinal Faulhaber and the honor of the church more generally; it consisted of many leading BVP figures but also represented a fairly broad cross-section of Munich Catholic society.[18] On 11 December 1923, the committee petitioned the Bavarian minister-president Eugen von Knilling himself to intervene on behalf of Munich Catholics in what was being portrayed increasingly as a new Protestant-*völkisch Kulturkampf*.[19] Over the next several months, the committee also spearheaded a massive press campaign that explicitly utilized *Kulturkampf* imagery, attempting to convince Catholics who had previously been involved in the Kampfbund (and especially the NSDAP) that the true anti-Catholic nature of the *völkisch* movement was at last being revealed, while continuing to shield Hitler from charges of anti-Christianity.[20] Throughout early 1924, a number of mass rallies were organized by the committee to demonstrate unwavering Catholic sympathy and support for Faulhaber as a unifying religious—and distinctly apolitical—figure. The largest of these occurred on 10 April 1924 in the Löwenbräukeller, at which a unified "pledge of loyalty to the church and to the leaders of the Catholic populace, especially to Cardinal Dr. von Faulhaber" was declared "without a single objection" from the Catholics present.[21] As in the case of the persecuted bishops during the nineteenth-century *Kulturkampf,* the *völkisch* campaign against Faulhaber made him increasingly into a heroic martyr figure and an integrative rallying point for Catholics of varying political hues.

Faulhaber himself seems to have made a special attempt to appeal, again as an explicitly apolitical religious leader, to *völkisch* Catholics who had previously supported Hitler and the NSDAP, offering an olive branch that the anti-Nazi partisans within the BVP were often unwilling to extend. In a well-publicized speech to a Catholic academic group in Munich on 15 February 1924, Faulhaber, in stark contrast to the bitterness of Hitler's critics in the BVP, issued a remarkably strong statement of praise for what he portrayed as the loyally Catholic political vision that had been represented by Hitler and the Nazi movement before the putsch, and he lamented the fact that the "initially pure spring" that fed the NSDAP's early activism had come to be "poisoned" by the anti-Catholic influence of Ludendorff and his followers:

> Adolf Hitler knew better than his rivals for leadership within the *völkisch* movement that German history did not begin in 1870 or 1517, that for the rebuilding of the German *Volk* the power source [*Kraftquelle*] of Christian culture is indispensable, and that this work of rebuilding cannot be accomplished through the worship of Germanic gods [*Wotanskult*] or through hatred of Rome. As a man of the people he knew the soul of the south German populace better than the others and recognized that the soul of the people cannot be won over by a movement that at the same time battles against the

[Catholic] Church. There is a shocking tragedy in the fact that this initially pure spring came to be poisoned by subsequent influences and [turned into] a *Kulturkampf.*[22]

Such a clear statement from a figure of Faulhaber's stature amounted in effect to a powerful endorsement of the religious legitimacy of the Catholic-oriented crusade that had helped to fuel the Nazi movement's growth in 1923, while it also pointed out to *völkisch* Catholics who may have earlier been drawn to the NSDAP that those better days, now poisoned, were irretrievably gone. Similarly, while the speakers at the pro-Faulhaber rally on 10 April made no secret of their anger at Ludendorff, the organizer of the rally, Johann Rauch, paid Hitler an important (if somewhat backhanded) compliment, distinguishing the Nazi leader and his "healthy" movement from the influence of Ludendorff and implying that the current explosion of anti-Catholicism was the regrettable result of Hitler's lack of control over the movement.[23] Ludendorff's followers and other Protestant-oriented *völkisch* activists effectively agreed with this assessment, frequently blaming Hitler and the NSDAP for having been in essence "too Catholic" and having therefore contributed at least in part to the eventual Catholic sabotage of the *völkisch* cause. Abandoning the earlier distinction between religious and political Catholicism and equating the Catholic faith with ultramontanism across the board, Albrecht Hoffmann claimed shortly after the putsch, "Hitler...failed because he did not recognize the immense danger of ultramontanism clearly enough."[24] Hitler's otherwise hagiographic biographer, the Protestant Georg Schott, implied in early 1924 that Hitler's "sincere" Catholic religious faith had made him dangerously naïve, stating with reference to the NSDAP's more Catholic orientation before the putsch:

In his soul there was simply no room for consideration of such devilish [Catholic] trickery. He clearly recognized the Jewish treachery, but was not capable of the thought that the devil had crept into the eucharistic vessel and was deceiving the childishly believing populace. He was not capable, that is, until life taught him this hard lesson. What level of pain this experience caused him, this sincere Catholic and deeply pious man, requires no further discussion.[25]

The initial divisions that were visible in the immediate aftermath of the putsch would eventually blossom into open animosity between Hitler and Ludendorff.

In early 1924, remnants of the former NSDAP in Munich made the decision to enter electoral politics for the first time, running in both the Landtag elections of April 1924 and the Reichtsag elections of May and December 1924 as part of an amalgamation known as the Völkischer Block, which problematically pledged its official loyalty to the leadership of both Hitler and Ludendorff.[26] One important aspect of the Block's energetic electioneering in Munich was the attempt by certain former Nazis to maintain Catholic support, or at least to hinder a mass exodus of Catholics from the movement. The Hochschulring leader Kleo Pleyer, who was raised Catholic but eventually left the church completely and later achieved some fame as a Nazi historian, led the campaign for the Völkischer Block at the university. In attempting to counteract the influence of the anti-Catholic crusade by essentially denying its existence, Pleyer asserted that the *völkisch* movement was "not at all in conflict with the Catholic faith" and made the unconvincing claim that "the attempt to conjure up a new *Kulturkampf* did not originate from *völkisch* groups but rather from certain political parties that have laid claim to Catholicism as their hereditary right."[27] Quite different and considerably more effective in pursuing the objective of keeping believing Catholics in the movement were the two mass meetings held in Munich in late April 1924 on the theme "Can a Catholic Be *Völkisch?*" Strongly reminiscent of the propagandistic speeches given jointly by Lorenz Pieper and Max Sesselmann (under the title "Can a Catholic Be a National Socialist?") during the Catholic-oriented membership drive the previous year, these heavily publicized events were convened in the Bürgerbräukeller and the Löwenbräukeller and were headlined by Sesselmann and two other believing Catholics who had been long-time members of the NSDAP: Hans Dauser, a former BVP leader who had defected to the NSDAP in 1920, and Friedrich Ferrari (see fig. 5.1).[28]

The police observer present at the meeting in the Bürgerbräukeller on 25 April 1924 noted an attendance of more than a thousand and recorded that Sesselmann, who "spoke for two full hours," protested the treatment of *völkisch* Catholics as "second-class Catholics" by the BVP press and stressed the continued Christian nature of the movement's "moral battle against the degeneration of the German national soul."[29] Ferrari launched into an extended personal testimonial that echoed the earlier theme of warrior Christianity and highlighted for his audience his own experience of wrestling with deep issues of faith, an experience he saw as foreign to the complacent and lukewarm Catholics in the BVP:

Figure 5.1. Max Sesselmann (early 1920s).
Source: Sesselmann and Hoffmann, *Deutschlands Erwachen*.

I am a believing Catholic, but I first had much to work through. Events have constantly brought me back to the question: why [am I a Catholic]? I have wrestled with God, but I have persevered to arrive at my positive Catholic faith. Anyone who has to struggle in life will have to struggle with his faith. A doubter who has fought his way through becomes stronger than someone who has always been comfortable.

Ferrari continued by describing how his strong Catholic faith bolstered his commitment to the Nazi mission and emphasized the consistent support for the Catholic faith by Hitler, who had "never in his life made a single attack on religion or the church." In urging *völkisch*-oriented Catholics to remain in the movement, Ferrari asserted that the majority of actively believing Catholics still opposed the opportunistic policies of the BVP and insisted that "this is best illustrated when one visits Munich's churches on Sundays, where one will by no means merely find people from the Bavarian People's Party."[30] Both the meeting at the Bürgerbräukeller and the related rally at the Löwenbräukeller culminated in impassioned and clearly worded declarations of loyalty to the principle of religious Catholicism, rejecting the anti-Catholic attacks of Ludendorff and his followers while pledging, in transcendence of the detrimental phenomenon of political Catholicism, unwavering spiritual allegiance to the pope and to Cardinal Faulhaber personally:

> We Catholics of Munich (and of all the German-speaking territories) who belong to the *völkisch* movement are in no way waging a war against the cross, the symbol of Christianity, against the Catholic Church, against the Holy Father, or against our archbishop.... We *völkisch* Catholics venerate in the Holy Father the honored head of our church, which we esteem as standing above the nations, untroubled by the personal sentiments of individuals. We venerate in his eminence, the cardinal-archbishop Dr. Faulhaber, our honorable diocesan shepherd, whom we continue to recognize as standing above the parties.[31]

This statement should be read at least in part as a response to the olive branch offered by Faulhaber to *völkisch*-oriented Catholics weeks earlier. It was also explicitly in this spirit that Franz Schrönghamer-Heimdal ran, ultimately unsuccessfully, as a candidate for the Völkischer Block in the spring of 1924.[32]

While these and other such efforts encountered considerable success in the early months of 1924, in the end they proved unable either to drown out the never-ending chorus of anti-Catholic invective coming from Ludendorff's followers within the movement or to definitively stave off the reality of decline, which became increasingly undeniable as the year progressed. This development can be traced in part by looking at the electoral fortunes of the Völkischer Block in Munich during 1924. In the Landtag elections of April 1924, the popularity of the movement (while perhaps somewhat residual, riding the wave of publicity generated by Hitler's trial) was considerable, with the block garnering 34.9 percent of the Munich vote—the largest total of any single party—before slipping to a still-impressive 28.5 percent in the Reichstag elections the next month.[33] At the same time, however, unmistakable signs of disillusion on the part of many *völkisch* Catholics, especially the movement's priestly supporters, became increasingly apparent through the spring and summer. Abbot Alban Schachleiter, whose commemorative mass for Albert Leo Schlageter the previous summer at St. Boniface had done much to strengthen the growing Catholic-Nazi synthesis, expressed the bitterness felt by growing numbers of *völkisch* Catholics toward the disastrous impact of Ludendorff and his anti-Catholic followers, noting in a letter to Oswald Spengler in late May 1924: "What a disaster for the Fatherland! One could almost scream over this state of affairs! Haven't we already been brought low enough? Our *Volk* has never been so leaderless as it is today. Ludendorff has completely thrown away the support of German Catholics.... God help us! May he grant us the strength to continue to work for our poor Fatherland."[34] Similarly, Christian Huber, the priest who had so energetically supported the Nazi cause between 1920 and 1923, distanced himself from the movement in the spring of 1924 explicitly as a result of Ludendorff's statements, as did the vast majority of priests who had engaged in *völkisch*-Nazi activism in the summer of 1923.[35] Given the increasingly widespread nature of these sentiments, it is not surprising that the declining fortunes of the Völkischer Block continued into free fall through the rest of the year, so that by the time of the Reichstag elections in December 1924, its support in Munich had withered to a mere 9.1 percent. The once-mighty movement had managed over the course of a few months to lose nearly three-fourths of its Munich constituency.[36] Ultimately, the movement would never, despite some effort, regain its former level of Catholic support in Munich, and following the refounding of the NSDAP in early 1925, the stronghold of the Nazi movement in Bavaria would no longer be Munich and its Catholic environs but rather the Protestant regions of Mittel- and Oberfranken.[37]

Not only did large numbers of believing Catholics abandon the movement over the course of 1924, but there is evidence that those early Munich Catholics who chose to remain often felt compelled to abandon their Catholic convictions as a result. For instance, Alfred Miller, the student of Joseph Schnitzer who in countless articles in the *Beobachter* had trumpeted the distinction between religious and political Catholicism, no longer viewed such a distinction as viable in the wake of the putsch. In a widely publicized pamphlet from January 1924 on the causes of the coup's failure, Miller initially blamed "Jesuitism" and ultramontanism rather than Catholicism across the board: "In these days it is to be decided which has the upper hand, the Jesuitical-ultramontane [world view] or the *völkisch* idea."[38] But as the year progressed, Miller came to see the *völkisch* and Catholic identities as increasingly incompatible, framing the contrast between the two as a stark either-or choice. By late 1924, Miller had made his choice increasingly clear, embracing a mystical form of distinctly non-Christian Nordic religiosity and announcing that he no longer saw any benefit in attempting in vain to awaken German Catholics to the dangers of political ultramontanism and indicating that he had essentially given up on the Catholic faith itself.[39] The fact that Miller completely abandoned not only the religious Catholicism he had once so vocally trumpeted but also Christianity more generally is demonstrated by his later publications, his work on the staff of Theodor Fritsch's Hammer Verlag beginning in the late 1920s, and a literal flood of bombastically anti-Christian books and articles published by Miller in the 1930s, during which time he served as a leading member of the anti-Christian Germanic Glaubensbewegung and helped to edit the movement's official journal, *Durchbruch*.[40]

Perhaps the most instructive example of the abandonment of Catholic identity in favor of the *völkisch* cause is provided by Heinrich Himmler, who was born into an extremely religious Catholic household in Munich in 1900—his father was a devout gymnasium teacher and personal tutor to the Wittelsbach royal family with good connections among the *Hofklerus*—and grew to young adulthood as a scrupulously practicing Catholic.[41] Numerous entries from Himmler's youthful diary reflect the central role of communion, confession, and attendance at mass in shaping the rhythm of his daily life.[42] Like Eckart and Schrönghamer, when the BVP was initially founded in November 1918, Himmler wrote to his family full of enthusiasm for the new party, proclaiming, "Father, you must join the Bayerische Volkspartei, it is the only hope."[43] While a student at the Technische Hochschule in Munich between 1919 and 1922, Himmler continued to be scrupulous in fulfilling his religious obligations, although he was plagued by periodic doubts arising from his membership in an interconfessional student fraternity that practiced the *Mensur* (student saber duel), which had been officially condemned by the church.[44] As Himmler became increasingly involved in the local *völkisch* milieu during his student years—evidenced in part by his meticulously kept reading list, which recorded a steadily increasing diet of racist and anti-Semitic texts—he was initially quite successful in reconciling this growing *völkisch* involvement with a continued commitment to his Catholic identity.[45]

In the summer of 1923, Himmler was clearly caught up in the NSDAP's Catholic-oriented membership drive, and he was almost certainly present at the St. Boniface memorial mass for Albert Leo Schlageter to hear the powerful eulogy given by Alban Schachleiter.[46] Along with countless other young Catholic men in Munich who were similarly attracted to the party, Himmler officially joined the NSDAP a few weeks after the Schlageter commemoration, receiving member number 42404, and went on to participate in the putsch that November.[47] Himmler seems to have engaged for several months after the putsch, in the midst of the rising tide of anti-Catholic invective, in an extended struggle to reconcile his Catholic faith with the imperatives of continued membership in the *völkisch* movement. It is clear from his diary entries that he continued to attend Catholic mass faithfully as late as February 1924, on the eve of the Hitler-Ludendorff trial.[48] While he continued to read Catholic-oriented *völkisch* works in early 1924, including earlier writings by Alfred Miller, Himmler was also at the same time coming increasingly under the influence of overtly anti-Catholic ideas, devouring books by Ernst Haeckel and Houston Stewart Chamberlain, in addition to a scurrilous pamphlet regarding sexual perversion in the Catholic priesthood.[49] Himmler's initial reaction to Haeckel's *Welträtsel,* which he read on 9 February 1924, was fairly negative, and he recorded in his book list his disagreement with Haeckel's anti-Christian stance and his "denial of a personal God," which Himmler judged as "simply terrible."[50] In any event, by the summer of 1924, while Hitler was still in jail, Himmler had decided to join the Nationalsozialistische Freiheitspartei, one of the Nazi successor groups that oriented itself specifically around the figure of Ludendorff and was often in opposition to the Munich-based remnants of the NSDAP.[51] Not coincidentally, Himmler's diary entries indicate that he had ceased attending mass entirely by the summer of 1924 at the latest. Apparently feeling that it was no longer possible to reconcile his Nazi identity with the Catholic faith in which he had been raised, Himmler would eventually become an ardent critic of Christianity.[52]

A New Beginning: Religious Identity and the Refounding of the NSDAP

When Hitler was released from prison in Landsberg in December 1924, the future direction and shape of his movement was uncertain at best. No doubt, the calamitous demise of the broader *völkisch* coalition, inescapably demonstrated in the elections earlier that December, proved fortuitous for Hitler's rapid reassertion of control in a political sense.[53] In light of the rabid anti-Catholicism that had characterized the majority of *völkisch* activism while Hitler was in prison, however, the question of the religious orientation to be taken during the process of rebuilding the Nazi movement remained open. What would the principle of Positive Christianity come to mean in these altered circumstances?

Initially, starting in early 1925, some superficial trappings of the movement's pre-putsch Catholic flavor were revived, at least briefly, as Hitler and his most loyal Munich-based followers attempted to regain at least part of the Catholic support they had lost in the Bavarian capital. In a meeting on 4 January 1925 with BVP leader Heinrich Held, who had become Bavarian minister-president the previous July, Hitler pledged to personally oppose the harsh anti-Catholic course that had been pursued by the *völkisch* movement since the putsch. The meeting had been arranged by the staunchly pious Catholic businessman Theodor von Cramer-Klett, and Hitler's apparent sincerity contributed greatly to Held's decision, however reluctant, to allow both the refounding of the NSDAP and the reappearance of the *Beobachter* as its Munich-based organ beginning in February 1925.[54] On the front page of the first issue of the reestablished *Beobachter,* Hitler did in fact publish a programmatic condemnation of the *Kulturkämpfer* who had misused *völkisch* sentiments to wage war on the Catholic Church, and Hitler claimed he was willing to give up entirely the use of the term *völkisch* to avoid future confusion with the counterproductive efforts of Catholic-baiters.[55] Despite early attempts to patch up differences between Hitler and Ludendorff—including the Nazis' initial support for Ludendorff's candidacy in the first round of presidential elections in March 1925—it was no secret that these comments were aimed directly at the overt anti-Catholicism of Ludendorff and his followers.[56] Initial efforts were made to revive the image of religious Catholicism cultivated so successfully before the putsch, including the use of devotional reflections by Alfons Heilmann, the priest who had begun his career as an advocate of prewar Reform Catholicism and had launched the short-lived journal *Der Deutsche Geist* in Munich in 1920.[57] In the spring of 1925, the NSDAP, attempting to rally Catholics around the figure of the newly freed Hitler, founded its own Munich-based Katholikenbund, mirroring in many ways the Katholiken-Ausschuss of the Deutschnationale Volkspartei (DNVP), which was gaining increasing national recognition throughout Germany behind leading figures like Martin Spahn.[58] The Nazi Katholikenbund, which was headed by retired military officer Wilhelm Starck, made a brief splash in Munich and then, tellingly, disappeared completely by the summer of 1925.[59] Hitler himself continued on public occasions to invoke the principle of Positive Christianity and to associate the NSDAP with a vague form of Christian activism.[60] Hitler also continued strongly to condemn *völkisch* anti-Catholicism—a theme that emerged clearly in his criticisms of the Austrian Los-von-Rom movement in the first volume of *Mein Kampf,* which appeared in 1925—and this stance led directly to sustained conflict with overtly anti-Catholic forces within the broader *völkisch* movement.[61] Protestant *völkisch* activists, most notably Albrecht von Graefe, attacked Hitler energetically throughout 1925 and 1926 for attempting to reconstitute the strong Catholic orientation of the pre-putsch NSDAP and operating "in league with Rome, working with the Jesuits, being dependent on the Bavarian People's Party, and being engaged to a well-known ultramontane lady."[62] Hitler's lengthy response—which was finally read publicly at a mass meeting on 17 March 1926 by Hermann Esser since Hitler was at the time banned from speaking publicly in Bavaria—rejected the allegations decisively yet tactfully.[63] Nonetheless, anti-Catholic *völkisch* activists, often associated with Ludendorff, would continue to make the assertion that Hitler was essentially too pro-Catholic even into the 1930s.[64]

Despite these assertions and the Nazis' initial attempts to revive earlier Catholic-oriented imagery, the religious identity of the movement (and of Hitler in particular) was unmistakably different following the re-founding of the NSDAP in February 1925. Occasional references to Positive Christianity and the heroism of Christ aside, Hitler was no longer portrayed either as a believing Catholic or as an energetic advocate of Christianity. Even the adulation showered on Hitler by the newly founded Katholikenbund in Munich in the spring of 1925 stopped well short of invoking Hitler's own personal faith or Catholic background; the furthest that founder Wilhelm Starck was allowed to go was to insist that Hitler would not "make the support of us Catholics impossible," that he "respected our religious convictions" and would never "seek to influence the religious beliefs of his followers."[65] Similarly, Hitler's seemingly positive remarks about the Catholic Church in *Mein Kampf* were no longer those of a committed member of the church, but those of one who merely respected its organizational strength and was willing to tolerate, not necessarily celebrate, the continued presence of Catholic-Christian convictions within his movement.[66] This public willingness to *tolerate* Christianity—rather than preaching it or claiming to represent it—and Hitler's insistence on keeping religious disputes out of the movement have been viewed by some as an indication of pro-Catholic sentiment cultivated more than anything for reasons of political opportunism.[67] What these sentiments seem to reveal is a growing indifference that contrasts starkly with the religious identity cultivated by Hitler before the putsch, as seen in his April 1922 public profession of faith in his "Lord and Savior" or Lorenz Roder's December 1923 claim that Hitler was a "convinced Catholic." Whatever else he claimed to have learned while in prison, Hitler clearly emerged from Landsberg with an unwavering sense of his own messianic political mission.[68] It is equally clear in retrospect that this growing political messianism would ultimately leave little or no room for any genuine Catholic or Christian sentiment among the Nazi leadership. Initially, however, the Nazi appeal to the principle of Positive Christianity was not abandoned entirely in the early life of the refounded NSDAP; rather, in moving away from its original Munich-based Catholic inflection, the movement began to assume a more Protestant-oriented identity in keeping with the party's dramatic expansion throughout Protestant regions in northern Bavaria in 1925 and 1926.

Whereas the pre-putsch Nazi movement had excoriated political Catholicism while defending and advocating religious Catholicism, the refounded NSDAP tended increasingly—initially somewhat imperceptibly, then more overtly—toward outright anti-Catholicism, despite Hitler's public insistence on avoiding confessional disputes. In a sensational and brutally critical series beginning in the spring of 1925, the *Beobachter* lambasted the (entirely nonpolitical) activities of the Benedictine missionary house on Munich's Königinstrasse, which was accused of heartlessly driving out poverty-stricken Protestants living in a neighboring building to acquire living space for Benedictine missionaries returning home from overseas service.[69] In contrast to the positive imagery that had been associated with the Nazis' earlier support for Catholic religious education in the schools, a new set of much more critical images emerged in the Nazis' emphatic opposition to the establishment of the concordat between Bavaria and the Vatican.[70] This stance was accompanied by numerous unflattering remarks regarding the papal nuncio Pacelli, particularly at the time of his move from Munich to Berlin in the summer of 1925.[71] Over time, this imagery went far beyond the standard political criticism of the BVP or Center Party, as Nazi publicity turned increasingly against the Catholic Church as an institution. In a series of articles entitled "Church and High Finance," the church itself was accused of corruption, greed, and (perhaps worst of all) collaborating scandalously with Jewish bankers in New York to arrange advantageous loans not available to German organizations more generally.[72] Additionally, the German bishops were attacked frequently and in an increasingly personal way, mocked and ridiculed as corrupt and greedy "Jewish lackeys" who were steeped in the dishonorable "spirit of Erzberger."[73]

By far the harshest criticism was reserved for Cardinal Faulhaber who had, prior to his well-publicized defense of Munich Jews on the eve of the putsch, typically been treated with a fair amount of deference and respect by the early NSDAP, even in cases of direct disagreement. Throughout 1925 and 1926, the *Beobachter* engaged in a veritable orgy of blatantly disrespectful insults and demeaning remarks directed at Faulhaber's person. During the 1925 legal case lodged by Faulhaber against Rainer Hupperz, the Nazi editor of the Hamburg paper *Vaterland*, who had publicly called Faulhaber a "traitor" and accused him of dooming the 1923 putsch, the *Beobachter* not only sided with Hupperz but compared Faulhaber directly to Kurt Eisner and his Jewish "comrades."[74] Further *Beobachter* coverage of the Hupperz trial labeled Faulhaber a pacifist traitor and, for good measure, reflected back derisively on his initial emergence as a "pious Jew-friend" in November 1923.[75] When Faulhaber criticized what he saw as excessive nationalistic posturing on the issue of Germans living in the Italian-controlled South Tyrol—Faulhaber called it "pathological nationalism"—the *Beobachter* mobilized immediately against Faulhaber, calling his perspective not only wrong but "dishonorable."[76] In addition to personal attacks on his honor, Faulhaber was openly labeled a hypocrite and, in a barely veiled insinuation, characterized as nothing more than a common liar.[77]

As a corollary to this gradual public shift in orientation, it should be noted that the numerous Catholic priests who had emerged as pro-Nazi propagandists throughout Bavaria before the putsch, especially in 1923, ceased virtually all such activity in the refounded NSDAP. An important turning point seems to have been reached initially in September 1923, following Josef Roth's impassioned field mass for the Nazi SA at the Deutstcher Tag events in Nuremberg. Writing on 8 September 1923, Munich Vicar General Buchberger censured Roth for the flaming nature of his sermon, noting that "you have inflicted unfathomable damage on the church."[78] At the same time, Catholic priests throughout the archdiocese of Munich-Freising were forbidden—apparently informally but no less definitively—from attending Nazi meetings in the fall of 1923.[79] In the aftermath of the wave of *völkisch* anti-Catholicism that followed the putsch, figures like Philipp Haeuser and Josef Roth clearly continued to sympathize with the newly refounded NSDAP, allowing some of their writings to be reprinted in the Nazi press even as they personally avoided open propagandistic activity.[80] Lorenz Pieper remained in Westphalia and also continued to sympathize strongly with the NSDAP, although the entries in his *Brieftagebuch* indicate that he attended only one Nazi event throughout the remainder of the 1920s—a Hitler gathering in Braunschweig on 4 November 1925—and there is no indication of Pieper engaging directly in any propaganda activities before the early 1930s. Disgusted by the fact that the anti-Catholicism of Ludendorff and his followers had driven believing Catholics out of the *völkisch*-Nazi movement in droves throughout 1924—as reflected in his May 1924 letter to Oswald Spengler—Alban Schachleiter increasingly distanced himself from the NSDAP in the mid-1920s, although he maintained an idealized image of Hitler personally (which would fuel the renewal of their close relationship in the early 1930s) and found himself occasionally being defended in the Nazi press.[81] Few other Catholic priests who had been active on behalf of the Nazi movement before the putsch continued this activism publicly after 1924.[82] Despite the fact that several priestly figures would attempt to revive their Nazi propaganda activities in the 1930s, the absence of any visible engagement on the part of Catholic priests in the refounded NSDAP in the mid-1920s is striking.

In stark contrast, Protestant pastors—who had been almost entirely absent from the NSDAP's Positive Christian appeal before the putsch—began to emerge openly and in increasing numbers as *völkisch* and Nazi spokesmen. During the period in which the NSDAP was banned, numerous Protestant pastors throughout Bavaria had embraced the Völkischer Block and, especially, the striking cult of heroism surrounding Ludendorff, even as Catholic members were beginning to engage in a corresponding mass exodus. In the April 1924 Bavarian Landtag elections, pastor Hellmuth Johnsen from Coburg was elected overwhelmingly as a candidate for the Völkischer Block, riding the tide of publicity surrounding Ludendorff's inflammatory trial comments.[83] In May 1924, at the yearly Protestant youth conference held at the Franconian retreat Burg Hoheneck, which was owned by the Protestant *völkisch* publicist Julius Friedrich Lehmann, pastors like Wilhelm Stählin from St. Lorenz in Nuremberg idealized the figure of Ludendorff and energetically advocated the participation of young Protestant clergy in the *völkisch* movement.[84] Whereas Stählin's Burg Hoheneck speech had also warned against a potential for *völkisch* excess that could lead to doctrinal problems, other Protestant pastors, including Emerich Eder of Lehenthal, Heinrich Derleder of Kasendorf, Christian Richter of Weiden, and Konrad Hoefler of Nuremberg, emerged throughout 1924 as even stronger *völkisch* advocates of Ludendorff.[85] Many of these pastors continued to side with Ludendorff after the refounding of the NSDAP in February 1925 and, partly as a result of running tensions between Ludendorff and Hitler, often did not become Nazi members themselves.[86] The absence of these Ludendorff supporters among the Nazi ranks was more than compensated, however, by the striking emergence of numerous other explicitly pro-Nazi Protestant pastors throughout Bavaria in 1925 and 1926.

In April 1925, when the *Beobachter* published its first Christian devotional reflection after its refounding, on the occasion of Good Friday, it was the Protestant Dekan of Munich, Hermann Lembert, who was tapped to write it.[87] This was significant, since despite having been a major figure in broader right-wing circles in Munich before the putsch, Lembert had never been affiliated with the NSDAP and certainly never had published anything (religious or otherwise) in the pre-putsch *Beobachter*.[88] In the wake of the death of former Munich police president and putsch co-conspirator Ernst Pöhner in April 1925, the *Beobachter* focused increasingly on the activities of Johannes Kreppel, Protestant pastor at the Christuskirche in Munich-Neuhausen, who presided over Pöhner's funeral.[89] Theo Schenk, pastor in Neulussheim, emerged as a leading figure in the NSDAP Ortsgruppe in nearby Frankenthal in August 1925, as did pastors Wilhelm Heerdegen within the Ortsgruppe Hof and Max Sauerteig in the Ortsgruppe Ansbach by the fall of 1925.[90] Perhaps the most notable Nazi propagandist among Protestant pastors in Bavaria was Martin Weigel of Nuremberg, who joined the NSDAP in December 1925. When the Nazis staged a massive event to consecrate the flags of the SA in Nuremberg on 1 August 1926, Weigel performed the ceremony in the Lorenzkirche and received the same type of coverage that the Catholic priest Josef Roth had received in September 1923, with the *Beobachter* lauding him as "the honorable pastor of the Almighty" and a "courageous servant of God."[91] Weigel's sermon was reprinted in its entirety on the front page of the *Beobachter*, which foregrounded the sacramental elements of the ceremony and noted that Weigel blessed each of the SA standards individually by pronouncing "a biblical word over each flag, along with the following prayer: 'God sanctify our hearts to resist all evil and give us the wisdom and strength and good will to serve our *Volk* loyally, until he leads us through the night and into the light.'"[92] Perhaps even more striking, however, was the fact that the Protestant Weigel was invited to Munich to preside over a massive consecration ceremony for Nazi standards on 11 September 1926, embodying the spirit of warrior Christianity with a clear Protestant inflection.[93] The sermon delivered in Munich by Weigel, who was described as a heroic "priest and warrior who is German to the core," made fairly typical appeals to Nazi racial imagery and character-ized Christ in explicitly Germanic terms as a "German *Volkskönig*."[94] But perhaps the most significant aspect of this event is the fact that a Nazi ceremonial sermon of this nature—in Munich, of all places—would without question have been performed by a Catholic priest before the putsch, effectively illustrating how vastly different the religious identity of the movement was in the process of becoming.

The propagandistic activism of Bavarian Protestant pastors was ac-companied, perhaps not surprisingly, by numerous other indications of the movement's increased Protestant orientation. Protestant organiza-tions and events throughout Germany received generous publicity in the *Beobachter,* including especially the attempt to fuse Germanic identi-ty and Christianity that characterized the *völkisch* Deutschkirchliche Bewegung and the related Bund für Deutsche Kirche.[95] The latter group was praised effusively for proposing at the Protestant general synod of March 1926 that Protestant religious education for children consist entirely of German heroes and "prophets," who would replace the more traditional Christian figures.[96] Martin Luther was held up on countless occasions as the quintessential national and spiritual hero; Nazi activist Richard Dingeldey, for instance, delivered a standard speech on Luther's convictions to numerous Nazi gatherings in the fall of 1925, claiming that "the life of Luther is our goal."[97] Luther's attacks against the Catholic Church, including his flaming 1545 missive "Wider das Papsttum in Rom,"[98] were reprinted on numerous occasions in the *Beobachter.* This idealization of Luther was in contrast to the almost complete absence of positive imagery regarding Catholic historical fig-ures.[99]

The Shape of Things to Come: Political Religion and the New Nazi Trajectory after 1925

In addition to the initial shift away from Catholic imagery toward a more overt Protestant orientation, the refounded NSDAP began pio-neering new sacramental practices outside of any Christian frame of reference, fostering a performative secular cult built upon both the heroic blood-based martyr imagery attached to those who had died in the putsch and an increasingly messianic portrayal of Hitler that were mediated by a new set of Nazi-oriented sacramental symbols and objects of veneration. Numerous historians and scholars have focused on the pseudo-religious cult of aesthetics that fueled Nazi political spectacle during the Third Reich.[100] Others have documented the transformation in Hitler's self-perception from a "drummer" for the *völkisch* movement to the near-omnipotent Führer, a process that began perhaps in late 1922 and was accelerated greatly during Hitler's time in prison.[101] Importantly, both of these trajectories—the pseudo-religious symbolic aesthetic and the messianic Hitler cult—merged for the first time in the aftermath of the failed putsch and became increasingly visible in the early years of the refounded NSDAP. It was at this point in the mid-1920s that National Socialism was essentially transformed from a political movement that had initially pitched itself as both a defender and champion of (Catholic-inflected) Positive Christianity into something that can accurately be considered a political religion in its own right.

It is well known that the concept of Nazism as a political religion was pioneered most prominently by the philosopher and political scientist Eric Voegelin, who fled from the Nazis in 1938 and spent much of his career at Louisiana State University.[102] What is often overlooked, however, is the fact that Voegelin, whose anti-Nazi credentials are undisputed, built in part on the eccentric yet deeply insightful earlier analysis of an early NSDAP member who had soured on the movement by 1924: the sociologist and journalist Carl Christian Bry.[103] Bry, whose real name was Carl Decke, founded the Heimkehr Verlag in the Pasing section of Munich in 1919 and joined the NSDAP in January 1921, serving briefly on the staff of the *Beobachter* while also contributing numerous essays in 1922 and 1923 to Karl Muth's *Hochland,* particularly on the English Catholic convert G. K. Chesterton.[104] By 1924, Bry had become, like so many others in the aftermath of the putsch, a staunch critic of the Nazis, and his own personal experience and insights were central to his argument that the NSDAP was beginning to develop into a "disguised" (*verkappte*) religion.[105] That process, which began before the putsch, became increasingly unmistakable throughout the mid-1920s.

Shortly after his arrest in November 1923, Hitler had demonstrated an increasing obsession with justifying his "mission" (*Sendung*) in near-messianic terms before the "court of history."[106] Hitler's early biographer Georg Schott structured his 1924 account of Hitler's life around a set of messianic one-word headings—"Teacher," "Awakener," "Führer"—and focused especially on the image of Hitler as the "Liberator" who was destined to be embraced by "millions of Germans" in their "innermost hearts."[107] By 1926, the messianic imagery had become even more overt, as seen, for instance, in the striking Easter issue of the *Beobachter* that featured a massive idealized portrait of Hitler accompanied by the caption "Unsere Osterbotschaft."[108] Members of the Nazi youth organization were encouraged to express their personal "faith" in Hitler,

foreshadowing in certain ways the Hitler-centric children's prayers of the
1930s.[109] Other portrayals focused on the near-divine presence of the
"Spirit of Hitler" throughout the movement.[110] One particularly striking
devotional poem, written by Otto Bangert expressly as a prayer to Hitler
in July 1926, captures the essence of this growing messianic imagery,
referring to Hitler alternately as "Savior" (*Retter*) and "Master" (*Meister*)
and emphasizing the "holy" nature of the Nazis' political mission, with
Hitler's "spirit" illuminating the empty night:

> He rose up from the primeval depths
> To tower like a mountain.
> And as we languished in misery,
> Crying fearfully for a Savior,
> He began his great holy work.
>
> He stood with outstretched hands,
> Facing the downfall of an entire world.
> Desperation reverberated everywhere,
> But as if with hot brands of fire
> His spirit illuminated the desolate night.
>
> He points to the distant morning glow,
> And all our hearts are inflamed.
> Lift up our fists and our spirits—
> And build for your *Volk,* O Master,
> A new, elevated Fatherland![111]

This poem is also illustrative of the dramatic differences between the
nature of the refounded NSDAP and the more straightforward Christian appeal of the 1923 membership drive, which had publicized devotional prayers on behalf of—not to—Hitler. The powerful messianic cult
that later characterized the Third Reich was both foreshadowed and, in
practical terms, pioneered already within the refounded NSDAP, as the
more overtly Catholic nature of the Nazis' earlier liturgical appeals faded
increasingly into the background.

Bangert's poem appeared in conjunction with the first national party
rally since the refounding of the NSDAP, held in Weimar on 3–4 July
1926, which further accelerated the secular-liturgical trajectory. Rather
than featuring Christian imagery or religious reflections delivered by
clergy, the sacramental aspects of the Parteitag events were presided over
by Hitler, who gave a particularly striking sermon at the central flag
consecration ceremony.[112] The first part of his sermon focused on the

theme of spiritual resurrection, emphasizing the rebirth not only of the party but especially of the SA and its standards: "The old SA lives, its spirit has been resurrected.... We could never abandon this flag, not even if someone ripped out of our bodies these hearts of ours which are filled with rock-solid faith in the German resurrection!" Hitler then proceeded to explicitly theological reflections on the symbolism of the individual elements of the Nazi standard, with the colors—red, white, and black—symbolizing the concepts of social unity, nationalism, and the spirit of work, while the entire flag served a homiletic function, to "preach the spirit of the liberation struggle" to the rest of Germany. This initial focus on the spiritual symbolism of the flag was then elevated to overtly salvific dimensions through the sanctifying power of the blood shed by the Nazi martyrs of the putsch and preserved in the Blood Flag, the central object of Nazi veneration that was unveiled publicly at the 1926 party congress for the first time:

> Many have fallen and shed their blood for our standards, and this is what gives them a holy consecration. For the first time since 1923 our holy relic [*Heiligtum*], the Blood Flag, stands once again before the public. It was loyally protected after the November treason up until the resurrection of our organization. This flag, with the blood of a party comrade who fell as a martyr of the idea on 9 November 1923, will now be maintained by the most loyal group within the SA.[113]

That most loyal group within the SA was the young Schutzstaffel (SS), whose leader, Josef Berchtold, then received the Blood Flag from Hitler "with an oath of loyalty unto death" and proceeded to assist Hitler in the task of consecrating the new standards of SA groups from across Germany. The *Beobachter* emphasized the personal sacramental touch of Hitler's hand in solemnly blessing the new set of flags, which each SA chapter "received from Adolf Hitler's hand with a pledge of loyalty."[114] On a more general level, the sixteen Hitler followers who had been killed in the putsch were elevated to the position of secular saints, eternally occupying sacred positions within the Nazi pantheon (see fig. 5.2).[115]

The spectacle of the Blood Flag consecration, with its striking cult of heroic martyrdom and salvific commemoration, was then replicated in numerous Nazi ceremonies through the coming months.[116] The Blood Flag would remain after 1933 as the centerpiece of the growing Nazi arsenal of religiously inflected artifacts on display, particularly during the yearly Nuremberg rallies, which were designed to produce both a "mystical ecstasy" and a "holy mania" among the participants.[117]

Die Gefallenen vom 9. November 1923

Figure 5.2. Pantheon of Beerhall Putsch "martyrs."
Source: Sesselmann and Hoffmann, *Deutschlands Erwachen*.

Additionally, the Nazi architectural refashioning of Munich's Königs-platz in the 1930s, particularly the construction of the two *Ehrentempel* with eternal flames commemorating the sixteen putsch "martyrs," further demonstrates this trajectory. It is important to note that this pseudo-sacral performative experience did not emerge sui generis, but should be seen as a sort of distant echo of the liturgical performativity of the Catholic-oriented early movement, which had itself already been emptied of most of its overt Catholic content by the time of the 1926 Parteitag.[118]

Finally, it is interesting to observe the extent to which these various trajectories within the refounded NSDAP—the initial attempt to revive the movement's Catholic appeal, the subsequent shift toward a more overt Protestant orientation, and the growing (secular) cult of messianic heroism, martyrdom, and blood—were reflected in the shifting commemoration of Albert Leo Schlageter, who had served as the fairly straightforward embodiment of a powerful Catholic-Nazi synthesis in the summer of 1923. In May 1925, on the second anniversary of Schlageter's execution, the newly revived *Beobachter* allowed a Catholic CV student from Düsseldorf, Willi Hess, to publish a tribute that emphasized Schlageter's identity as a member of the CV.[119] By the next month, however, it was explicitly Protestant figures like pastor Hellmuth Johnsen and the lay Protestant Hans Severus Ziegler who were tapped to preside over official Nazi-sponsored Schlageter commemorations.[120] At the same time, the overtly anti-Christian Joseph Stolzing was commissioned to write the official *Beobachter* tribute to Schlageter on the second anniversary of his death, which made absolutely no mention of Schlageter's religious faith nor of his insistence on confessing and receiving communion before his execution, treating him instead as a secular warrior who had died in the mode of a heroic Nordic figure.[121] This pagan-oriented imagery was emphasized further by Adalbert Jakob, who removed all reference to Christian elements and lauded Schlageter as the incarnation of the spirit of Siegfried.[122] The Nazi-sponsored Schlageter commemorations of 1926 were even more pagan-oriented, with *Edda*-based comparisons to the betrayal of Baldur by the conniving Loki structuring much of the imagery.[123] Throughout 1926, paralleling trends within the Nazi movement more broadly, secular political messianism progressively engulfed the commemorative imagery related to Schlageter. One particularly striking account, entitled "Schlageter's Transfiguration," treated Schlageter as a secular Nazi saint who had gone to an essentially non-Christian Germanic afterlife to engage in combat against the Jewish forces arrayed around Moses and the treacherous Judas.[124] Similarly, when the Nazi group in Munich-Neuhausen staged a play about Schlageter's "martyrdom" in the fall of 1926, the imagery of secular sainthood was married to powerful messianic imagery surrounding Hitler, whose giant wall-sized portrait provided the striking backdrop to the play itself.[125]

As the 1920s progressed, both the original Catholic orientation of the NSDAP and the initial turn toward Protestant imagery within the refounded party were increasingly submerged in the rising tide of political messianism. The power of this pseudo-sacral cult is illustrated by the fact that its more overtly Catholic-oriented roots were largely forgotten by the time the Nazis came to power.[126] Ultimately, this secular-political religiosity overshadowed all future attempts to revive the earlier Catholic orientation.

By early 1928, when the refounded NSDAP was preparing to enter its first full-fledged campaign for the upcoming Reichstag elections, an anonymous pro-Nazi Catholic theologian writing under the pen name J. A. Kofler published a propaganda pamphlet with the Nazis' Eher Verlag that lamented the dramatic demise of the earlier Catholic-Nazi synthesis and noted the altered nature of the movement after the putsch: "The *völkisch*-German movement has suffered a terrible setback since 1923. Many [Catholics] who were once enthusiastic supporters now offer nothing but condemnation. Only a few selfless souls have remained loyal."[127] Kofler's pamphlet argued forcefully for the continued full compatibility between the Catholic faith and Nazi anti-Semitism, but in his call for a revival of Catholic support for the NSDAP, he remained essentially a voice in the wilderness, as the Nazis garnered very little support or even attention in Catholic regions in the May 1928 election, polling only 2.6 percent of the vote and gaining a grand total of 12 out of 491 seats in the Reichstag.[128] Kofler's missive was reprinted, however, in the context of the September 1930 elections, when the Nazis experienced their first electoral breakthrough, gaining 107 seats and more than 18 percent of the total vote to become the second largest party in the Reichstag.[129] By that point, Kofler's authoritative tone and confident handling of theological complexities were causing significant consternation in official Catholic circles throughout Germany, as numerous Catholic leaders scrambled, ultimately unsuccessfully, to ascertain the identity of the mysterious theologian.[130] As it turns out, Kofler was none other than the priest from Indersdorf, Josef Roth, and his propagandistic missive was but an expanded version of the *Katholizismus und Judenfrage* text that the young Roth had published in installments in the *Beobachter* and then in book form with the Eher Verlag in the context of the Catholic-oriented membership drive in the summer of 1923.[131] In the late 1920s, Roth was part of a small circle of pro-Nazi priests including most notably Alban Schachleiter, Philipp Haeuser, and Lorenz Pieper who had largely retreated from public engagement on behalf of the NSDAP after the putsch but had not given up either their idealization of Hitler personally or their broader hope that the Nazi movement might still one day bring about a national and spiritual rebirth.[132]

In the years leading up to Hitler's appointment as chancellor, while continuing his pastoral duties at Munich's St. Ursula, Roth wrote several anonymous articles in the *Beobachter* in addition to his pseudonymous Kofler text.[133] While at St. Ursula's, Roth not only remained close to Alban Schachleiter, inviting him to perform mass on numerous occasions, but also exercised a strong influence on two of his priestly colleagues in the parish, Peter Schmittinger and Bernhard Weinschenk, both of whom later sympathized openly with the NSDAP after 1933.[134] Schachleiter himself had continued for years to be incensed about the destructiveness of Ludendorff's anti-Catholic crusade in the aftermath of the putsch,[135] although he continued both to idealize Hitler personally and to sympathize with the NSDAP. After maintaining his weekly Schola Gregoriana at the Allerheiligen-Hofkirche in Munich until 1930,[136] Schachleiter moved at that point to a newly built country house in Bad Feilnbach owned by his close friends Gildis and Wilhelm Engelhard, where he was still living when Hitler came to power in 1933.[137] Lorenz Pieper, who moved back to Westphalia in October 1923, had continued to sympathize strongly with Hitler and the NSDAP both during and after the putsch, portraying Hitler's release from prison in December 1924 as a "Christmas gift from God" and staying in touch over the next several years with Schachleiter and Roth in particular.[138] Philipp Haeuser had been active primarily in the DNVP in the aftermath of the putsch, running as a DNVP candidate in the December 1924 Reichstag election.[139] However, he made headlines throughout Bavaria for his central participation in a Christmas celebration for the NSDAP in Augsburg on 14 December 1930. In the aftermath of the dramatic Nazi electoral success of September 1930, Haeuser's Christmas speech was perhaps the most widely covered attempt before 1933 to revive some semblance of the earlier Catholic-Nazi synthesis.[140] Such a revival was made much more difficult when the Bavarian bishops conference, in partial response to the publicity generated by Haeuser, issued a binding directive in February 1931 forbidding Catholic priests from participating in the Nazi movement in any capacity and prohibiting any attempt to revive the striking sacramental practices of the summer of 1923, when Nazi organizations had participated in countless Catholic field masses and when Nazi standards had been blessed openly by Catholic clergy.[141] A broader discussion stretched through much of 1931 and 1932 regarding the impossibility of ever reconciling the Catholic faith with the now-resurgent NSDAP, with a number of powerful and convincing works arguing that the Nazi movement had become, regardless of its earlier (pre-putsch) development and its continued claims to represent Positive Christianity, utterly incompatible with Catholicism.[142] This discourse was, in turn, shaped in large part by the continually evolving stance of the broader German episcopate, initiated by the Fulda bishops conference but involving also the Bavarian bishops, which issued a vague collective condemnation of Nazi radicalism in August 1931 and then, in August 1932, announced a much more specific and sweeping prohibition on Catholic membership in the NSDAP.[143]

Following Hitler's appointment as chancellor in January 1933, Roth and the circle of pro-Nazi priests trumpeted their own heroic loyalty for having maintained faith in Hitler and the NSDAP throughout the so-called wilderness years.[144] Even as they gazed into the promised land of Nazi governing power, however, they recognized the unlikelihood of ever reviving the more overt Catholic orientation that had characterized the early Nazi movement. When Haeuser wrote to his bishop in the spring of 1933 claiming vindication for the pro-Nazi activism for which he had been disciplined, he pointed openly to the loss of the Catholic-Nazi symbiosis that had been so visible a decade earlier and lamented: "If the priest from Strassberg had been heeded rather than slandered during these last ten years, then the [Nazi] movement would rest today in the hands of Catholics!" Even in the otherwise exuberant aftermath of the March 1933 elections, Haeuser could not hide his pessimistic grief regarding both the missed opportunities of the past and the dark prospect of a future Nazi state in danger of being shaped by non- (or anti-) Catholic influences: "It is too late, and we are now at the mercy of the bishops to determine whether something can still be salvaged and whether the pains that threaten to ensue can still be prevented."[145] Similarly, as Schachleiter wrote to Cardinal Faulhaber later that spring: "It seems to me to be a catastrophe that the Holy Church stands aloof from the new freedom movement, whose triumph I foresaw, and that the massive uprising of the *Volk*, which is now lifting our poor Fatherland out of its misery and shame, may well go down in history as a triumph of Protestantism."[146] Through the remainder of 1933 and well into 1934, there were numerous Catholic figures, including prominent theologians and influential laymen, who attempted to counteract increasingly visible anti-Catholic currents within the Nazi leadership, working as "bridge builders" (*Brückenbauer*) to identify commonalities between Catholicism and Nazism and to urge Catholics to participate centrally in forging the new Nazi state rather than risk the consequences of remaining passively on the sidelines.[147] The decision by the German bishops, made public on 28 March 1933, to lift the previous prohibitions on Catholic involvement in the NSDAP made the prospect of participation both more enticing and, at least temporarily, more realistic.[148] Despite the lifting of the bishops' ban, however, the pseudo-sacral spectacle of the Nazi aesthetic continued on its own trajectory, developing outside—and, in many ways, in clear contrast to—any Catholic or Christian framework, with the trappings of the more overt Catholic content of the early movement continuing only in residual form. And unlike 1923, when Catholic clergy had been central to the planning and mediation of the religious spectacles at the heart of the Nazi membership drive, none of the Catholic priests who emerged as *Brückenbauer* in 1933 were involved in any capacity in the staging of the Nazis' striking performative aesthetic.

The possibilities and limitations of these bridge-building endeavors are illustrated in interesting ways through the fate of Alban Schachleiter, who seemed to many to be in the best position of all pro-Nazi Catholic priests to exert a significant public influence after 1933.[149] Schachleiter had been instructed by the Ordinariat in Munich not to engage in pro-Nazi activism after the putsch, and as late as May 1932 he had trumpeted his continuing loyal obedience in a letter to General Vicar Hindringer, stating, "I have never written or had written on my behalf any article, report, notice or anything else of any kind in the *Völkischer Beobachter*— not one word, not one syllable."[150] However, immediately upon Hitler's appointment as chancellor on 30 January 1933, and well in advance of the bishops' lifting of the Nazi ban in late March, Schachleiter resumed energetic pro-Nazi activities, publishing a major manifesto in the *Beobachter* that appealed to "strict believing Catholics" and emphasized the need to revive Catholic participation in the NSDAP to prevent "the National Socialist freedom movement from being a purely Protestant endeavor" and to avoid "the horrors of a new Thirty Years' War."[151] Faulhaber responded on 3 February by forbidding Schachleiter from performing masses within the archdiocese, and Schachleiter issued a statement a few days later accepting the ecclesiastical censure.[152] Schachleiter complied with the spirit of this disciplinary measure even to the point of reluctantly refusing Hitler's request for him to come to Berlin on 20 March 1933 to perform a personal mass for the Führer.[153] When the

Figure 5.3. Alban Schachleiter (*front row, third from left*) at 1934
Nuremberg rally.
Source: Engelhard, *Schachleiter.*

personal censure remained intact even after the German bishops lifted the
ban on the NSDAP on 28 March 1933, Schachleiter was encouraged by the
fact that Nazi authorities on various levels intervened to get the censure
removed, and he was heartened also by Hitler's well-publicized visit in mid-
May to personally congratulate him on his fiftieth anniversary as a Benedictine, leading Schachleiter to believe that a revival of genuine collaboration between Nazism and Catholicism might indeed be possible in the
dawning Third Reich.[154] Schachleiter's invitation to sit among the Nazi
dignitaries at the Nuremberg party rally in 1934—which has provided, via
Leni Riefenstahl's *Triumph of the Will,* some of the most enduring images
of the Nazis' political religiosity in practice—helps to illustrate both
the illusion of influence and the reality of his complete lack of direct
involvement.[155] Whereas he had been centrally involved in shaping the
commemorative imagery surrounding Albert Leo Schlageter more than
a decade earlier, Schachleiter was now not only content, but indeed thrilled,
to sit—literally—on the sidelines as the Nazis' striking, yet thoroughly
secularized, performative aesthetic played out before him (see fig. 5.3).

It took Schachleiter until 1936 to admit (and then only privately) that his hopes had been dashed and that his vision of Catholic-Nazi cooperation had likely been unrealistic from the outset of the Third Reich. Over the previous three years, much of his energy had been consumed in a campaign against what he saw as inauthentic attempts by peripheral Nazi leaders to hijack the party and lead it in a direction that was both anti-Catholic and anti-Christian more generally. The primary goal of Schachleiter's campaign had been to get Hitler to publicly disavow the (anti-Christian) ideology represented in Alfred Rosenberg's *Mythus des 20. Jahrhunderts,* which Schachleiter believed was the central impediment to a renewal of wide-ranging Catholic support for the NSDAP.[156] In an attempt to drive a wedge between Rosenberg's ideas and the official stance of the party, Schachleiter eventually wrote more than two dozen appeals to a variety of Nazi officials—most notably to Hans Lammers, the head of the Reichskanzlei—and was politely rebuffed (or ignored) on every occasion.[157] By the last year of his life, Schachleiter had resigned himself to the fact that a genuine marriage between Catholicism and Nazism was no longer possible, admitting privately to a friend in September 1936 that "a believing Christian can no longer participate [in the NSDAP]; they do not want believing Christians in the party."[158] Publicly, however, Schachleiter continued to profess his loyalty both to the Führer and to the church.[159] Following the abbot's death in June 1937, Nazi authorities made an initial show of support and reverence, ordering a moderately expensive state funeral arranged by Bavarian minister-president Ludwig Siebert.[160] At the same time, the fact that Hitler declined to attend the funeral and the further circumstance that Schachleiter's grave was soon severely neglected and overgrown despite an initial pledge of state provisions for its upkeep indicate how marginal Schachleiter, and his vision of a renewed Catholic-Nazi synthesis, had become.[161] On the one-year anniversary of Schachleiter's death, the editorial leadership of the *Beobachter,* under Josef Berchtold, refused all attempts to publish official commemorations honoring Schachleiter for the explicit reason that discussions of the "relationship between Christianity and National Socialism"—whose fruitful coexistence had been championed so energetically by Schachleiter—were "not desirable in any form at present."[162]

The dramatically altered religious identity of the NSDAP after 1933 can be further traced in the continually evolving imagery surrounding Albert Leo Schlageter. After the refounding of the NSDAP in 1925, Schlageter's image became increasingly contested, as his CV fraternity brothers continued over the ensuing years to commemorate his heroic

Catholic faith while Nazi and *völkisch* portrayals foregrounded secular or pagan-oriented imagery.[163] The contrast between these two trajectories was accentuated greatly in the spring of 1933, as preparations for the tenth anniversary of Schlageter's death were initiated. In the midst of the nationalist groundswell that accompanied the March 1933 election, the CV was quick to perceive in the image of Schlageter an opportunity to claim superiority over other student groups attempting to accommodate themselves to the realities of the new Germany. The April 1933 issue of the CV's official paper, *Academia,* celebrated the bishops' recent decision to rescind the prohibition against Catholic membership in the NSDAP, and each of the ensuing monthly issues through the remainder of 1933 contained ostentatious celebrations of the life and death of Schlageter, portraying him as the heroic incarnation of the harmony that was, it was alleged, still possible between Catholicism and Nazism.[164] This spirit infused the words of Alban Schachleiter, who spoke at a Nazi commemoration for Schlageter in the Trudering section of Munich on 25 May 1933, as he utilized Schlageter's image as a central component in his vision of a revived Catholic-Nazi collaboration, an image he had initially helped to fashion in the striking St. Boniface mass a decade earlier (see fig. 5.4).[165]

Although the covers of the *Academia* issues celebrating Schlageter had featured a large swastika throughout much of 1933, by January 1934 the swastika was removed completely and replaced by a simple Christian cross, as optimism regarding the possibility of genuine Catholic-Nazi cooperation waned. That same month, under pressure from the Nazi leadership of the Deutsche Studentenschaft, the CV was forced to disavow its Catholic identity entirely, and the emasculated fraternity federation limped along without much purpose or enthusiasm until it was dissolved entirely the following year.[166] Deeply disillusioned, CV leader Fritz Berthold informed Schachleiter of the deconfessionalization of the CV, seething with anger at the growing anti-Catholic currents within the Nazi leadership even as he nostalgically longed for the days before the putsch, when "Catholic students were the pioneers of National Socialism [*Vorkämpfer des Nationalsozialismus*]."[167] Once held up as paragons of the Nazi spirit of Positive Christianity, Catholic students were now forced to strip themselves of their overt Catholic identities in order to comply with the imperatives of the Third Reich.

Similarly, Catholic-oriented dramatists had initially seized optimistically on the image of Schlageter in early 1933, emphasizing his Catholic faith while blending it with explicitly Nazi imagery. But here as well, the

Figure 5.4. Alban Schachleiter at Schlageter ceremony (1933).
Source: Engelhard, *Schachleiter*.

secular-messianic current was too powerful to swim against. A striking example is provided by the hagiographic novel of the Catholic author Felix Nabor, which discussed in great detail Schlageter's early desire to enter the Catholic priesthood and his membership in the CV as a student.[168] In dramatizing Schlageter's decision to join the NSDAP in 1922, Nabor fused Schlageter's devotion to the Christian cross with his newfound love for the swastika, as his Catholic piety came to fuel his

Nazi activism.[169] The scene of the execution near Düsseldorf fore-grounded Schlageter's desire for Catholic confession and communion while intermingling imagery of him as a first-century Christian martyr and as a transfigured Nazi messianic figure in his own right.[170] Before the shots of the firing squad rang out, Schlageter was fashioned finally into the physical tapestry in which the heroic symbolism of the crucifix and the swastika, which his captors had forced him to remove, were seamlessly woven together: "With a quick movement Leo stuck the crucifix between the top two buttons of his vest, where once the swasti-ka—the cross of this world, of his *Volk*—had had its place. Now his breast was adorned with the cross of Heaven, the symbol of God, and it is under this symbol that he died."[171]

Despite Nabor's efforts to construct a harmonious interweaving of Catholic and Nazi symbols, the swastika ultimately came to displace the crucifix. Nazi idealizations of Schlageter after 1933 almost invariably either downplayed or completely omitted his Catholic identity, and these images quickly overshadowed all others.[172] By the fall of 1936, the overtly anti-Christian Nazi magazine *Durchbruch* was able to proclaim triumphantly that Schlageter's image had finally been rescued from the sinister Catholic attempt to "unjustly characterize him as Christian or Catholic," when in reality Schlageter was a "German hero" who "derived his courage not from the church and its teaching but rather from the harmony of a biological-racial world view."[173] Believing Catho-lics also began distancing themselves from Schlageter, whose image had effectively become so "Nazified" as to lose any alternative meaning or significance. In early 1937, angered by the bombastic *Durchbruch* article, Cardinal Faulhaber wrote to Hermann Fassbender, the priest who had given Schlageter his final communion, admitting that Schlageter's Nazi identity while alive was indeed deeply problematic yet refusing to abandon the Catholic significance of Schlageter's inspirational death: "A Catholic author recently explained to me that he would now refuse to write about Schlageter, during his life, as a Catholic hero. But in his death he was in every way a Catholic hero and, as such, we cannot allow him to be stolen away from us!"[174]

At the time of its triumphal anti-Catholic Schlageter article, the editor of *Durchbruch* was none other than Alfred Miller, who had begun his career as an idealistic member of the Catholic Hochland fraternity championing the Catholic Nazi cause in the pages of the *Beobachter*. The contrast between the early 1920s and the mid-1930s could not have been clearer.

Conclusion

Catholic identity is not dependent upon statistics. Neither can it be equated simply with orthodoxy.

—Pope Benedict XVI, 17 April 2008

When Pope Benedict XVI visited the United States in the spring of 2008, he attempted to articulate his vision of Catholic identity within the particular context of American university culture and its pursuit of academic freedom. While this pope cannot be accused in any way of being soft on the question of theological orthodoxy, his statements point to the important fact that defining Catholic "identity" is often anything but a straightforward process, despite the ostensibly clear-cut hierarchical nature of the church and its authority structures. What entitles a Catholic university to lay claim to Catholic identity, the pontiff asked, and what does it mean more generally to be a Catholic in an American university setting, particularly in the twenty-first century?[1] Without question, temporal and geographic contexts matter a great deal. Given the pope's own personal biography, one wonders similarly what it meant for the young Joseph Ratzinger to be a Bavarian Catholic nearing university age during the waning days of the Third Reich, as the Nazis' once seemingly invincible secular-messianic facade was crumbling?[2] What, for that matter, did this same question mean more than two decades earlier for Catholic university students—or Catholics more generally—in Munich in the immediate aftermath of the First World War? If, as Pope Benedict hinted, neither statistics nor orthodoxy are the sole measures of "authentic" Catholic identity, how should one go about the task of assessing the religious identity of the early Nazi movement, particularly in light of the later (anti-Catholic) nature of the Third Reich? And what should one make of the often unorthodox religious ideas of many professing Catholics within the early NSDAP?

Despite the profusion of works on broader issues of identity and identity politics, the study of religious identity—and particularly

Catholic identity—is still in its infancy in many ways.[3] In his landmark 1987 presidential address to the Society for the Scientific Study of Religion, Phillip Hammond differentiated between religious identity in the premodern context, which he characterized as "collective-expressive" and therefore essentially involuntary, and in the modern era, in which religious identity emerges primarily as a result of choice and voluntary self-identification.[4] This is not to say that, when applied to the study of Catholicism, religious identity is completely fungible or that church teaching and orthodox theology are in any way unimportant in the forging and definition of Catholic identity, but merely that authority and orthodoxy should not necessarily be seen as all-encompassing or exclusively hegemonic. At any given time, the authoritative teachings of the church may (or may not) be both clearly articulated and broadly perceived as such, but in analytical terms those teachings cannot be considered entirely coterminous with Catholic identity, which instead is forged in practice through a complex series of negotiations on both personal and collective levels. This perspective seems much more applicable after the pivotal Second Vatican Council, to be sure, but it must also be taken into account in examinations of earlier periods.[5] This negotiated relationship among the church's teachings, its official hierarchy and structures, and individual Catholics is a relationship that needs to be continually examined and problematized, with close attention given to temporal and geographic specificity.[6]

By contrast, historical approaches to the relationship between Catholicism and Nazism have typically subsumed the issue of religious identity within a blanket equation linking Catholic authenticity to the perceived nature of the Catholic milieu and the support for ultramontanism and political Catholicism that underpinned it. The early Nazi movement could not have had genuine Catholic support, the common argument runs, since "authentic" Catholics supported the Center Party and BVP. The present work has argued that this equation is a poor starting point for understanding the Catholic-Nazi relationship. But even if we accept that Catholic identity should not be viewed merely through the prism of Center Party or BVP support, does that mean that Catholic identity could ever, in actuality, be brought into true harmony with Nazi ideology? Or should historians now, in retrospect, agree with the Nazis' opponents in the BVP who argued, often for their own self-interested reasons, that Catholic supporters of the NSDAP had forfeited their legitimacy as Catholics? What if respected priests were openly advocating the virtues of the Nazis' brand of Positive Christianity? And what if, in the earliest years, there were no official ecclesiastical directives regarding the Nazi phenomenon to be obeyed or, as the case may be, disobeyed?

Beyond the need to pay attention to temporal and geographic specificity, a distinction between "internal-ideal" and "external-historical" categories of analysis can be of use in sorting out the complexities of Catholic-Nazi identity in and around Munich.[7] On the most general level, an internal-ideal approach would explore religious identity primarily in terms of putative authenticity and orthodoxy; that identity would be perceived as objective and timeless despite the reality of being interpreted, of necessity, within the subjective temporal and ideational context of the observer. Thus, an ideological position seen as contravening church teaching could be dismissed as inauthentic in a fairly straightforward sense, regardless of the very real differences that may separate the context of the observer from the period and locale under examination.[8] On the other hand, an external-historical approach would focus not so much on the perception of "timeless" internal authenticity as on the reality—or, at the very least, the plausibility—of public attribution, recognition, and classification of religious identity within a temporally specific context. For example, the brutality of the inquisitorial extermination launched against the medieval Cathars would have to be considered incompatible today with virtually any conceivable internal-ideal definition of Catholic-Christian theology or orthodoxy. In an external-historical sense, however, it is an undeniable fact that the persecution was undertaken by figures laying plausible claim to Catholic-Christian identity within that temporally specific context, and it would be historically inaccurate to characterize them otherwise. It is possible, indeed necessary, to deplore the tragic and errant nature of inquisitorial zeal in thirteenth-century southern France while also recognizing its problematic, yet nonetheless real, contextual Christian legitimacy.

In striving to characterize accurately the activities of early Nazi Catholics in and around Munich, the distinction between the internal-ideal and external-historical perspectives helps to navigate around a central conundrum: avoiding the appearance of indicting Catholicism (as an institutional entity or in ideational terms) for the tragic excesses of the Nazis while at the same time recognizing the important and very real role played by Nazi Catholic clergy and laypeople who, acting as Catholics and in pursuit of what they perceived to be a legitimate form of Catholic identity, were indeed central to the stabilization and spread of the early Nazi movement. Although the pronounced anti-ultramontanism and often bizarre theological eccentricities of certain early Nazi lay Catholics—Schrönghamer and Eckart are good examples—would make their religious identities problematic in an internal-ideal sense, it would also be inaccurate to discount summarily, in the scholarly pursuit of retroactively debunking the Nazis' putatively obfuscatory religious facade, the vehement professions of Catholic identity made by such influential early Nazis, which were widely perceived as authentic at the time. It seems important both to maintain a skeptical and critical perspective on Nazi professions and utterances and to take them seriously enough to recognize their potential effectiveness within their specific contemporary context.[9]

A good case in point is the issue of Nazi racial anti-Semitism, which has been condemned as un-Christian from a variety of theological positions.[10] In an internal-ideal sense and from the perspective of the present day, this characterization is convincing, since full-blown racial anti-Semitism ultimately denies the unity of humanity and thus the possibility of redemption through the figure of Jesus Christ. In an external-historical sense, however, the issue is not so straightforward. Building on existing prejudices in and around Munich and in the radicalized context of the immediate aftermath of the First World War, figures within the early Nazi movement drew largely on New Testament imagery—framing the *Judenfrage* in terms of a Catholic-oriented religious crusade akin to Christ's driving of the money-changers out of the temple—and thus condemned Jewish "immorality" as being rooted ultimately in Jewish blood and in the racial identity of the Jews as a *Volk*. In other words, implicit in the New Testament antipathy toward the Jews was a sort of proto-racial sensibility—the notion that God had rejected and condemned the Jews specifically as a race and not merely as individuals. Within the early movement, when Nazi ideology was still fluid, the logical conclusions of racial anti-Semitism could thus remain at least partially obscured, particularly when shrouded in New Testament moral imagery and when articulated by clerical spokesmen like Josef Roth or Lorenz Pieper. Later, as Nazi ideology crystallized and assumed increasingly all-encompassing dimensions, the religious-oriented proto-racial approach was supplanted by a purer, more overtly secular form of racial anti-Semitism.[11] At that point, especially in light of the official ecclesiastical condemnations of the early 1930s, the mutual exclusivity of the Catholic and Nazi world views came into clearer focus, even if the dichotomy was denied for as long as possible by *Brückenbauer* like Alban Schachleiter.[12]

Similarly, in order to make sense of the religious identity of leading Nazis like Hitler, an external-historical approach that pays attention to temporal specificity can be helpful. In the late 1960s, the brilliant (if idiosyncratic) Austrian historian Friedrich Heer put forward an insightful and controversial sketch of what he called Hitler's "political religiosity," arguing against the grain of conventional wisdom that Hitler's religious identity and Catholic background were worthy of examination and should be taken seriously on at least a basic level.[13] Subsequent historiographic interpretations, however, have been much more dismissive of Hitler's Catholic background, concluding almost invariably that Hitler completely abandoned at a very early age the faith in which he was raised and that he maintained a consistent and thorough aversion to all forms of Christianity throughout the entirety of his political career.[14] This interpretive line of argumentation—that Hitler's personal rejection of both Catholicism and Christianity was deep and essentially unchanging from early adulthood through the time of his death—is typically supported by reference to rumors that Hitler had desecrated the eucharistic host as a child by spitting it out and stuffing it into his pocket;[15] by statements from Hitler's acquaintances from childhood and from before the First World War claiming that Hitler expressed distaste and open contempt for Christianity;[16] and, most notably, by his private ruminations once in power, whether in the form of 1933 comments reported famously by Hermann Rauschning and others or in the anti-Christian tone of many of Hitler's so-called table talks in the early 1940s.[17] While there is little doubt that Hitler was a staunch opponent of Christianity throughout the duration of the Third Reich, I would caution against viewing Hitler's religious identity in static terms. Rather, it seems to me that Hitler's religious stance underwent a significant evolution over time, particularly in an external-historical sense but quite possibly internally as well. Before the Beerhall Putsch, Hitler made public statements of devotion to his "Lord and Savior" that would never have been made—either publicly or privately—at a later date. In the context of his 1924 trial, his identity as a believing Catholic was still (at the very least) eminently plausible, and it should be noted that all rumors and reports of Hitler's scandalous aversion to Christianity, including the host desecration rumor, were publicized without exception *after* the putsch and would almost certainly not have been accorded public plausibility if they had been circulated in Munich earlier. At the same time, a shift is already visible in the pages of *Mein Kampf* away from energetic and open advocacy to a much more subdued tolerance of Christianity, a respect for the institutional strength of the Catholic Church, and a practical desire to avoid interconfessional squabbles within the movement. It seems to me that the dramatic transformation in Hitler's self-perception—from drummer boy before the putsch to messianic Führer figure after his release from prison—brought with it important consequences for Hitler's religious identity, as he came to see his political mission in increasingly all-encompassing messianic terms. When coupled with the striking secular-political religiosity that characterized the performative cult surrounding the martyrs of the Beerhall Putsch and the veneration of the Blood Flag, there was ultimately little or no room within the Nazi ideological universe for any "genuine" (internal-ideal or external-historical) Catholic or Christian substance during Hitler's tenure in power.

This leads, finally, to the question of the broader significance of the religious identity of the early Nazi movement. If the Third Reich can be characterized as generally anti-Catholic and perhaps overtly anti-Christian, then why bother with the role of religion in the early movement? If the full-blown Nazi and Catholic world views were in many ways incompatible and if Catholicism, broadly construed, did not play a central role in somehow creating or directly shaping Nazi ideology, then of what importance are the earliest years of the NSDAP? In addition to reasons of historical curiosity, it seems to me a fruitful endeavor in and of itself to continually rethink and reexamine the immediate roots of Nazism on at least two levels: first, in terms of the early movement's survival during its vulnerable infancy; and second, in regard to the origins of the performative political religion that later characterized the Third Reich. Numerous historical studies have already focused on Nazism's longer-term ideational roots, examining individual figures, movements, and intellectual currents—ranging from race theories to Social Darwinism to national syndicalism—that can be seen in various ways as precursors to National Socialism or the fascist mindset.[18] Similarly, broader continuities have been sought in examinations of the twists and turns taken by the so-called German *Sonderweg*.[19] Much less attention has been given, however, to the continuities between the prewar and interwar periods specifically with regard to Munich. What attention that existing works have devoted to these local continuities has focused primarily on Hitler's brief contact with the dark underbelly of Munich's bohemian Schwabing culture before the war or on small esoteric and racist cell groups like the Germanenorden or the Thule-Gesellschaft.[20] In light of the marginal connections both between Hitler and prewar Schwabing culture and between the Thule-Gesellschaft and the early (NS)DAP, this volume's examination of the issue of religious identity has been an attempt to illuminate a less recognized, yet undeniably significant, aspect of the local context within which the Nazi "roots" dug in and proliferated.

The movement's ability to survive its infancy in the tumultuous atmosphere of Munich's *völkisch* milieu was directly related to Hitler's skill as an organizer and speaker, to be sure, but one should not overlook the importance of the NSDAP's early Catholic orientation in helping to stabilize the movement in its earliest and most vulnerable years. Building on the distinctive tradition of Catholic anti-ultramontanism and opposition to political Catholicism in Munich, the party was able to skillfully deploy the interconfessional ideal of Positive Christianity within an overwhelmingly Catholic context. It embraced the principle of religious Catholicism and thus distinguished itself from other *völkisch* groups, pitching itself ultimately as the most viable option for *völkisch*-oriented Catholics in Munich. The liturgical performativity of the early Catholic-Nazi events, such as Schachleiter's ceremony for Schlageter or Josef Roth's sermon at the Deutscher Tag in Nuremberg, was striking. The subsequent flood of anti-Catholic venom that flowed in the wake of the failed putsch drove large numbers of believing Catholics out of the movement and led many of those who remained to essentially sacrifice their Catholic identities. But although the movement was emptied of much of the straightforward Catholic content of its early years, it ultimately maintained many of the external liturgical trappings. After the refounding of the NSDAP in early 1925, a religious impulse unquestionably remained, finding expression first in an attempt to regain Catholic support in Munich, then adopting a more Protestant-inflected public face as the party spread throughout the Protestant Franconian regions, and finally coalescing around the striking imagery of secular martyr-saints and objects of veneration like the Blood Flag.[21] This pseudo-sacral trajectory should be seen in many ways as an offshoot or by-product, however hollow and indistinct, of the earlier liturgical performativity of the young Catholic-oriented movement.[22] Ultimately, despite attempts by the so-called *Brückenbauer* in the 1930s to revive the earlier Catholic-Nazi synthesis, the current of secular messianism—which had been born in the context of the putsch and accelerated in the ensuing years—proved too strong to overcome, eventually burying even the existence of the movement's early Catholic orientation beneath the waves of an all-encompassing party mythology.

It was into this figurative black hole that Franz Schrönghamer-Heimdal's *Das kommende Reich,* and the broader Catholic-*völkisch* activism it represented, disappeared after it arrived at Nazi party headquarters in the fall of 1933. After riding out the Nazi era in relative obscurity in the Passau area, Schrönghamer managed after the Second

World War, with the energetic complicity of local Catholic elites, to obfuscate his role in the early Nazi movement almost completely. At that point, the unceremonious burial of his early *völkisch* activism by Nazi leaders worked clearly to his advantage. In his brief trial in June 1948, Schrönghamer's legal defender admitted his client's early Nazi involvement but differentiated strongly between the Catholic-oriented early Nazi movement and the murderous Third Reich: "The first NSDAP was dissolved on 9 November 1923 and refounded in 1925. The accused [Schrönghamer] insists reliably that he had nothing more to do with the party . . . after 1923." In discussing Schrönghamer's continued marginalization during the Third Reich, the defense emphasized his impeccable Catholic credentials in the Passau area and throughout Bavaria, thereby drawing on the widely accepted image of incompatibility between Nazism and Catholicism: "The accused was from 1933 on the editor of the *Altöttinger Liebfrauenboten,* a well-known Catholic Sunday paper that was under the official ecclesiastical supervision of the Passau cathedral chapter."[23] Schrönghamer was, predictably, acquitted and three years later, in 1951, was proclaimed an honored citizen of the city of Passau by Mayor Stephan Billinger.[24] Largely cleansed of the stains of his fanatical anti-Semitic activism in the 1920s by his omission from the Nazis' mythology in the 1930s, Schrönghamer lived out the rest of his days as a local Catholic celebrity, receiving numerous commendations from the diocese of Passau and continuing to write folksy stories and poems until his death; he was never forced publicly to confront his role in the early Nazi movement.[25] Coincidentally, at the time of Schrönghamer's death in September 1962, preparations were in full swing for the opening of the Second Vatican Council in Rome, which convened in October 1962 and was infused in many ways by the same reformist impulses that had shaped the prewar Reform Catholic movement in Munich.[26] While it would be inaccurate to draw any kind of direct relationship between the irenic theological openness of the 1960s and the religious Catholicism espoused by early Nazis—such an examination would, in any case, vastly exceed the boundaries of the present study—it is nonetheless interesting to note the extent to which the discarding of the Nazis' early Catholic orientation allowed the trajectory of prewar reformist Catholicism to emerge almost miraculously unblemished after 1945, its exculpatory narrative having been largely written and disseminated by the (anti-Catholic) Nazi mythologizers themselves.

In any event, as Schrönghamer and countless other Catholics were drifting increasingly away from the movement in the mid-1920s, it seems that Hitler sensed the momentous nature of the changes already under way then, during the so-called wilderness years, even as he simultaneously claimed to lament the loss of the Catholic orientation of the early movement. In an important passage from the second volume of *Mein Kampf,* published in 1926, he pointed bitterly to the anti-Catholic crusade of Ludendorff and his followers after the putsch as an unmistakable and tragic caesura, which Hitler claimed had destructively "torn open the *völkisch* movement." In pledging to steer the NSDAP clear of such errors in the future, Hitler went on nostalgically to reminisce about the party's religious stance in the days before coming under the increased influence of Ludendorff in the fall of 1923:

> It will always be the supreme duty of the leadership of the National Socialist movement to offer the keenest opposition to any attempt to put the movement at the disposal of such [confessional] fights, and instantly to drive the propagators of such a scheme from the ranks of the movement. And, in fact, down to the autumn of 1923 this was thoroughly done. The most believing Protestant could stand in the ranks of our movement next to the most believing Catholic, without either [one of them] having to come into the slightest conflict of conscience with his religious convictions. . . . And this notwithstanding the fact that, in those very years, the movement fought most bitterly against the Center Party, not of course on religious grounds, but exclusively on questions of national, racial, and economic policy. Success proved us right then, just as today it proves the know-it-alls wrong.[27]

Of course, the truth was that it was Hitler's own decision to join the Kampfbund in September 1923 which, in sacrificing the organizational independence of the NSDAP on the altar of a vain and premature attempt to seize power, had opened the party to the increased influence of Ludendorff and his anti-Catholic followers, and was ultimately most responsible for the movement's loss of Catholic support in Munich. And while Hitler would cling doggedly to the claim that Munich would forever remain the *Hauptstadt der Bewegung,* it was increasingly clear that this early support would never be fully recovered. The space that had previously existed within which Nazi and Catholic identities could peacefully and fruitfully cohabit had essentially disappeared in the flood of anti-Catholic invective that washed over the fractured movement in the wake of the failed putsch, an early victim of Hitler's already massive—and increasingly messianic—political ambition.

Notes

Introduction

1. Schrönghamer, *Reich* (1933), 247–48, 261–62. The 1918 original was published by Haas & Grabherr in Augsburg.

2. Inscription dated 28 Oct 1933; see also Gassert and Mattern, *Hitler Library,* 396.

3. Schrönghamer's member number was 722, and Hitler's was 555; the tiny party, of course, began numbering at 500 to make its membership seem larger.

4. Even Richard Steigmann-Gall, who has argued that Nazism should be seen as a broadly Christian phenomenon, emphasizes the overwhelmingly Protestant (and anti-Catholic) orientation of pro-Christian Nazi rhetoric during the Third Reich; see his *Holy Reich.*

5. There are numerous examples of the retroactive Nazi falsification of the party's early history, as seen, for example, in the 1940 conflict between Anton Drexler and the Nazi leadership over the deliberate marginalization of Drexler's early influence; see Phelps, "Arbeiterpartei," 891; and the materials in NSDAP/HA-R3, fols. 77–78. Also, more generally, Bräuninger, *Kontrahenten,* 19–37.

6. Schrönghamer managed to exculpate himself almost completely by the late 1940s; he was acquitted in his *Spruchkammerverfahren* before Allied authorities in June 1948 and then was proclaimed an honored citizen of the city of Passau in 1951. See the Spruchkammer Passau report, 15 June 1948, and Beschluss aus der Stadtratssitzung, 28 June 1951, Schrönghamer papers, StAP, sch. 11. He lived out his days as a Bavarian Catholic celebrity, writing fiction and poetry and receiving numerous commendations from the diocese of Passau up until his death in 1962.

7. Kohn, *Roots;* Butler, *Roots;* Stern, *Despair;* Mosse, *Origins;* also see Glaser, *Roots.*

8. Gasman, *Origins;* Weikart, *Darwin;* Goodrick-Clarke, *Occult;* Goodrick-Clarke, *Black Sun;* Poewe, *New Religions;* Vieler, *Roots.*

9. Parsons, "Structure"; Moore, *Origins;* Abel, *Movement;* Brustein, *Origins.* For a Marxist-structuralist perspective, see Neumann's masterful *Behemoth.*

10. Franz-Willing, "Munich," 319–34; Franz-Willing, *Ursprung;* Maser, *Frühgeschichte;* also Auerbach, "Lehrjahre," 1–45.

11. Orlow, *Nazi Party;* Bracher, *Diktatur;* Schulz, *Aufstieg;* Fischer, *Rise;* Benz, *Geschichte;* Evans, *Coming;* Piper, *Kurze Geschichte.*

12. The best biographical accounts remain Fest, *Hitler;* and Kershaw, *Hubris.* Two outstanding studies that also shed broader light on Munich are Joachimsthaler, *Hitlers Weg;* and Tyrell, *Trommler.*

13. Kellogg, *Russian Roots;* Lohalm, *Radikalismus;* Horn, *Parteiorganisation;* McKale, *Courts;* Waite, *Vanguard;* Jones, *Freikorps.*

14. For useful portraits of pre-1923 Nazi developments in Munich, see Large, *Ghosts,* chaps. 4–5; Prinz and Mensing, *Irrlicht;* Bauer, *München.* The two most impressive studies dealing with the rise of the movement in its Munich-based and broader Bavarian context (Pridham, *Hitler's Rise;* and Rösch, *NSDAP*) begin explicitly after the Beerhall Putsch of 1923. Of the monographs on the putsch itself, the best is still Gordon, *Putsch.* Exemplary regional studies that do begin before 1923, albeit outside the realm of Munich, include Wagner, *Passau;* Albrecht, *Coburger NSDAP;* McElligott, *Altona;* Möller, *Region;* Paul, *NSDAP;* Franke, *Düsseldorf;* Krause, *Hamburg;* Koshar, *Marburg;* Reiche, *Nürnberg;* Heinacher, *Flensburg;* Grill, *Baden;* Behrend, *Beziehungen;* Bohnke, *Ruhrgebiet;* Schön, *Hessen;* Noakes, *Saxony;* Jochmann, *Hamburg.*

15. For the most comprehensive early membership lists, see NSDAP-HA R10, fol. 215; R2a, fol. 230; R8, fol. 171. See also Kater, "Soziographie," 124–59; Kater, *Party;* Orlow, "Organizational History," 208–26; Douglas, "Parent Cell," 55–72; Madden, "Characteristics," 34–56; Schieder, "NSDAP vor 1933," 141–53; Mühlberger, *Social Bases;* also Genuneit, "Probleme," 34–66, on the general difficulties involved in any statistical-demographic approach to the early Nazi membership.

16. The Zentralkartei (BDC, ser. A3340-MFKL) and the Ortskartei (BDC, ser. A3340-MFOK) typically contain no confessional identification at all, and while the SA files (BDC, ser. A3341-SA), the SS files (BDC, ser. A3343-SSO), and the Party Correspondence Files (BDC, ser. A3341-PK) do frequently contain information on religious affiliation—as does the extensive 1939 Party Census—all of that material dates invariably from the 1925 refounding of the party or later. Similarly, the multivolume *Partei-Statistik* (Munich, 1935) contains information only on those members who joined after 1925.

17. Lewy, *Church,* 7; also Morsey, "Volksminderheit," 9–24.

18. Mensing, "Münchener Protestantismus," 424. Mensing's broader work on the Protestant clergy in Bavaria, however, admits that it is difficult to identify the participation of Protestants (especially clergy) in the Nazi movement before 1925; Mensing, *Pfarrer,* 92.

19. The "church struggle," as the conflict between the Nazi regime and the Christian churches was identified at the time, quickly generated a substantial literature. See Lepier, *Struggle;* Schuster, *Army;* Means, *Conflict;* Untermeyer, *Destruction;* Gurian, *Hitler;* Kraft, *Christ versus Hitler;* Frey, *Cross;* Duncan-Jones, *Struggle;* Micklem, *Church;* Buxton, *Christendom;* Marinoff, *Heresy;* Herman, *Souls;* Carmer, *War.*

20. Neuhäusler, *Kreuz;* Preysing, *Kampf;* also Muckermann, *Widerstandsbewegung;* Portmann, *Galen;* Strobel, *Bewährung;* Hoffmann, *Schlaglichter;* Carsten, *Aktenstücke;* Kuehn, *Blutzeugen;* Adolph, *Schatten.*

21. See the famous blue-bound series of the Kommission für Zeitgeschichte, which was inaugurated in 1965 by the Catholic publishing house of Grünewald in Mainz and continues to be published by the Schöningh Verlag in Paderborn; also the publications of the Görres-Gesellschaft, such as *HJ.*

22. The critical reevaluation of the Catholic-Nazi relationship began in earnest with Böckenförde, "Katholizismus," 215–39. See also Lewy, *Church;* Amery, *Kapitulation;* Zahn, *Catholics;* Breuning, *Vision.* Debate on the role of Pius XII first reached a wide public with Hochhuth, *Stellvertreter.* For a more sympathetic interpretation, see Conway, *Persecution;* Scholder, *Kirchen;* Helmreich, *Churches;* Dietrich, *Citizens.*

23. Denzler, *Anpassung;* Denzler and Fabricius, *Kirchen;* Faber, "Politischer Katholizismus," 136–58; Faber, *Lateinischer Faschismus.* In contrast, see the skillful apologetic approach of Hürten, *Katholiken,* esp. 342–61.

24. Goldhagen, *Reckoning.* In addition to the oversimplistic nature of Goldhagen's ruminations, the accusatory literature occasionally reached near-comic proportions, as in the deeply flawed broadside by Cornwell, *Hitler's Pope.* But see also the more nuanced and balanced, if no less devastating, findings of Zuccotti, *Windows;* Carroll, *Sword;* Godman, *Vatican;* Rittner and Roth, *Pius XII.* For exculpatory approaches, see Dalin, *Myth;* McInerney, *Defamation.* By far the best and most thoughtful treatment of this thorny topic is the outstanding study by Phayer, *Church.*

25. Griech-Polelle skillfully examines the complicated identity of one of the most iconic figures in the Catholic anti-Nazi resistance paradigm in her *Galen.* See also Spicer, *Resisting.* Valuable additional studies include Krieg, *Theologians;* Burkard and Weiss, *Theologie.* For a sharp critique of the lack of resistance among Catholic leaders, see Denzler's insightful *Widerstand.* For much less convincing apologetic approaches, see Senninger, *Glaubenszeugen;* Gross, *Kirche.*

26. Spicer, *Hitler's Priests.*

27. See his discussion of the influence of prewar *Kulturprotestantismus* in Steigmann-Gall, *Holy Reich,* 37–41. See also the analysis of prewar liberal Protestant biblical scholarship in Bergen, *Twisted Cross,* 141–45; Heschel, *Aryan Jesus.* For critical assessments of Steigmann-Gall's work, see Ruff, "Religionspolitik," 252–67; and the essays by Manfred Gailus, Ernst Piper, Stanley Stowers, Doris Bergen, and Irving Hexham in *JCH* 42 (2007).

Steigmann-Gall's response was published in the next *JCH* issue as "Christianity," 252–67.

28. Heilbronner, *Countryside;* Heilbronner, "Failure," 531–49; Heilbronner, "Plight," 219–35; Heilbronner, "Achilles' Heel," 221–51.

29. See Voegelin, *Religionen.* On the theological underpinnings of Voegelin's thought, see Morrissey, *Consciousness;* Emberley and Cooper, *Faith.* More generally, see Franz, *Revolt;* Webb, *Voegelin.*

30. See Burleigh, *Third Reich;* Burleigh, *Sacred Causes;* Gentile, *Politics as Religion;* Bärsch, *Religion;* Burrin, "Political Religion," 321–49; Strohm, *Gnosis;* Maier, *Totalitarianism.* For a critical perspective, see Steigmann-Gall, "Revival," 376–96; Steigmann-Gall, "Religious Politics," 386–408. For a useful overview of the literature, see Maier, "Political Religion," 5–16.

31. Lepsius, "Parteiensystem," 371–93.

32. See Klöcker, "Milieu," 241–62; Arbeitskreis, "Katholiken," 588–654; Lönne, "Katholizismusforschung," 128–70; Schlank, *Kölsch-katholisch.*

33. See, e.g., the essays in Blaschke and Kuhlemann, *Religion;* also Weichlein, *Sozialmilieus;* Damberg, *Abschied vom Milieu?*

34. Munich at the time was located in the political-administrative region of upper Bavaria (Oberbayern), which largely coincided with the territory of the archdiocese of Munich-Freising. The population of upper Bavaria was 89.8 percent Catholic in 1916 and 89 percent in 1925, whereas the population of Munich itself remained 80–85 percent Catholic; see Seiler, "Statistik," 287.

35. Schauff, *Katholiken,* 174–75. Schauff's extensive statistical study of Catholic voting behavior has stood the test of time remarkably well. Jonathan Sperber notes that, while Schauff's methodology shares some of the limitations of its era, it is "unusually comprehensive in its scope and demonstrates great care (not always shared by more recent authors with more possibilities at their disposal) in handling the available election returns"; *Kaiser's Voters,* 16. One partial exception to upper Bavaria's claim to the lowest Catholic support for political Catholicism took place between 1903 and 1907 in the district of Oppeln (upper Silesia), where the Center Party's percentage of the Catholic vote dropped from 66 percent to 34.7 percent in connection with the rise of the Polish nationalist party under Korfanty; see Smith, *Nationalism,* 196–99; Bjork, "Neither," chap. 4.

36. By comparison, Catholic support for the Center Party in prewar Münster remained in the 80–90 percent range (90.1 percent in 1903, 83.2 percent in 1912) and was still 73.6 percent in December 1924. In Cologne, the Center Party got 73.8 percent of the Catholic vote in 1903, 70.6 percent in 1912, and still a respectable 55.7 percent in December 1924; Schauff, *Katholiken,* 175.

37. Thränhardt, *Wahlen,* 173.

38. Burnham, "Immunization," 1–30.

39. Pohl, *Arbeiterbewegung,* esp. 85–90; Pohl, "Sozialdemokraten," 233–53.

40. Pohl, "Sozialdemokraten," 252–53.

41. Blaschke and Kuhlemann conclude that Pohl's "surprising discovery" was likely due to the fact that "the weaker the influence of religion, the easier it was to step out of the religious sphere and into other [spheres]"; Blaschke and Kuhlemann, "Religion," 53. In this common yet circular interpretation, the failure to align one's political identity with the perceived borders of the Catholic milieu—and with the forces of ultramontane piety and political Catholicism that were seen as holding it together—is evidence of a sort of religious deficiency, which itself is then interpreted as the root cause of the ability to cross milieu boundaries in the first place. Blaschke and Kuhlemann do, however, attempt to differentiate among micro-, meso-, and macro-milieus (ibid., 54–55), making it possible, at least by extrapolation, to view Munich and its environs as a distinctive micro-milieu within the broader German Catholic macro-milieu.

42. In 1924, despite accelerating secularization trends, Schauff's study still found that a full 80 percent of Catholics in the archdiocese of Munich-Freising were religiously practicing, compared to 76.8 percent in Cologne and only 53.6 percent in Berlin; Schauff, *Katholiken,* 178.

43. For a concise overview of the founding of the archdiocese see Müller, "Zwischen," 85–130; also Schwaiger, *Erzbistum,* 15–45. It should be noted that the western suburbs of Munich were part of the neighboring diocese of Augsburg, which will also be included as necessary in the chapters that follow.

44. Munich's population growth was comparatively modest in the years at the heart of this study, however, growing from 596,000 in 1910 to 680,000 in 1925; *Ortschaften-Verzeichnis;* also *Statistisches Jahrbuch der Landeshauptstadt München* (Munich, 2004), 16–18.

45. Figures are from the year 1910, and there was only incremental expansion thereafter; *Schematismus,* 1910, 259–64.

46. Faulhaber was named cardinal in 1921, after serving as Munich's archbishop for four years. On his life and career, see Pfister et al., *Faulhaber.*

47. Schwaiger, *Georgianum.*

48. Despite the fact that the Nazi regime opposed these Catholic fraternities after 1933, several of the most visible Nazi propagandists in the earliest years of the movement were members of these same fraternities. The CV was the oldest and largest of the Catholic fraternity federations in Germany, originating from the mid-nineteenth-century founding of CV Aenania in Munich. Its official journal, *Academia,* was edited and published in Munich; see Dölken, *Cartellverband.* On the KV, see Löhr, *KV-Studententum.* Unlike the CV and KV, Rhaetia was only open to Catholic students from Bavaria; Bruner, *Festschrift.* The HV was smaller and was founded on the eve of the First World War; Klövekorn, *Hochland.* See, more generally, Jarausch, *Students,* 258–65; Swartout, "Identities"; Dowe, *Bildungsbürger;* Schwarz, *Studenten;* Kater, *Studentenschaft;* Grüttner, *Studenten.*

49. On Catholic workers' organizations in Munich, see Denk, *Arbeiterbewegung;* Krenn, *Arbeiterbewegung.* The influential Volksverein was almost

non-existent in and around Munich, as was the Rhenish-based Borromäusverein—both of which were pillars of the Catholic milieu elsewhere in Germany. Instead, local and regional (Bavarian) organizations, such as the Bavarian Pressverein, filled similar roles; see, e.g., Spael, *Deutschland,* 129–32; Klein, *Volksverein;* Zalar, "Knowledge." On prewar Munich in particular, see Nesner, *Erzbistum.*

50. For a detailed overview of Catholic publications in Munich, see esp. Nesner, *Erzbistum,* chap. 4; Pörnbacher, "Literatur," 845–62; Schwaiger, "Zeitenwende," 147–59.

51. Pfister, *Blutzeugen;* Schwaiger, *Herrschaft.* Critical voices have been few; see, e.g., Laube, *Fremdarbeiter;* Denzler, "Gebetssturm," 124–53.

Chapter 1

1. Funk, "München im katholischen Geistesleben der deutschen Gegenwart," *Hochland* 19:11 (Aug 1922): 499–500.

2. On tensions remaining at the end of the *Kulturkampf,* see Weber, *Politik;* Baumeister, *Parität.*

3. Funk, "München," 504–5.

4. See Stehkämper, *Katholikentagspräsident,* and the press clippings in NL Faulhaber, fol. 3502.

5. Joseph Joos explicitly referenced the anti–Center Party hostility cultivated in the "peculiar atmosphere [*eigenartige Atmosphäre*] that has grown in the Bavarian capital in recent years"; Joos, "Der Münchener Katholikentag," *Das Zentrum* 19 (1 Sep 1922); see also "Münchener Katholizismus," *AR* 37 (16 Sep 1922).

6. For years, the historiography on Wilhelmine and Weimar era Catholicism was virtually synonymous with the Center Party. Notable exceptions include Blackbourn, *Marpingen;* Mergel, *Zwischen;* Busch, *Frömmigkeit;* Kotulla, *Nach Lourdes.*

7. Quote from Funk, "Vom Münchener Katholizismus," *NJ* 29 (21 July 1912): 354. Funk was a leading member of the Reform Catholic movement in Munich, which will be discussed later in this chapter, and he fashioned the paper *Das Neue Jahrhundert* into a leading organ of Catholic anti-ultramontane sentiment; see Engelhardt, *Funk,* 187–222.

8. Raab, "Ultramontan," 159–73; Weiss, "Ultramontanismus," 821–77.

9. Weber, *Phalanx;* Sperber, *Popular Catholicism,* 55–91; Gross, *War,* 29–62.

10. For examples of these two trajectories, see Buchheim, *Demokratie;* Weber, "Ultramontanismus," 20–45.

11. Schlossmacher, "Antiultramontanismus," 164–98. On the Rhineland and Black Forest regions, see Mergel, "Ultramontanism," 151–74; Mergel, *Zwischen;* Heilbronner, *Freiheit.*

12. On the variety of Catholic attitudes toward *kleindeutsch* German nationalism after 1866–1871, see esp. Windell, *Catholics;* Morsey, "Nationalstaat,"

31–64; Gründer, "Nation," 65–88; Smith, *Nationalism*. On the earlier nineteenth century, see Altgeld, *Katholizismus*.

13. Funk did not mention the Nazis explicitly and, although he clearly sympathized with certain aspects of the young movement's nationalism and anti-ultramontanism, his attitude toward the earliest Nazis is not clearly documented. Funk eventually habilitated in history at the University of Munich in 1925 and left to assume a chair in history first at Braunsberg and then at Freiburg. Although his closest colleague in Freiburg in the 1930s was the pro-Nazi philosopher Martin Heidegger, Funk was clearly opposed to the Nazi regime after 1933; see Engelhardt, *Funk,* 448–52.

14. Kapfinger, *Eoskreis,* 17–25; Vanden Heuvel, *Görres,* esp. 293–303; Buchheim, *Demokratie;* also, more generally, Mayring, *Bayern.*

15. Laube, *Fest,* esp. 224–28; Blessing, *Staat,* esp. 132–36; Weiss, *Redemptoristen;* Phayer, *Religion.*

16. On Döllinger's transformation from ultramontanist to liberal nationalist, a process dating primarily to the 1850s, see Schwedt, "Döllinger," 107–66. The general literature on Döllinger is vast; on his later career, see Bischof, *Theologie.*

17. See the account of Döllinger's most famous student, Lord Acton, in his "Doellinger's Historical Work," *EHR* 5 (1890): 700–744.

18. "Vergangenheit und Gegenwart der katholischen Theologie," reprinted in Finsterhölzl, *Döllinger,* 227–63, quote from 251.

19. Ibid., 242. For brilliant evocations of the ultramontane mental universe that Döllinger was at such pains to differentiate from his Munich-based vision, see Blessing, *Staat,* chap. 4; Weiss, *Redemptoristen,* chaps. 5–8. For an insightful analysis of both of these works, see Anderson, "Piety," 681–716.

20. Döllinger, "Theologie," 256–57. On alleged connections between ultramontanism and the feminization of Catholicism, see Olenhusen, "Feminisierung," 9–21; also McLeod, "Frömmigkeit," 134–56; Habermas, "Religiosität," 125–48.

21. The dogma of papal infallibility was proclaimed at the First Vatican Council, which convened in Rome in December 1869. Döllinger had been invited to Rome as a theological advisor to the German bishops and, in the months of preparation before the convening of the council, wrote a famous series of letters to Munich's *Allgemeine Zeitung* under the pen name Janus that criticized both the idea of dogmatizing papal infallibility and the ultramontane mental universe that called it forth; Brandmüller, *Döllinger,* 147–80. On Döllinger's continued piety and refusal to join the Old Catholic movement after his excommunication, see Bischof, *Theologie,* 352–83.

22. On the *Hofklerus* after the death of Döllinger, primarily at Munich's St. Kajetan, where Döllinger had served as ecclesiastical provost (*Stiftspropst*), see Koegel, *Hofkirche;* Möckl, "Hofgesellschaft," 183–235.

23. Andersch, *Vater;* on Himmler and Patin, see chaps. 3–4 below.

24. In contrast to many later Catholic anti-ultramontanes, by the 1880s Döllinger came to reject extreme anti-Semitism; Kornberg, "Döllinger's *Die Juden,*" 223–45.

25. Hartmannsgruber, *Patriotenpartei,* chap. 6; Möckl, *Prinzregentenzeit,* 212–28.

26. On the broad influence of Döllinger and his followers on Bauernbund leaders, see, e.g., Möckl, *Prinzregentenzeit,* 119–20; more generally Abbott, "Peasants"; Hundhammer, *Geschichte;* Hochberger, *Bauernbund.*

27. Farr, "Anti-Catholicism," 249–68; also Farr, "Populism," 136–59; Farr, "Peasant Protest," 110–39.

28. On the related anti-Semitic *Deutsches Volksblatt* of the Austrian Christian Socials, which was edited by Ernst Vergani, see Boyer, *Radicalism,* 72–78.

29. Satzungen, 10 Nov 1892, SAM-PD, fol. 633.

30. On Böckel, see Massing, *Rehearsal,* chap. 6; Pulzer, *Anti-Semitism;* Brustein, *Roots,* 137–38; Mosse, *Final Solution,* 166–67.

31. Police report, 12 Apr 1893, SAM-PD, fol. 613.

32. Tiedemann, "Antisemitismus," 306. On the ensuing Landtag election of July 1893, see Möckl, *Prinzregentenzeit,* 454–64.

33. Geisler to Polizeidirektion, 15 Aug 1893; SAM-PD, fol. 667; also the notice in *DV* 67 (17 Aug 1893).

34. "Kauft nicht bei Juden," *DV* (29 Oct 1893).

35. Boyer, *Radicalism,* 122–83; Boyer, "Religion," 40–42; Pauley, *Prejudice,* 38–44. For Hitler's later idealization of Lueger, see *Mein Kampf,* 98–101.

36. Boyer, *Radicalism,* 372–409.

37. Wenng to Polizeidirektion, 8 Aug 1896, SAM-PD, fol. 667.

38. Flyer, "Bayerische antisemitische Volkspartei," SAM-PD, fol. 667.

39. Police report, 11 Aug 1896, SAM-PD, fol. 667; see also the oppositional coverage, *MP* 181 (12 Aug 1896).

40. Ludwig Quidde (the head of the local Demokratischer Verein who would later become a famous pacifist and winner of the Nobel Peace Prize) spent months trying to arrange Brunner's visit; Quidde to Polizeidirektion, 26 Oct 1899; Meixner to Quidde, 28 Oct 1899; Meixner to Quidde, 31 Jan 1900, SAM-PD, fol. 1004.

41. "Wegen Kohlenmangel werden hier Juden verbrannt," *DV* 10 (11 Mar 1900). See also Wenng's public letter in *NMT* 72 (13 Mar 1900); "Gesprengte Volksversammlung," *MNN* 111 (7 Mar 1900); "Gesprengte Versammlung," *NBZ* 56 (8 Mar 1900); "Aufgelöste Versammlung," *BK* 65 (8 Mar 1900). See also the opaque reference in Blaschke, *Antisemitismus,* 233.

42. Wenng also gained increased attention with numerous anti-Semitic pamphlets; see, e.g., Wenng, *Die Judenfrage* (Munich, 1901).

43. Tiedemann, "Antisemitismus," 306; Abbott, "Peasants," 159–62; Möckl, *Prinzregentenzeit,* 68–70, 120–26.

44. Tiedemann, "Antisemitismus," 309.

45. Schnepper eventually split from Wenng in 1903 to form the rival Christlich-Sozialer Zentralverein; see "Die Vorstandschaft des christlich-

sozialen Zentralvereins für Bayern," *MCSZ* 6 (12 July 1903), and the organization's July 1903 bylaws, SAM-PD, fol. 480. By 1905, Wenng managed to restore a working relationship between his and Schnepper's organizations; "Kundgebung," *DV* (5 Nov 1905).

46. Police report, 11 Mar 1900, SAM-PD, fol. 1495; also "Kirchlicher Reform," *MFP* 54 (7 Mar 1900); "Erster katholischer Reformverein," *BK* 70 (13 Mar 1900).

47. Müller was ordained in Bamberg in 1877 and spent more than a decade in a variety of pastoral positions in the Bamberg area before gaining permission to pursue higher studies; he obtained a doctorate in philosophy under Richard Falckenberg at Erlangen in 1894 and transferred to the archdiocese of Munich-Freising thereafter; see Müller's memoir, published initially as an article series entitled "Mein Leben" in his journal *Renaissance* in 1903 and then in book form as *Das Leben eines Priesters in unseren Tagen* (Munich, 1903).

48. Müller, *Reformkatholizismus.* Although Müller wrote more than a dozen other monographs, this remains by far his best-known work.

49. See, e.g., Schröder, *Aufbruch;* Schwaiger, *Aufbruch;* Trippen, *Theologie;* Loome, *Reform Catholicism;* Weiss, *Modernismus;* Wolf, *Antimodernismus.* For a concise historical sketch of Reform Catholicism, see Nipperdey, *Umbruch,* 32–38.

50. "Reformkatholizismus," *MNN* 40 (25 Jan 1900).

51. The subscribers among the *Hofklerus* included Jakob von Türk—Döllinger's closest protegé and successor as *Stiftspropst* at St. Kajetan, who was also the personal confessor to Prince Regent Luitpold—as well as Joseph Koegel, Wilhelm Müller, and Corbinian Ettmayr; "Zur Beachtung," *Ren* 3:2 (Feb 1902). Although it briefly appeared in an overly optimistic printing of 6,000, at its height in 1902 *Renaissance* had a circulation of around 3,000. For the majority of its existence, however, its circulation remained slightly more than 1,000; "An die Leser," *Ren* 8:1 (Jan 1907).

52. The circulation of the *Jahrhundert* reached around 2,000 by 1904, which was quite respectable for a publication targeting an educated readership of students and academics; see *20Jh* 26 (26 June 1904). In comparison, the circulation of the prestigious national liberal *Grenzboten* remained between 1,200 and 2,000; Schlawe, *Zeitschriften,* 10–11. The *Rundschau* straddled the divide between Reform Catholic opponents of political Catholicism and educated supporters of the right wing of the Bavarian Center Party; see Mennekes, *Herausforderung,* 15–17. *Hochland* quickly transcended the limits of Munich's Reform Catholic community, reaching a truly impressive circulation of more than 10,000 and becoming perhaps the leading Catholic cultural journal in the entire German-speaking world; Körling, *Hochland,* 18–19. The circulation of *Hochland* surpassed such prestigious rival monthlies as the *Preussische Jahrbücher;* see Schlawe, *Zeitschriften,* 80–81; more generally, Nipperdey, *Umbruch,* 36–38; Osinski, *Literatur,* 339–402; Becker, "Muth," 396–402; Spael, *Deutschland,* 106–20; Hüffer, *Muth.*

53. "Verein Renaissance," *Ren* 5:3 (Mar 1904); "Einladung," *Ren* 5:7 (July 1904). On the KG, see esp. Haustein, *Krausgesellschaft.*

54. Nipperdey, *Umbruch,* 34. The theological literature on Schell is huge; see, e.g., Hausberger, *Schell;* Hasenfuss, *Schell;* Greiner, "Schell," 427–54; O'Meara, *Culture,* chap. 6.

55. Schell, *Prinzip.* In Schell's eyes, the "Roman spirit" of the ultramontane movement exercised an especially unhealthy influence on German Catholicism, burdening it with childish, superstitious, southern European cultural baggage that ultimately had nothing to do with the noble essence of the Catholic faith; see, e.g., Schell, *Prinzip,* 60.

56. Ibid., 61. Despite the fact that Schell demonstrated sufficient humility to avoid severe ecclesiastical discipline for his controversial writings (he remained in the priesthood and was allowed to continue his theological teaching duties at Würzburg until his death in 1906), comparisons with Döllinger came quickly; see historian Ludwig von Pastor's diary entry of 9 May 1897 in *Tagebücher,* 302.

57. Police report, 21 Oct 1902, SAM-PD, fol. 5138; also "Einladung," *20Jh* 40 (4 Oct 1902); "Versammlung," *20Jh* 43 (25 Oct 1902); more generally, Weiss, *Modernismus,* 226–30; Haustein, *Krausgesellschaft,* 49–53.

58. KG bylaws, 11 June 1904, SAM-PD, fol. 2803. On Kraus, see Weber, *Kraus.*

59. See the minutes of the KG Ausschuss from 1909 to 1914, KG-Archiv, BSB; also Haustein, *Krausgesellschaft,* 306–11.

60. Ibid. The influence of the KG in Munich greatly exceeded its deliberately narrow membership, which likely never exceeded 200; see Haustein, *Krausgesellschaft,* 74–89.

61. Briemann achieved the highest rank within the early NSDAP of all the former KG members, serving as treasurer of the party from early 1922 to early 1923 and then taking over as secretary from 29 January 1923 up through the putsch, after which he did not rejoin the party.

62. Lachner, "Schnitzer," 582–88; also Schröder, *Aufbruch,* 419–31.

63. Georg Stipberger, "Joseph Schnitzer 80 Jahre alt," *VB* 166 (15 June 1939); also see the obituary by former Schnitzer student Joseph Bernhart in *Hochland* 37:6 (Mar 1940).

64. See, e.g., Schnitzer, "Epilog zur Rottenburger Bischofsrede," *Ren* 4:3 (Mar 1903): 184–92. On his role in the Isarlust event, see the diary entry of 30 Mar 1903, Schnitzer, "Tagebuch," 148–50.

65. Schnitzer was labeled a "modernist" in large part due to his acceptance of biblical higher criticism; for the details of the famous "Fall Schnitzer," see Trippen, *Theologie,* esp. 268–349.

66. On Catholic student participation in the Isarlust event, see Bernhart, *Erinnerungen,* 1:197–200; also police report, 21 Oct 1902, SAM-PD, fol. 5138.

67. Pieper's 1903 dissertation was awarded the distinction summa cum laude. See also the correspondence between Pieper and Brentano in NL Pieper, AK.

68. On Pieper's devotion to Schell, see the unpublished ms. in NL Pieper, "Vielfalt des Lebens," 19. Pieper's *Nachlass* also includes the large number of books he collected about Franz Xaver Kraus, in addition to Pieper's own personal file of press clippings on Kraus dating all the way up to the celebration of Kraus's 100th birthday in 1940. Pieper's fascination with Döllinger is reflected in his purchase of a rare copy of the proceedings from the 1863 St. Boniface conference and his personal collection of more than two dozen different portraits and photos of Döllinger.

69. Pieper was a subscriber to and supporter of the *Jahrhundert,* which was affiliated with the KG, and kept the bound version of all of the journal's issues from the controversial year 1907 as part of his personal library. It is possible (perhaps likely) that Pieper contributed to the *Jahrhundert* anonymously between 1906 and 1911, the period in which he wrote numerous signed contributions in *Academia,* the Munich-based organ of the CV.

70. Police report, 11 Mar 1900, SAM-PD, fol. 1495; also "Reformverein," *BK* 70 (13 Mar 1900); "Mitteilung," *Ren* 1:3 (May 1900). Although he did not move to Munich until taking over in 1910 as editor of the KG's *Jahrhundert,* Philipp Funk had been deeply influenced by Josef Müller while he was a theology student in Rottenburg, and it was Müller who published the first essays Funk ever wrote; Funk, "Custos quid de nocte?" *Ren* 7:4 (Apr 1906); "Zur Psychologie und Mystik von Fogazzaros Il Santo," *Ren* 7:10 (Oct 1906); "Legendenstudien," *Ren* 7:11 (Nov 1906).

71. Schrönghamer later noted that he initially entered the seminary under (well-intentioned) pressure from his family and local priest; see his autobiographical entry in Zils, *München.*

72. Schrönghamer remained an active member of Rhaetia's local alumni association (Philisterverein) in Munich for years; see, e.g., his personal entry in the *Korrespondenzblatt des Philisteriums der kath. bayer. Studentenverbindung Rhaetia* 18 (1911).

73. See, e.g., Müller, "Zum Semesterschluss," *Ren* 4:6 (June 1903); "Musenalmanach katholischer Studenten 1903," *Ren* 4:7 (July 1903). See also Karl Muth, "Zwei akademische Musenalmanache," *Hochland* 1:1 (Oct 1903).

74. See the announcement in "Verein Renaissance," *Ren* 5:3 (Mar 1904).

75. Schrönghamer's later career is discussed in chap. 2 below. The *Fliegende Blätter* were somewhat overshadowed by Munich's more famous satirical journals *Simplicissimus* and *Jugend,* which were both much racier and generally more offensive to Catholic sensibilities; see Allen, *Satire.* In 1912, Schrönghamer purchased an ancient estate near Passau and began at that point to split his time between Munich and the Passau area; H. P. Heller, "Vom Waldbauernbüberl zum Heimatdichter," *PNP* 60 (12–13 Mar 1960); also the materials in Schrönghamer's papers, StAP, sch. 11.

76. See, e.g., Scheicher's controversial comments criticizing ultramontanism at the 1902 Austrian Clerustag, where he echoed explicitly the ideas of Herman Schell and Josef Müller; Boyer, *Radicalism,* 141–42. Schindler

emerged as a central defender of the Reform Catholic theologian Albert Ehrhard during a major controversy in Vienna in 1901–1902 and was celebrated as a hero among Reform Catholics in Munich; ibid., 156. See also the energetic idealization of Schindler and Ehrhard in the pages of the *Jahrhundert* (e.g., "Abschiedskommers der 'Austria' zu Ehren Professor Ehrhard's," *20Jh* 28 [12 July 1902]).

77. Defining *root paradigms* as "cultural models in the heads of the main actors," which help to structure their political actions, Turner argued that these discursive paradigms should not be viewed as "systems of univocal concepts, logically arrayed; they are not, so to speak, precision tools of thought." Rather, root paradigms influence political activity in more indirect and subtle ways, going "beyond the cognitive and even the moral to the existential domain, and in so doing become clothed with allusiveness, implicitness, and metaphor." These paradigms tend to emerge particularly during times of strife and tension or, as Turner termed it, during "life crises"; Turner, "Paradigms," 64; also more generally, Turner, *Ritual;* Turner, *Image.*

78. Walter Goetz, "Franz Xaver Kraus und der religiöse Katholizismus," *MNN* 72 (12 Feb 1902), reprinted in Weber, *Kraus,* 430–38. See also the biography by KG member Ernst Hauviller, *Kraus,* esp. 35–50; "Franz Xaver Kraus und die Schweiz," *Hochland* 1:12 (Sep 1904).

79. See esp. "Politischer und religiöser Katholizismus. I," *Ren* 3:6 (June 1902); "Politischer und religiöser Katholizismus. II," *Ren* 3:9 (Sep 1902); also *Reformkatholizismus,* chap. 1.

80. "Politik und Religion," *Ren* 3:1 (Jan 1902). See also "Centrumstheologie," *Ren* 2:10 (Oct 1901); "Nochmals 'Centrumstheologie,'" *Ren* 2:12 (Dec 1901); "Politik und Religion," *Ren* 3:3 (Mar 1902); "Politik und Religion," *Ren* 4:5 (May 1903); "Geschäftskatholizismus," *Ren* 4:12 (Dec 1903); "Hierarchie und Demagogentum," *Ren* 6:10 (Oct 1905); "Zum Thema: Politik und Religion," *Ren* 7:3 (Mar 1906); "Politik und Religion," *Ren* 7:4 (Apr 1906); "Politik und Klerus," *Ren* 7:6 (June 1906); "Politik und Religion," *Ren* 8:3 (Mar 1907).

81. Müller, *Reformkatholizismus,* 2:59.

82. "Einladung," *20Jh* 40 (4 Oct 1902); "Versammlung," *20Jh* 43 (25 Oct 1902).

83. Muth, "Ein Vorwort zu 'Hochland,'" *Hochland* 1:1 (Oct 1903): 3–4.

84. "Politischer Katholizismus," *20Jh* 3 (16 Jan 1904); also "Freiherr von Hertling und das Zentrum," *20Jh* 16 (16 Apr 1905); "Zu den Landtagswahlen," *20Jh* 18 (30 Apr 1905); "Religiöses Bekenntnis und Parteizugehörigkeit," *NJ* 40 (3 Oct 1909); "Ist das Zentrum eine christliche Partei?" *NJ* 40 (2 Oct 1910); "Politik im Namen der Religion?" *NJ* 48 (26 Nov 1911); "Ist das katholische Christentum eine Religion oder ein politisches System?" *NJ* 53 (31 Dec 1911); "Erlöset den deutschen Katholizismus von der Politik!" *NJ* 4 (28 Jan 1912).

85. "Katholiken Bayerns, Deutschlands!" *NJ* 52 (11 Dec 1911).

86. Bumüller, "Was bedeutet ultramontan?" *20Jh* 24 (14 June 1902); also Müller, "Ultramontaner Kampfesweise," *Ren* 3:3 (Mar 1902); and, on a slightly more moderate level, Karl Muth, "Ultra montes," *Hochland* 1:6 (Mar 1904). See also "Was wir wollen!" *20Jh* 50 (13 Dec 1902); the multipart series "Katholisch oder ultramontan?" *20Jh* 47 (20 Nov 1904); 48 (27 Nov 1904); 49 (4 Dec 1904); "Über welschen und deutschen Katholizismus," *20Jh* 18 (5 May 1907); "Roms Sünden gegen Deutschland," *NJ* 25 (19 June 1910); "Ein positives Programm zur Selbsterhaltung gegenüber dem Ultramontanismus," *NJ* 27 (3 July 1910).

87. Schnitzer, "Ultramontane Frivolität," *NJ* 14 (6 Apr 1913); 15 (13 Apr 1913); 16 (20 Apr 1913); 17 (27 Apr 1913); 18 (4 May 1913). Herman Schell consistently characterized kitschy ultramontane religiosity as "childish superstition" that must be distinguished from the maturity and nobility of the Germanic Catholic conception of God's nature; Schell, "Gottesbegriff und Aberglaube," *Ren* 6:1 (Jan 1905); 6:2 (Feb 1905); 6:3 (Mar 1905); 6:4 (Apr 1905).

88. See Koch's *Katholizismus und Jesuitismus* (Munich, 1913), which exercised a powerful influence in the early Nazi movement over anti-Jesuit Catholics, such as Alfred Miller. Other KG figures openly equated ultramontanism and Jesuitism across the board; see, e.g., "Jesuitismus–Ultramontanismus," *20Jh* 47–48 (1 Dec 1907); Bumüller, "Der Jesuitismus," *20Jh* 25 (21 June 1902); "Häresie in der jesuitischen Lehre," *NJ* 7 (13 Feb 1910); Müller, *Jesuiten;* more broadly, Healy, *Specter.*

89. Reformverein bylaws, 31 Mar 1900, SAM-PD, fol. 1495; also Müller, "Die Religion," *Ren* 4:1 (Jan 1903).

90. A 1910 KG flyer in the papers of *Hochland* founder Karl Muth identified the purpose of the group to be "the deepening of religious life and the fostering of a personal and manly Christianity"; NL Muth, BSB, fol. V.E.61. The founding program of the KG had also defined religious Catholicism succinctly as "the internalization of Christianity"; *20Jh* 29 (17 July 1904).

91. "Schutz der Sittlichkeit," *20Jh* 2 (9 Jan 1904); "Der Student und die Religion," *20Jh* 35 (28 Aug 1904); "Sittlichkeitskongress," *20Jh* 42 (21 Oct 1906); "Die religiöse Krisis der Gegenwart und ihre Lösung," *Ren* 6:1 (Jan 1905), 6:2 (Feb 1905).

92. Josef Müller's strong admiration for Döllinger, for example, was tempered by the conviction that Döllinger had erred disastrously by allowing himself to be "driven out" of the church in the 1870s, and Müller insisted on the importance of remaining loyally within the church, "in whose divinity we believe"; *Reformkatholizismus,* 2:155; also "Döllingers letzte Stellungnahme," *Ren* 7:8 (Aug 1906); "Döllingers letzte Lebensjahre," *Ren* 7:10 (Oct 1906); "Die Frage der Unfehlbarkeit auf dem Vatikanum," *Ren* 8:1 (Jan 1907).

93. See esp. "Möchten wir doch die Kirche nicht verlieren!" *NJ* 6 (5 Feb 1911); "Warum wir in die Kirche bleiben," *NJ* 5 (2 Feb 1913).

94. For a clear statement that Old Catholicism was a "heresy," see "Das 20. Jahrhundert und der Altkatholizismus," *20Jh* 23 (7 June 1902). See also the KG's principled rejection of the attempt to get its leaders to join forces with the Old Catholic Church at the height of the modernist controversy, *Altkatholizismus und Reformkatholizismus* (Bonn, 1908). After some initial cooperation with the AUR, the KG rejected all further cooperation; see "Zur Frage des Antiultramontanen Reichsverband," *NJ* 10 (8 Mar 1914). On the AUR more generally, see Gottwald, "Antiultramontaner Reichsverband," 41–43.

95. "Religiöser und politischer Katholizismus," *NJ* 4 (22 Jan 1911).

96. The founding of the Christlich-Sozialer Verein in 1900 had been occasioned in part by the agitation of the Los-von-Rom movement in Munich, led by the anti-Catholic publisher J. F. Lehmann, who also cofounded the Munich branches of the Pan-German League and the Evangelischer Bund; see the clippings in SAM-PD, fol. 1002; also "Zur Los von Rom-Bewegung," *Ren* 3: 2 (Feb 1902); "Die Los von Rom-Bewegung," *Ren* 6:7 (July 1905). On the movement's Austrian context, see Albertin, "Nationalismus"; Smith, *Nationalism,* 206–30.

97. "Weltgeschichte in Charakterbildern," *20Jh* 36 (6 Sep 1902).

98. See, e.g., "Ein positives Programm zur Selbsterhaltung gegenüber dem Ultramontanismus," *NJ* 27 (3 July 1910); also "Der konfessionelle Friede," *20Jh* 32 (9 Aug 1902); "Irenik im 20. Jahrhundert," *Ren* 5:1 (Jan 1904); *Ren* 5:5 (May 1904); "Auch ein Wort zum konfessionellen Frieden," *20Jh* 31 (31 July 1904); "Konfession und soziale Politik," *NJ* 4 (28 Jan 1906); "Ein Wort zum konfessionellen Frieden," *20Jh* 19 (13 May 1906); "Wiedervereinigungsbestrebungen," *20Jh* 29 (22 July 1906); "Religiöses Bekenntnis und Parteizugehörigkeit," *NJ* 40 (3 Oct 1909); "Die Arbeit für den konfessionellen Frieden," *NJ* 2 (9 Jan 1910); "Die Stellung der Krausgesellschaft zu der Kirche, zu den Mitkatholiken, zu fremden Lagern," *NJ* 23 (7 June 1914).

99. "Ein Vorwort zu 'Hochland,'" *Hochland* 1:1 (Oct 1903).

100. On Lienhard's leading position in the broader *völkisch* movement, see Chatellier, "Lienhard," 114–30. Muth's *Nachlass* contains nearly 500 letters from Lienhard to Muth alone (plus those written from Muth to Lienhard); see also Muth, "Friedrich Lienhard: Ein Gedenkblatt," *Hochland* 26 (1929).

101. "Vorwort," 2; also "Katholizismus und Deutschtum," *Hochland* 1:3 (Dec 1903). Josef Müller's vision of Reform Catholicism as the "religion of the future for the educated of all confessions" was predicated on "positive" cooperation with irenically minded Protestants; see also Schell, "Katholizismus und Protestantismus," *Ren* 2:5 (May 1901); Schell, "Das Christentum Christi," *Ren* 3:2 (Feb 1902); Schell, "Lehrende und lernende Kirche," *Ren* 5:1 (Jan 1904).

102. 1896 BAVP Flyer, SAM-PD, fol. 667; BAVP bylaws, Nov 1894, SAM-PD, fol. 613.

103. See the explicit reference to "all segments of society" at the founding of the KG; "Einladung," *20Jh* 29 (29 June 1904). The SPD was frequently characterized as a "terroristic group" unworthy of support from believing Catholics; "Die Sozialdemokraten und die Schillerfeier," *20Jh* 21 (21 May 1905).

104. "Geistige Selbständigkeit und Katholizismus," *20Jh* 8 (24 Feb 1907); also "Nationalismus und Katholizismus," *20Jh* 3 (20 Jan 1907); "Stichwahl-parolen," *20Jh* 7 (12 Feb 1905). These prewar attacks on socialist "atheism" were milder than the later rhetoric used by the early Nazi movement, in part due to the relative tolerance toward Catholicism displayed by some SPD leaders in Munich; see Pohl, *Arbeiterbewegung,* 85–90.

105. Müller attempted to build upon and rework the ideas of Friedrich Naumann; "Sozialismus und Christentum," *Ren* 2:10 (Oct 1901).

106. The roots of social student activism in Munich can be traced to the 1908 founding of the journal *Akademiker;* "Münchener sozial-caritativen Studentenvereinigung," *Akademiker* 1:1 (Nov 1908); "Die sozial-caritativen Vereinigungen kath. Studenten," *Akademiker* 1:2 (Dec 1908).

107. See the bitter lament by Nischler's close friend and mentor Karl Muth, "Karl Nischler," *Hochland* 10:5 (Feb 1913).

108. Ibid., 640; also "Karl Nischler: Nachruf," *Akademiker* 5:4 (Feb 1913).

109. "Student und Jugend," *Akademiker* 5:1 (Nov 1912); on Nischler's *völkisch* activism and close relationship to Muth, see Sack, *Semester,* 4–6.

110. "Alte und neue Studentenideale," *Akademiker* 5:8 (June 1913).

111. See, e.g., "Isolierung des jüdischen Studenten," *DV* (9 Mar 1902); also police reports on the conspicuous presence of Catholic university students at Christian Social gatherings, SAM-PD, fols. 613, 633, 667. On ties between the Austrian Christian Socials and CV students, see Skalnik, *Lueger,* 143–58.

112. Kausen, "Kampf gegen die öffentliche Unsittlichkeit," *AR* 25 (23 June 1906).

113. Membership list, 25 May 1906, SAM-PD, fol. 4475. The right wing of the Bavarian Center Party was somewhat more acceptable to Reform Catholics than the broader Center Party. The group soon numbered more than 2,000 members; *AR* 51 (22 Dec 1906).

114. Report on Gruber speech, 21 Nov 1907, BHSA, MInn-73589, fol. 227. On Gruber, see also Weindling, *German Politics,* 147–50, 312–20.

115. "Massenvergiftung," *AR* 3:4 (27 Jan 1906); also Muth, "Sittliche Zucht und nationale Kraft," *Hochland* 3 (1906).

116. Despite Kausen's initial offer to include a Munich rabbi, the Männerverein was exclusively Christian; "Warum brauchen wir interconfessionelle Männervereine?" *AR* 11 (14 Mar 1908).

117. On the broader *völkisch* movement, see Puschner et al., *Handbuch;* Puschner, *Bewegung.*

118. *20Jh* 23 (7 June 1902).

119. "Erklärung des Titelbildes," *Ren* 3:4 (Apr 1902).

120. Rohling, *Talmudjude.* Rohling retired as theology professor at the German university in Prague in 1899 and contributed numerous articles to Müller's *Renaissance;* see, e.g., "Der Theodicee," *Ren* 4:2 (Feb 1903): 65–93; "Es wird werden eine Herd, ein Hirt," *Ren* 4:4 (Apr 1903): 242–55; "Schell und Stufler," *Ren* 4:9 (Sep 1903): 518–29. On Rohling more generally, see Patschovsky, "Talmudjude," 13–27; Massing, *Rehearsal,* 14–16; Mosse, *Final Solution,* 138–39; Katz, *Prejudice,* 285–87; Pulzer, *Anti-Semitism,* 152–58; Blaschke, *Antisemitismus,* 49–50.

121. See, e.g., "Die jüdische Blutmorde" *DV* (24 June 1894). Wenng's dissemination of Rohling's pamphlet *Talmud-Auszug (Schulchan Aruch)*—advertised throughout 1894 in the *Volksblatt* with the heading "Zur Massenverbreitung bestimmt!"—brought about a legal case that was not settled until 1897; see "München," *IDR* 6 (June 1897), and materials in SAM-PD, fol. 613. This case was the basis, at least in part, for Wenng's 1899 drive to expel *Ostjuden* from Munich; see "München," *IDR* 12 (Dec 1899).

122. See chap. 3 below. On the four 1899 meetings, see SAM-PD, fol. 667.

123. See, e.g., "Ein Zucht-Problem," *Ren* 5:8 (Aug 1904); "Abstammungslehre," *Ren* 5:10 (Oct 1904); "Schwäche unserer nationalen Presse," *Ren* 5:12 (Dec 1904); "Korrespondenz," *Ren* 6:2 (Feb 1905); "Los von Rom Bewegung," *Ren* 6:7 (July 1905); also "Rasse und Kultur," *Ren* 4:6 (June 1903); "Rasse und Kultur," *Ren* 4:8 (Aug 1903). On Fritsch, see Bönisch, "Hammer-Bewegung," 341–65.

124. Daim, *Liebenfels.* See the publicity for Lanz's books in *Ren* 6:6 (June 1905), and *Ren* 6:8 (Aug 1905); also Müller, "Otto Weininger," *Ren* 5:7 (July 1904).

125. Fendt had been ordained into the Catholic priesthood in July 1905 and then completed an award-winning dissertation under the direction of Schnitzer in 1906; Fendt, *Wirksamkeit.*

126. Ironically, unlike most other Reform Catholic figures, Fendt later (in 1918) did convert to Protestantism; see Wiggermann, "Fendt."

127. "Germanischer Katholizismus," *20Jh* 17 (28 Apr 1907); also Scheicher, "Über welschen und deutschen Katholizismus," *20Jh* 18 (5 May 1907).

128. Karl Muth's friend Luzian Pfleger made sure to emphasize repeatedly that "Gobineau was a practicing Catholic"; see, e.g., "Eine Gobineaubiographie," *Hochland* 11:10 (July 1914).

129. Schell, "Worte Christi: Das Charakterbild Jesu nach Houston Stewart Chamberlain," *Hochland* 2:7 (Apr 1905). See Georg von Hertling's critical response upon that issue's advance release; Hertling to Muth, 19 Mar 1905, NL Muth, BSB.

130. "Gobineaus Amadis," *Hochland* 6:12 (Sep 1909).

131. Alfons Scherer, "Gobineau und die deutsche Kultur," *Hochland* 8:4 (Jan 1911).

132. "Arische Weltanschauung," *20Jh* 4 (28 Jan 1906); see also "Nationalismus und Katholizismus," *20Jh* 3 (20 Jan 1907).

133. "Bausteine zu einer germanischen Weltanschauung," *20Jh* 42 (18 Oct 1908).

134. See, e.g., "Über Ritualmord," *20Jh* 49 (3 Dec 1905).

135. "Zerfall des deutschen Judentums," *Hochland* 11:11 (Aug 1914).

136. *Ren* 3:8 (Aug 1902): 510. Despite his criticisms, Müller committed himself to remaining celibate; see *Ren* 3:12 (Dec 1902): 765–66.

137. "Zölibat und Priestertum," *Ren* 5:4 (Apr 1904): 206–7.

138. "Unterfruchtige Völker im Lichte der Biologie," *Hochland* 4:1 (Oct 1906); "Einfluss der Arbeit auf die völkische Entwicklung," *Hochland* 10:2 (Nov 1912), 10:3 (Dec 1912); "Der Geburtenrückgang," *Hochland* 10:4 (Jan 1913). Grassl had written his 1905 dissertation, "Blut und Brot," on the relationship between racial hygiene and economics. On the broader race hygiene movement, see Proctor, *Hygiene,* 10–45; Weindling, *German Politics,* 141–54.

139. *Efeuranken* published the works of Schrönghamer and other *völkisch*-oriented Reform Catholics; see also Persch, "Thrasolt," 1504–8.

140. Reinecke, "Feuer," 164–69.

141. See Stauff, "Guido von List gestorben," *MB* 17 (24 May 1919). On the radicalism of Stauff's racial anti-Semitism, see Thrasolt's editorial postscript to Stauff's essay "Die Semiten," *DHF* 1:4 (Jan 1914).

142. "Gegen völkische Entartung," *DHF* 1:5 (Feb 1914): 358–59; also "Das Heilige Feuer," *DHF* 1:1 (Oct 1913).

143. Hallermeyer joined the KG Ausschuss in Nov 1910; minutes, 5 Nov 1910, KG-Archiv, BSB.

144. The KG also monitored racial hygiene movements elsewhere in the world; see, e.g., Hallermeyer, "Die Rassenhygiene in den Vereinigten Staaten von Nordamerika," *NJ* 8 (22 Feb 1914).

145. Hallermeyer, "Das Problem der Entartung," *NJ* 8 (22 Feb 1914).

146. See also Hastings, "Fears," 34–56. On later Catholic attitudes toward eugenics, see Dietrich, "Eugenics," 575–601; Richter, *Eugenik.*

147. Verhey, *Spirit;* Missalla, *Gott;* Pressel, *Kriegspredigt;* Hoover, *Gospel.*

148. Evans, *Center Party,* 203; more generally, see Morsey, "Nationalstaat," 31–64; Dülmen, "Katholizismus," 347–76; Heinen, "Integration," 183–222.

149. On the *Burgfrieden,* see Chickering, *War,* 13–18.

150. "Gut und Blut für das Vaterland!" *NJ* 32 (9 Aug 1914); also "Was die Stunde lehrt," *NJ* 31 (2 Aug 1914).

151. "An die Leser," *NJ* 33 (27 Sep 1914): 385–86.

152. "Unsere Aufgabe," *Hochland* 12:1 (Oct 1914): 112; also "Vom gerechten Krieg," *Hochland* 12:1 (Oct 1914); "An die Pforten des Weltkrieges," *Hochland* 12:1 (Oct 1914); "Die sittliche Berechtigung und Bedeutung des Krieges," *Hochland* 12:6 (Mar 1915); "Der Krieg als Wissenschaft und Kunst," *Hochland* 12:6 (Mar 1915); "Positionskrieg und Sittlichkeit," *Hochland* 12:8 (May 1915); "Der Genius des Krieges," *Hochland* 13:1 (Oct 1915); "Christus und der Krieger," *Hochland* 13:1 (Oct 1915).

153. "Völkische Lebensfähigkeit und Religion," *Hochland* 11:12 (Sep 1914): 667.

154. Wolf, "Deutsche Volkskraft," *Hochland* 12:8 (May 1915).

155. Guenther, "Der Krieg und das Rassenproblem," *Hochland* 12:9 (June 1915): 260–61. For the culmination of Guenther's racial thought, see his *Rasse und Heimat* (Berlin, 1936).

156. On Wirth, see Wiwjorra, "Vorgeschichtsforschung," 200–206.

157. Wirth, *Rasse;* "Russland und der Panslavismus," *Hochland* 12:1 (Oct 1914); "Die irische Frage," *Hochland* 12:6 (Mar 1915); "Die Orientpolitik Österreichs," *Hochland* 12:8 (May 1915); "Entwicklung und Bedeutung des Dreibundes," *Hochland* 12:9 (June 1915). On Wirth's centrality to the early Nazi group in Burghausen, see Grypa, *Kampfzeit,* 3–4.

158. Thrasolt, "Deutsch-*völkisch,*" *DHF* 2:3 (Dec 1914): 131–32.

159. See, e.g., Thrasolt, "Gelöbnis," *AGD* 1 (1918–19); Thrasolt, "Einem Bauern," *AGD* 1 (1918–1919); Schrönghamer, "Advent," *AGD* 1 (1918–19); Schrönghamer, "Das Sonnengebot," *AGD* 1 (1918–1919).

160. One insightful observer noted that the immediate postwar years represented the "darkest chapter" in the history of liberal religious movements like Reform Catholicism: "This movement, once so powerful, reached its lowest point in this period. Its exit reminds one of the ending of a Shakespearean play in which all the heroes lay slain on the floor"; Nigg, *Geschichte,* 394. On the broader turn away from prewar progressive subjectivism to harsh postwar objectivism, see, e.g., Gay, *Weimar,* 119–27.

161. Giliard to Joseph Bernhart, 11 Mar 1919, NL Bernhart, BSB.

162. Undated internal note, SAM-PD, fol. 2803.

163. On the almost complete eclipsing of prewar Reform Catholic subjectivism in the 1920s, see Ruster, *Nützlichkeit,* esp. 72–95. On connections between Reform Catholicism and Vatican II, see Wolf, *Antimodernismus.*

Chapter 2

1. NSDAP, *Wesen, Grundsätze und Ziele der NSDAP* (Munich, 1923), 43.

2. Conway, *Persecution,* 5–6; Scholder, *Kirchen,* 1:85; Steinhoff, *Widerstand,* 27–28; Zipfel, *Kirchenkampf,* 1–11. More recently, Richard Steigmann-Gall has taken the interconfessionality of Positive Christianity at something closer to face value, arguing persuasively that early Nazi statements on religion should be accorded a good degree of plausibility since the Nazis did not yet engage in electoral politics and their ideas were thus presented unvarnished, without the overriding concerns of political expediency; see Steigmann-Gall, *Holy Reich,* 13–15.

3. Geyer, *Verkehrte Welt.* See also Mitchell, *Revolution;* Bosl, *Umbruch;* Grunberger, *Rising;* Hillmayr, *Terror.*

4. On postwar Catholic attitudes more generally, see Berning, "Neubesinnung," 47–98. On broader German apocalypticism, see Redles, *Millenial Reich,* 14–45; Vondung, *Apocalypse;* Rhodes, *Movement;* Geyer, "Warfare."

5. Faulhaber, "Hirtenwort," *Amtsblatt* 33 (14 Nov 1918).

6. For Faulhaber's brash pro-war sermons, see, e.g., his *Schwert*. On the dramatic impact of the war and its aftermath on Eugenio Pacelli, the future Pope Pius XII who served as papal nuncio in Munich from 1917 to 1925, see O'Shea, *Cross Too Heavy*, 151–78.

7. *Amtsblatt* 36 (20 Dec 1918) and 6 (27 Feb 1919). See also "In die Krisis hinein," *HPB* 162 (Dec 1918); "Was die Stunde fordert," *HPB* 162 (Dec 1918). On Catholic attitudes toward the Eisner regime, see Kanzler, *Bayerns Kampf*, 13–16; Grau, *Eisner*, chap. 8; Blessing, "Kirchenglocken," 403–20.

8. Bauer, *Eisner*, 378–79; Hennig, *Hoffmann*, 109–12, 140–41.

9. *Amtsblatt* 3 (31 Jan 1919); "Die bayerischen Bischöfe gegen die Verordnung vom 25. Januar 1919," *Amtsblatt* 4 (5 Feb 1919); also the earlier warning, "Am Beginn des Kulturkampfes," *AR* 50 (14 Dec 1918).

10. Hillmayr, "München," 480–81.

11. On pervasive anti-Semitism in Catholic Bavaria, see Fenske, *Konservativismus*; Large, *Einwohnerwehr*, 27–28.

12. Quoted in Breuer, *Wandel*, 311–12. On broader Catholic anti-Semitism, see Greive, *Theologie*, 31–61.

13. "Freimaurerei," *MKK* 9 (2 Mar 1919); Wichtl, *Weltfreimaurerei*.

14. "Vom Büchertisch," *AR* 22 (31 May 1919). On the strong alignment of the *Rundschau* with the BVP, see Mennekes, *Herausforderung*, 15–16.

15. Schwend, *Bayern;* Schönhoven, *Volkspartei*. On Erzberger's politics, see Epstein, *Erzberger;* Leitzbach, *Erzberger*.

16. "Bayerische Volkspartei," *BK* 317 (14 Nov 1918); also "Die Bayerische Volkspartei entsteht!" *BK* 321 (18 Nov 1918); "Gründung der Bayerischen Volkspartei," *BK* 326 (21 Nov 1918).

17. Ringelmann, *Handbuch*, 5.

18. On Munich reactions to the uprising in Berlin, see Pelz, *Spartakusbund*, 284–87.

19. On the relationship between the BVP and Center Party, see Schönhoven, *Volkspartei*, 35–42.

20. BVP *Flugblatt* 2 (22 Nov 1918); cited in Schönhoven, *Volkspartei*, 28. On BVP anti-Semitism, see Speckner, "Ordnungszelle," 138–42.

21. Rost, "Zersetzungserscheinungen im modernen Judentum," *AR* 4 (25 Jan 1919).

22. Rost, "Die Entartung des Judentums," *AR* 13 (29 Mar 1919); also "Die moderne Jüdin," *AR* 6 (8 Feb 1919); "Das Judentum im öffentlichen Leben," *AR* 20 (17 May 1919). See also Rost's *Erinnerungen*.

23. "Unser Elend," *HPB* 163 (Jan 1919); also "Gott allein kann helfen," *HPB* 163 (Jan 1919). For more on the conservative *HPB*, see Mennekes, *Herausforderung*, 13–14.

24. Karl, *Schreckensherrschaft*.

25. "Münchener, seid dankbar!" *MKK* 19 (11 May 1919). The article contained a footnote condemning the "terrible" murder of the twenty-one members of the Catholic Gesellenverein mistaken for Red activists, but did not suggest that the arbitrary shooting of hundreds of Jewish and communist figures was anything but morally acceptable.

26. "Kommunismus?" *MKK* 22 (1 June 1919).

27. "Wirrnisse in Bayern," *HPB* 163 (May 1919); "Politik ohne Gott," *HPB* 163 (May 1919).

28. "Niederlage der Sozialdemokratie in Bayern," *AR* 26 (28 June 1919); also "Ursachen des revolutionären Sieges des Proletariats," *HPB* 164 (June 1919).

29. See Schrönghamer's autobiographical entry in Zils, *München.*

30. See Schrönghamer, *Kriegssaat; Helden; Dörfl; Volke.*

31. See Greive, *Theologie,* 34–36.

32. Schrönghamer, *Ende,* viii–ix.

33. Ibid., 5.

34. Ibid., iv.

35. Schrönghamer, *Antichrist,* 2.

36. Ibid., 46–47. Schrönghamer was also influenced by Sebastian Wieser, an anti-Semitic priest in Waal, with whom he had been especially close since their student days together; see Wieser, *Antichrist.* On their later *völkisch* collaboration, see "Deutschtum und Christentum," *VB* 95 (31 Oct 1920).

37. Schrönghamer, *Reich* (1918), 5–6. He saw the "coming Reich" alternately in spiritual terms, as an "epoch of the Holy Spirit," and in economic terms, in which the Germanic *Walddorfgeist* would triumph over the Jewish *Warenhausgeist.*

38. Ibid., 38, 106.

39. Ibid., 262–63.

40. Ibid., 188–207. On mystical word-play within the broader *völkisch* movement, see Puschner, *Bewegung,* 27–48.

41. See, for example, the central discussion of his *Arbeit–Arbot–Sonnengebot* formulation at the Nazis' first mass meeting in February 1920, below.

42. Schrönghamer blamed political Catholicism, which he identified as the "old party spirit" that was based merely on an "external confession of faith," for stifling the internal "renewal" to which religious Catholicism aspired; *Reich* (1918), 11–12.

43. See, e.g., *AR* 5 (1 Feb 1919); *AR* 13 (29 Mar 1919); *Hochland* 17:2 (Nov 1919).

44. Schrönghamer, *Auferstehung.*

45. Schrönghamer, *Geist.*

46. Schrönghamer, *Kapitalismus.*

47. Schrönghamer, *Weltfeind,* 6.

48. Schrönghamer, *Waldsegen;* Schrönghamer, *Glück;* Schrönghamer, *Daheim.*

49. "Weltensturz: Zeitgedanken," *AR* 34 (23 Aug 1919).

50. Ibid.

51. On the similar ideas of Chamberlain, see Field, *Evangelist,* 310–12. While influenced by such Protestant thinkers, Schrönghamer viewed his own thought as distinctive in laying claim to an older Catholic-Christian identity that predated the Reformation; see also *Reich* (1918), 182–84.

52. "Bolschewismus, Kapitalismus, Imperialismus," *AR* 35 (30 Aug 1919).

53. See *AR* 32 (9 Aug 1919); *AR* 45 (8 Nov 1919); also Schrönghamer's "Verwandlung," *AR* 39 (27 Sep 1919); "Sei froh!" *AR* 49 (6 Dec 1919); "Junges Mädchen," *AR* 52 (27 Dec 1919); "Gebet," *AR* 8 (21 Feb 1920); "Das Webergärtlein," *AR* 25 (19 June 1920).

54. The second Hoffmann cabinet, which consisted of an SPD-BVP-Democrat coalition, almost dissolved in the late summer due to internal tensions, but was rescued by an agreement pledging joint cooperation signed by the coalition parties in late October; Schwend, *Bayern,* 552–53; "Bayerisch-politische Umrisse," *HPB* 164 (Dec 1919); "Neujahr 1920," *HPB* 165 (Jan 1920). The subsequent turn away from radical anti-Semitism within BVP circles was interpreted by many anti-Semites as a craven concession to the "Jewish" SPD and as a dishonorable abandonment of principle for purely political gain.

55. Geyer, *Verkehrte Welt,* 283–84; Krenn, *Arbeiterbewegung,* 294–95. Pfeiffer's hagiographic biographer largely overlooks his anti-Semitism; Reuter, *Eminenz.*

56. On Kausen, see Munro, *Moenius,* 27–29.

57. "Zur Judenfrage," *AR* 47 (22 Nov 1919).

58. Joseph Lippl, "Der Talmud nach dem Urteil der getenwärtigen Forschung," *AR* 47 (22 Nov 1919).

59. Kausen, "Die Judenfrage als Rassenproblem," *AR* 50 (13 Dec 1919). For a charitable interpretation of Kausen's thought, see Greive, *Theologie,* 66–67.

60. Caspar Hartl, "Jüdische und christliche Arbeiterführer," *AR* 2 (10 Jan 1920).

61. "Errungenschaften der Revolution," *HPB* 164 (Dec 1919); "Überwindung der Sozialdemokratie," *HPB* 165 (Jan 1920).

62. Schrönghamer, "Ihr Schläfer, erwacht!" *MB* 63 (19 Nov 1919); "Reaktion," *MB* 71 (17 Dec 1919).

63. Schrönghamer not only trumpeted the ideas of Eckart but encouraged Catholic readers of the *Rundschau* to support *Auf gut deutsch;* "Bolschewismus," *AR* 35 (30 Aug 1919).

64. Plewnia, *Eckart;* Engelman, *Eckart;* Rosenberg, *Vermächtnis;* Reich, *Eckart;* Euringer, *Eckart;* Grün, *Publizist.*

65. Eckart was in contact with Reform Catholic playwright Carl Scapinelli, who helped to publicize his works in Munich; Scapinelli, "Der Froschkönig," *BK* 34 (6 Mar 1906); also the reviews in *MNN* 108 (6 Mar 1906); *AZ* 104 (4 Mar 1906). On the formation of Eckart's world view after moving to Munich, see Bärsch, *Religion,* 52–63.

66. "Christus, Buddha, Nietzsche," *MZ* 31 (2 Feb 1917); also "Der Heilige und der Narr," *UV* 1 (Dec 1916).

67. On Catholic Vaterlandspartei support in Munich, see Hagenlücke, *Vaterlandspartei,* 212–15.

68. Lorenz Pieper is but one example; see BTB entries of 20 May 1920, 22 Mar 1921, 5 Apr 1921, 21 Feb 1922.

69. "Schönheitsfehler," *AGD* 1 (7 Dec 1918); "Randbemerkungen," *AGD* 3 (17 Jan 1919).

70. "Zwiesprache," *AGD* 2 (10 Jan 1919).

71. This pattern was followed by a number of Catholic nationalist figures who originally supported the BVP, including early Nazi activists like Hans Dauser, who had been an influential BVP figure in 1918 and 1919; see, e.g., Dauser's SS *Lebenslauf,* BDC A3343-SSO, reel 137.

72. See, e.g., Schrönghamer, "Advent," *AGD* 16 (30 May 1919); Schrönghamer, "Das Sonnengebot," *AGD* 36 (31 Oct 1919); Thrasolt, "Gelöbnis," *AGD* 11–12 (4 Apr 1919); Thrasolt, "Einem Bauern," *AGD* 11–12 (4 Apr 1919); Fischer, "Und die Kirche . . . ?" *AGD* 17–18 (13 June 1919); Fischer, "Nicht Geld! Eine Tat!" *AGD* 22 (17 July 1919).

73. Eckart also had a deeply conflicted view of the person of St. Paul, seeing him as a heroic figure as long as he was serving as a representative of Christ against the Jews (as in Acts 23) while also blaming him at least in part for preventing early Christianity from breaking completely with its Jewish roots; see "Das Judentum in und ausser uns," *AGD* 2 (10 Jan 1919). On the more radical rejection of Paul by non-Catholic *völkisch* pioneers like Paul de Lagarde, see Scholder, *Kirchen,* 1:81–83. Eckart's criticism of ultramontanism also became stridently bitter on numerous occasions; "Erzberger," *AGD* 22 (17 July 1919); "Tagebuch," *AGD* 32–33 (10 Oct 1919).

74. Meisl was born in Munich in 1887 and was ordained in 1913. After serving for six years in neighboring Dachau, Meisl returned to Munich in 1919 to edit the *Kirchenzeitung;* PA-Meisl, AEMF; *Schematismus,* 1923.

75. The Jews were identified as "a particular nationality [*Nationalität*], not simply a religious party," whose identity was maintained through the "non-mixing of blood"; "Wie entstand der Internationalismus der Freimaurerei?" *MKK* 7 (15 Feb 1920).

76. "Das kommunistische Ostjudentum in Österreich," *MKK* 14 (4 Apr 1920).

77. "Judenbekehrungen in Ungarn," *MKK* 14 (4 Apr 1920). On Hungarian Catholicism in the aftermath of the Bela Kun regime, see Hanebrink, *Defense,* 77–107.

78. "Der jüdische Imperialismus," *MKK* 15 (11 Apr 1920).

79. "Wo steht der Gegner?" *MKK* 19 (9 May 1920). It is possible that Meisl solicited this anonymous piece, which exhibits strong similarities with the ideas of Schrönghamer, rather than writing it himself.

80. See the later coverage in *VB* 54 (9 June 1920). Müller was born in 1876, ordained in 1902, and appointed head of the Pressverein after receiving a doctorate in law from Munich; *Schematismus,* 1929, PA-Müller, AEMF.

81. "Nicht Judenhass, sondern Christenschutz!" *MKK* 18 (2 May 1920).

82. Meisl's transfer was dated 15 May 1920, and he was eventually replaced as editor by Justin Maag. Meisl's new title was merely "assistant" upon his transfer to the Kloster der Frauen vom guten Hirten; see *Schematismus,* 1920.

83. See *Qualifikations-Noten,* 14 Feb 1921 and 23 Jan 1922, Meisl personnel file, AEMF.

84. "Katholiken und Judenfrage," *VB* 54 (9 June 1920).

85. Franz-Willing, *Ursprung,* 62–75; Phelps, "Arbeiterpartei," 974–86; Orlow, *Nazi Party,* 11–45; Deuerlein, *Aufstieg,* 56–61; Auerbach, "Lehrjahre," 1–45; Joachimsthaler, *Hitlers Weg,* 250–68.

86. Phelps, "Drexler," 1134–43; Evans, *Coming,* 169–72; also Drexler's 1935 "Lebenslauf," in Deuerlein, *Aufstieg,* 59.

87. In its earliest months, the DAP's leadership committee consisted of Drexler, sportswriter Karl Harrer, railroad locksmith Michael Lotter, carpenter Franz Xaver Girisch, and two engineering students, Adolf Birkhofer and Johann Baptist Kölbl; see also Joachimsthaler, *Hitlers Weg,* 259.

88. Drexler was also specific in framing his appeal to Munich workers: "Only Christian Socialism can give you the power to survive and triumph"; *Erwachen,* 48. See also, e.g., Drexler's extreme idealization of Jesus in "Dürfen Sozialisten Judengegner sein?" *VB* 46 (12 June 1921).

89. Mühlberger, *Voice,* 1:25–28; Layton, "Beobachter," 353–54.

90. The group had, at its height, a membership of around 250 in Munich; Franz-Willing, "Munich," 319–34; Phelps, "Before Hitler," 245–61; Hatheway, "Origins," 443–62; more generally, see Rose, *Thule;* Gilbhard, *Thule.*

91. Sebottendorff, whose real name was Adam Alfred Rudolf Glauer, was the most influential figure; see Sebottendorff, *Bevor;* and Goodrick-Clarke, *Occult,* 123–48.

92. Tavernaro, *Verlag,* 19–24.

93. "Halte dein Blut rein!" *MB* 19 (12 Oct 1918).

94. "Warum das Zentrum umfiel," *MB* 20 (19 Oct 1918).

95. "Nationalliberale Partei Münchens," *MB* 29 (21 Dec 1918); "München als Fremdenstadt," *MB* 1 (11 Jan 1919); "Nationalliberale Landespartei in Bayern," *MB* 3 (18 Jan 1919). Contrary to common attribution, Eckart was never an official member of the Thule-Gesellschaft; Rose, *Thule,* 108–20.

96. "Was wir wollen," *MB* 25 (22 Nov 1918).

97. There were rumors that Sebottendorff was running from the law and had possibly played a role in betraying the seven members of the Thule-Gesellschaft who ended up among the hostages executed by the Soviet regime in late April 1919; see "Eine Klarstellung," *MB* 21 (21 June 1919). On the seven Thule members who were killed, see, e.g., Rose, *Thule,* 58–66.

98. Both had connections to the Deutsch-Sozialistische Partei, which strongly influenced the Nazi program, and both discussed their Catholic identity publicly; see, e.g., "Bekanntmachung," *VB* 37 (12 May 1921). Sesselmann was from a very prominent Catholic family in Steinwiesen that also included his cousin Josef "Ochsensepp" Müller, who later cofounded the CSU and served as Bavarian minister-president after 1945. The two were

born only weeks apart in 1898 and were close childhood friends; Hettler, *Müller,* 10–12.

99. Both joined the DAP in December 1919, Sesselmann with member number 628 and Müller with member number 613. Sebottendorff, Hering, and Nenner were never members.

100. Tavernaro, *Verlag,* 24.

101. "Kann ein Katholik Antisemit sein?" *MB* 19 (7 June 1919).

102. "Kann ein Katholik Antisemit sein?" *AGD* 17–18 (13 June 1919). The same issue also featured an article by the anti-Semitic Catholic priest Anton Fischer.

103. "Eingesandt," *MB* 20 (14 June 1919).

104. Although there was not much serious attempt to conceal his identity, Stempfle's articles in the *Beobachter* often appeared under the pseudonym Redivivus; see the clippings in NL Stempfle, BHSA.

105. On Stempfle's work with Catholic students, see *Akademiker* 7:3 (May 1915). He remained active among Catholic student groups in Munich into the early 1920s; Stempfle to Rudolf Kanzler, 10 Mar 1921, NL Stempfle, fol. 3. Among the *Hofklerus,* Stempfle was closest to the anti-Semitic Dr. Max Fastlinger, who had served as the official diocesan librarian in Munich since 1899 and who had held—alongside future Nazis Georg Stipberger, Johannes Heldwein, and Wilhelm August Patin (first cousin of Heinrich Himmler)—the position of canon (*Kanonikus*) at St. Kajetan since 1913; PA-Fastlinger, AEMF. When Fastlinger died in 1918, Stempfle became the executor of Fastlinger's literary estate; "Vereinbarung," NL Stempfle, fol. 5.

106. Stempfle's Latin compilation of Fastlinger's works was listed officially in the "Schriftstellerische Arbeiten des Diözesan-Klerus," *Schematismus,* 1920, 205.

107. "Die jüdische Tagespresse," *MB* 39 (27 Aug 1919); "Pogrommärchen," *MB* 48 (20 Sep 1919); "Und bei uns?" *MB* 61 (12 Nov 1919); "Ein katholischer Bischof und die Judenfrage," *MB* 48 (20 Sep 1919).

108. Stempfle to Hugo Machhaus, 12 Apr 1921, NL Stempfle, fol. 3. On Stempfle's leading role in Orka, see Kanzler, *Bayerns Kampf,* 86–94.

109. Hoffmann, *Hitler,* 52.

110. Roth's younger brother Franz served as Faulhaber's doorman and personal concierge from October 1919 to September 1923. See Faulhaber to Franz Roth, 25 Sep 1929, Faulhaber to Josef Roth (father), 16 June 1931, NL Faulhaber, fol. 9606; also Josef Roth (son) to Faulhaber, 5 Apr 1929, NL Faulhaber, fol. 7269. Roth's other brother Leonhard joined the Dominican order in 1924; see Füllenbach, "Leonhard Roth," 1167–71; Göttler, *Leonhard Roth.*

111. Studentenkartei, UAM. Roth had fought on the western front in 1917–1918 and was awarded the Iron Cross, second class; on the impact of his combat experience, see Roth, "Der Weg der Frontsoldaten," *GH* 6 (1929): 319–23.

112. The standard history remains Lohalm, *Radikalismus.*

113. Ibid., 168.

114. Ibid., 290–92. On the dramatic growth of groups like the DVST among students in 1919–1920, see Bleuel and Klinnert, *Studenten,* 91–97; Kater, *Studentenschaft,* 80–95.

115. Roth, "An die Münchener Studentenschaft," *MB* 28 (19 July 1919). See also the collective letter of the Munich DVST to Faulhaber, 16 Nov 1919, appealing to "all Catholic Christians"; NL Faulhaber, fol. 7221.

116. Roth, "Studentenschaft"; see also Karl Brassler, "Kommilitonen!" *MB* 33 (6 Aug 1919).

117. Roth, "Über die Stellung der Katholiken zur völkischen Wiedergeburt," *MB* 33 (6 Aug 1919).

118. "Eingesandt," *MB* 35 (13 Aug 1919).

119. Roth and Alfred Miller, a Catholic Nazi student who venerated his mentor Schnitzer for decades, may have met as students in Schnitzer's course "Allgemeine Religionsgeschichte"; see *Vorlesungstätigkeit,* Schnitzeriana, BSB. On the close student friendship of Roth and Miller, see Baumgärtner, *Weltanschauungskampf,* 71.

120. Schrönghamer's marriage of Catholic imagery and the nordic *Edda* permeated Roth's early writings, echoing clearly in the references to Baldur, Hödur, and Loki in his DVST appeal; Roth, "Studentenschaft."

121. On Roth's membership, see his Studentenkartei entry, UAM. On the importance of the Munich DVST to early Nazi history, see Auerbach, "Nationalsozialismus," 13–28.

122. "Der versäumte Friede" and "Kapitalismus," *MB* 33 (6 Aug 1919). The former was the lead article on the front page; it appeared almost exactly at the height of Schrönghamer's parallel *Rundschau* activism.

123. From August through December 1919, Schrönghamer wrote over thirty major *Beobachter* pieces, literally saturating the paper. He also wrote nearly twenty *Beobachter* pieces in the first few months of 1920.

124. *MB* 35 (13 Aug 1919).

125. Deuerlein, "Eintritt," 195–96; Franz-Willing, *Ursprung,* 66–67.

126. See Maser, *Frühgeschichte,* 263–65.

127. On Hitler's modest early DAP speeches, see Kershaw, *Hubris,* 140–43. Feder was the brother-in-law of historian Karl Alexander von Müller, who was involved in prewar Reform Catholic circles but later abandoned his Catholic faith; Müller, *Gärten,* 427–29.

128. "Zusammenbruch," *MB* 40 (30 Aug 1919); also his "Das Wirken des Judentums," *MB* 52 (11 Oct 1919); "Kultur und Judentum," *MB* 53 (15 Oct 1919); "Politik und Judentum," *MB* 55 (21 Oct 1919).

129. *MB* 52 (11 Oct 1919); *MB* 56 (25 Oct 1919). The book was soon distributed directly from the *Beobachter* offices; *MB* 60 (8 Nov 1919).

130. Schrönghamer held out the possibility that Christ's power was miraculous enough to perhaps redeem even some Jews, although this caveat was largely out of sync with the brutality of his anti-Semitism; *Weltfeind,* 4–6.

131. Schrönghamer, "Kapitalismus," *MB* 33 (6 Aug 1919). Feder's first *Beobachter* contributions, which both dealt with interest slavery, were

published in the very next issue, *MB* 34 (9 Aug 1919). More generally, see Schrönghamer, *Reich,* 228–36, which was published in the fall of 1918 and predated Feder's *Manifest* by several months. Feder later claimed that he had formulated his ideas already in November 1918; Feder, "Innere Geschichte der Brechung der Zinsknechtschaft," *VB* 72 (12 Aug 1920); also Tyrell, "Feder," 48–57.

132. "Ihr Schläfer, erwacht! Ein Heimruf zum lebendigen Gott," *MB* 63 (19 Nov 1919); see also "Selbstbetrug und Selbstbefreiung," *MB* 51 (8 Oct 1919); "Staatsschulden," *MB* 52 (11 Oct 1919); "Politik," *MB* 55 (21 Oct 1919); "Politik und Judentum," *MB* 55 (21 Oct 1919); "Die wahre Volksschule," *MB* 58 (1 Nov 1919); "Der Kapitalismus im sozialistischen Staat," *MB* 59 (5 Nov 1919); "Abbau der Preise," *MB* 62 (15 Nov 1919); "Ehre," *MB* 69 (10 Dec 1919); "Reaktion," *MB* 71 (17 Dec 1919); "Staatsformen," *MB* 72 (20 Dec 1919).

133. "Weihnacht," *MB* 72 (24 Dec 1919).

134. "Gemeinwohl vor Eigennutz"; see esp. Schrönghamer, "Verantwortung," *MB* 50 (4 Oct 1919).

135. Franz-Willing, *Ursprung,* 80–81; Joachimsthaler, *Hitlers Weg,* 268–71; Maser, *Frühgeshichte,* 202–6.

136. Franz-Willing, *Ursprung,* 68–69; Maser, *Frühgeschichte,* 201–3.

137. Maser notes that even before his expulsion, Harrer's primary loyalty to the Thule-Gesellschaft was out of step with the DAP; *Frühgeschichte,* 170–71; also Tyrell, *Trommler,* 25–33.

138. Franz-Willing, *Ursprung,* 77–79, credits Hitler with a significant role in formulating the program, whereas Maser, *Frühgeschichte,* 206, portrays Hitler as being only marginally involved.

139. Drexler to Uetrecht, 24 Feb 1941; also Rudolf Schüssler to Uetrecht, 11 Mar 1941; both in NSDAP/HA-R4, fol. 110.

140. See Wiegand's minutes of the meeting, with a copy of the "Grundsätze" attached; Akte Wiegand, NSDAP/HA-R4, fol. 111.

141. "Grundsätze," Akte Wiegand, NSDAP/HA-R4, fol. 111. Drexler made the caveat, which was eventually included in point 24 of the party program, that religious ideas that threatened the "existence of the German *Volk*" could not be supported by the state.

142. Ibid. The "Grundsätze" were quite general and should not be seen as a direct encapsulation of the 25 Points; their significance lies in the fact that Drexler cited them as central to the evolution of the broader ideals eventually represented in the party's program.

143. Wiegand minutes, NSDAP/HA-R4, fol. 111. Schrönghamer later stated that Drexler had essentially pushed him into the party; Spruchkammerverfahren, 15 June 1948, StAP, sch. 11.

144. Additionally, the phrase continued to echo frequently in postwar Catholic circles. See the official diocesan condemnation of a nudist group whose "principles and views are in conflict with Positive Christianity and Catholic religious exercise"; *Amtsblatt* 5 (22 Feb 1922). The BVP also

represented its ideals explicitly in terms of Positive Christianity; see, e.g., "Katholizismus und Deutschnationale Volkspartei," *BVC* (6 Nov 1922).

145. Hasselbach, "Entstehung," 22–23; see also the copy in NSDAP/HA-R4, fol. 107.

146. There is general overlap with almost all of the 25 Points, but see most explicitly point 11 (on interest slavery), cf. *Reich* (1918), 228–29, 236; point 13 (nationalization of trusts), cf. *Reich* (1918), 241; point 14 (division of profits in heavy industry), cf. *Reich* (1918), 241; point 16 (creation of healthy *Mittelstand,* nationalization of retail outlets), cf. *Reich* (1918), 20–22; point 17 (on land reform), cf. *Reich* (1918), 230; point 19 (replacing Roman law with Germanic law), cf. *Reich* (1918), 107.

147. The program of the DSP was printed in *MB* 18 (31 May 1919). On its influence on the 25 Points, see Tyrell, *Trommler,* 77–78; Franz-Willing, *Ursprung,* 78.

148. For Hitler's exaggerated account, see *Mein Kampf,* 373–74; also Kershaw, *Hubris,* 144–46; Tyrell, *Trommler,* 32–33.

149. On Hitler's Passau speech, see the report in *Donau-Zeitung* 78 (22 Feb 1920); also Moosbauer, *Passau,* 2–3; Wagner, *Passau,* 23; Becker, "Organisation," 137–43.

150. Phelps, "Arbeiterpartei," 983–84. See also Drexler's 26 Feb 1920 letter of thanks to Dingfelder, crediting him with the "remarkable" success of the evening; NSDAP/HA-R4, fol. 111.

151. Dingfelder contributed, along with Schrönghamer, to *Auf gut deutsch* in 1919–1920. Franz-Willing claimed that Dingfelder was acquainted with Anton Drexler already in 1917 through the local branch of the Vaterlandspartei (*Ursprung,* 73), but Dingfelder's retrospective account stated that he had never met Drexler until Drexler approached him in early 1920 about speaking at the DAP event; Dingfelder, "Wie es kam" (undated), NSDAP/HA-R52, fol. 1214. Several of Dingfelder's Bauernbund speeches from 1897—focusing, not surprisingly, on the perceived evils of ultramontanism and political Catholicism—are also contained in the same file.

152. On Dingfelder's collaboration with Schrönghamer's *Königsbote* in early 1920, see chap. 3 below.

153. After Schrönghamer, Dingfelder was perhaps the next most prolific contributor to the *Beobachter* at the time, writing often under the pen name Germanus Agricola; Fenske, *Konservatismus,* 282.

154. *Reich* (1918), 207–24. A copy of Dingfelder's speech is included in its entirety in NSDAP/HA-R52, fol. 1214.

155. The German original from Schrönghamer's 1918 text reads:

Was heisst denn Arbeit? Dem Wörtlein, wie es dasteht, merkt man den Ursprung nicht an. Die volkstümliche Mundart weist uns auch hier den richtigen Weg. Nicht "Arbeit" sagt das Volk, sondern "Arbot." "Ar" heisst aber Sonne und "bot" bedeutet Gebot. Also heisst Arbeit soviel wie Sonnengebot. (*Reich,* 190–91)

By comparison, the relevant section from Dingfelder's speech reads in the German original: "Was heisst denn arbeiten? Es heisst: bewusst schöpferisch tätig sein. Arbeit = Arbot (noch heute im Fränkischen noch gebräuchlich), ist das göttliche Sonnengebot"; Dingfelder speech, NSDAP/HA-R52, fol. 1214.

156. Schrönghamer, "Das Sonnengebot," *AGD* 36 (31 Oct 1919). Eckart attached a friendly editorial note praising Schrönghamer's *Reich* as "ein urgesundes Buch."

157. "Deutsche Arbeiterpartei," *VB* 17 (28 Feb 1920).

158. "War Jesus ein Jude? Eine deutsche Antwort," *VB* 16 (25 Feb 1920), 17 (28 Feb 1920), 18 (3 Mar 1920), 19 (6 Mar 1920), and 20 (10 Mar 1920). The fact that the pseudonym was not meant to conceal Schrönghamer's identity fully can be seen in a comparison of Widar Wälsung, "Bayern den Bayern!" *BKB* 1 (2 Apr 1920) and Schrönghamer, "Staat und Stadt," *VB* 30 (10 Apr 1920).

Chapter 3

1. The Hoffmann government, which had attempted to stabilize Bavarian politics after the upheaval of the *Räterepublik,* was finally dissolved in the aftermath of the March 1920 Kapp Putsch in Berlin; Hennig, *Hoffmann;* Seipp, "Scapegoats," 35–54.

2. "Bayern," *Donauwacht* 306 (31 Dec 1921).

3. Rosenberg, *Wesen.*

4. "War Jesus ein Jude? Eine deutsche Antwort," *VB* 16 (25 Feb 1920); *VB* 17 (28 Feb 1920), *VB* 18 (3 Mar 1920), *VB* 19 (6 Mar 1920), *VB* 20 (10 Mar 1920).

5. *VB* 16 (25 Feb 1920).

6. The journal was founded in 1916 as the *Deutsche Katholikenzeitung: Organ für Religion und Kirchenpolitik* and underwent several name alterations. Although it was published in Munich, Wieser's parish was located in the Bavarian town of Waal, some fifty miles south and west of Munich. Wieser and Schrönghamer had been close friends since their student days together.

7. "Die jüdische Sittenlehre," *DKZ* 4:8 (29 Feb 1920).

8. Pestalozza's initial open letter to Wieser, dated 1 Mar 1920, along with Schrönghamer's response on Wieser's behalf were reprinted in "Deutschtum und Christentum," *VB* 95 (31 Oct 1920).

9. Miller, "Demokratisches Demagogentum und seine Folgen," *VB* 87 (16 Nov 1921).

10. On the BKP within the context of other Catholic-oriented monarchist groups, see Garnett, *Monarchism,* 97–113.

11. Mayer-Koy, "In Treue fest," *BK* 1 (2 Apr 1920). On the BKP founding, see *BKB* 2 (9 Apr 1920). On Mayer-Koy, see Large, *Einwohnerwehr,* 52–53; Thoss, *Ludendorff-Kreis,* 135–36.

12. Editorial note, *BKB* 1 (2 Apr 1920).

13. Schrönghamer attacked prewar monarchical institutions as hopelessly decrepit, while also excoriating Bavarian separatists within the BVP who were rumored to want a south German Danubian monarchy; Schrönghamer, "Was wir wollen," *BKB* 1 (2 Apr 1920).

14. Dingfelder wrote an open letter explicitly linking his activities in the *Beobachter* to his willingness to contribute to the new *Königsbote; BKB* 2 (9 Apr 1920). One of the early contributors to come out of the Reform Catholic movement was Hermine Diemer, whose husband and brother-in-law (Michael and Markus Diemer) were prominent members of the KG; minutes, 26 Jan 1911 and 8 Jan 1914, KG-Archiv, BSB; Haustein, *Krausgesellschaft,* 286, 334; Diemer entry in Zils, *München;* also Diemer, "An den Königsboten!" *BKB* 2 (9 Apr 1920); "Eine Märtyrin," *BKB* 6 (23 Apr 1920); "Monarchie und Bürgerkrieg," *BKB* 15 (5 June 1920). Another collaborator was Therese Tesdorpf-Sickenberger, the sister of KG chair Otto Sickenberger; see, e. g., her "Der Königsbote," *BKB* 4 (13 Apr 1920); and her entry in Zils, *München.*

15. Haeuser did nothing to modify Schrönghamer's flaming anti-Semitism; Haeuser, "Die Königstreuen," *BKB* 2 (9 Apr 1920).

16. On the continuing flirtation between monarchist and *völkisch* circles, see Garnett, *Monarchism,* 224–42; Thoss, *Ludendorff-Kreis,* 187–89.

17. In May 1920, Mayer-Koy began publicly disavowing Schrönghamer's anti-Semitism; *BKB* 11 (11 May 1920). After the departure of Schrönghamer, the editorial position was offered initially to former Krausgesellschaft leader Philipp Funk, who agreed with the *völkisch* and anti-Semitic aspects of the program but was ultimately too "burdened with responsibility" to accept the position; Funk to Helene Raff, 16 Dec 1920, NL Raff, BSB. See also the partial account in Engelhardt, *Funk,* 281–82.

18. "Protestlerbund oder Kampfpartei?" *BKB* 44 (28 Oct 1921); "Mayer-Koy gegen Schrönghamer-Heimdal," *DZ* 490 (25 Nov 1921); also Schrönghamer, "Die 'judenreine' Königspartei und Mayer-Koy," *VB* 97 (21 Dec 1921); Eckart, "Nochmals Mayer-Koy und die Königspartei," *VB* 100–101 (31 Dec 1921); "F. Schrönghamer-Heimdal," *BKB* 51 (17 Dec 1921).

19. The initial *Beobachter* statement, which explicitly foregrounded Heilmann's role, appeared alongside a review of Catholic theologian Robert Klimsch's anti-Semitic *Juden,* a gushing advertisement for Schrönghamer's *Kapitalismus,* and the announcement for an upcoming NSDAP meeting at which Hitler was the advertised speaker; "Der deutsche Geist," *VB* 18 (2 Mar 1920).

20. Hagen, *Reformkatholizismus,* 100–101; Weiss, *Modernismus,* 345–47.

21. On the depth of Heilmann's reformist ideals, see Bernhart, *Erinnerungen,* vol. 1, 719.

22. On his continuing relations with KG figures, see Weiss, *Modernismus,* 354–56; Engelhardt, *Funk,* 155–56; Bernhart, *Erinnerungen,* vol. 1, 741. See also Heilmann, *Volksbibel.*

23. On Heilmann's influence, see Zoller, "Steppes," esp. 151–52. On Steppes' close relationship with Eckart beginning in early 1919, see, e.g., Eckart, "Entweder—oder!" *AGD* 5 (31 Jan 1919).

24. *DG* 1 (Apr 1920), 6.

25. On the widespread coding of Jews as "internal enemies" in the aftermath of the First World War, see Bartov, "Enemies," 775–76.

26. Heilmann, "Der deutsche Geist," *DG* 1 (Apr 1920), 2–3.

27. See the list of founding signatories in *DG* 1 (Apr 1920), 7. On Steppes' role as an early Nazi art critic, see his "Völkische Kunst," *VB* 89 (10–11 May 1923). Doerfler joined the NSDAP on 17 September 1920 (number 2100). On Heilmayer's Reform Catholic activism, see chap. 1 above; on his later abandonment of his Catholic identity and embrace of an aestheticized Nazi identity, see his "Die Stadt Adolf Hitlers," *SM* 33 (Dec 1935). Kotzde did not live in Munich but appeared at a major local event alongside Hitler on his thirty-first birthday; *VB* 36 (24 Apr 1920). See also the diocesan praise for Kotzde in "Gute Bücher," *MKK* 27 (2 July 1922).

28. Eckart supported Heilmann's journal so energetically that he mailed sample copies to all of his subscribers in April 1920 along with the current issue of *AGD;* see, e.g., the attached issue of *Der Deutsche Geist* included in the microfilm copy of *AGD* at Duke University.

29. See Heilmann, "Christ ist entstanden!" *VB* 14 (12–13 Apr 1925).

30. Hehl, *Priester,* 932.

31. Minutes, 19 Jan 1912, KG-Archiv, BSB; also Haustein, *Krausgesellschaft,* 310–11.

32. Huber, "Fragebogen für die ersten Mitglieder der NSDAP," 31 Oct 1933, BDC, ser. A3341-PK, reel F054. Since there were certainly numerous men from Rosenheim named Hans Huber, this biographical information was central to determining that both the Nazi Huber and the KG Huber were the same Johann Baptist Huber, born 30 March 1879 in Wiedergeltingen.

33. Huber's founding membership was dated 18 April 1920 (number 1074). On the founding of the Ortsgruppe Rosenheim, see Miesbeck, *Gründung;* Ullrich, "Rosenheim," 11–15.

34. Huber became progressively estranged from the NSDAP, although he never renounced his early party membership. He continued to express pride in the decisive role he had played in the early Nazi movement, when it still fought for Catholic-Christian ideals, while excoriating the anti-Catholic nature of the Nazi regime in power; Huber to Bouhler, 26 Mar 1940, Huber file, BDC.

35. Stegmaier joined the Ortsgruppe Rosenheim on 12 May 1920 (number 1157); on his role alongside Huber in the KG, see Haustein, *Krausgesellschaft,* 310–11.

36. Fuchs joined the NSDAP on 1 May 1920 (number 994); Böhm joined on 17 September 1920 (number 2094).

37. Briemann, born in Munich in 1873, joined the NSDAP in June 1920 (number 1184) and went on to serve as assistant treasurer of the party from 30 January 1922 to 29 January 1923, at which time he took over as secretary; see "Aus der Bewegung," *VB* 11 (8 Feb 1923); Joachimsthaler, *Hitlers Weg,* 294–95. On Briemann's role in the KG campaign against the antimodernist oath, see Gustav Ziegler to Polizeidirektion, 23 Dec 1910, along with the attached "Aufruf," SAM-PD, fol. 2803.

38. Sickenberger, a former chair of the KG, founded his own short-lived *völkisch* group called the Volksbund in 1918. By 1922, he settled in the Passau area and emerged as a vocal member of the NSDAP's Ortsgruppe Passau; *VB* 33 (26 Apr 1922); also *Lebenslauf,* 8 Aug 1934, MK-44612, BHSA. Koch was ordained in 1893 and joined the KG in 1910, eventually abandoning his Catholic faith in favor of the Nazi world view; Baumgärtner, *Weltanschauungskampf,* 71–72; Weiss, *Modernismus,* 343; Wesseling, "Koch," 210–15. Müller, born in 1881 in Oberhäuser, was ordained in 1907 and served on the leadership committee of the KG between 1910 and 1912; Haustein, *Krausgesellschaft,* 289–95. He was posted to a small parish in the Bavarian village of Röfingen, where he came into contact with the NSDAP in the early 1920s. He attempted to maintain his Catholic and Nazi loyalties after the putsch, founding the Ortsgruppe Röfingen in 1929 and coming into conflict with his ecclesiastical superiors as a result; see his file, BDC, A3341-PK, reel I185.

39. Sigmund, *Frauen,* pt. 3, 333–57; *Frauenleben,* 125–30.

40. It is important to note that this was a Catholic nursing order and not a religious order. Although she was not a nun, her public identification as a Catholic *Ordensschwester* helped to reinforce the Catholic-oriented charitable activism that the early Nazis were eager to embrace; see also Holzhaider, "Schwester Pia," 101–14.

41. Sigmund, *Frauen,* 339–40; Holzhaider, "Teufeln."

42. Early membership lists indicate that she was given member number 506; see, e.g., NSDAP-HA/R8, fol. 171. Other sources list her as having number 512; e.g., Holzhaider, "Schwester Pia," 102–3.

43. See "Achtung Münchener!" *VB* 36 (24 Apr 1920).

44. "Eine Gerichtsverhandlung!" *VB* 39–43 (11 May 1920). The *Beobachter* had been banned by the authorities from 29 April through 11 May, which delayed its report on the trial; "Verbot," *VB* 39–43 (11 May 1920).

45. "Kleine Nachrichten," *VB* 89 (10 Oct 1920); see also the publicity in *VB* 90 (14 Oct 1920); *VB* 92 (21 Oct 1920). Sister Pia later achieved notoriety for overseeing a detachment of Dachau prisoners who renovated her apartment in Schwabing in the early 1940s. She claimed to be caring for these prisoners—none of whom were killed or severely mistreated, it should be stated—but the work was unquestionably forced labor. She was also later accused of having looked the other way when Polish prisoners in Dachau were used for

medical testing. On the other hand, numerous Catholic priests held in Dachau claimed that she used her influence to better their conditions; see the comments of priests Bernhard Josef Seitz and Otto Pies in Thoma and Weiler, *Geistlichen,* 397–99. The priest Johann Huber, who fell ill and died in Dachau, was comforted by Sister Pia in a "truly motherly way" before his death, according to Huber's sister Therese; Holzhaider, "Teufeln," 8. The priest Leopold Arthofer also noted that she helped to win the release of several priests and secretly brought the inmates food, showing "a heart in which feminine goodness had not yet died out"; Arthofer, *Priester,* 101.

46. See the list in *VB* 91 (17 Oct 1920). On Heldwein, see Haustein, *Krausgesellschaft,* 258, 279. Prechtl, a twenty-three-year-old medical student, joined the NSDAP on 5 November 1920 along with his younger brother Wilhelm (numbers 2360 and 2361). Maurer will be discussed later in this chapter.

47. Kater, *Party,* 242–43; Madden, "Characteristics," 44–46; also Bleuel and Klinnert, *Studenten,* 89–95.

48. On Quickborn, which was founded in 1909, see Binkowski, *Quickborn.*

49. Studentenkartei, UAM. On the idealization of Philipp Funk, see Miller, *Schuldbuch,* 125–27. The ideas of Hugo Koch were cited and praised liberally throughout Miller's writings.

50. Vorlesungstätigkeit, Schnitzeriana, BSB; PA-Schnitzer, UAM. Having initially enrolled as a student of veterinary medicine, Miller switched to philosophy fairly quickly.

51. Despite their clear ideological differences at the time, the dedication to Miller's *Völkerentartung* still read: "Meinem hochverehrten Lehrer und väterlichen Freund Herrn Univ. Prof. Dr. J. Schnitzer—München in bleibender Dankbarkeit gewidmet." On Miller's later anti-Christian activities, see his party file, BDC, ser. A3341-PK, reel I087.

52. Studentenkartei, UAM. On the relationship between older Catholic fraternities and the HV, see "Quickborn," *Academia* 33:8–9 (20 Jan 1921); "Nachklänge zur Quickborntagung," *Academia* 34:5–6 (Sep–Oct 1922); more generally, Spael, *Deutschland,* 74–75.

53. Jedin, *Lebensbericht,* 29–30, 69–70.

54. Weinzierl is not included on any of the early party membership lists, although this does not necessarily discredit Jedin's perception of Weinzierl's early support for the NSDAP. He completed his medical studies at Munich in 1923.

55. Klara Schätz to Faulhaber, 13 Gilbhard (October) 1920; also Ludwig Schätz to Faulhaber, 19 Scheiding (September) 1919, both in NL Faulhaber, fol. 6557. Germanic phraseology like this was characteristic of Quickborn and several other youth groups.

56. See Faulhaber to Quickborn founder Bernhard Strehler, 24 Feb and 26 Apr 1921; Faulhaber to A. M. Mitnacht, 7 Aug 1921; all in NL Faulhaber, fol. 6557.

57. Between 1920 and 1922, Miller wrote at least 120 *Beobachter* contributions (signed as Alfred Miller, A. Miller, A.M., -ll-, or M., all of which are indisputably Miller), in addition to what is likely a sizable number of others that were either unsigned or perhaps written under unverifiable signatures. On the rise of Rosenberg's influence, see Piper, *Rosenberg,* 80–85.

58. "Friedensbund deutscher Katholiken," *VB* 10 (4 Feb 1920). On Schrönghamer's influence, see, e.g., Miller, "Judas der Würger," *VB* 64 (15 July 1920); "Judas der Weltfeind," *VB* 66 (22 July 1920); "Christentum und Antisemitismus," *VB* 80 (9 Sep 1920); "Judentum und Bolschewismus sind eins," *VB* 88 (7 Oct 1920).

59. "Anti-ultramontaner Reichsverband und Freimaurerei," *VB* 80 (22 Oct 1921).

60. "Staat, Religion, Kirche," *VB* 1–2 (6 Jan 1921); also "Christus am Kreuz—ein öffentliches Ärgernis!" *VB* 83 (19 Sep 1920); "Ein antisemitischer Bischof," *VB* 84 (23 Sep 1920); "Verfolgung deutscher Katholiken," *VB* 90 (26 Nov 1921); "Katholische Kirche und Judentum," *VB* 95 (14 Dec 1921).

61. "Staat, Religion, Kirche," *VB* 1–2 (6 Jan 1921).

62. See esp. "Die katholische Kirche und das Judentum," *VB* 76 (26 Aug 1920); 77 (29 Aug 1920); 78 (2 Sep 1920); 79 (5 Sep 1920).

63. Years later, in the mid-1930s, when Maurer was appointed editor of a staunchly Catholic paper in Würzburg despite clerical concerns over his earlier Nazi involvement, the major justification offered by Maurer's priest, Max Rössler, was the fact that Maurer "had come out of the Catholic youth movement"; Schmidt, *Maurer,* 72.

64. Maurer's first article appeared in *VB* 44 (13 May 1920). His first issue as chief editor was dated 15 July 1920 and featured a front-page lead article by Alfred Miller that echoed Schrönghamer's ideas; Miller, "Judas der Würger," *VB* 64 (15 July 1920).

65. See the initial announcement, *VB* 51 (29 May 1920).

66. Eder to Polizeidirektion, 26 July 1920, NSDAP-HA/R89, fol. 1864; also "Einladung," *VB* 65 (18 July 1920).

67. "Protokoll über die Gründungs-versammlung des Bundes der Beobachterfreunde im Katholischen Gesellschaftshaus," NSDAP-HA/R83, fol. 1691; also "Gründungsversammlung," *VB* 69 (31 July 1920).

68. After the Nazi purchase of the *Beobachter,* the BdB was no longer deemed necessary; its last meeting was held on 17 January 1921; NSDAP-HA/R83, fol. 1691.

69. *VB* 53 (5 June 1920). His NSDAP membership was dated 18 December 1920 (number 2603), but he had been an official Nazi speaker long before that date.

70. On the founding of the Landshut Ortsgruppe, see Auerbach, "Wurzeln," 72–74. The elder Maurer was a brewer by trade and joined the NSDAP on 4 October 1920 (number 2485). Kölbl joined on 2 August 1921 (number 4273); he was born in 1887 and took up his post in

Deggendorf in 1920. Kölbl did not rejoin the NSDAP after the putsch and eventually became an opponent of the Nazis; Hehl, *Priester,* 1296.

71. "Kampf gegen Wucher und Schiebertum," *VB* 100 (18 Nov 1920).

72. On the Nazi acquisition, see Layton, *"Beobachter,"* 353–82.

73. "Judenfrage und katholische Kirche. Von einem katholischen Geistlichen," *VB* 84 (23 Sep 1920). Maurer announced in an editorial preface: "We are hereby happy to be able to turn things over to the editorial colleague who is responsible for this question [*in dieser Frage zuständigen Mitarbeiter*], and we advise our readers to give his comments the utmost special attention."

74. Huber to parents, 28 June 1912, PA-Huber, ABA; also Spicer, *Hitler's Priests,* 39. For more on the KG campaign against the antimodernist oath, see Haustein, *Krausgesellschaft,* 156–75.

75. *MA* (9 Oct 1919); *MA* (10 Oct 1919); Spicer, *Hitler's Priests,* 39.

76. "Wegen Krankheit beurlaubt"; see Huber's entry in the 1920 *Schematismus.*

77. Quote from diocesan statement, 3 Feb 1948, in NL Faulhaber, fol. 5402.

78. "Judenfrage und katholische Kirche," *VB* 84 (23 Sep 1920); "Zentrum und Löwenstein," *VB* 100 (18 Nov 1920); "Geistlichkeit und Antisemitismus," *VB* 103 (28 Nov 1920); "Heute genau wie einst!" *VB* 108 (16 Dec 1920); see also the (mild) anti-ultramontanism of "Der Vatikan und England," *VB* 101 (21 Nov 1920).

79. "Freilicht-Passionspiel," *VB* 65 (18 July 1920); also the major publicity in *VB* 69 (31 July 1920). See also "Passionsfreilichtspiele," *MKK* 29 (18 July 1920); "Passionsspiel," *AR* 31 (31 July 1920).

80. "Katholische Heimatmission," *VB* 77 (29 Aug 1920); see also *MKK* 35 (29 Aug 1920).

81. Schärl, *Beamtenschaft,* 347–48; "Kath. Heimatmission," *MKK* 15 (2 Apr 1922); "Heimatmission," *Amtsblatt* 7 (6 Apr 1922); also Möckl, *Prinzregentenzeit,* 537–40.

82. Maurer, who was listed alternately as a student of veterinary medicine (med. vet.) and, erroneously in one entry, as a medical student (med.), was initiated (*geburscht*) as "Hans Maurer" according to the Aenania records; *Academia* 33:5 (20 Sep 1920). Maurer only used the distinctive "Hansjörg" in his journalistic endeavors and otherwise went by Hans Maurer or Hans Georg Maurer, which is how his name is listed on his NSDAP card; BDC, ser. A3340-MFKL, reel L091. His membership seems to have been short-lived (he is not listed in *Academia* 33:11 [25 Mar 1921]), and he was certainly not a central figure. I was unable to find further information (beyond verification of his initial membership) in the CV-Archiv in Regensburg.

83. *Academia* 33:5 (20 Sep 1920). On Hofmann's Nazi involvement, see Spicer, *Hitler's Priests,* 257.

84. The Stoeckle family was deeply religious but critical of political Catholicism. Hermann was ordained in 1912, joined the ranks of the

reform-oriented *Hofklerus* in 1918, and was appointed vicar at St. Kaje-tan (alongside future Nazis Patin and Stipberger); *Schematismus,* 1921. He was transferred to a position in Rome in 1931, ostensibly because of his friendliness toward the NSDAP. Unlike Edmund—who eventually left the Catholic Church, joined the SS, and declared himself *gottgläu-big*—Hermann never fully embraced Nazism, although a 1938 Gestapo report (BDC, ser. A3343-SSO, reel 162B) did note that "from time to time he has been willing to send information from Rome here [to Gestapo headquarters]."

85. See 1940 *Lebenslauf* and 9 June 1937 Stoeckle letter to Heinrich Himmler, both in Stoeckle SS file, BDC.

86. Andreas Stoeckle saw to it that all four of his sons—Hermann, Edmund, Alfons, and Josef—joined CV-Aenania, while he also served as president of the local Aenania alumni association until the early 1930s; Stitz, *CV,* 70–73.

87. The seven individual fraternities that constituted the Münchener-CV were Aenania, Burgundia, Langobardia, Moenania, Rheno-Franconia, Tuiskonia, and Vindelicia. An eighth Munich CV fraternity, Trifels, was founded in early 1923; *Academia* 36:1–4 (1 Aug 1923).

88. Birnbaum, "Studenten," esp. 120–23. On the initial pro-democratic stance of postwar students, see Stickler, "Verbindungen," 85–107.

89. Stoeckle was a decorated veteran and a celebrated athlete (most notably as a track-and-field star in the 110-meter hurdles); see "Leichtathle-tik," *VB* 177 (1 Sep 1923); "Meisterschaften," *BHZ* 4:7 (3 July 1922); "Zum Marburger Olympia," *BHZ* 5:4 (19 July 1924); Stoeckle, *Leibesübungen.* He was elected head of the Munich ASTA from 1920 to 1923 and served as editor of the *BHZ* in 1922; *Lebenslauf,* Stoeckle SS file, BDC. The most important spiritual leadership role within the Munich CV was assumed by the priest Erhard Schlund; see Fellner, "Schlund," 139–43.

90. On the HDA, see Kater, *Studentenschaft,* 21–24; Giles, *Students;* Steinberg, *Sabers,* 51–60.

91. Brandl, "Brauchen wir eine Arbeitsgemeinschaft der vaterländischen Verbände?" *Academia* 33:8–9 (20 Jan 1921).

92. Pfeiffer, "Schulungswoche des Deutschen Hochschulringes," *Acade-mia* 34:9–10 (Jan–Feb 1922); "Hochschulring und Münchener CV," *Acade-mia* 36:10 (15 Feb 1924); "CV und Hochschulring," *Academia* 34:3 (25 July 1921); "Zum Kampf um den Hochschulring," *Academia* 34:11–12 (Mar–Apr 1922); also the HDA materials in CV-Archiv (Regensburg), fol. 57.

93. "Hochschulring," *VB* 83 (2 Nov 1921); also "Deutsche Studenten!" *VB* 99 (14 Nov 1920); "Deutsche Studenten!" *VB* 1 (1 Jan 1921); "Treibereien gegen den Hochschulring," *VB* 17 (25 Feb 1921); "Zum Semester-Heil!" *VB* 36 (8 May 1921).

94. "Aus der Bewegung," *VB* 101 (21 Nov 1920); also Stoeckle to Himm-ler, 9 June 1937, Stoeckle SS file, BDC. Despite internal debate over the expulsion of Max Ettlinger (a CV alumnus, prominent philosophy

professor, and Jewish convert), the Aryan clause stood; "Rundschreiben," 7 Jan 1921, CV-Archiv, fol. 51.

95. Liebel was born in Munich on 9 April 1900 and received NSDAP member number 823; see also "Mitgliederverzeichnis," *Academia* 33:3 (15 July 1920).

96. Vianden, born on 17 December 1894 in Elberfeld and identified as a medical student on both the CV and Nazi membership lists, joined the NSDAP on 1 June 1920 (number 1351). He went on to obtain his medical doctorate in 1923. Mayer, born 21 February 1896 and listed as a medical-dental student, joined the NSDAP on 8 July 1920 (number 1637). Schreiber, born 28 November 1897 and identified on both the CV and Nazi membership lists as an architecture student, joined the NSDAP on 8 October 1920 (number 2246). Brücklmayr, born on 23 October 1885 and living at Arnulfstrasse 26 in Munich in 1920, joined the NSDAP on 25 June 1920 (number 1531); cf. "Verzeichnis der Rechtsanwälte und Notare des CV," *Academia* 33:5 (20 Sep 1920); and NSDAP/HA-R10, fol. 215.

97. Total membership in the NSDAP had grown to some 2,300 by late 1920; Manstein, *Mitglieder,* 115; Kater, *Party,* 242. By the summer of 1921, the number of student members of the NSDAP had grown to 229; Douglas, "Parent Cell," 64–65; Maser, *Frühgeschichte,* 255.

98. The *Beobachter* praised Stoeckle's "forceful words"; "Reichsgründungsgedanken," *VB* 6 (21 Jan 1921).

99. See, e.g., the blood-soaked symbolism of Stoeckle's speech the next year; "Totengedächtnisfeier," *BHZ* 3:11 (21 Jan 1922).

100. *VB* 15 (20 Feb 1921).

101. See, e.g., "Student und Arbeiter: Zur letzten Massenversammlung der NSDAP," *VB* 37 (12 May 1921).

102. On the continuing overrepresentation of students within the overall Nazi membership, which had grown to over 3,000 by the spring of 1921, see Madden, "Characteristics," 44–46.

103. For a contrasting account of the broader Catholic social-student movement elsewhere in Germany, which often did cooperate with the Center Party, see Spael, *Deutschland,* 61–75.

104. Weigl, who joined the NSDAP on 25 May 1920 (number 1187), consistently emphasized the religious (apolitical) aspects of the movement in the official diocesan press, noting for instance that "the social-student movement represents the principle of practical Christianity" in contrast to the allegedly complacent and hypocritical piety of political Catholicism; Weigl, "Die sozialstudentische Zentrale München," *MKK* 23 (8 June 1919). Karl Debus was a member of the Freie Vereinigung katholischer Studenten, with which Bernhard Stempfle was involved, and joined the NSDAP on the same day as Weigl, 25 May 1920 (number 1172). On Debus's activism, see the 1922 memo "Völkische Arbeit und katholischer Akademiker," CV-Archiv, fol. 57.

105. "Die sozialstudentische Bewegung," *BHZ* 2:3 (6 Nov 1920).

106. "Sozialstudentische Tagung in München," *VB* 100 (18 Nov 1920); also "Sozialstudentische Tagung," *BHZ* 2:4 (13 Nov 1920). Beck also kept Faulhaber informed of the HV's activities; Beck to Faulhaber, 15 Jan 1923, NL Faulhaber, fol. 6557.

107. Ludwig Schätz, "Zur sozialstudentischen Arbeit," *Hochland-Buch* 4 (1918).

108. "Vom Geiste deutscher Jugend und deutschem Führertum," *VB* 5 (18 Jan 1922); the offending work was Nettmann, *Fuchs.*

109. "Der korrekte Fuchs," *BHZ* 3:7 (3 Dec 1921); also "Der korrekte Fuchs," *Academia* 34:7–8 (Nov–Dec 1921).

110. Glasebock, *Studentenschaft,* 7–8, 9–11. Glasebock distanced himself from the Nazi movement after the putsch but later, in 1933, joined the Nazi SA for opportunistic reasons. His Catholic faith, however, brought him into conflict with his superiors within the SA, and he was expelled for being a "schwarze Bruder" who was more loyal to his old CV comrades than to the NSDAP; memo, 31 Mar 1935, Glasebock SA file, BDC, ser. A3341-SA, reel 175.

111. On Hirschfeld, see Stümke, *Homosexuelle,* esp. 21–52; Wolff, *Hirschfeld;* Kotowsky and Schoeps, *Hirschfeld.*

112. "Volkswohl und Nationalgedanke," *VB* 95 (31 Oct 1920).

113. Miller, "Hirschfeld und seine Jünger von der 'homosexuellen Sache,'" *VB* 94 (28 Oct 1920); also Miller, "Die jüdische Filmseuche," *VB* 94 (28 Oct 1920).

114. Miller, "Volksvergiftung: Ein Wort zum Vortrag Reitzenstein," *VB* 96 (4 Nov 1920).

115. "Kampf gegen die öffentliche Unsittlichkeit," *VB* 99 (14 Nov 1920).

116. Maurer, *Homosexualität;* "Die Homosexuellen," *VB* 59 (28 July 1921); "Der homosexuelle Sturmlauf," *VB* 62 (7 Aug 1921); "In eigener Angelegenheit," *VB* 69 (1 Sep 1921); "Vom Mädchenhandel," *VB* 69 (1 Sep 1921); "Sexualwissenschaftliche Preisaufgabe," *VB* 82 (29 Oct 1921); "Das Ziel der jüdischen 'Kultur'-Pioniere," *VB* 90 (26 Nov 1921); "Die neue Sittlichkeit," *VB* 92 (3 Dec 1921).

117. See his entry in *Schematismus,* 1922. Hecker was born in Osterhofen in 1860, was ordained in Munich in 1884, and was still alive as of the printing of the 1941 *Schematismus.* His personnel file is missing entirely from the archdiocesan archive in Munich.

118. Hecker, *Weltregierung,* 3–4. Hecker is mentioned briefly in Greive, *Theologie,* 38.

119. Hecker, *Weltregierung,* 32–33.

120. Hecker was particularly incensed about the anti-Christian policies of the Bolsheviks, exclaiming with no qualification: "In Russia the battle against Bolshevism means the extermination [*Ausrottung*] of the Jews"; ibid., 163.

121. Ibid., 177–81, quote from 177. Despite his energetic support for the NSDAP in 1921, Hecker distanced himself from the Nazi movement after the putsch.

122. See esp. ibid., 125–30.

123. One positive *Beobachter* review of Hecker's book concluded: "We welcome this brave priest as our fellow soldier [*Mitkämpfer*]. May he find many followers"; *VB* 89 (23 Nov 1921).

124. "Christentum und Antisemitismus," *VB* 80 (9 Sep 1920).

125. The Nazis continued to praise, whenever possible, the local anti-Semitic activism of priests like Franz Lukas, chaplain at Munich's Heilig-Geist-Kirche, who gave a flaming speech on the moral justification of anti-Semitism on 14 October 1920; *VB* 93 (24 Oct 1920); also Miller, "Ein antisemitischer Bischof," *VB* 84 (23 Sep 1920); "Schlafen die christlichen Geistlichen?" *VB* 93 (24 Oct 1920); "Geistlichkeit und Antisemitismus," *VB* 103 (28 Nov 1920); "Die Not der kirchlichen Angestellten," *VB* 109 (19 Dec 1920); "Christentum–Deutschtum–Judentum," *VB* 45 (9 June 1921); "Ein neues Verschleierungsmanöver," *VB* 88 (19 Nov 1921).

126. On the activism of Munich's Protestant clergy in non-Nazi *völkisch* groups, see Mensing, *Pfarrer,* 72–74.

127. "Jüdischer Mädchenhandel aus 'Religiosität,'" *VB* 95 (31 Oct 1920). The influence of Schrönghamer is unmistakable; compare, e.g., to his "Bolschewismus," *AR* 35 (30 Aug 1919).

128. Maurer reprinted, with appropriate "outrage," passages from the *Toldoth Jeschu* that characterized Jesus as a "bastard" conceived when a drunk Joseph raped Mary while she was "menstruating," who grew up to be an "arrogant magician"; Maurer, "Zentralverein," *VB* 43 (2 June 1921).

129. Maurer, "Vergehen gegen die Religion," *VB* 44 (5 June 1921); "Wie die Rasse, so der Geist," *VB* 45 (9 June 1921). By this time, Maurer's Catholic-*völkisch* crusade had made him into a minor local celebrity. On 10 June 1921, seventeen-year-old Fritz Lauböck received an autographed inscription from Maurer that admonished the young Catholic to "always remember your Christian faith"; NSDAP/HA-R53, fol. 1242. Fritz Lauböck served briefly as Hitler's secretary in 1923.

130. Maurer, "Der abgeblitzte Zentralverein"; "Die Wahrheit geht ihren sicheren Weg"; "Dem Zentralverein zu Ehren," all in *VB* 46 (12 June 1921). The judgment did not set the precedent Maurer claimed; the charges were merely dropped due to lack of evidence.

131. "Aufruf an die Schriftleitungen deutschvölkischer Zeitungen!" *VB* 47–48 (19 June 1921); "Bibel und Politik," *VB* 49 (23 June 1921).

132. "Zur Beachtung!" *NS* 1 (26 June 1921); also "An unsere Leser!" *NS* 1 (26 June 1921); and "Die talmudischen Weltverbrecher in katholischer Beleuchtung," *NS* 8 (21 July 1921).

133. "An die Adresse des Herrn Trasybulos im 'Bayer. Kurier,'" *VB* 34 (1 May 1921).

134. Dickel had gained respect in *völkisch* circles with his *Auferstehung des Abendlandes* (Augsburg, 1920), which was envisioned as a parallel to Oswald Spengler's more famous *Untergang des Abendlandes* (Vienna, 1918).

135. Tyrell, *Trommler,* 120–22; Kershaw, *Hubris,* 162–65; Eckart, "Der Gaunerstreich gegen Hitler," *VB* 61 (4 Aug 1921).

136. *VB* 61 (4 Aug 1921).

137. "Erzberger," *VB* 69 (1 Sep 1921).

138. "Der Verrat!" *VB* 70–73 (14 Sep 1921).

139. "Die göttliche Reichsregierung," *VB* 70–73 (14 Sep 1921); also "Der Betrug des Dr. Wirth," *VB* 62 (7 Aug 1921).

140. "Gimpelfang," *VB* 76 (5 Oct 1921); also "Juda und das Zentrum," *VB* 63 (11 Aug 1921); "Erzberger und das Zentrum," *VB* 64 (14 Aug 1921); "Der Retter des Zentrums," *VB* 64 (14 Aug 1921).

141. "Politik der Hetze," *BK* 260 (17 Sep 1921); "In München," *VB* 74–75 (1 Oct 1921).

142. On Lerchenfeld's tenure, see Schwend, *Bayern,* 182–98.

143. "Graf Lerchenfeld," *VB* 76 (5 Oct 1921). On the resulting ban, see "Verbot," *VB* 77–78 (15 Oct 1921).

144. "Graf Lerchenfelds jüdische Umgebung," *VB* 91 (30 Nov 1921); "Und das 10. Gebot, Graf Lerchenfeld?" *VB* 14 (18 Feb 1922); "Abrechnung mit dem Grafen Lerchenfeld," *VB* 15 (22 Feb 1922); "Pharisäer," *VB* 17 (1 Mar 1922).

145. *VB* 22 (18 Mar 1922); *VB* 25 (29 Mar 1922); *VB* 28 (8 Apr 1922).

146. See the mocking response of Eckart, "Graf Lerchenfeld," *VB* 28 (8 Apr 1922).

147. "Versammlung im Bürgerbräukeller," *VB* 30 (15 Apr 1922). Reprinted as "Die 'Hetzer' der Wahrheit!" in Boepple, *Reden,* 6–21. See also the police report, NSDAP/HA-R65, fol. 1480.

148. *VB* 30 (15 Apr 1922); also "Rundschreiben" (15 Apr 1922), 26, NSDAP-HA/R4, fol. 97.

149. The pamphlet, *Hetzer,* appeared on 22 April 1922. Within a week, the first run of 20,000 copies had been exhausted and a new printing was needed; *VB* 34 (29 Apr 1922).

150. "Kirchenkonzert"; Miller, "Das wahre Gesicht des Zentrums," both in *VB* 68 (26 Aug 1922).

151. *VB* 69 (30 Aug 1922). On the uproar caused by Faulhaber's speech, see Stehkämper, *Katholikentagspräsident,* and the materials in NL Faulhaber, fol. 3503.

152. Faulhaber's awkward term, "Katholiken reinrassiger Art," was open to more than one interpretation; see "Zeichen der Zeit," *VB* 69 (30 Aug 1922); "Gedanken zum Katholikentag," *VB* 69 (30 Aug 1922); also "Ansprache Sr. Eminenz," NL Faulhaber, fol. 3502.

153. "Leitsätze für den Katholikentag," *VB* 69 (30 Aug 1922); "Rom und Juda," *VB* 76 (23 Sep 1922); "Das Hakenkreuz als Wegweiser," *VB* 77 (27 Sep 1922). Alfred Rosenberg had begun to comment increasingly on religious issues in the *Beobachter* upon Alfred Miller's departure for Breslau in the summer of 1922; for Rosenberg's religiously indifferent interpretation, see "Katholikentag und Nationalsozialismus," *VB* 70 (2 Sep 1922).

154. On 1922 membership, see Tyrell, *Trommler,* 32. Statistics varied, since a number of German states progressively banned the NSDAP in the

fall of 1922 as part of the longer-term fallout from the assassination of Walther Rathenau; Maser, *Frühgeschichte,* 345.

155. *BVC* (28 Oct 1922); "Kulturpolitik," *BVC* (25 Oct 1922); "Landesversammlung," *BVC* (29 Oct 1922). For the Nazi response, see *VB* 86 (28 Oct 1922); *VB* 88 (4 Nov 1922).

156. Bea, "Antisemitismus, Rassentheorie und Altes Testament," *SdZ* 100 (Dec 1920).

157. "Arisches Glaubentum," *VB* 4 (13 Jan 1921); see also the rebuttal of Bea in "Antisemitismus, Rassentheorie und Altes Testament," *VB* 31 (17 Apr 1921); Schrönghamer, "Wie das Geld 'verdient' wird," *VB* 1 (1 Jan 1921); Miller, "Staat, Religion, Kirche," *VB* 1–2 (6 Jan 1921).

158. "Die nationalsozialistische Bewegung," *BVC* (21 Nov 1922). For the Nazi response, see *VB* 92 (18 Nov 1922).

159. "Die Nationalsozialisten und die Bayer. Volkspartei," *BVC* (13 Dec 1922); also "Nationalsozialistisches," *BVC* (1 Dec 1922); *BVC* (28 Jan 1923); *BVC* (1 Feb 1923).

160. "Der Nationalsozialismus und die Religion," originally published in installments in the *APZ* and reprinted months later as "Der Nationalsozialismus," *Politische Zeitfragen* 5–6 (May–June 1923).

161. "Der Nationalsozialismus," *BVC* (16 Jan 1923), *BVC* (18 Jan 1923).

162. *BVC* (16 Jan 1923).

163. "Der Münchener Nationalsozialismus und die Religion," *AR* 31 (2 Aug 1923).

Chapter 4

1. "Vermählung von Pg. Hermann Esser," *VB* 134 (6 July 1923). As a nineteen-year-old aspiring journalist, Esser had joined the NSDAP on 8 March 1920 (member number 881) and began contributing regularly to the *Beobachter* alongside Hansjörg Maurer in May 1920. Although he did not typically write on religious issues, which remained the purview of Maurer and Alfred Miller, Esser's pronounced Catholic identity was clear even in his first *Beobachter* contribution, which praised the prewar Christian Social movement and approvingly quoted one of its Viennese leaders: "We have been accused of simply being priestly lackeys [*Pfaffenknechte*]. I can report that we are not, but it is better—a thousand times better—to be a priestly lackey than a Jewish lackey!" Esser, "Aus ungeheltenen Reden," *VB* 51 (29 May 1920). On Hitler's reluctance to give a lengthy speech at the wedding dinner, see Hoffmann, *Hitler,* 46.

2. "Bayerische Priester als Hakenkreuzler," *Vorwärts* 320 (11 July 1923).

3. Held to Faulhaber, 6 Oct 1923, NL Faulhaber, fol. 5402; reprinted in Volk, *Akten,* 1:314–15. As will be seen, Faulhaber did speak out specifically against *völkisch* anti-Semitism several weeks later, on the eve of the putsch.

4. Schlund, "Der Münchener Nationalsozialismus und die Religion," *AR* 31 (2 Aug 1923).

5. "Der fromme Betrug," *VB* 8 (27 Jan 1923).

6. This potentiality can be seen in the case of Karl Debus, the socially minded Catholic student who had joined the NSDAP alongside Martin Weigl in May 1920. Debus left the Nazi movement in the context of the BVP enlightenment campaign in late 1922 and emerged as a critic of the NSDAP, albeit still a rather sympathetic one who continued to refer to himself as a spokesman of the "patriotically inflamed Catholic student body" in Munich; see esp. Debus, "Rauchen die Flammenzeichen?" *AR* 4 (27 Jan 1923); also Debus, "Nationalsozialismus und Massenseele," *AR* 45 (11 Nov 1922); "An die Zeit," *AR* 1 (6 Jan 1923).

7. Michael Schmitt, "Christentum und Nationalsozialismus," *VB* 98 (9 Dec 1922); see also "Volksbetrug durch Zentrum und Bayer. Volkspartei," *VB* 98 (9 Dec 1922).

8. On Gött's academic studies, see the materials in PA-Gött, ABA. Schnitzer had taught church history in Dillingen until he moved to the University of Munich in 1903.

9. The column was entitled "Wie es geht und steht in der Welt"; see Hoser, "Kirche," 476–77.

10. *LA* (1 Dec 1918).

11. *LA* (2 Mar 1919).

12. *LA* (12 Jan 1919).

13. *LA* (6 Sep 1919); *LA* (24 Apr 1920).

14. Gött, "Ein Wort an Hochw. Herrn Benefiziat Huber in Kronburg," *LA* (25 Nov 1922); Hoser, "Kirche," 478.

15. G.M. [Gött], "Nationalsozialismus und Religion," *VB* 7 (24 Jan 1923).

16. Schrönghamer, "Der Feldzug der Verleumdung," *VB* 23 (22 Feb 1923).

17. "Unsere Weihnachtsfeier," *VB* 101 (20 Dec 1922); in contrast, see "Bolschewistische Weihnachtsfeier," *VB* 102–103 (23 Dec 1922). Esser's Christmas speech to the Ortsgruppe Bad Tölz stated that the "teachings of Christ" would remain "the bedrock and foundation" of the NSDAP; "National-Sozialisten-Weihnachtsfeier," *MA* 288 (12 Dec 1922).

18. Hitler, *Wahrheit*, 5.

19. See the central references to Christ in Drexler, "Dürfen Sozialisten Judengegner sein?" *VB* 46 (12 June 1921).

20. Hitler quoted in "Der Nationalsozialismus und die Beamten," *VB* 62 (8–9 Apr 1923).

21. "Propagandafeldzug gegen Lüge und Verleumdung"; see "Aus der Bewegung," *VB* 62 (8–9 Apr 1923).

22. "An die Ortsgruppen," *VB* 78 (27 Apr 1923); also "Aus der Bewegung," *VB* 70 (18 Apr 1923).

23. "Aus der Bewegung," *VB* 85 (5 May 1923).

24. On the "success of the past four weeks of propagandistic activity" and the extension of the membership drive, see "Deutschlands Erwachen," *VB* 90 (12 May 1923).

25. Catholic masses were foregrounded, beginning with "Sonntags-Gottesdienst," *VB* 80 (29–30 Apr 1923), and ran in every weekend edition of the *Beobachter* throughout the summer.

26. "Zuvor hat jeder Junge seinen sonntäglichen Kirchenbesuch zu machen"; "Jugendbund," *VB* 127 (28 June 1923). On the contrasting anti-Catholic nature of the Hitler Youth after 1933, see, e.g., Kater, *Youth,* 22–23.

27. "Aus der Bewegung: Wanderzunft," *VB* 137 (10 July 1923).

28. See the publicity for the "powerful proclamation of religious faith" exhibited in the Patrona Bavariae procession on 13 May 1923; "Eine grosse religiöse Kundgebung," *VB* 92 (15 May 1923); also "Fronleichnamstag," *VB* 104 (1 June 1923); "Kirchenmusik," *VB* 128 (29 June 1923); "Kirchenmusik," *VB* 134 (6 July 1923).

29. Kernstock, "Das Hakenkreuz: Ein Widmungsgedicht," *VB* 85 (5 May 1923); also Kernstock, "Gebet vor der Hunnenschlacht," *VB* 149 (29–30 July 1923). Another devotional poem, written anonymously in the form of a prayer, expressed the fever pitch of anger and frustration reached during the summer of 1923: "Herr, lehre uns hassen," *VB* 155 (5–6 Aug 1923). Like so many others, Kernstock distanced himself from the Nazi movement after the putsch, and before his death in 1928 he complained that the Nazis were continuing to use his poem against his will; see Liebmann, "Kernstock," 381–93.

30. *VB* 97 (20–21 May 1923).

31. See, e.g., "Kampfgebet," *VB* 165 (18 Aug 1923); "Das Gotteszeichen," *VB* 184 (9–10 Sep 1923).

32. Esser, a member of the St. Rupert parish in Munich, opened a mass meeting on 21 June 1923 by reemphasizing the common image of Hitler's loyal Catholic faith and noting, "The Führer has said to me: It especially grieves me that I, as a Catholic, am attacked so unkindly by other Catholics [in the BVP]. This is all the more painful since there is absolutely no other movement that champions the cause of Christianity as ours does"; quoted in "Nationalsozialismus und Christentum," *VB* 123 (23 June 1923).

33. "Aus der Bewegung," *VB* 69 (17 Apr 1923). See also the continuing publicity surrounding his work in "Buchbesprechung," *VB* 91 (13–14 May 1923); Schrönghamer, "Der Staat als Treuhänder," *VB* 118 (17–18 June 1923); Schrönghamer, "Bayerns Pflicht in letzter Stunde," *VB* 190 (16–17 Sep 1923).

34. "Bayerische Priester als Hakenkreuzler," *Vorwärts* 320 (11 July 1923).

35. Björn Mensing notes the activities in Munich of Protestant pastors like Hermann Lembert, Friedrich Langenfass, and Martin Joch in the DNVP and in other local anti-Semitic and *völkisch* groups in the early 1920s, but finds no engagement with the early NSDAP itself; Mensing, *Pfarrer,* 74–75. Mensing also cites a Munich police report from 9 May 1923 that found "not a single [Protestant] pastor or even a theology student" who was involved notably in the Nazi movement; ibid., 92–93.

36. "Zeichen der Zeit," *VB* 101 (20 Dec 1922). Braun was born on 30 April 1877, served for several decades at the Frauenkirche in Nürnberg,

and eventually distanced himself completely from the Nazi movement after the Beerhall Putsch. By the 1930s, he had become a committed opponent of the NSDAP and was jailed by the Nazi regime for nine months in 1942; Hehl, *Priester,* 438.

37. "Nationalsozialismus und Religion," *VB* 8 (27 Jan 1923).

38. Patin was born in Würzburg in 1879 but grew up in Munich and was ordained there in June 1904. He was appointed at St. Kajetan's in 1907 and stayed there until the 1930s. Patin recalled in a March 1934 autobiographical sketch that he had been among Hitler's "most enthusiastic listeners" at numerous early Nazi mass meetings and had discussed the "significance of the NSDAP for the salvation of our embattled Fatherland" with his cousin Himmler; 9 Mar 1934, *Lebenslauf,* Patin SS file, BDC-A3343/SSO, reel 365A.

39. Haeuser had worked closely with Schrönghamer in spreading *völkisch* ideas among Catholic monarchists in the BKP in 1920. On Miller's strong admiration for Haeuser's "astonishing courage," see his comments in *VB* 15 (21 Feb 1922). Haeuser's career is discussed in some detail in Spicer, *Hitler's Priests,* 101–34.

40. See the account in Haeuser's unpublished autobiographical manuscript, "Mein Werden," 17–18, Haeuser materials, Stadtarchiv Bobingen. Haeuser had previously given this lecture before a meeting of the Landshut branch of the Heimat- und Königsbund; see the notice in *LZ* 303 (8 Nov 1922).

41. "Jüdische Anmassung und bischöfliche Schwäche," *VB* 99 (13 Dec 1922). The unnamed priest was almost certainly either Christian Huber or Magnus Gött; see also "Berichtigung," *VB* 7 (24 Jan 1923).

42. Addressing "sport-loving youth" in particular, the *Beobachter* proclaimed: "Archbishop Balduin of Trier was one of the most virile men to ever sit on the bishop's throne, and he girded himself with the sword when it was necessary....He engaged in sprinting, jumping, and stone throwing, and was not easily bested by anyone in strength and agility." The portrait closed by challenging Balduin's successors among the present-day Catholic bishops to cut a more vigorous and heroic profile; "Der sporttreibende Bischof," *VB* 14 (11–12 Feb 1923).

43. "Bücherschau," *VB* 8 (27 Jan 1923).

44. "Bücherschau," *VB* 31 (3 Mar 1923).

45. Haeuser's works were literally saturated with images of Jesus as a warrior: "Only he who recognizes Pharisaism knows that a Jesus-nature—whether Jesus himself or a disciple of Jesus—can never be a pacifist, only a warrior"; Haeuser, "Mein Werden," 6.

46. See the excerpt from his 1918 diary in NSDAP/HA-R55, fol. 1327; see also "Der Umsturz in Böhmen, Emaus und Abt Alban," *KVZ* 510 (9 July 1920); and clippings in NL Schachleiter, BHSA, abt. 5, fol. 1.

47. In a letter to Philipp Haeuser, 9 Feb 1922, Ludendorff referred to Schachleiter as his "friend" and said he first received a copy of Haeuser's *Wir deutschen Katholiken* as a gift from Schachleiter; cited in Haeuser, "Mein

Werden," 14. For more on Schachleiter's energetic *völkisch* activism throughout Bavaria, see "Eine grossdeutsche Agitation an der böhmisch-bairischen Grenze," *ZHDS* 3:5 (May 1922); "Gegen die Schuldlüge,"
Isar-Bote 77 (4 July 1922); "Vermischtes," *Kötzinger Anzeiger* 75 (20 Sep 1922).

48. See Faulhaber to Schachleiter, 16 Sep 1922, NL Schachleiter, BHSA, fol. 6. On the Bund Bayern und Reich more generally, see Gordon, *Putsch,* esp. 109–16. On Schachleiter's contact with right-wing and monarchist circles surrounding Bavarian crown prince Rupprecht, see Ludwig Graf von Holnstein to Schachleiter, 6 Oct 1922, Schachleiter papers, NSDAP/HA-R55, fol. 1326.

49. Müller had first become close to KG leaders Philipp Funk and Joseph Schnitzer in 1913, meeting with them at the Cafe Heck every Tuesday evening and eventually becoming involved in the KG in 1914; see Müller, *Gärten,* 427–29; and Haustein, *Krausgesellschaft,* 231–32, 341. On Helene Raff's close relationship with Philiipp Funk, see their extensive correspondence in NL Raff, BSB.

50. Müller, *Wandel,* 130–31. On Helene Raff more generally, see her *Blätter.*

51. Müller, *Wandel,* 129; Hanfstaengl, *Zwischen,* 107–8. The date of 1922—rather than 1923, as stated by Sauser ("Schachleiter," 1301–3) and Bleistein ("Schachleiter," 170–87)—is given definitively by Georg Löffelholz von Colberg in his unpublished reflections after his close friend Schachleiter's death; "Abt Albanus Schachleiter zum ehrenden Gedächtnis," NL Schachleiter, BHSA, Abt. 5, fol. 3. Schachleiter kept in touch over the years (albeit sporadically at times) with Karl Alexander von Müller, and in March 1936, Müller, who was by then one of the leading Nazi historians, fondly reminded Schachleiter of their common "circle of friends" and mentioned Helene Raff by name; Müller to Schachleiter, 10 Mar 1936, NSDAP/HA-R55, fol. 1330.

52. On Stempfle's role at the *Miesbacher Anzeiger,* see Kirmayer, "Miesbacher Anzeiger," 67–70; and the correspondence in NL Stempfle, BHSA, Abt. 5, fol. 1.

53. "Bayern," *Donauwacht* 306 (31 Dec 1921).

54. "Hitler," *MA* 266 (16 Nov 1922); also "Das Hakenkreuz," *MA* 255 (3 Nov 1922); "Nationalismus," *MA* 274 (24 Nov 1922); "Der National-Sozialisten-Weihnachtsfeier," *MA* 288 (12 Dec 1922); "Hakenkreuz und Sowjetstern," *MA* 292 (16 Dec 1922); "Eine Erklärung Hitlers," *MA* 26 (2 Feb 1923); "Gegen die 'Radi-Nazi,'" *MA* 29 (6 Feb 1923); "Der 'Völkische Beobachter' verboten!" *MA* 30 (7 Feb 1923); "Piepke-Pupke gegen Hitler," *MA* 31 (8 Feb 1923); "Wie Israel Deutschland höhnt," *MA* 57 (10 Mar 1923); "Juden und Judenfrage," *MA* 85 (13 Apr 1923). On the Nazis' close relationship with Stempfle and the *Anzeiger,* see also "Bayerische Rundschau," *VB* 136 (7 July 1923).

55. Hoffmann calls Stempfle a "man of strong personality" and states that "Hitler was originally suspicious of him and thought him a spy of the

[BVP]," although Stempfle was able to gain Hitler's "full confidence" in discussions on the Catholic Church; Hoffmann, *Hitler,* 52.

56. Entries of 17 Dec 1920 and 15 May 1921, BTB, NL Pieper, AK. On the Catholic response to groups like the Jungdo, see esp. Vogel, *Kampfverbände.* On the Jungdo more generally, see the insightful study by Ganyard, *Mahraun.*

57. On Pieper's contact with and admiration for Eckart, see esp. BTB entries for 20 May 1920, 22 Mar 1921, 5 Apr 1921, and 21 Feb 1922. On publicizing the *Beobachter,* see, e.g., the entry for 11 Mar 1921; on publicizing the *MA,* see the entries for 23 July 1921 and 30 Mar 1922.

58. Pieper was also later issued member number 15406; see Beck, *Kampf und Sieg,* 24. On the founding of the Ortsgruppe Hagen in March 1922, see *VB* 23 (22 Mar 1922). Pieper began praising Esser and Hitler personally in early 1922 (see BTB, 21 Feb and 30 Mar 1922); on Pieper's early contact with the Nazi group in Hagen before joining officially, see the entries for 21 May, 22 June, 26 July, and 16 Aug 1922.

59. BTB entries for 8 and 25 Oct, 9 and 16 Nov 1922, 18 Feb 1923.

60. *VB* 62 (8–9 Apr 1923); Tröster, "Pieper," 54.

61. Pieper's "Positive Christian–German world view" was held up as a shining example; "Dr. Pieper Nationalsozialist?" *VB* 84 (4 May 1923); also *MA* (4 May 1923).

62. *LA* (7 Apr 1923). Less than a week after this statement, the Ortsgruppe Legau was formed; Hoser, "Kirche," 478.

63. "Denkmalsweihe in der St.-Peters-Kirche," *VB* 69 (17 Apr 1923). On Attenberger's further activities, see, e.g., "Enthüllungsfeier der Kriegergedächtnistafel," *VB* 127 (28 June 1923). Attenberger was born 20 October 1877 in Grünthal and was ordained in Munich in 1903; he was eventually, in 1925, appointed Stadtpfarrer at St. Lorenz in Munich-Oberföhring. There is no record of pro-Nazi or *völkisch* activism on his part after the putsch.

64. "Fahnenweihe," *VB* 82 (2 May 1923). Knogler was born on 11 February 1882 and was ordained in Munich alongside Peter Widmann of St. Rupert's in 1908; *Schematismus,* 1925. He later became an opponent of the NSDAP; Hehl, *Priester,* 945.

65. "Denkmalseinweihung," *VB* 81 (1 May 1923); "Denkmalsweihe," *VB* 85 (5 May 1923); "Der Einser- und Zweiertag," *VB* 87 (8 May 1923). Widmann was Stadtpfarrer in Munich-Haidhausen from 1901 to 1931, serving as Meisl's supportive superior after his dismissal as *Kirchenzeitung* editor in 1920; see chap. 2 above.

66. Lukas organized a "patriotic evening" fundraiser at the Hofbräuhaus in May 1923 and an organ concert fundraiser in July; "Kriegergedächtniskapelle in der Hl.-Geist-Kirche," *VB* 81 (1 May 1923); "Orgelvortrag in die Heilig-Geist-Kirche," *VB* 149 (29–30 July 1923). Lukas, born on 16 March 1883 and ordained in Munich alongside Josef Knogler in 1908, had drawn praise from the Nazis for his flaming anti-Semitism as early as 1920; see chap. 2 above.

67. "Ingolstadt," *VB* 81 (1 May 1923); also "Ingolstadt," *VB* 80 (29–30 Apr 1923). Wagner was born in 1869 and had received his doctorate in Munich under Lujo Brentano (like Lorenz Pieper) in 1905. After the putsch, Wagner had nothing more to do with the *völkisch*-Nazi movement and was appointed cathedral advisor (*Domkapitular*) in Eichstätt in July 1924 and then Vicar General (*Generalvikar*) in Eichstätt in May 1925; Hausfelder, "Ingolstadt," 314; Buchner, *Bistum Eichstätt,* 588–89.

68. "Ingolstadt," *VB* 80 (29–30 Apr 1923); *Ingolstädter Zeitung* (30 Apr 1923); Straub, "Ingolstadt," 46.

69. *Freie Presse* (27 Apr 1923); *Ingolstädter Tagblatt* (28 Apr 1923); Straub, "Ingolstadt," 49. Götz was born in 1872 and, like Wagner, distanced himself from the Nazi movement after the putsch; Hehl, *Priester,* 541.

70. *VB* 102 (30 May 1923); on the further activities of the same priest, see *VB* 114 (13 June 1923) and *VB* 154 (4 Aug 1923). Fischer also distanced himself from the Nazi movement after the putsch, moving from Rieden to a parish in Durach in 1930 (*Schwäbisches Volksblatt* 290 [17 Dec 1930]) and eventually becoming an opponent of the NSDAP; Hehl, *Priester,* 342.

71. Roth, "Katholizismus und Judentum. I," *VB* 108 (6 June 1923).

72. Roth, "Katholizismus und Judentum. II," *VB* 109 (7 June 1923).

73. Roth, "Katholizismus und Judentum. III," *VB* 110 (8 June 1923).

74. Ibid.

75. Roth, *Katholizismus und Judenfrage* (Munich, 1923). The *Beobachter* publicity for the pamphlet began in *VB* 151 (1 Aug 1923). The article series also appeared in the *Katholischer Korrespondenzblatt* of the DNVP.

76. Schlund, *Katholizismus und Vaterland* (Munich, 1923), 32–33.

77. The speech was entitled "Aufstieg oder Niedergang." Coverage in the *Beobachter* praised the impact of Haeuser's words in the highest possible terms: "Very rarely has this lecture hall heard more enthusiastic applause. . . . It was for us a ray of hope for the future of our *Volk* to be able to hear this German priest"; "Aus der Bewegung," *VB* 121 (21 June 1923).

78. Schedule announced in "Deutscher Tag," *VB* 117 (16 June 1923).

79. "Der Tag von Passau," *VB* 120 (20 June 1923). On broader associated events, see Moosbauer, *Passau,* 10; Wagner, *Passau,* 32–34.

80. Stadler was born in 1881, was ordained in Munich in 1905, and eventually rose to the position of *Domkapitular* by 1935; *Schematismus,* 1941. On Stadler's "gripping sermon" at a *völkisch*-oriented paramilitary ceremony in Munich, see "Ehrung der Gefallenen des 11. Stadtbezirks," *VB* 116 (15 June 1923). See also the coverage of the flaming *Feldgottesdienst* performed by Pater Theodor for the Nazi-affiliated Reichsflagge on 17 June 1923 in *VB* 122 (22 June 1923). Foohs spoke at a massive paramilitary ceremony on 27 June 1923, giving an "inspiring address that resonated in an oath of loyalty for the Fatherland"; *VB* 131 (3 July 1923).

81. See the report on Huber's speech, "Antisemitismus und die national-sozialistische Stellung zum Eigentum," *VB* 146 (26 July 1923). It is likely that Krimm, who served as prior in Ottobeuren from 1912 until his death in 1930, first became affiliated with the NSDAP upon the formation of

the Ottobeuren Ortsgruppe in March 1923. Interestingly, the vice-chair (*2. Vorstand*) of the Ottobeuren Ortsgruppe at its founding was identified as "A. Grimm" in *VB* 43 (17 Mar 1923), and the fact that I have been unable to find any Grimm among the early Nazi membership lists makes the possibility that this may have been "A. Krimm" somewhat tantalizing. In any case, Krimm disassociated himself from the movement after the putsch, and local Nazi organizations in the area remained notably weak well into the early 1930s; see Fröhlich, "Memmingen," 549–50.

82. Announced in "An alle Ortsgruppen der NSDAP," *VB* 162 (14 Aug 1923), which urged Nazi members from Munich to attend and emphasized "participation in the mass at the magnificent Klosterkirche."

83. "Deutscher Tag in Ottobeuren," *VB* 168 (22 Aug 1923).

84. Entry for 5 June 1923, NL Pieper, AK.

85. "Aus der Bewegung," *VB* 135 (7 July 1923), emphasis in original.

86. Ibid.; also see a later incarnation, "Kann ein Katholik Nationalsozialist sein?" *VB* 170 (24 Aug 1923).

87. On the life and career of Görres, see Vanden Heuvel, *Görres;* Raab, *Görres.*

88. "Sprechabend Neuhausen," *VB* 134 (6 July 1923). See also the internal party report in "Protokoll der Ortsgruppe Neuhausen," NSDAP/HA-R1a, fol. 218.

89. Quote from speech "Wesen des Nationalsozialismus" given in Ustersbach on 9 July 1923; "Mitteilungen," *VB* 141 (14 July 1923).

90. Quote from Pieper speech in Biberach on 22 July 1923; "Mitteilungen auswärtiger Ortsgruppen," *VB* 148 (28 July 1923).

91. Quoted in the extensive report on Pieper's speech in "Protokoll der Ortsgruppe Neuhausen," NSDAP/HA-R1a, fol. 218. For a related but separate discussion, see "Die Heiligkeit des Hakenkreuzes," *VB* 137 (10 July 1923).

92. Quotes taken from another of Pieper's standard stump speeches, entitled "Nationalsozialismus und Christentum," delivered in Rosenheim on 26 July 1923 and in Traunstein on 27 July 1923; "Rosenheim," *VB* 151 (1 Aug 1923); "Traunstein," *VB* 152 (2 Aug 1923).

93. Report in *VB* 170 (24 Aug 1923).

94. "Mitteilungen auswärtiger Ortsgruppen: Regensburg," *VB* 173 (28 Aug 1923). This line of thought was also pursued in Pieper's speech on 14 August 1923 delivered to the NSDAP's Ortsgruppe Legau at the invitation of his fellow Nazi priest Magnus Gött; Hoser, "Kirche," 478.

95. On Schlageter, see Zwicker, *Märtyrer,* 25–73; Baird, *Heroes,* 13–40, though both Zwicker and Baird tend to overlook the larger significance of Schlageter's Catholic faith.

96. "Der CV bekennt sich zu Albert Leo Schlageter," *Academia* 46:1 (15 May 1933); "Der CV gedenkt seines toten Cartellbruders," *Academia* 46:3 (15 July 1933).

97. "Schlageter und die NSDAP," *Hannoverscher Anzeiger* 122 (25 May 1933); NSDAP/HA-R53, fol. 1265. On the difficulties of documenting

the definitive dates and details of Schlageter's Nazi membership, see Zwicker, *Märtyrer,* 51–52.

98. "Schlageter in München," *Academia* 46:3 (15 July 1933). The mass meeting on 1 June 1923 was opened by Esser: "We mourn in Schlageter the loss of our best and most loyal party comrade"; *VB* 106 (3–4 June 1923).

99. The ads for Schlageter keepsakes ran for weeks in the summer of 1923, e.g., "Schlageter-Gedenkmarken," *VB* 128 (29 June 1923); "Schlage-terlied," *VB* 156 (7 Aug 1923); "Zwei Schlageter-Broschüren," *VB* 157 (8 Aug 1923).

100. See, e.g., "Schlageter-Motorradstafette der SA," *VB* 117 (16 June 1923); "Nachruf für Schlageter," *VB* 117 (16 June 1923); "Schlageterfeier der SA," *VB* 122 (22 June 1923); "Schlageterfeier," *VB* 123 (23 June 1923); "Schlageter-Abend," *VB* 128 (29 June 1923); "Deutscher Abend," *VB* 144 (25 July 1923). See also "Ein Schlageter-Denkmal," *VB* 116 (15 June 1923); "Zur Frage eines Schlageter-Denkmals," *VB* 117 (16 June 1923); "Schlageter-Kranz-Spende," *VB* 118 (17–18 June 1923); "Schlageter-Denkmal," *VB* 131 (3 July 1923); "Schlageter-Denkmal," *VB* 146 (26 July 1923); "Schlageter-Denkmal," *VB* 156 (7 Aug 1923); "Schlageter-Gedächtnisbund," *VB* 161 (12–13 Aug 1923); "Gedenkfeier zum Geburtstag Albert Leo Schlagteter," *VB* 164 (17 Aug 1923).

101. "Zu Schlageters Hinrichtung," *VB* 114 (13 June 1923).

102. "Schlageters letzte Augenblicke," *VB* 113 (12 June 1923); also "Zum Tode Schlageters," *VB* 114 (13 June 1923).

103. "Albert Leo Schlageter zum Gedächtnis," *VB* 112 (10–11 June 1923).

104. *VB* 110 (8 July 1923). Although the Nazis participated in the broader Königsplatz rally, the leading organizer was the Protestant Hermann Kriebel and the only clergyman present was the Protestant pastor Martin Joch, providing a stark contrast to the Catholic Nazi nature of the St. Boniface ceremony.

105. Franz-Willing, *Krisenjahr,* 77–85.

106. Hanfstaengl, *Witness,* 86–87; also Hanfstaengl, *Zwischen,* 108.

107. See the hagiographic reference to Schlageter and other CV students who had been "the pioneers of National Socialism"; Fritz Berthold to Schachleiter, 28 Jan 1934, NSDAP/HA-R55, fol. 1327.

108. Hanfstaengl, *Zwischen,* 109.

109. *VB* 113 (12 June 1923).

110. Ibid.

111. Hinkel, *Einer unter Hunderttausend* (Munich, 1938), 99.

112. "Aus der Bewegung," *VB* 125 (26 June 1923).

113. "Schlageter-Gedenkfeier in Innsbruck," *VB* 128 (29 June 1923).

114. "Eine Schlageterfeier der Berliner Studentenschaft," *VB* 131 (3 July 1923). See also the discussion of the CV in "Schlageter-Denkmal," *VB* 137 (10 July 1923).

115. Weiss, "Albert Leo Schlageter," *Academia* 36:1–4 (1 Aug 1923). In her literary analysis of commemorative Schlageter literature, *Erschaffung,* Elisabeth Hillesheim overlooks its powerful Catholic orientation in 1923.

116. Priemer, "Albert Leo Schlageter," *Academia* 36:1–4 (1 Aug 1923).

117. "Schlageter und der katholische Jugendverein," *VB* 151 (1 Aug 1923).

118. "Aus der Bewegung," *VB* 116 (15 June 1923); "Der Tag von Passau," *VB* 121 (21 June 1923).

119. "Aus der Bewegung," *VB* 121 (21 June 1923).

120. For instance, in addition to the aforementioned events on 10 June and 17 June 1923, on Sunday, 24 June 1923, the NSDAP organized Catholic-oriented Schlageter memorial ceremonies in Oettingen (see report in *VB* 129 [30 June 1923]), Landsberg (*VB* 131 [3 July 1923]), and Freising (*VB* 137 [10 July 1923]), with ceremonies on Sunday, 1 July 1923, in Ipsheim (complete with a "Kirchenparade"; see advance publicity in *VB* 127 [28 June 1923]) and Staffelstein (*VB* 132 [4 July 1923]), followed by an official Catholic mass and Schlageter rally in Holzkirchen, near Miesbach, on Sunday, 8 July 1923 ("Schlageterfeier in Holzkirchen," *VB* 137 [10 July 1923]), and so on.

121. "Hochamt für Schlageter," *VB* 137 (10 July 1923).

122. "Schlageterfeier in Passau," *VB* 160 (11 Aug 1923).

123. "Die abgelehnte kirchliche Fahnenweihe," *VB* 161 (12–13 Aug 1923).

124. See also "Kann ein Katholik Nationalsozialist sein?" *VB* 170 (24 Aug 1923).

125. Roth, "Fahneneid der Wehrbereiten: Predigt vom 2.9.1923," *Bayern und Reich* 32 (8 Sep 1923); reprinted in Nusser, *Wehrverbände,* 22–26. See also "Der Deutsche Tag," *MA* 204 (5 Sep 1923).

126. Program, "Deutscher Tag in Nürnberg, 1. und 2. Sept. 1923," in NSDAP/HA-R4, fol. 105; see also the related materials in NSDAP/HA-R65, fol. 1481.

127. Haeuser to Hitler, 14 Oct 1923, NSDAP/HA-R53, fol. 1242.

128. "Strohfeuer oder Organisation," *VB* 177 (1 Sep 1923).

129. Maser, *Frühgeschichte,* 376.

130. On the broader effects of the devastating inflation, see Widdig, *Inflation,* and, for Munich in particular, Geyer, *Verkehrte Welt,* chap. 9.

131. On the Kampfbund, see Franz-Willing, *Krisenjahr,* 107–21; Tyrell, *Trommler,* 161–64; Gordon, *Putsch,* 93–95, 116–18; Maser, *Frühgeschichte,* 419–23.

132. The NSDAP had, however, participated in a looser grouping of *völkisch* organizations known as the Arbeitsgemeinschaft earlier in 1923; see Maser, *Frühgeschichte,* 377–80; Franz-Willing, *Krisenjahr,* 36–43.

133. On the undoubtedly artificial, yet nonetheless effective, image of the march on Rome, see, for example, Knox, *Threshold,* 361–71; Lyttleton, *Fascism,* 67–70; Bosworth, *Dictatorship,* chap. 7.

134. See, e.g., "Der Siegeslauf des Faschismus," *AR* 45 (11 Nov 1922). A BVP leader noted: "Since Mussolini's coup the Nazi movement has become for many [Bavarians] the focal point of all hope"; *BVC* (21 Nov 1922).

135. Hermann Esser quoted in *VB* 89 (8 Nov 1922); see also "Hitler," *MA* 266 (16 Nov 1922); "Der Bayerische Mussolini," *Tegernseer Zeitung* 133 (11 Nov 1922).

136. Ian Kershaw notes that the fall of 1922, in the aftermath of Mussolini's seizure of power, "marked the symbolic moment when Hitler's followers invented the Führer cult"; Kershaw, *Hubris,* 180. David Redles locates Hitler's messianic tendencies in his childhood development; Redles, *Millenial Reich,* 108–16. See also Tyrell, *Trommler,* 150–64.

137. Tyrell, *Trommler,* 160–62, 274–75; also Tyrell, "Wie er der 'Führer' wurde," 20–48.

138. Quoted in Binion, *Hitler,* 136; also Redles, *Millenial Reich,* 113.

139. Hitler speech of 4 May 1923, cited in Kershaw, *Hubris,* 184; see also Kershaw, *Hitler Myth,* esp. 13–25.

140. Quoted in Kershaw, *Hubris,* 184; see also Franz-Willing, *Verbotszeit,* 56.

141. Hanfstaengl, *Zwischen,* 109.

142. The other leading groups in the Kampfbund were the Bund Oberland, led by the Protestant Friedrich Weber, and the Reichskriegsflagge under Ernst Röhm, who was also from a Protestant background; see Deuerlein, *Hitler-Putsch,* 488–89. The Nazi SA came under the increased control of Hermann Kriebel (also Protestant), who had been appointed overall military leader of the Kampfbund; Franz-Willing, *Krisenjahr,* 119–21.

143. Thoss, *Ludendorff-Kreis,* 249–61.

144. "Ludendorffs völkisches Bekenntnis," *VB* 195 (22 Sep 1923). See also the large front-page portrait of Ludendorff, *VB* 202 (30 Sep 1923); "Ludendorffhetze," *VB* 211 (18 Oct 1923); "Ein Hebräer als Verleumder General Ludendorffs," *VB* 211 (18 Oct 1923). It was also Ludendorff who wrote the movement's last programmatic ideological statement before the putsch: "Die völkische Bewegung," *VB* 223 (1 Nov 1923).

145. *VB* 188 (14 Sep 1923). Mencke was born in 1882 and ordained in Munich in 1907; after serving in numerous brief pastoral positions, he was appointed Stadtpfarrer in Garmisch in July 1923; *Schematismus,* 1925. Mencke abandoned his *völkisch* activism after the putsch. After numerous run-ins with the Nazi authorities in the mid-1930s, Mencke was denounced to the Gestapo for listening to foreign radio by fellow priest (and Nazi member) Leonhard Götz, serving a year in Gestapo custody in 1940–1941; see Hehl, *Priester,* 958, and the materials in NL Faulhaber, fol. 5402. Würzberger had been ordained in the Bamberg diocese in 1893, coming into contact with the Reform Catholic priest Josef Müller (also from Bamberg) and publishing in Reform Catholic circles before the First World War; see his "Der Kampf gegen die kirchliche Reaktion," *MAZ* 39 (25 Jan 1908). He served as parish priest in Kleukheim (now part of Markt Ebensfeld, near Bamberg) from 1905 to his retirement in 1936. On his 7 October 1923 Nazi-oriented mass in Bamberg, see Breuer, *Wandel,* 47–48.

146. "At home as a person everyone can be either Protestant or Catholic, but as political figures we must be first and foremost Germans"; speech, 27 Sep 1923, in Hitler, *Aufzeichnungen,* 1018.

147. See the advance publicity in *VB* 194 (21 Sep 1923). Obermayr was born in 1875, was ordained in Munich in 1900, and began as a parish priest in Schliersee in 1916; *Schematismus,* 1926. Obermayr also distanced himself from the Nazi movement after the putsch, but he is not listed among the priests persecuted by the Nazis in Hehl, *Priester.*

148. "Gedenksteinenthüllung in Schliersee," *VB* 203 (1 Oct 1923); also "General Ludendorff bei der Oberlandsgedächtnisfeier in Schliersee," *VB* 204 (2 Oct 1923).

149. See the coverage of Heerdegen's central participation in Kampfbund activities in the Hof area on 16 September 1923; "Der 'Deutsche Tag' in Hof," *VB* 196 (23–24 Sep 1923). See also the important role played by Leuthel in a major Kampfbund event near Bayreuth in late September, in which the ailing Houston Stewart Chamberlain also participated; Joseph Stolzing, "Der Deutsche Tag in Bayreuth," *VB* 205 (3 Oct 1923).

150. Schlund, *Heidentum,* 63.

151. Stempfle had begun to voice discontent over Ludendorff's Protestantism shortly after the formation of the Kampfbund; see "Ludendorff in Bayern," *MA* 211 (13 Sep 1923); also "Wie der Hass geschürt wird," *MA* 240 (17 Oct 1923); "Vershlungene Wege," *MA* 256 (6 Nov 1923). Stempfle's denunciation of Ludendorff elicited a sharply critical response from Alfred Rosenberg in "Der Stempfle enthüllt sich!" *VB* 225 (4–5 Nov 1923); and "Der Stempfle enthüllt sich weiter," *VB* 227 (7 Nov 1923).

152. See Eckart's October 1923 letter to Max Amann, cited in Joachimsthaler, *Hitlers Weg,* 279.

153. Tröster, "Pieper," 54.

154. Kershaw, *Hubris,* 199–200; Orlow, *Nazi Party,* 43–44. Hitler announced his decision to accept the position of political leader of the Kampfbund in *VB* 198 (26 Sep 1923).

155. See Volk, *Akten,* 1:318–19.

156. "Kardinal Faulhaber als Judenschützer," *VB* 226 (6 Nov 1923). A separate frontal attack on Faulhaber played up the image of hypocrisy, posing the question: "Which Cardinal Faulhaber should the good Catholic believe? The one from last year's Katholikentag or the one from the last few days?" The *Beobachter* connected this behavior to the inconsistent stance regarding the Jews cultivated by the BVP over the previous few years; "Kardinal Faulhaber," *VB* 228 (8 Nov 1923).

157. See, e.g., "Kirchliche Rundschau," *AR* 47 (22 Nov 1923).

Chapter 5

1. Franz-Willing, *Verbotszeit,* 66–131; Gordon, *Putsch,* 270–409; Maser, *Frühgeschichte,* 443–64; Deuerlein, *Hitler-Putsch;* Mommsen, "9. November," 33–48.

2. Franz-Willing, *Verbotszeit,* 191–271; Jablonsky, *Dissolution,* 53–128; Pridham, *Hitler's Rise,* 11–35; Gritschneder, *Bewährungsfrist.*

3. Gordon, *Putsch,* 413–15.

4. Guttenberg, "Das nationale Ziel und Bayern," *VB* 211 (19 Oct 1923). On Kahr's appointment, see Schwend, *Bayern,* 215–41. On Guttenberg's later prominence in the anti-Nazi resistance during the Second World War, see Bottlenberg-Landsberg, *Guttenberg.*

5. "Die Novembervorgänge an der Münchener Universität," *Academia* 36:5–8 (15 Dec 1923); also Erhard Schlund, "Die Münchener Universitäts-Studenten und der 12. November," *APZ* 295 (25 Dec 1923).

6. Hoffmann, *9. November,* 15.

7. Quoted in "Religionskrieg," *BK* 58 (27 Feb 1924).

8. Quoted in "Kein Born der Weisheit," *BV* 54 (4 Mar 1924).

9. "Religionskrieg," *BK* 58 (27 Feb 1924); also *BVZ* 47 (23 Feb 1924).

10. Matt to Innenminister Schweyer, 13 Feb 1924, BHSA, MInn-73548.

11. See the account in "Patriotismus 'der Tat,'" *BK* 48 (18 Feb 1924).

12. "Die ersten Bilder vom Hitler-Prozess," *Münchener Illustrierte Presse* 56 (4 Mar 1924); "Die Haputangeklagten im Hitlerprozess," *Volk und Zeit* (9 Mar 1924); "Das Urteil im Hitlerprozess," *MAA* (1 Apr 1924); also see Ludendorff quotes in Gruchmann and Weber, *Hitler-Prozess,* 262–64, 1057–58, 1183–84; and Steger, "Hitlerprozess," 441–66.

13. Gruchmann and Weber, *Hitler-Prozess,* 1314.

14. See, e.g., "Eine Abrechnung Ludendorffs mit seinen Gegnern," *Völkischer Kurier* 117 (26 Apr 1924).

15. This host-desecration rumor was circulated most energetically after the putsch by Georg Sponsel, a pro-BVP priest in Ansbach; Hambrecht, *Aufstieg,* 285.

16. For the text of Roder's statment, see Hitler, *Aufzeichnungen,* 1059; also Kern, *Hitler,* 18.

17. Schlund, *Heidentum,* 63.

18. Rauch to Faulhaber, 19 Nov 1923, NL Faulhaber, fol. 7156; also the notice in *BK* 345 (12 Dec 1923); "Zurückweisung der Angriffe gegen den Kardinal," *MNN* 28 (29 Jan 1924).

19. Rauch to Eugen von Knilling, 11 Dec 1923, SAM-PD, fol. 6687. See also Cremer, "Kulturkampf."

20. See the clippings in SAM-PD, fol. 6687; NSDAP/HA-R64, fol. 1466. One article featured a picture of a Nazi dagger, with a swastika on the handle, severing a row of rosary beads and plunging through a Bible; "Sind die Deutschvölkischen kirchenfeindlich?" *BK* 87 (27 Mar 1924).

21. See the police report, SAM-PD, fol. 6687.

22. The speech was published the following year under the title *Deutsches Ehrgefühl und katholisches Gewissen* (Munich, 1925), quote from p. 13.

23. Rauch quoted in police report, SAM-PD, fol. 6687.

24. Hoffmann, *9. November,* 8.

25. Schott, *Hitler,* 165.

26. Probst, *NSDAP,* 23–38; Jablonsky, *Dissolution,* 54–57.

27. *Deutsche Presse* 3 (Jan 1924), also quoted in "Kulturkampf," *BK* 33 (2 Feb 1924). On Pleyer's later career, see Walter Frank's obituary essay, "Kleo Pleyer: Ein Kampf um das Reich," *HZ* 166 (1942): 507–53.

28. These meetings were heavily covered in the press on all sides; see "Kann ein Katholik völkisch sein?" *BK* 112 (25 Apr 1924); "Kann ein Katholik völkisch sein?" *APZ* 97 (26 Apr 1924); "Kann ein Katholik völkisch sein?" *MZ* 116 (26 Apr 1924); "Kann ein Katholik völkisch sein?" *GZ* 73 (28 Apr 1924).

29. Police report, SAM-PD, fol. 6687.

30. Ferrari quoted in "Kann ein Katholik völkisch sein?" *GZ* 73 (28 Apr 1924).

31. *GZ* 73 (28 Apr 1924). The police report noted that the declaration was opposed by only 5 of the more than 1,000 Catholics in attendance.

32. See the discussion in his 1948 *Spruchkammerverfahren,* StAP, sch. 11.

33. The bulk of support for the Völkischer Block had come at the expense of the BVP; Thränhardt, *Wahlen,* 172–73.

34. Schachleiter to Spengler, 31 May 1924, in Spengler, *Briefe,* 325.

35. See the comments of Magnus Gött in *LA* (1 Apr 1924); also Hoser, "Kirche," 478–79. Huber eventually rejoined the NSDAP in 1933, ultimately at the expense of his Catholic identity, as he eventually left both the priesthood and the church entirely; "Suspendierte und abgefallene Geistliche," 3 Feb 1948, NL Faulhaber, fol. 5402.

36. Thränhardt, *Wahlen,* 173.

37. Hambrecht, *Aufstieg.*

38. Miller, *Jesuitismus als Volksgefahr,* 17.

39. Miller, *Rom,* 16.

40. See, e.g., Miller, "Christentum im Weltgericht," *Durchbruch* 3:42 (15 Oct 1936); also Miller's anti-Christian manifestos, *Völkerentartung* and *Zeichen.*

41. Smith's *Himmler;* Padfield, *Reichsführer.* The fragments of Himmler's diaries discovered after the Second World War are on deposit at the Hoover Institution; see Smith and Angress, "Diaries," 206–24; also NSDAP-HA/R98, fols. 1–9; R99, fols. 9–16; R17a, fol. 1; R18a, fol. 11.

42. Smith and Angress, "Diaries," 214–17; Smith, *Himmler,* 29–30.

43. Himmler to parents, 29 Nov 1918, NSDAP/HA-R98, fol. 2. This letter is cited in a somewhat different context in Smith, *Himmler,* 59. Himmler remained active in the BVP (even agitating on the party's behalf) at least through 1921.

44. Himmler was a member of Apollo, part of the Rothenburger Verband schwarzer Verbindungen; Smith, *Himmler,* 87; Smith and Angress, "Diaries," 217; Himmler to parents, 20 Mar 1920, NSDAP/HA-R98, fol. 2.

45. Himmler's partial reading list c. 1919–1924 contains nearly 350 titles; NSDAP/HA-R18a, fol. 11. On his early involvement in various *völkisch* groups, see Smith, *Himmler,* 124–26, 131–33.

46. Himmler was a member of the Vereinigte Vaterländische Verbände Bayerns (VVVB), which mandated attendance at the Königsplatz event; *VB* 110 (8 June 1923). Himmler's almost certain attendance at the St. Boniface ceremony and the impact of Schlageter on his life are indicated by Himmler's central involvement in the festivities surrounding the one-year

anniversary of Schlageter's death. On the back of his personal *Ehrenkarte* for the 26 May 1924 Bürgerbräukeller ceremony, which he saved for posterity, Himmler recorded proudly: "Was present in uniform and carried the flag"; NSDAP/HA-R98, fol. 1.

47. Bradley Smith interprets (wrongly, in my opinion) Himmler's entrance into the NSDAP as the almost accidental result of simply "stumbl[ing] along" in the wake of the decision of the popular Ernst Röhm, leader of the Reichsflagge (one of the several *völkisch* groups to which Himmler belonged), to join the NSDAP; Smith, *Himmler,* 134. On Himmler's participation in the putsch, see ibid., 136; Gordon, *Putsch,* 345–46.

48. See, e.g., the entries for 17–24 Feb 1924 in Smith and Angress, "Diaries," 217.

49. In February 1924, Himmler read Miller's *Ultramontanes Schuldbuch* alongside Eckart's *Bolschewismus;* NSDAP/HA-R18a, fol. 11. During the same month, Himmler also read Haeckel's *Die Welträtsel* (Bonn, 1899), Chamberlain's *Die Grundlagen des 19. Jahrhunderts* (Munich, 1899), and Carl Friedrich von Schlichtegroll, *Ein Sadist im Priesterrock* (Leipzig, 1924).

50. Reading list, NSDAP/HA-R18a, fol. 11.

51. Smith, *Himmler,* 154. For more details, see Jablonsky, *Dissolution,* 85–92; Stachura, *Strasser,* 35–37. Himmler's SS file indicates that he rejoined the NSDAP in August 1925; BDC, A3343-SSO, reel 099A.

52. See esp. Dierker, *Glaubenskrieger,* 123–28; Padfield, *Reichsführer,* 170–74.

53. Kershaw, *Hubris,* 225–26.

54. On Cramer-Klett's role, see Schwend, *Bayern,* 298; Pridham, *Hitler's Rise,* 35. On Cramer-Klett's earlier involvement with Nazi and *völkisch* circles, see Kellogg, *Russian Roots,* 126.

55. Hitler, "Zum Wiedererstehen unserer Bewegung!" *VB* 1 (26 Feb 1925).

56. On the initial Nazi support for Ludendorff's candidacy, see "Ludendorff als Kandidat," *VB* 4 (21 Mar 1925); "Aufruf!" *VB* 5 (25 Mar 1925).

57. See chap. 2 above. Heilmann himself had no personal contact with the NSDAP after the putsch, although his publisher, the Herder Verlag, did give the *Beobachter* permission to reprint excerpts from Heilmann's devotional *Stunden der Stille* (Freiburg, 1919); see Heilmann, "Christ ist entstanden!" *VB* 14 (12–13 Apr 1925).

58. On the DNVP's Catholic committee, see esp. the outstanding study by Jones, "Catholics," 221–67; also Clemens, *Spahn;* Gründer, "Rechtskatholizismus," 107–55.

59. Starck, "Katholiken!" *VB* 6 (28 Mar 1925).

60. At a Nazi Christmas celebration in December 1925, Hitler focused on the heroism of Christ's Aryan identity, pledging to replicate his "fanatical faith" and to act "not only as Germans but also as Christians"; reported in "Adolf Hitler in Dingolfing," *VB* 222 (17 Dec 1925). See also the separate Christmas 1925 speech cited in Grieswelle, *Propaganda,* 56–57.

61. Hitler, *Mein Kampf,* esp. 108–17.

62. Quoted by Hitler in "Nationalsozialisten!" *VB* 63 (17 Mar 1926); see also Graefe's claim that Hitler had "capitulated before Rome," cited in "Nationalsozialisten!" *VB* 45 (24 Feb 1926).

63. See "Hitlers offene Antwort an Herrn von Graefe," *VB* 65 (19 Mar 1926).

64. See esp. Ludendorff, *Hitlers Verrat der Deutschen an den römischen Papst* (Munich, 1931), which claimed that in early 1925 the NSDAP made the fateful decision to "give up the battle against Rome," which had been pursued by *völkisch* forces since the failure of the 1923 putsch, and that the party thereafter continued to "recognize as binding the world view of the Roman pope" (3).

65. Starck, "Katholiken!" *VB* 6 (28 Mar 1925).

66. See, e.g., Hitler's speech on 12 June 1925 in which he praised the church as a "grandiose mechanism"; Hitler, *Reden,* 1:93.

67. Conway, *Persecution,* 1–5; Scholder, *Kirchen,* 91–98.

68. Tyrell, *Trommler,* 165–74; Redles, *Millenial Reich,* 116–29; more generally, Schreiner, "Retter," 107–60.

69. "Christenaustreibung aus Frömmigkeit," *VB* 50 (27 May 1925); *VB* 57 (5 June 1925); *VB* 68 (19 June 1925).

70. See, e.g., "Deutschland und das bayer. Konkordat: Rede des Nationalsozialisten Frick," *VB* 69 (20 June 1925).

71. "Aufgeregte Scheinheiligkeit," *VB* 124 (25 Aug 1925); "Zur Übersiedlung des Nuntius Pacelli," *VB* 93 (18 July 1925); "Das Wesen der Nuntiaturen," *VB* 123 (23–24 Aug 1925).

72. "Kirche und Hochfinanz," *VB* 55 (7–8 Mar 1926); see also later installments in *VB* 66 (20–21 Mar 1926); *VB* 138 (19 June 1926); *VB* 149 (2 July 1926); also "Fromme Korruption," *VB* 1 (1 Jan 1926).

73. See "Ein Kardinal als Judenknecht," *VB* 170 (27 July 1926), which also accused the Dutch cardinal Willem van Rossum (stationed in Rome) of collaborating with the "finance Jews of Wall Street"; see also "Ein schmachvolles Dokument," *VB* 166 (13 Oct 1925); "Jesuiten und Juden," *VB* 234 (9 Oct 1926).

74. "Der Prozess des Kardinals," *VB* 86 (10 July 1925).

75. "Um den Kardinalsprozess," *VB* 87 (11 July 1925); "Fromme Judenfreunde," *VB* 126 (27 Aug 1925). Faulhaber's appeal was ultimately successful in getting Hupperz sentenced to six months in prison; "Beleidigungsprozess Faulhaber–Hupperz," *VB* 262 (12 Nov 1926).

76. "Die Bedeutung der Rede des Kardinals Faulhaber," *VB* 34 (11 Feb 1926); "Kardinal Faulhaber und Südtirol," *VB* 33 (10 Feb 1926); also "Eine Rede Faulhabers," *VB* 165 (21 July 1926).

77. See esp. "Kardinal Faulhaber und das achte Gebot," *VB* 250 (28 Oct 1926).

78. Roth's close friend Philipp Haeuser recorded this encounter between Roth and Buchberger in his unpublished memoirs and asserted (in an almost certain fabrication) that Buchberger told Roth that an

unnamed Jewish figure in Munich had approached the diocesan authorities and threatened to withdraw a major financial donation to the church unless Roth was officially disciplined for his pro-Nazi agitation; Haeuser, "Mein Werden," 177–78.

79. In a November 1926 statement that corroborates the account of Roth and Haeuser, Hermann Esser declared under oath that "in September 1923 the relationship of the Catholic clergy to the [Nazi] movement became different. They were no longer allowed to attend our meetings"; cited in the trial proceedings against Hupperz, *VB* 262 (12 Nov 1926).

80. See Haeuser, "Aufruf!" *VB* 10 (21 Apr 1925). Roth allowed his *Katholizismus und Judenfrage* to be reprinted as a six-part series under the title "Katholizismus und Judentum" in the Bamberg-based Nazi paper *Die Flamme* between 9 Mar 1926 and 16 Apr 1926. On Faulhaber's dissatisfaction with Roth's activities, see Roth to Faulhaber, 4 Nov 1926, NL Faulhaber, fol. 9606.

81. The *Beobachter* opportunistically defended Schachleiter on occasions when he clashed with diocesan officials; see "Die wahren Kulturkampfhetzer," *VB* 76 (2–3 Apr 1926); "Unerhörte Priesterverfolgung," *VB* 80 (9 Apr 1926); "Zum Predigtverbot," *VB* 102 (5 May 1926).

82. In addition to the continued pro-Nazi sympathies of Roth, Haeuser, Patin, Stempfle, and Pieper, Magnus Gött corresponded with Hitler in 1927; see Hoser, "Kirche," 473–92. For a list of pro-Nazi Catholic priests, most of whom became involved with the Nazis after 1933, see Spicer, *Hitler's Priests,* 240–99.

83. Kuessner, *Johnsen,* 18–22.

84. See Stählin, *Die völkische Bewegung und unsere Verantwortung* (Sollstedt, 1924). The pamphlet was published by the Bund Deutscher Jugendvereine, which was led by Stählin. On Lehmann's increasing prominence in Nazi circles in the late 1920s and into the 1930s, see Lehmann, *Verleger,* 76–85.

85. Mensing, *Pfarrer,* 79–83; Hambrecht, *Aufstieg,* 63–64.

86. Hellmuth Johnsen is a good example of this tendency; Kuessner, *Johnsen,* 22.

87. Lembert, "Karfreitag," *VB* 12 (10 Apr 1925).

88. Lembert did, however, publicly defend the Kampfbund in a controversial sermon on the Sunday following the putsch; Mensing, "Sendung," 100–101.

89. See, e.g., "Pöhners Bestattung," *VB* 18 (18 Apr 1925).

90. "Aus Bayern und Reich," *VB* 110 (7 Aug 1925); "Aus der Bewegung," *VB* 126 (27 Aug 1925); "Aus der Bewegung," *VB* 175 (23 Oct 1925). On Sauerteig, see Mensing, *Pfarrer,* 93; Hambrecht, *Aufstieg,* 245–46.

91. "Nat.-Soz. Bannerweihe in Nürnberg," *VB* 176 (3 Aug 1926); "Aus der Bewegung," *VB* 174 (31 July 1926).

92. "Deutsche Priesterworte aus Frankens Hauptstadt," *VB* 177 (4 Aug 1926). On Weigel, see also Reiche, *Nürnberg,* 62.

93. Advance publicity trumpeted Weigel's role; "Deutsche Volks-genossen!" *VB* 203 (3 Sep 1926); "Aus der Bewegung," *VB* 204 (4 Sep 1926).

94. "Die Standarten-Weihe in München," *VB* 212 (14 Sep 1926). The racial aspects of Weigel's sermon were rather stereotypically blood-based and were delivered with evangelistic zeal: "Your German blood! That alone creates the spirit, the faith, the deed! Join the racial struggle [*Hinein in den Rassenkampf*]!"

95. "Tagung Deutschkirchlicher und Vaterländischer Führer," *VB* 154 (29 Sep 1925); "An die Christgläubigen," *VB* 228 (24 Dec 1925); "Bund für deutsche Kirche," *VB* 265 (16 Nov 1926); "Weltkonferenz für praktisches Christentum," *VB* 120 (20 Aug 1925); "Landesfest des Evangelischen Bundes in Bayern," *VB* 209 (10 Sep 1926); "Märkertag," *VB* 241 (17–18 Oct 1926).

96. "Deutschtum und evangelische Kirche," *VB* 63 (17 Mar 1926).

97. "Aus der Bewegung," *VB* 162 (8 Oct 1926); Dingeldey, "Rasse und Persönlichkeit," *VB* 176 (24 Oct 1925).

98. "Lutherworte," *VB* 240 (16 Oct 1926); "Luthergedanken," *VB* 119 (25 May 1926); "Advent 1925," *VB* 215 (9 Dec 1925); "Gotteszeugen—Gottesglauben!" *VB* 1 (1 Jan 1926); "Pfingsten" and "Pfingstgedanken," *VB* 119 (25 May 1926).

99. For instance, when reflecting on the 150th anniversary of the birth of Görres, the *Beobachter* focused almost entirely on his early career, only mentioning his return to Catholicism in negative terms: "The fate of Görres after the wars of liberation has to be characterized as tragic.... The Reaction triumphed and in his disappointment Görres turned in his later years more and more to ecclesiastical and religious issues"; "Joseph von Görres," *VB* 20 (26 Jan 1926).

100. Spotts, *Aesthetics,* esp. 311–98; Bartetzko, *Illusionen;* Karow, *Opfer;* Reichel, *Faszination.*

101. Tyrell, *Trommler,* 150–64; Kershaw, *Hubris,* 221–53. The death in December 1923 of Hitler's one-time mentor Dietrich Eckart, whose unorthodox theological views had been combined with a continued dogged profession of Catholic identity, may also have impacted the nature of Hitler's ideological and psychological evolution thereafter; see Bärsch, *Religion,* 86–91.

102. Burrin, "Political Religion," 321–49; Burleigh, *Sacred Causes;* Burleigh, *Third Reich,* esp. 9–10; Bärsch, *Religion;* Maier, "Political Religion," 5–16.

103. Bry's influence is occasionally mentioned in the literature—e.g., by Scholder (*Kirchen,* 1:596–97), Burleigh (*Sacred Causes,* 29–31), and Burrin ("Political Religion," 326)—but his Nazi connection is not.

104. Bry, *Verkappte Religionen* (Gotha, 1924); also see the materials in Bry NL, BHSA, abt 5. He was born in 1892 and joined the NSDAP on 13 January 1921 (member number 2685); NSDAP/HA-R8, fol. 171. On his

time on the official editorial staff of the *Beobachter,* see, e.g., "Mitteilung," *VB* 37 (12 May 1921).

105. Bry also provided a remarkably prescient analysis (especially in the context of 1924) of Nazi racial obsession and anti-Semitism: "The anti-Semites of 1924 do not exactly know what they would do with the Jews after coming to power. The wildest among them envision concentration prisoner camps for Jews [*Konzentrations-Gefangenenlager für Juden*]"; Bry, *Verkappte Religionen,* 115. Bry/Decke died in 1926 (at age thirty-four) and never witnessed the tragic realization of his prophetic remarks.

106. Gritschneder, *Bewährungsfrist,* 37–38; also Schreiner, "'Retter,'" 115–20.

107. Schott, *Volksbuch,* 231, and passim; also see the expanded imagery in the 1941 edition, pp. 219ff.

108. The portrait, which echoed imagery of the resurrected Christ's Easter tidings, was intended to foster unity behind the drive to repeal the speaking ban on Hitler, to "resurrect" Hitler, in effect, as a public figure; "Unsere Osterbotschaft," *VB* 77 (4–6 Apr 1926).

109. See, e.g., "Jugendbewegung und Hitlerglaube," *VB* 93 (24 Apr 1926).

110. See, e.g., "Hitlergeist in allen Gauen," *VB* 150 (3 July 1926); more generally, Bärsch, *Religion,* 136–78.

111. Bangert, "Adolf Hitler," *VB* 150 (3 July 1926). The poem was reissued in 1934 and circulated widely during the Third Reich, but most accounts have overlooked its origins in the mid-1920s; see, e.g., Eder, "Hitler," 153–54.

112. See the advance publicity on the flag consecration, "Reichsparteitag der NSDAP in Weimar," *VB* 150 (3 July 1926); "Programm für den Reichsparteitag," *VB* 150 (3 July 1926).

113. "Adolf Hitlers Rede bei der Fahnen- und Standartenübergabe," *VB* 152 (6 July 1926).

114. Ibid.

115. On the post-1933 significance of this martyr imagery, see Baird, *Heroes,* chap. 3.

116. On the major consecration ceremony in Munich, see "Aus der Bewegung," *VB* 162 (17 July 1926); also the blood-drenched martyr imagery of the putsch commemoration that year: "Wir gedenken den Toten," "Die Totenfeiern für unsere Helden," and "Weihestunde für unsere gefallenen Freiheitskämpfer," all in *VB* 259 (9 Nov 1926); "Trauerfeier der Münchener Nationalsozialisten," *VB* 262 (12 Nov 1926).

117. Quoted in Thamer, "Reichsparteitage," 353; see also Thamer, "Rituale," 79–98; Meyer, *Blutfahne;* Spotts, *Aesthetics,* 105–7; Doosry, "Sakrale Dimension," 205–24.

118. Joseph Goebbels, the former Catholic who was just beginning his engagement with the NSDAP in 1926, emerged only later as a driving force behind this trajectory in the 1930s; see, e.g., Bärsch, *Religion,* 91–130.

119. Hess, "Schlageter und kath. Farbenstudententum," *VB* 51 (28 May 1925). The fact that Hess was from Düsseldorf, not Munich, is significant.

On the decision by the Munich CV not only to abandon connections with the NSDAP, which had in any case been outlawed, but also to secede from the *Hochschulring* in the aftermath of the putsch, see "Hochschulring," *Academia* 10 (15 Feb 1924). On the Munich CV's continuing refusal to collaborate with the refounded NSDAP after 1925, see the materials in CV-Archiv, fol. 61.

120. Johnsen was scheduled to preside over a Nazi-sponsored Schlageter ceremony in June 1925, but when he was unable to attend Ziegler presided instead; "Ein Schlageter-Denkmal," *VB* 76 (28–29 June 1925). Ziegler went on to be a major figure within the Deutsche Christen movement; see also his Protestant-Nazi devotional reflection "Advent," *VB* 215 (9 Dec 1925).

121. Stolzing, "Schlageter," *VB* 49 (26 May 1925).

122. Jakob, "Schlageter," *VB* 54 (31 May–1 June 1925); also "Schlageter-feier," *VB* 62 (11 June 1925); "Grosse Schlageter-Gedenkfeier," *VB* 201 (22–23 Nov 1925); "Schlageter-Kundgebung," *VB* 215 (9 Dec 1925); "Schlageter-Gedächtnis-Feier!" *VB* 218 (12 Dec 1925); "Schlageter-Kundgebung," *VB* 219 (13–14 Dec 1925); "Unser Schlageter," *VB* 102 (5 May 1926).

123. "Schlageter," *VB* 118 (26 May 1926); also A. Schönauer, "Heldentum: Eine Erinnerung an Albert Leo Schlageter," in the same issue, as well as "Schlageter und der Nationalsozialismus," *VB* 120 (28 May 1926). In contrast to the earlier mixture of Catholic and *Edda* imagery employed by Schrönghamer, this pagan-oriented veneration of Schlageter generally lacked any reference to Christianity; see, more generally, Ulbricht, "Baldur," 164–65.

124. "Schlageters Verklärung," *VB* 118 (26 May 1926).

125. The play, *Schlageters Heldentod,* was staged on 20 October 1926; "Unser Vormarsch," *VB* 247 (24–25 Oct 1926); see also the related "Enthüllung eines Denkmals für Schlageter," *VB* 255 (4 Nov 1926).

126. Much of the literature on the development of this imagery has noted connections with Catholic cultic-liturgical impulses but has typically done so only in passing; see, e.g., Reichel, *Faszination,* esp. 371–75; Spotts, *Aesthetics,* 311ff.; Karow, *Opfer;* Bartetzko, *Illusionen;* Lane, *Architecture;* Taylor, *Stone.*

127. Kofler, *Katholische Kirche,* 5.

128. Johannes Schauff, "Zur Soziologie der Wahlen," *Weckruf* 4:7 (1 July 1928). On the inability of the NSDAP to gain any real political traction among Catholics in Munich, see Rösch, *NSDAP,* 49–56.

129. On the September 1930 elections, see, e.g., Orlow, *Nazi Party,* 185–92; Schulz, *Wandel,* chap. 2; Falter, *Wähler,* 30–34; Falter, "Mobilization," 202–31.

130. In addition to the extensive investigation of Catholic journalist Peter Pfeiffer in 1929, the *Bayerischer Kurier* revisited the issue in a 1931 article entitled "Who Is Dr. Theol. Kofler?" but was unable to proffer a convincing answer. Subsequent historians also failed to identify Kofler; Mazura, *Zentrumspartei,* 211–16; Greive, *Theologie,* 291; Noack, *Unbelehrbar,* 345–50.

131. That this has apparently gone unnoticed by scholars is rather surprising, given the fact that the identical wording appears in the two

opening paragraphs of both the 1923 and 1928–1930 editions. The Ordinariat in Munich had its suspicions that Roth was the author; see, e.g., the related discussion in Generalvikar Hindringer to Roth, 4 Apr 1929, NL Faulhaber, fol. 7269.

132. See, e.g., the private letter, marked *streng vertraulich,* from Roth to Hitler, 7 Jan 1931, copy in NL Schachleiter, BHSA, fol. 11.

133. See "Katholizismus und Nationalsozialismus," *VB* 54 (21 Feb 1929); "Für den Katholizismus, gegen das Konkordat," *VB* (25 June 1929).

134. Schmittinger was born in 1893 and ordained in Munich in 1918. He and Roth served together at Munich's St. Ursula from October 1924 to March 1925 and remained close thereafter. Schmittinger joined the NSDAP on 1 May 1933 with member number 1930597. After the war, U. S. authorities asked that he be removed from his parish post in Günzlhofen because of his "adverse political activities"; Capt. Leo Knuti to Ordinariat, 5 Nov 1945, PA-Schmittinger, AEMF. Weinschenk was ordained in 1917 in Strassburg and served alongside Josef Roth at St. Ursula's from May 1925 to September 1931. By September 1933, he was openly supporting the NSDAP Ortsgruppe in nearby Bruck bei Grafing; see Weinschenk to Schachleiter, 6 and 17 Sep 1933, both in NL Schachleiter, BHSA, fol. 9. Weinschenk eventually had numerous run-ins with Nazi authorities; Witetschek, *Lage,* 1:325–26; Hehl, *Priester,* 990; Spicer, *Hitler's Priests,* 296–97. Schmittinger and Weinschenk died on 9 January 1960 and 27 January 1990, respectively.

135. See, e.g., his 18 June 1929 letter to Hindenburg, NL Schachleiter, BHSA, abt. 5, fol. 5.

136. See "Schola Gregoriana in München," *Musica Sacra* 61:2 (Feb 1931): 47–51.

137. The large country house, known as *Haus Gott-Dank,* now houses the Bärenstub'n restaurant. On diocesan attempts to get Schachleiter to move out of the Engelhard house, see the materials in NL Faulhaber, fol. 5537.

138. Entries of 21 and 31 Dec 1924, BTB, NL Pieper, AK.

139. Haeuser, "Mein Werden," 180–81, 237–38; also DNVP Munich to Faulhaber, 13 Nov 1924, and Haeuser to Faulhaber, 18 Nov 1924, both in NL Faulhaber, fol. 7603.

140. See "Nationalsozialistische Weihnachtsrede," *APZ* 291 (19 Dec 1930); "Ein katholischer Pfarrer als Hitleragitator," *MP* 292 (18 Dec 1930); "Ein Apostel der Wahrheit," *Stürmer* 52 (Dec 1930); "Kampfgeist gegen Pharisäertum," *VB* 300 (18 Dec 1930). Haeuser's ecclesiastical superiors forbade him from speaking publicly on behalf of the Nazis, a rule Haeuser obeyed until early 1933; Haeuser, "Mein Werden," 203–7. See also "Redeverbot," *BK* 354 (20 Dec 1930); "Der Fall Haeuser," *BK* 357 (23 Dec 1930); "Der Fall Haeuser," *APZ* 295 (24 Dec 1930); "Massregelung," *VB* 304 (23 Dec 1930); "Redeverbot," *VB* 305 (24 Dec 1930).

141. "Nationalsozialismus und Seelsorge," *Amtsblatt* 4 (10 Feb 1931); also Donohue, *Opponents,* 32–34. The Bavarian bishops' statement echoed in many ways earlier bishops' statements from elsewhere in Germany; see, e.g., the forceful words of Breslau's Cardinal Bertram, who issued a directive

on 31 December 1930 identifying National Socialism as "a religious delusion which has to be fought with all possible vigor"; Bertram, *Stellung,* 7–8. On the strong September 1930 statement by the *Generalvikar* of of Mainz, see Lewy, *Church,* 8.

142. Nötges, *Nationalsozialismus;* Wild, *Nationalsozialismus;* Gerdemann and Winfried, *Christenkreuz;* Wild, *Hitler;* Eberle, *Kampf;* Rost, *Christus.* For the argument that a reconciliation was still possible, see Senn, *Katholizismus;* Senn, *Halt;* Stark, *Nationalsozialismus.*

143. Unlike the 1932 statement, the 1931 directive did not mention Nazism by name; *Protokoll 1931; Protokoll 1932;* also Lewy, *Church,* 10–15.

144. See, e.g., Schachleiter to Josef Roth, 30 Jan 1933; Roth to Schachleiter, 1, 6, 9 Feb and 12 Mar 1933, all in NL Schachleiter, BHSA, fol. 11; Haeuser to Schachleiter, 5 Feb and 27 Mar 1933, NL Schachleiter, BHSA, fol. 10.

145. Haeuser to Kampfmüller, 16 Mar 1933, PA-Haeuser, ABA.

146. Schachleiter to Faulhaber, 28 Apr 1933, NL Schachleiter, BHSA, fol. 6.

147. On the *Brückenbauer,* who typically became disillusioned after the Röhm purge in the summer of 1934, see Breuning, *Vision,* esp. chap. 3; Hürten, *Katholiken,* 214–30; Krieg, *Theologians,* 27–30; Denzler, *Widerstand,* 48–82; Spicer, *Hitler's Priests,* 12–28. Representative contemporary texts include Karl Adam, "Deutsches Volkstum und katholisches Christentum," *TQ* 114 (1933): 40–63; Brauer, *Katholik;* Eschweiler, "Die Kirche im neuen Reich," *Deutsches Volkstum* 15 (1933): 451–58; Nobel, *Katholik;* Kaller, "Unsere katholischen Aufgaben von heute," *Zeit und Volk* 1:3 (5 Aug 1933): 91–94; Mirgeler, "Die deutschen Katholiken und das Reich," *Schildgenossen* 13 (1933–1934): 53–56; Lortz, *Zugang;* Schmaus, *Begegnungen.*

148. Reprinted in Müller, *Dokumente,* 76–78.

149. Josef Roth held a fairly high government position but worked mainly behind the scenes; Kreutzer, *Reichskirchenministerium,* 160–82.

150. Schachleiter to Hindringer, 17 May 1932, NL Schachleiter, BHSA, Abt. 5, fol. 6.

151. Schachleiter, "Zum Linzer Hirtenbrief: Ein Wort zur Beruhigung für strenggläubige Katholiken," *VB* 32 (1 Feb 1933). He was responding to the 21 January 1933 statement by the bishop of Linz condemning Nazism as incompatible with Catholicism. Schachleiter's manifesto had been written in advance and left in the hands of Josef Roth, awaiting Hitler's appointment as chancellor. On 30 January 1933, Schachleiter cabled Roth, instructing him to deliver the manifesto to the offices of the *Beobachter,* where it arrived in time to appear in the paper's triumphal issue on 1 February; Schachleiter to Roth, 30 Jan 1933, NL Schachleiter, BHSA, fol. 11.

152. "Eine Erklärung des Abtes Schachleiter," *MNN* (6 Feb 1933); also Buchweiser to Schachleiter, 3 Feb 1933, NL Schachleiter, BHSA, fol. 6; "Das Münchener Ordinariat gegen Abt Alban Schachleiter," *TTB* 29 (4 Feb 1933); "Abt und Hakenkreuz," *BVZ* (6 Feb 1933); "Zelebrationsverbot," *NMT* 38 (7 Feb 1933).

153. Bleistein, "Schachleiter," 178–79.

154. "Gewaltige Kundgebung für Abt Albanus Schachleiter," *VB* 84–85 (25–26 Mar 1933); "Der 74 jährige Abt Schachleiter wird wegen seiner Hitlertreue weiter verfolgt," *VB* 96 (6 Apr 1933); "Der Reichskanzler bei Abt Schachleiter," *VB* 137 (17 May 1933). Nazi official Alarich Seidler met with diocesan officials in late May to demand the "rehabilitation of Abbot Schachleiter"; meeting minutes, 27 May 1933, BHSA-StK, fol. 7279/I. The censure was finally lifted in early September; Volk, *Akten,* 1:741.

155. On Riefenstahl's portrayal of Nazi liturgical performativity, see Peucker, "Choreography," 279–97.

156. On the similar attempts in Rome by the pro-Nazi Austrian bishop Alois Hudal to separate the "healthy" Nazism represented by Hitler from the unhealthy anti-Christian sentiments of Rosenberg and others, see Burkard, *Häresie,* as well as Hudal's *Grundlagen;* more generally, see Baumgärtner, *Weltanschauungskampf.*

157. See esp. their correspondence from March 1935, NSDAP/HA-R55, fol. 1326.

158. Schachleiter to Wilhelm Widmann, 8 Sep 1936, Schachleiter papers, BHSA-StK, fol. 7279/I. Widmann, who was cathedral choral director (*Domkapellmeister*) in Eichstätt, continued over the next several months to try to get Schachleiter to state publicly what he had admitted privately: "it is your duty and a matter of honor to announce to the public your true thoughts on the matter"; Widmann to Schachleiter, 1 Jan 1937, BHSA-StK, fol. 7279/I.

159. One of his final letters to Rudolf Hess proclaimed: "My final greeting is *Heil Hitler!* And now I go to face God, faithful unto death to my Führer and his glorious movement"; Schachleiter to Hess, 8 Mar 1937; cited in Spicer, *Hitler's Priests,* 91.

160. The funeral cost approximately 11,000RM; internal note, 22 July 1937, BHSA-StK, fol. 7279/I.

161. In January 1938, Schachleiter's caretaker Gildis Engelhard complained that the abbot's grave had gone completely untended throughout the recent holiday season, whereas the neighboring graves of Nazi functionaries were decorated richly with party wreaths; Engelhard to Siebert, 5 Jan 1938, BHSA-StK, fol. 7279/I. Schachleiter's grave was originally adorned with a huge steel cross and was located in section 137 in Munich's Waldfriedhof; after the war, his grave was moved to the priests' section (142a), and both the giant steel cross and the original prime location in section 137 were eventually used for the graves of Duchess Anna (1874–1958) and Duke Christoph (1879–1963) of Bavaria. Schachleiter's identification plate was removed entirely from the priests' section at some later point, leaving a blank spot in that row to the present day.

162. Artur Bäuml to Siebert, 17 June 1938; Siebert to Gildis Engelhard, 18 June 1938; BHSA-StK, fol. 7279/II.

163. For the continuing idealization of Schlageter's Catholic identity, see Sengstock and Fassbender, *Schlageter,* esp. 63–93 (Fassbender was the

Catholic priest who had heard Schlageter's final confession on the morning of his execution). See also the CV tribute edited by Hagen, *Schlageter;* "Zum Todestag Schlageters," *Academia* 45:2 (15 June 1932); "Albert Leo Schlageter," *Academia* 45:6 (15 Oct 1932). For secular and pagan-*völkisch* portrayals, see Brandt, *Schlageter,* whose discussion of Schlageter's student days (11–13) explicitly omitted any reference to the CV and whose account of the execution (92–101) reduced the importance of Schlageter's final communion and confession to a brief partial sentence. Also see Glaser, *Stahlkreuz;* Mahnke, *Schlageter;* and Rehbein, *Tod,* which made only one passing reference to the CV (99).

164. "CV und Nationalsozialismus," *Academia* 45:12 (15 Apr 1933). Of the more than fifty individual *Academia* articles on Schlageter through the remainder of 1933, see esp. "Der CV bekennt sich zu Albert Leo Schlageter," *Academia* 46:1 (15 May 1933); "Schlageter in seinen Briefen," *Academia* 46:1 (15 May 1933); "Die nationale Erhebung und der katholische Akademiker," *Academia* 46:2 (15 June 1933); "Schlageter-Feiern im CV," *Academia* 46:2 (15 June 1933); "Der Schlageter-Gedenktag," *Academia* 46:3 (15 July 1933); "Schlageters Begräbnis," *Academia* 46:3 (15 July 1933); "Begegnung eines CVers mit Schlageter im Gefängnis," *Academia* 46:3 (15 July 1933); "Schlageters Persönlichkeit," *Academia* 46:4 (15 Aug 1933); "Schlageter-Erinnerungen," *Academia* 46:4 (15 Aug 1933); "Persönliche Erinnerungen an Schlageter," *Academia* 46:5 (15 Sep 1933); "Bund Schlageter," *Academia* 46:5 (15 Sep 1933); "Wehrhafter Student und politischer Soldat," *Academia* 46:5 (15 Sep 1933).

165. See his handwritten notes, "Schlageter-Rede in Wald-Trudering," NL Schachleiter, BHSA, fol. 5; also the report in *VB* 147 (26 May 1933).

166. Individual groups for CV alumni continued to exist in some cities until July 1938; see Stitz, *CV,* 352–85.

167. Berthold continued by recalling the obvious fact that "Schlageter was a Catholic student and a *Bundesbruder* of ours!" In the same letter, Berthold notified Schachleiter that the Nazi regime had "demanded that the last pillars and supports of the church, the Catholic student fraternities, deconfessionalize themselves!...Under these conditions the CV will probably fail, and we would rather in any case voluntarily dissolve ourselves, since a forfeiture of the Catholic ideal would go against our honor!!" Berthold to Schachleiter, 28 Jan 1934, NSDAP/HA-R55, fol. 1327; also Berthold to Schachleiter, 21 Dec 1933, NSDAP/HA-R55, fol. 1330.

168. Nabor, *Schlageter,* 17–19, 25–29. Nabor, whose real name was Karl Allmendinger, had written a number of popular Catholic devotional works earlier in his career.

169. The relevant chapter was entitled "Das Sonnenkreuz"; Nabor, *Schlageter,* 51–60.

170. Schlageter's preparation for death was portrayed as "an image out of the time of the Christian martyrs in the catacombs under the bloody tyrannical rule of Nero," and his walk to the execution site was characterized as a messianic transfiguration: "A truly majestic, supernatural

illumination shone from his face and his demeanor was so heroic that the Germans present looked upon him in wonderment"; ibid., 182–83.

171. Ibid., 186. For other attempts to fuse Schlageter's Catholic and Nazi identities, see also Hessdörffer, *Schlageter;* and the work by CV alumnus Josef Magnus Wehner, *Schlageter.*

172. Most famously, Johst, *Schlageter;* see also the CV's review by Wehner, "Hanns Johsts Schlageter-Drama," *Academia* 46:1 (15 May 1933). Johst's portrayal, while certainly downplaying Schlageter's Catholic faith, is fairly moderate when compared to flaming Nazi accounts that attempted to establish Schlageter as a purely secular Germanic messianic figure, such as Beyer, *Düsseldorfer Passion.* See also Schmiedel, *Schlageter;* Freitag, *Schlageter;* Kürten, *Schlageter;* Sommer, *Schlageter;* Knorreck, *Schlageter;* Wentzke, *Schlageter;* Albert, *Schlageter;* Zaum, *Schlageter;* Glombowski, *Organisation Heinz;* Grote, *Schlageter;* Grote, *Ruf;* Kurfess, *Schlageter;* the official SA account by Priesack, *Schlageter;* Thuermeister, *Schlageter;* Wiest, *Schlageter;* Hotz, *Schlageter.*

173. "Weltanschauung auf biologischer Grundlage," *Durchbruch* 3:43 (22 Oct 1936). Among the angry Catholic responses, see esp. "Schlageter zu unrecht Christ?" *Der Katholik* 49 (6 Dec 1936).

174. Faulhaber to Fassbender, 13 Mar 1937, NL Faulhaber, fol. 7278.

Conclusion

1. Byrne, "Benedict."

2. See Kissler, *Benedikt,* esp. chaps. 2–3.

3. See the brilliant analysis of Dillon, *Identity.* For a good overview of the vast recent literature on broader identity studies, see Burke et al., *Advances,* 1–10; also Vryan et al., "Identity," 367–90; Appiah and Gates, *Identities,* 1–6.

4. Hammond, "Persistence," 1–11.

5. Dillon, *Identity,* esp. 242–55. See also the insightful analysis of the longer-term formation of Catholic "faith-identity experience" by the Dutch Jesuit theologian Franz Josef van Beeck, *Identity,* 11–26; more generally, Graf, *Wiederkehr,* 203–25.

6. Nancy Ammerman has emphasized the importance of official church institutions and structures to the study of religious identity, while arguing convincingly that these institutions have never been the sole source of the religious narratives that serve to structure the identities of individual adherents; see her "Religious Identities," 207–24. For a nuanced treatment of Catholic identity within the defined geographic and temporal context of early twentieth-century Boston, see the outstanding Kane, *Separatism.*

7. See Bergen, "Partners?" esp. 28–29; also Bergen, "Gläubige," 542–74, and her discussion of "canonicity" in *Twisted Cross,* 143–48.

8. For a discussion of this type of perspectival challenge in assessing reform-oriented theologians condemned as "modernists" in the early twentieth century, see esp. Weiss, *Modernismus,* 594–601.

9. Steigmann-Gall's *Holy Reich* has been criticized for, among other things, taking Nazi statements too often at face value and according too much credence to the public utterances of Nazi figures; see, e.g., Hexham, "Reading," 59–65.

10. Carroll, *Sword,* 475–78; also Krieg, "Views"; Füllenbach, "Shock"; Forstner, "Katholizismus contra Antijudaismus"; Spicer, *Antisemitism.*

11. On the relationship between earlier forms of Catholic anti-Semitism and emerging pseudo-scientific racial currents, see Blaschke, *Antisemitismus,* 91–106; Greive, *Theologie,* 129–34.

12. See, more broadly, Phayer, "Guilt"; Brown-Fleming, *Conscience;* Phayer, "German Catholic Church," 151–67.

13. Heer, *Glaube.* See also Heer's initial foray, *Liebe.*

14. See Hesemann, *Hitlers Religion;* Rissmann, *Hitlers Gott;* Läpple, *Psychogramm;* also, in a slightly different vein, Pois, *Nature.*

15. Heer, *Glaube,* 32–33; Läpple, *Psychogramm,* 125–26; Hesemann, *Hitlers Religion,* 51–52.

16. Statements by early aquaintances on the young Hitler's anti-Christian views include Kubicek, *Jugendfreund,* esp. 95–100; and Hanisch, "Hitler"; see also Hamann, *Hitler's Vienna,* 163–65, 249–52.

17. Hermann Rauschning claimed that Hitler stated privately in early 1933 that his goal was to "stamp out Christianity in Germany, root and branch. One is either a Christian or a German. You can't be both"; Rauschning, *Hitler Speaks,* 55. For a critical discussion that dismisses Rauschning's recollections as unreliable, see Steigmann-Gall, *Holy Reich,* 28–29. On Hitler's table talks in the early 1940s, which were saturated with deeply unflattering references to Christianity, see Picker and Ritter, *Tischgespräche.* For an attempt to undermine the reliability of the anti-Christian statements, see Carrier, "Table Talk," 561–76.

18. In addition to works on Germany discussed in the introduction, see the literature on its Austrian roots, e.g., Whiteside, *Austrian;* Whiteside, *Fools;* Strong, *Seedtime.* On fascist ideological roots within French national syndicalism and revolutionary antiliberalism, see, e.g., Sternhell, *Neither;* more generally, Sternhell, *Birth.*

19. Wehler, *Empire;* Eley and Blackbourn, *Peculiarities.*

20. Large, *Ghosts,* chaps. 4–5; Wilhelm, *Fememörder,* 57–76.

21. For an attempt to connect overtly Protestant impulses to the political religiosity of the Third Reich, see Hardtwig, "Political Religion," 1–14.

22. The fusion of residual elements from the early movement's liturgical performativity with a Protestant-nationalist orientation can be seen, for example, in the striking image from President Paul von Hindenburg's 1934 funeral on the cover of this book.

23. Spruchkammer Passau report, 15 June 1948, Schrönghamer papers, StAP, sch. 11.

24. "Beschluss aus der Stadtratssitzung," 28 June 1951, StAP, sch.11.

25. See the gushing diocesan tributes "Franz Schrönghamer-Heimdal 70 Jahre alt," *Passauer Bistumsblatt* 28 (15 July 1951); "Der bayerische Rosegger:

Franz Schrönghamer-Heimdal zu seinem 75. Geburtstag," *Passauer Bistumsblatt* 28 (8 July 1956). In the 1990s, amateur historian Anna Rosmus (whose earlier experiences as a student were dramatized in the Michael Verhoeven film *Das schreckliche Mädchen*) succeeded in having Schrönghamer's name removed from the Passau street that had been named in his honor; see Rosmus, *Out of Passau,* 98.

26. See, e.g., Wolf, *Antimodernismus.*

27. Hitler, *Mein Kampf,* 829.

Bibliography

Archival Materials

Abtei Königsmünster (AK), Meschede
  Nachlass Lorenz Pieper
Archiv der Bayerischen Franziskanerprovinz (St. Anna, Munich)
  Nachlass Erhard Schlund
Archiv des Bistums Augsburg (ABA)
  Personal-Akten
Archiv des Bistums Regensburg
  CV-Archiv
Archiv des Erzbistums München und Freising (AEMF)
  Faulhaber-Archiv (NL Faulhaber)
  Personal-Akten
Bayerisches Hauptstaats-Archiv (BHSA), Munich
  Abteilung V: Nachlässe
  Kultusministerium (MK)
  Ministerium des Innern (MInn)
Bayerische Staatsbibliothek (BSB)
  Handschriften-Abteilung: Nachlässe
  Krausgesellschaftiana
  Schnitzeriana
Berlin Document Center (microfilm), National Archives, College Park, Md.
(BDC)
  Partei Korrespondenz, A-3341-PK
  SA Kartei, A-3341-SA
  SS Frauen, A-3343-SF
  SS Personal-Akten, A-3343-SSO
  Zentralkartei, A-3340-MFKL
Institut für Zeitgeschichte, Munich
  Presseausschnittsammlung
  Sammlungen und Nachlässe

NSDAP Hauptarchiv (microfilm), Hoover Institution, Stanford, Calif.
  Collection Himmler
  Collection NSDAP Hauptarchiv
Staatsarchiv München (SAM)
  Polizeidirektion
Stadtarchiv Augsburg
  Dienst-Personalakten des Stadtrats
Stadtarchiv Bobingen
  Philipp Haeuser Materials
Stadtarchiv Mönchengladbach
  KV-Archiv
Stadtarchiv München
  Bürgermeister und Rat
Stadtarchiv Passau (StAP)
  Sammlung Franz Schrönghamer-Heimdal
Universitätsarchiv, München (UAM)
  Personal-Akten
  Studentenkartei
Universitätsbibliothek, Würzburg (UBW)
  Archiv des Instituts für Hochschulkunde

Published Materials

CONTEMPORARY NEWSPAPERS AND PERIODICALS

Academia
Der Akademiker
Akademische Monatsblätter
Allgemeine Rundschau
Allgemeine Zeitung
Amtsblatt für die Erzdiozese München und Freising
Auf gut deutsch
Augsburger Postzeitung
Bayerische Hochschulzeitung
Das Bayerische Vaterland
Bayerische Volkspartei Correspondenz
Bayerische Volkszeitung
Bayerischer Königsbote
Bayerischer Kurier
Der Deutsche Geist
Deutsche Katholikenzeitung
Deutsches Volksblatt: Bayerische antisemitische Zeitung für Stadt und Land
Donauwacht
Donau-Zeitung
Fliegende Blätter
Gelbe Hefte

Grossdeutsche Zeitung
Historisch-politische Blätter für das katholische Deutschland
Hochland
Hochland-Buch
Im Deutschen Reich
Jugend
Kölnische Volkszeitung
Korrespondenzblatt des Philisteriums der kath. bayer. Studentenverbindung Rhaetia
Landshuter Zeitung
Legauer Anzeiger
Miesbacher Anzeiger
Münchener-Augsburger Abendzeitung
Münchener Freie Presse
Münchener Illustrierte Presse
Münchener Katholische Kirchenzeitung
Münchener Neueste Nachrichten
Münchener Post
Der Nationalsozialist
Neue Bayerische Zeitung
Das Neue Jahrhundert
Neues Münchener Tagblatt
Passauer Neue Presse
Quickborn
Renaissance
Schematismus der Geistlichkeit des Erzbistums München und Freising
Simplicissimus
Der Stürmer
Süddeutsche Monatshefte
Völkischer Kurier
Vorwärts
Das zwanzigste [20.] Jahrhundert

PRIMARY SOURCES

Adam, Karl. "Deutsches Volkstum und katholisches Christentum." *TQ* 114 (1933).
Adolph, Walter. *Im Schatten des Galgens: Zum Gedächtnis der Blutzeugen in der nationalsozialistischen Kirchenverfolgung.* Cologne, 1953.
Albert, Wilhelm. *Albert Leo Schlageter.* Berlin, 1934.
Altkatholizismus und Reformkatholizismus: Fünf Schriftstücke zur kirchlichen Zeitgeschichte. Bonn, 1908.
Andersch, Alfred. *Der Vater eines Mörders.* Zurich, 1980.
Arthofer, Leopold. *Als Priester im Konzentrationslager: Erlebnisse in Dachau.* Graz, 1947.

Bauer, Franz, ed. *Die Regierung Eisner 1918/19: Ministerratsprotokolle und Dokumente*. Düsseldorf, 1987.

Beck, Friedrich Alfred, ed. *Kampf und Sieg: Geschichte der NSDAP im Gau Westfalen-Süd*. Dortmund, 1938.

Bernhart, Joseph. *Erinnerungen 1881–1930*, ed. M. Weitlauff. 2 vols. Weissenhorn, 1992.

Bertram, Adolf. *Die Stellung der katholischen Kirche zu Radikalismus und Nationalismus*. Breslau, 1930.

Beyer, Paul. *Düsseldorfer Passion: Ein deutsches National-Festspiel*. Munich, 1933.

Birnbaum, Immanuel. "Studenten machen Politik." In *Denk ich an München: Ein Buch der Erinnerung*, ed. H. Probst and K. Ude. Munich, 1966.

Boepple, Ernst, ed. *Adolf Hitlers Reden*. Munich, 1925.

Brandt, Rolf. *Albert Leo Schlageter: Leben und Sterben eines deutschen Helden*. Hamburg, 1926.

Brauer, Theodor. *Der Katholik im neuen Reich: Seine Aufgabe und sein Anteil*. Munich, 1933.

Bruner, Ludwig. *Festschrift zum 50. Stiftungsfest der katholischen bayerischen Studentenverbindung Rhaetia 1881–1931*. Munich, 1931.

Bry, Carl Christian. *Verkappte Religionen: Kritik eines kollektiven Wahns*. Gotha, 1924.

Buchner, F. X. *Das Bistum Eichstätt: Historisch-statistische Beschreibung*. Eichstätt, 1937.

Buxton, D. *Christendom on Trial: Documents of the German Church Struggle*. London, 1939.

Carmer, Carl. *The War against God*. New York, 1943.

Carsten, Wilhelm, ed. *Kölner Aktenstücke zur Lage der katholischen Kirche in Deutschland 1933–1945*. Cologne, 1949.

Deuerlein, Ernst. *Der Aufstieg der NSDAP in Augenzeugenberichten*. Düsseldorf, 1968.

Deuerlein, Ernst, ed. *Der Hitler-Putsch: Bayerische Dokumente zum 8./9. November 1923*. Stuttgart, 1962.

Drexler, Anton. *Mein politisches Erwachen*. Munich, 1919.

Eberle, Joseph. *Zum Kampf um Hitler*. Vienna, 1931.

Eckart, Dietrich. *Der Bolschewismus von Moses bis Lenin: Zwiegespräch zwischen Adolf Hitler und mir*. Munich, 1924.

Eschweiler, Carl. "Die Kirche im neuen Reich." *Deutsches Volkstum* 15 (1933).

Euringer, Richard. *Dietrich Eckart: Leben eines deutschen Dichters*. Hamburg, 1938.

Faulhaber, Michael von. *Deutsches Ehrgefühl und katholisches Gewissen*. Munich, 1925.

———. *Schwert des Glaubens: Kriegspredigten*. Freiburg, 1917.

Feder, Gottfried. *Manifest zur Brechung der Zinsknechtschaft*. Munich, 1919.

Fendt, Leonhard. *Die Dauer des öffentlichen Wirksamkeit Jesu*. Munich, 1906.

Freitag, Martin. *Albert Leo Schlageter: Ein deutscher Held*. Reutlingen, 1933.

Frey, Arthur. *Cross and Swastika: The Ordeal of the German Church*. London, 1938.

Gerdemann, Wilhelm, and Heinrich Winfried. *Christenkreuz oder Hakenkreuz?* Cologne, 1931.

Glasebock, Willy. *Katholische Studentenschaft und völkische Bewegung* (Munich, n.d. [c. 1921–1922]).

Glaser, W. *Stahlkreuz an der Ruhr: Albert Leo Schlageters Leben und Sterben*. Stuttgart, 1930.

Glombowski, F. *Organisation Heinz: Das Schicksal der Kameraden Schlageters*. Berlin, 1934.

Grassl, Josef. *Blut und Brot: Der Zusammenhang zwischen Biologie und Volkswirtschaft bei der bayerischen Bevölkerung im 19. Jahrhundert*. Munich, 1905.

Grote, Hans. *Albert Leo Schlageter: Der deutschen Jugend Vorbild*. Cologne, 1934.

————. *Ein Ruf erging: Der Roman Albert Leo Schlageters*. Leipzig, 1935.

Gruchmann, Lothar, and Reinhard Weber, eds. *Der Hitler-Prozess 1924: Wortlaut der Hauptverhandlung vor dem Volksgericht München I*. Munich, 1997.

Grün, Wilhelm. *Dietrich Eckart als Publizist*. Munich, 1944.

Guenther, Konrad. *Rasse und Heimat*. Berlin, 1936.

Haeuser, Philipp. *Jud und Christ, oder Wem gebührt die Weltherrschaft?* Regensburg, 1923.

————. "Mein Werden." Unpublished ms., Stadtarchiv Bobingen, 1942.

————. *Wir deutschen Katholiken und die moderne revolutionäre Bewegung*. Regensburg, 1922.

Hagen, Hermann. *Albert Leo Schlageter: Gesammelte Aufsätze aus der Monatsschrift des CV*. Munich, 1932.

Hanfstaengl, Ernst. *Unheard Witness*. Philadelphia, 1957.

————. *Zwischen Weissem und Braunem Haus*. Munich, 1970.

Hanisch, Reinhold. "I Was Hitler's Buddy." *New Republic* (12 Apr 1939).

Hasselbach, Ulrich von. "Die Entstehung der NSDAP.1919–1923." Ph.D. diss., Leipzig, 1931.

Hauviller, Ernst. *Franz Xaver Kraus: Ein Lebensbild aus der Zeit des Reformkatholizismus*. Munich, 1905.

Hecker, Alfons. *Vor Judas Weltregierung?* Passau, 1921.

Heilmann, Alfons. *Katholische Volksbibel*. Munich, 1912.

Herman, S. W. *It's Your Souls We Want*. New York, 1943.

Hessdörffer, Gerhard. *Schlageter*. Mönchengladbach, 1933.

Hinkel, Hans. *Einer unter Hunderttausend*. Munich, 1938.

Hitler, Adolf. *Die "Hetzer" der Wahrheit*. Munich, 1922.

————. *Mein Kampf*, trans. Ralph Mannheim. Boston, 1943.

————. *Reden, Schriften, Anordnungen: Februar 1925 bis Januar 1933*, ed. Clemens Vollnhalls. Munich, 1992.

————. *Sämtliche Aufzeichnungen 1905–1924*, ed. E. Jäckel and A. Kuhn. Stuttgart, 1980.

Hoffmann, Albrecht. *Der 9. November im Lichte der völkischen Freiheitsbewegung: Vortrag gehalten vor Studierenden der Universität München.* Munich, 1924.

Hoffmann, Heinrich. *Hitler Was My Friend.* London, 1955.

Hotz, Wilhelm. *Albert Leo Schlageter.* Essen, 1940.

Hudal, Alois. *Die Grundlagen des Nationalsozialismus.* Leipzig, 1936.

Hundhammer, Alois. *Geschichte des Bayerischen Bauernbundes.* Munich, 1924.

Jedin, Hubert. *Lebensbericht.* Mainz, 1984.

Johst, Hanns. *Schlageter: Schauspiel.* Munich, 1933.

Kaller, Maximilian. "Unsere katholischen Aufgaben von heute." *Zeit und Volk* 1 (1933).

Kanzler, Rudolf. *Bayerns Kampf gegen den Bolschewismus.* Munich, 1931.

Karl, Josef. *Die Schreckensherrschaft in München und Spartakus im bayerischen Oberland.* Munich, 1919.

Klimsch, Robert. *Die Juden, ein Beweis für die Gottheit Jesu und ein Mahnruf für die Christen der Gegenwart.* Regensburg, 1919.

Klövekorn, Anton. *Hochland! Eine Feldgabe von Mitgliedern des Verbandes der katholischen neustudentischen Verbindungen Hochland.* Munich, 1918.

Knorreck, Alfred. *Schlageter: Wie ein deutscher Held lebte, litt und starb.* Breslau, 1933.

Koch, Hugo. *Katholizismus und Jesuitismus.* Munich, 1913.

Koegel, Joseph. *Geschichte der St. Kajetans-Hofkirche, der Theatiner und des Kgl. Hofstiftes in München.* Munich, 1901.

Kubicek, August. *Adolf Hitler, mein Jugendfreund.* Graz, 1953.

Kurfess, Franz. *Albert Leo Schlageter.* Breslau, 1935.

Kürten, Michael. *Albert Leo Schlageter: Ein deutscher Freiheitskämpfer.* Bochum, 1933.

Lehmann, Melanie. *Der Verleger J. F. Lehmann: Ein Leben im Kampf für Deutschland.* Munich, 1935.

Liebenfels, Jörg Lanz von. *Katholizismus wider Jesuitismus.* Frankfurt, 1903.
————. *Theozoologie.* Vienna, 1905.

Lortz, Joseph. *Katholischer Zugang zum Nationalsozialismus.* Münster, 1934.

Ludendorff, Erich. *Hitlers Verrat der Deutschen an den römischen Papst.* Munich, 1931.

Mahnke, Johannes. *Schlageter: Ein deutsches Heldenleben in harter Zeit.* Langensalza, 1930.

Maurer, Hansjörg. *Eine kritische Betrachtung des Problems der Homosexualität.* Munich, 1921.

Meyer, Herbert. *Kaiserfahne und Blutfahne.* Weimar, 1933.

Micklem, Nathaniel. *National Socialism and the Roman Catholic Church.* London, 1939.

Miller, Alfred. *Im Zeichen des Kreuzes.* Leipzig, 1936.

————. *Der Jesuitismus als Volksgefahr: Eine Betrachtung zu den Münchener Novemberereignissen*. Munich, 1924.

————. *Rom und die deutsche Gegenwart*. Lorch, 1925.

————. *Ultramontanes Schuldbuch*. Breslau, 1922.

————. *Völkerentartung unter dem Kreuz*. Leipzig, 1936.

Mirgeler, Albert. "Die deutschen Katholiken und das Reich." *Schildgenossen* 13 (1933–1934).

Moosbauer, Max. *Die nationalsozialistischen Bewegung in Passau 1920–1933*. Passau, 1934.

Müller, Hans. *Katholische Kirche und Nationalsozialismus: Dokumente 1930–35*. Munich, 1963.

Müller, Josef. *Erlaubt die Kirche die eidliche Ableugnung einer wissenschaftliche Tatsache? Eine Verteidigung der katholischen Kirche gegen die Jesuiten und Ehrendomherrn*. Munich, 1896.

————. *Das Leben eines Priesters in unseren Tagen*. Munich, 1902.

————. *Der Reformkatholizismus: Die Religion der Zukunft für die Gebildete aller Bekenntnisse*. Würzburg, 1898.

Müller, Karl Alexander von. *Aus Gärten der Vergangenheit: Erinnerungen 1881–1914*. Stuttgart, 1958.

————. *Im Wandel einer Welt: Erinnerungen 1919–1932*. Stuttgart, 1958.

————. *Mars und Venus: Erinnerungen 1914–1919*. Stuttgart, 1954.

Nabor, Felix. *Schlageter, ein deutsches Heldenschicksal: Roman*. Darmstadt, 1933.

Nettmann, Adolf Leo. *Der korrekte Fuchs: Ein Ratgeber für alle Farbenstudenten*. Köln, 1921.

Neuhäusler, Johannes. *Kreuz und Hakenkreuz: Der Kampf des Nationalsozialismus gegen die katholische Kirche und der kirchliche Widerstand*. Munich, 1946.

Nigg, Walter. *Geschichte des religiösen Liberalismus: Entstehung–Blütezeit–Ausklang*. Zurich, 1937.

Nobel, Alfons. *Der Katholik im neuen Reich*. Augsburg, 1933.

Nötges, Jakob. *Nationalsozialismus und Katholizismus*. Cologne, 1931.

NSDAP, ed. *Partei-Statistik*. Munich, 1935.

Ortschaften-Verzeichnis für den Freistaat Bayern. Munich, 1928.

Pastor, Ludwig von. *Tagebücher, Briefe und Erinnerungen*, ed. W. Wühr. Heidelberg, 1950.

Picker, Henry, and Gerhard Ritter, eds. *Hitlers Tischgespräche im Führerhauptquartier 1941–42*. Bonn, 1951.

Preysing, Konrad. *Dokumente aus dem Kampf der katholischen Kirche im Bistum Berlin gegen den Nationalsozialismus*. Berlin, 1946.

Priesack, August. *Albert Leo Schlageter: Sein Leben und Sterben*. Bamberg, 1935.

Protokoll der Verhandlungen der Fuldaer Bischofskonferenz vom 3. bis 5. August 1931. Fulda, 1931.

Protokoll der Verhandlungen der Fuldaer Bischofskonferenz vom 18. bis 19. August 1932. Fulda, 1932.

Raff, Helene. *Blätter vom Lebensbaum*. Munich, 1938.

Rauschning, Hermann. *Hitler Speaks*. London, 1939.

Rehbein, Arthur. *Für Deutschland in den Tod: Leben und Sterben Albert Leo Schlageters*. Berlin, 1928.

Reich, Albert. *Dietrich Eckart: Ein deutscher Dichter und Vorkämpfer der völkischen Bewegung*. Munich, 1933.

Ringelmann, Richard. *Die Bayerische Volkspartei: Ein Handbuch für die Wählerschaft*. Munich, 1920.

Rohling, August. *Der Talmudjude*. Münster, 1873.

Rosenberg, Alfred. *Dietrich Eckart, ein Vermächtnis*. Munich, 1928.

————. *Der Mythus des 20. Jahrhunderts*. Munich, 1931.

Rosenberg, Alfred, ed. *Wesen, Grundsätze und Ziele der NSDAP*. Munich, 1923.

Rost, Hans. *Christus, nicht Hitler!* Augsburg, 1932.

————. *Erinnerungen aus dem Leben eines beinahe glücklichen Menschen*. Augsburg, 1962.

Roth, Josef. *Katholizismus und Judenfrage*. Munich, 1923.

————[as J. A. Kofler]. *Katholische Kirche und Judentum*. Munich, 1928.

Sack, Anton. *Ein Semester in München*. Munich, 1913.

Schauff, Johannes. *Die deutschen Katholiken und die Zentrumspartei: Eine politisch-statistische Untersuchung der Reichstagswahlen seit 1871*. Cologne, 1928.

Schell, Herman. *Der Katholizismus als Prinzip des Fortschritts*. Würzburg, 1897.

Schlund, Erhard. *Katholizismus und Vaterland*. Munich, 1923.

————. *Neugermanisches Heidentum im heutigen Deutschland*. Munich, 1924.

Schmaus, Michael. *Begegnungen zwischen katholischem Christentum und nationalsozialistischer Weltanschauung*. Münster, 1934.

Schmiedel, Ulrich. *Schlageter: Der Mythos eines deutschen Soldaten*. Berlin, 1933.

Schnitzer, Joseph. "Aus dem Tagebuch eines deutschen Modernisten." In *Aufbruch*, ed. Schwaiger.

Schott, Georg. *Das Volksbuch von Hitler*. Munich, 1924.

Schrönghamer-Heimdal, Franz. *Auferstehung: Ein Wegweiser durch den Weltensturz zur Menschwerdung*. Augsburg, 1919.

————. *Dem deutschen Volke: Deutsche Kriegsworte für deutsche Friedenswerk*. Freiburg, 1917.

————. *Das grosse Glück: Geschichten von allerhand Lebenskünstlern*. Augsburg, 1919.

————. *Helden der Heimat: Kriegserzählungen und Erlebnissen*. Freiburg, 1915.

————. *Judas, der Weltfeind. Was Jeder über die Juden wissen muss*. Munich, 1919.

————. *Kapitalismus: Sein Wesen, seine Wirkung und seine Wandlung*. Augsburg, 1919.

————. *Das kommende Reich: Entwurf einer Weltordnung aus dem deutschen Wesen.* Augsburg, 1918.

————. *Das kommende Reich.* Niederalteich, 1933.

————. *Kriegssaat und Friedensernte: Gesammelte Aufsätze eines Mitkämpfers.* Freiburg, 1915.

————. *Mein Dörfl im Krieg.* Freiburg, 1916.

————. *Vom Antichrist: Ein Büchlein von Gott und Geld, vom deutschen Wesen und vom ewigen Juden.* Augsburg, 1918.

————. *Vom Ende der Zeiten: Das Wissen vom Weltende nach Edda, Wissenschaft und Weissagung.* Augsburg, 1918.

————. *Vom Geist der Liebe.* Augsburg, 1919.

————. *Waldsegen: Geschichten aus der Heimat.* Augsburg, 1918.

————. *Wie's Daheim war: Geschichten aus meinem Jugendlande.* Augsburg, 1919.

Sebottendorff, Rudolf von. *Bevor Hitler kam.* Munich, 1933.

Sengstock, Paul, and Hermann Fassbender. *Albert Leo Schlageter: Seine Verurteilung und Erschiessung durch die Franzosen.* Düsseldorf, 1927.

Senn, Wilhelm Maria. *Halt! Katholizismus und Nationalsozialismus: Meine zweite Rede an den deutschen Katholizismus und—nach Rom.* Munich, 1932.

————. *Katholizismus und Nationalsozialismus.* Münster, 1931.

Sesselmann, Max, and Heinrich Hoffmann. *Deutschlands Erwachen in Wort und Bild.* Munich, 1924.

Sommer, Theo. *Albert Leo Schlageter.* Düsseldorf, 1933.

Spengler, Oswald. *Briefe 1913–1936,* ed. Anton Koktanek. Munich, 1963.

Stark, Johannes. *Nationalsozialismus und katholische Kirche.* Munich, 1931.

Stoeckle, Edmund. *Die Entwicklung der Leibesübungen an den deutschen Universitäten.* Munich, 1926.

Strobel, Ferdinand, ed. *Christliche Bewährung: Dokumente des Widerstandes der katholischen Kirche in Deutschland 1933–1945.* Olten, 1946.

Thuermeister, Robert. *Albert Leo Schlageter: Ein deutscher Held.* Halle, 1936.

Untermeyer, S. *A Call to Arms against Hitler's Destruction of Christianity.* New York, 1935.

Voegelin, Eric. *Die politische Religionen.* Vienna, 1938.

Volk, Ludwig, ed. *Akten Kardinal Michael von Faulhabers 1917–1945.* 2 vols. Mainz, 1975.

Wehner, Josef Magnus. *Albert Leo Schlageter.* Berlin, 1934.

Wenng, L. *Die Judenfrage vor der Bayerischen Kammer der Abgeordneten.* Munich, 1901.

Wentzke, Paul. *Schlageter und der Ruhrkampf.* Lübeck, 1934.

Wichtl, Friedrich. *Weltfreimaurerei, Weltrevolution, Weltpolitik.* Munich, 1919.

Wieser, Sebastian. *Der Antichrist: Trilogie.* Munich, 1911–1912.

Wiest, Hugo. *Albert Leo Schlageter und sein Geschlecht.* Görlitz, 1939.

Wild, Alfons. *Hitler und das Christentum.* Augsburg, 1931.

————. *Nationalsozialismus und Religion: Kann ein Katholik Nationalsozialist sein?* Augsburg, 1931.

Wirth, Albrecht. *Rasse und Volk.* Halle, 1914.

Witetschek, Helmut. *Die kirchliche Lage in Bayern nach den Regierungspräsidentenberichten 1933–1943.* Mainz, 1966.

Zaum, Karl. *Albert Leo Schlageter.* Leipzig, 1934.

Zils, W., ed. *Geistiges und künstlerisches München.* Munich, 1913.

SECONDARY SOURCES

Abbott, John. "Peasants in the Rural Public: The Bavarian *Bauernbund,* 1893–1933." Ph.D. diss., University of Illinois, Chicago, 2000.

Abel, Theodore. *The Nazi Movement: Why Hitler Came to Power.* New York, 1965.

Albertin, Lothar. "Nationalismus und Protestantismus in der österreichischen Los-von-Rom Bewegung." Ph.D. diss., University of Cologne, 1953.

Albrecht, Joachim. *Die Avantgarde des Dritten Reiches: Die Coburger NSDAP während der Weimarer Republik 1922–1933.* Frankfurt, 2005.

Allen, Ann Taylor. *Satire and Society in Wilhelmine Germany: Kladderadatsch and Simplicissimus, 1890–1914.* Lexington, Ky., 1984.

Altgeld, Wolfgang. *Katholizismus, Protestantismus, Judentum: Über religiös begründete Gegensätze und nationalreligiöse Ideen in der Geschichte des deutschen Nationalismus.* Paderborn, 1992.

Amery, Carl. *Die Kapitulation, oder Deutscher Katholizismus heute.* Hamburg, 1964.

Ammerman, Nancy. "Religious Identities and Religious Institutions." In *Handbook,* ed. Dillon.

Anderson, Margaret Lavinia. "Piety and Politics: Recent Work on German Catholicism." *JMH* 63 (1991).

————. *Practicing Democracy: Elections and Political Culture in Imperial Germany.* Princeton, N.J., 2000.

————. *Windthorst: A Political Biography.* Oxford, 1981.

Appiah, Kwame, and Henry Louis Gates. *Identities.* Chicago, 1995.

Arbeitskreis für kirchliche Zeitgeschichte Münster. "Katholiken zwischen Tradition und Moderne: Das katholische Milieu als Forschungsaufgabe." *Westfälische Zeitschrift* 43 (1993).

Auerbach, Hellmuth. "Hitlers politische Lehrjahre und die Münchener Gesellschaft 1919–1923." *VfZ* 24 (1977).

————. "Nationalsozialismus vor Hitler." In *Der Nationalsozialismus: Studien zur Ideologie und Herrschaft,* ed. Wolfgang Benz et al. Frankfurt, 1993.

————. "Regionale Wurzeln und Differenzen der NSDAP.1919–1923." In *Region,* ed. Möller et al.

Baird, Jay. *To Die for Germany: Heroes in the Nazi Pantheon.* Bloomington, Ind., 1990.

Baranowski, Shelley. *The Sanctity of Rural Life: Nobility, Protestantism, and Nazism in Weimar Prussia*. Oxford, 1995.

Bärsch, Claus-Ekkehard. *Die politische Religion des Nationalsozialismus*. Munich, 1998.

Bartetzko, Dieter. *Illusionen in Stein: Stimmungsarchitektur im deutschen Faschismus*. Reinbek, 1985.

Bartov, Omer. "Defining Enemies, Making Victims: Germans, Jews, and the Holocaust." *AHR* 103 (1998).

Bauer, Richard, ed. *München, "Hauptstadt der Bewegung": Bayerns Metropole und der Nationalsozialismus*. Munich, 1992.

Baumeister, Martin. *Parität und katholische Inferiorität: Untersuchungen zur Stellung des Katholizismus im deutschen Kaiserreich*. Paderborn, 1987.

Baumgärtner, Raimund. *Weltanschauungskampf im Dritten Reich: Die Auseinandersetzung der Kirchen mit Alfred Rosenberg*. Mainz, 1977.

Becker, Winfried. "Carl Borromäus Johann Baptist Muth." *BBKL* 6 (1993).

———. "Die Organisation der NS-Volksgemeinschaft in Passau." In *Passau*, ed. Becker.

Becker, Winfried, ed. *Passau in der Zeit des Nationalsozialismus*. Passau, 1999.

Beeck, Franz Josef van. *Catholic Identity after Vatican II*. Chicago, 1985.

Behrend, Hanna. *Die Beziehungen zwischen der NSDAP-Zentrale und dem Gauverband Süd- Hannover-Braunschweig 1921–1933*. Frankfurt, 1980.

Benz, Wolfgang. *Geschichte des Dritten Reiches*. Munich, 2000.

Bergen, Doris. "Die 'Deutschen Christen' 1933–1945: Ganz normale Gläubige und eifrige Komplizen?" *GG* 29 (2003).

———. "Nazism and Christianity: Partners or Rivals?" *JCH* 42 (2007).

———. *Twisted Cross: The German Christian Movement in the Third Reich*. Chapel Hill, N.C., 1996.

Berning, V. "Geistig-kulturelle Neubesinnung im deutschen Katholizismus vor und nach dem Ersten Weltkrieg." In *Religiös-kulturelle Bewegungen im deutschen Katholizismus seit 1800*, ed. Anton Rauscher. Paderborn, 1986.

Beyer, Hans. *Von der Novemberrevolution zur Räterepublik in München*. Berlin, 1957.

Binion, Rudolf. *Hitler among the Germans*. New York, 1976.

Binkowski, J. *Jugend als Wegbereiter: Der Quickborn von 1909 bis 1945*. Stuttgart, 1981.

Bischof, Franz Xaver. *Theologie und Geschichte: Ignaz von Döllinger (1799–1890) in der zweiten Hälfte seines Lebens*. Stuttgart, 1996.

Bjork, James. "Neither German nor Pole: Catholicism and National Ambivalence in Upper Silesia, 1980–1914." Ph.D. diss., University of Chicago, 1999.

Blackbourn, David. *Class, Religion, and Local Politics in Wilhelmine Germany: The Centre Party in Württemberg before 1914*. New Haven, Conn., 1980.

———. *Marpingen: Apparitions of the Virgin Mary in a Nineteenth-Century German Village*. New York, 1993.

Blaschke, Olaf. *Katholizismus und Antisemitismus im Deutschen Kaiserreich.* Göttingen, 1997.

Blaschke, Olaf, and Frank-Michael Kuhlemann. "Religion in Geschichte und Gegenwart." In *Religion*, ed. Blaschke and Kuhlemann.

Blaschke, Olaf, and Frank-Michael Kuhlemann, eds. *Religion im Kaiserreich: Milieus, Mentalitäten, Krisen.* Gütersloh, 1996.

Bleistein, Roman. "Abt Alban Schachleiter, OSB: Zwischen Kirchentreue und Hitlerkult." *HJ* 115 (1995).

―――. "Überläufer im Sold der Kirchenfeinde: Josef Roth und Albert Hartl, Priesterkarrieren im Dritten Reich." *BAK* 42 (1996).

Blessing, Werner K. "Kirchenglocken für Eisner? Zum Weltanschauungskampf in der Revolution von 1918/19 in Bayern." *Jahrbuch für fränkische Landesforschung* 53 (1992).

―――. *Staat und Kirche in der Gesellschaft: Institutionelle Autorität und mentaler Wandel in Bayern während des 19. Jahrhunderts.* Göttingen, 1982.

Bleuel, Hans-Peter, and Ernst Klinnert. *Deutsche Studenten auf dem Weg ins Dritte Reich: Ideologien, Programme, Aktionen 1918–1935.* Gütersloh, 1967.

Böckenförde, Ernst-Wolfgang. "Der deutsche Katholizismus im Janre 1933." *Hochland* 53 (1961).

Bohnke, Wilfried. *Die NSDAP im Ruhrgebiet 1920–1933.* Bonn, 1974.

Bönisch, Michael. "Die Hammer Bewegung." In *Handbuch*, ed. Puschner et al.

Bosl, Karl, ed. *Bayern im Umbruch. Die Revolution von 1918: Ihre Voraussetzungen, ihr Verlauf und ihre Folgen.* Munich, 1968.

Bosworth, R. J. B. *Mussolini's Italy: Life under the Dictatorship, 1915–1945.* New York, 2006.

Bottlenberg-Landsberg, Maria von. *Karl Ludwig Freiherr von und zu Guttenberg (1902–1945): Ein Lebensbild.* Berlin, 2003.

Boyer, John W. *Culture and Political Crisis in Vienna: Christian Socialism in Power, 1897–1918.* Chicago, 1995.

―――. *Political Radicalism in Late Imperial Vienna: The Origins of the Christian Social Movement, 1848–1897.* Chicago, 1981.

―――. "Religion and Political Development in Central Europe around 1900: The View from Vienna." *Austrian History Yearbook* 25 (1994).

Bracher, Karl-Dietrich. *Die deutsche Diktatur: Entstehung, Struktur, Folgen des Nationalsozialismus.* Cologne, 1969.

Brandmüller, Walter, ed. *Handbuch der Bayerischen Kirchengeschichte.* St. Ottilien, 1991.

―――. *Ignaz von Döllinger am Vorabend des 1. Vatikanums: Herausforderung und Antwort.* St. Ottilien, 1977.

Bräuninger, Werner. *Hitlers Kontrahenten in der NSDAP.1921–1945.* Munich, 2004.

Bredohl, Thomas. *Class and Religious Identity: The Rhenish Center Party in Wilhelmine Germany.* Milwaukee, Wis., 2000.

Breuer, Thomas. *Verordneter Wandel? Der Widerstreit zwischen nationalso-zialistischem Herrschaftsanspruch und traditionaler Lebenswelt im Erzbistum Bamberg*. Mainz, 1992.

Breuning, Klaus. *Die Vision des Reiches: Deutscher Katholizismus zwischen Demokratie und Diktatur 1929–1934*. Munich, 1969.

Brown-Fleming, Suzanne. *The Holocaust and Catholic Conscience: Cardinal Aloisius Muench and the Guilt Question in Germany*. Notre Dame, Ind., 2006.

Brustein, William. *The Logic of Evil: Social Origins of the Nazi Party*. New Haven, Conn., 1996.

———. *The Roots of Hate: Antisemitism in Europe before the Holocaust*. Cambridge, 2003.

Buchheim, Karl. *Ultramontanismus und Demokratie: Der Weg der deutschen Katholiken im 19. Jahrhundert*. Munich, 1963.

Bullock, Alan. *Hitler: A Study in Tyranny*. New York, 1952.

Burkard, Dominik. *Häresie und Mythus des 20. Jahrhunderts: Rosenbergs nationalsozialistische Weltanschauung vor der Tribunal der Römischen Inquisition*. Paderborn, 2005.

Burkard, Dominik, and Wolfgang Weiss. *Katholische Theologie im Natio-nalsozialismus*. Würzburg, 2007.

Burke, Peter, et al., eds. *Advances in Identity Theory and Research*. New York, 2003.

Burleigh, Michael. *Sacred Causes: The Clash of Religion and Politics from the Great War to the War on Terror*. New York, 2007.

———. *The Third Reich: A New History*. New York, 2000.

Burnham, Walter Dean. "Political Immunization and Political Confession-alism: The United States and Weimar Germany." *Journal of Interdisci-plinary History* 3 (1972).

Burrin, Philippe. "Political Religion: The Relevance of a Concept." *History & Memory* 9 (1997).

Busch, Norbert. *Katholische Frömmigkeit und Moderne: Die Sozial- und Mentalitätsgeschichte des Herz-Jesu-Kultes in Deutschland*. Gütersloh, 1997.

Butler, Rohan. *The Roots of National Socialism, 1789–1933*. London, 1941.

Byrne, Richard. "Pope Benedict Thanks Educators and Addresses Aca-demic Freedom in Talk at Catholic U." *Chronicle of Higher Education* (18 Apr 2008).

Carrier, Richard. "Hitler's Table Talk: Troubling Finds." *GSR* 26 (2003).

Carroll, James. *Constantine's Sword: The Church and the Jews*. New York, 2001.

Chatellier, Hildegard. "Friedrich Lienhard." In *Handbuch*, ed. Puschner et al.

Chickering, Roger. *Imperial Germany and the Great War*. Cambridge, 1998.

———. *We Men Who Feel Most German: A Cultural Study of the Pan-German League*. Boston, 1984.

Clemens, Gabriele. *Martin Spahn und der Rechtskatholizismus in der Weimarer Republik*. Mainz, 1983.

Conway, John. *The Nazi Persecution of the Churches, 1933–1945*. London, 1968.

Cornwell, John. *Hitler's Pope: The Secret History of Pius XII*. New York, 1999.

Cremer, Douglas. "To Avoid a New Kulturkampf: The Catholic Workers' Associations and National Socialism in Weimar-Era Bavaria." *Journal of Church and State* 41 (1999).

Daim, Wilfried. *Der Mann, der Hitler die Ideen gab: Jörg Lanz von Liebenfels*. Vienna, 1954.

Dalin, David. *The Myth of Hitler's Pope*. Washington, D.C., 2005.

Damberg, Wilhelm. *Abschied vom Milieu? Katholizismus im Bistum Münster und in den Niederländen 1945–1980*. Paderborn, 1997.

Denk, Hans Dieter. *Die christliche Arbeiterbewegung in Bayern bis zum Ersten Weltkrieg*. Mainz, 1980.

Denzler, Georg. "Ein Gebetssturm für den Führer: Münchens Katholizismus und der Nationalsozialismus." In *Irrlicht*, ed. Prinz and Mensing.

———. *Widerstand ist nicht das richtige Wort: Katholische Priester, Bischöfe und Theologen im Dritten Reich*. Zurich, 2003.

———. *Widerstand oder Anpassung: Katholische Kirche und Drittes Reich*. Munich, 1984.

Denzler, Georg, and Volker Fabricius. *Die Kirchen im Dritten Reich: Christen und Nazis Hand in Hand?* Frankfurt, 1984.

Deuerlein, Ernst. "Hitlers Eintritt in die Politik und die Reichswehr." *VfZ* 7 (1959).

Dierker, Wolfgang. *Himmlers Glaubenskrieger: Der Sicherheitsdienst der SS und seine Religionspolitik*. Paderborn, 2002.

Dietrich, Donald. *Catholic Citizens in the Third Reich*. New Brunswick, N.J., 1988.

———. "Catholic Eugenics in Germany, 1920–1945: Hermann Muckermann SJ and Josef Mayer." *Journal of Church and State* 34 (1992).

Dillon, Michelle. *Catholic Identity: Balancing Reason, Faith, and Power*. Cambridge, 1999.

Dillon, Michelle, ed. *Handbook of the Sociology of Religion*. Cambridge, 2003.

Dölken, T. A., ed. *140 Jahre Cartellverband*. Munich, 1997.

Donohue, James. *Hitler's Conservative Opponents in Bavaria, 1930–1945*. Leiden, 1961.

Doosry, Yasmin. "Die Sakrale Dimension des Reichsparteigeländes in Nürnberg." In *Politische Religion*, ed. Ferber.

Douglas, Donald M. "The Parent Cell: Some Computer Notes on the Composition of the First Nazi Party Group in Munich, 1919–21." *CEH* 10 (1977).

Dowe, Christopher. *Auch Bildungsbürger: Katholische Studierende und Akademiker im Kaiserreich*. Göttingen, 2006.

Dülmen, Richard van. "Der deutsche Katholizismus und der Erste Weltkrieg." *Francia: Forschungen zur westeuropäischen Geschichte* 2 (1974).

Duncan-Jones, A.S. *The Struggle for Religious Freedom in Germany*. London, 1938.

Eder, Manfred. "Hitler und die Bibel: Anmerkungen zu einem merkwürdigen Verhältnis." In *Das Buch, ohne das man nichts versteht: Die kulturelle Kraft der Bibel*, ed. G. Steins and F. G. Untergassmair. Münster, 2005.

Eley, Geoff. *Reshaping the German Right: Radical Nationalism and Political Change after Bismarck*. New Haven, Conn., 1980.

Eley, Geoff, and David Blackbourn. *The Peculiarities of German History: Bourgeois Society and Politics in Nineteenth-Century Germany*. Oxford, 1984.

Elste, Alfred, et al., eds. *Auf dem Weg zur Macht: Beiträge zur Geschichte der NSDAP in Kärnten von 1918 bis 1933*. Vienna, 1997.

Emberley, Peter, and Barry Cooper, eds. *Faith and Political Philosophy: The Correspondence between Leo Strauss and Eric Voegelin*. University Park, Pa., 1993.

Engelhard, Gildis. *Abt Schachleiter: Der deutsche Kämpfer*. Munich, 1941.

Engelhardt, Roland. *"Wir schlugen unter Kämpfen und Opfern dem Neuen Bresche": Philipp Funk (1884–1937) Leben und Werk*. Frankfurt, 1997.

Engelman, Ralph. "Dietrich Eckart and the Genesis of Nazism." Ph.D. diss., Washington University, 1971.

Epstein, Klaus. "Erzberger's Position in the Zentrumsstreit before World War I." *CHR* 44 (1958).

———. *Matthias Erzberger and the Dilemma of German Democracy*. Princeton, N.J., 1959.

Evans, Ellen Lovell. *The German Center Party, 1870–1933*. Carbondale, Ill., 1981.

Evans, Richard J. *The Coming of the Third Reich*. New York, 2003.

———. "Nazism, Christianity and Political Religion: A Debate." *JCH* 42 (2007).

Evans, Richard J., ed. *Society and Politics in Wilhelmine Germany*. London, 1978.

Faber, Richard. *Lateinischer Faschismus*. Berlin, 2001.

———. "Politscher Katholizismus: Die Bewegung von Maria Laach." In *Religions- und Geistesgeschichte der Weimarer Republik*, ed. Hubert Cancik. Düsseldorf, 1982.

Falter, Jürgen. *Hitlers Wähler*. Munich, 1991.

———. "The National Socialist Mobilization of New Voters." In *The Formation of the Nazi Constituency, 1919–1933*, ed. Thomas Childers. London, 1986.

Farr, Ian. "From Anti-Catholicism to Anti-Clericalism: Catholic Politics and the Peasantry in Bavaria, 1860–1900." *European Studies Review* 13 (1983).

———. "Peasant Protest in the Empire: The Bavarian Example." In *Peasants and Lords in Modern Germany: Recent Studies in Agricultural History*, ed. Robert Moeller. Boston, 1986.

————. "Populism in the Countryside: The Peasant Leagues in Bavaria in the 1890s." In *Society*, ed. Evans.

Fellner, Michael. "Pater Erhard Schlund OFM (1888–1953) und seine Auseinandersetzung mit der völkischen Bewegung und dem National-sozialismus." *BAK* 43 (1998).

Fenske, H. *Konservatismus und Rechtsradikalismus in Bayern nach 1918.* Bad Homburg, 1968.

Ferber, Richard, ed. *Politische Religion, religiöse Politik.* Würzburg, 1997.

Fest, Joachim. *Hitler: Eine Biographie.* Frankfurt, 1973.

Field, Geoffrey. *Evangelist of Race: The Germanic Vision of Houston Stewart Chamberlain.* New York, 1981.

Finsterhölzl, Johann. *Ignaz von Döllinger.* Graz, 1969.

Fischer, Conan. *The Rise of the Nazis.* Manchester, England, 1995.

Forstner, Thomas. "Katholizismus contra Antijudaismus: Dr. Franz Rödel (1891–1969), ein Priesterleben im Dienst der christlich-jüdischen Verständigung." *HJ* 125 (2005).

Franke, Volker. *Der Aufstieg der NSDAP in Düsseldorf.* Essen, 1987.

Franz, Michael. *Eric Voegelin and the Politics of Spiritual Revolt.* Baton Rouge, La., 1992.

Franz-Willing, Georg. *Die Hitlerbewegung: Der Ursprung 1919–1922.* Hamburg, 1962.

————. *Krisenjahr der Hitlerbewegung 1923.* Preussisch-Ohlendorf, 1975.

————. "Munich: Birthplace and Center of the NSDAP." *JMH* 29 (1957).

————. *Putsch and Verbotszeit der Hitlerbewegung.* Preussisch-Ohlendorf, 1977.

Frauenleben in München: Lesebuch zur Geschichte des Münchener Alltags. Munich, 1992.

Frevert, Ute, ed. *Bürgerinnen und Bürger: Geschlechterverhältnisse im 19. Jahrhundert.* Göttingen, 1988.

Fritzsche, Peter. *Germans into Nazis.* Cambridge, Mass., 1998.

Fröhlich, Elke. "Politische und soziale Macht auf dem Lande: Die Durchsetzung der NSDAP im Kreis Memmingen." *VfZ* 25 (1977).

Füllenbach, Elias. "Leonhard Roth." *BBKL* 17 (2000).

————. "Shock, Renewal, Crisis: Catholic Reflections on the Shoah." In *Antisemitism*, ed. Spicer.

Ganyard, Clifton. *Arthur Mahraun and the Young German Order: An Alternative to National Socialism in Weimar Political Culture.* Lewiston, Maine, 2008.

Garnett, Robert. *Lion, Eagle, and Swastika: Bavarian Monarchism in Weimar Germany, 1918-1933.* New York, 1991.

Gasman, Daniel. *The Scientific Origins of National Socialism: Social Darwinism in Ernst Haeckel and the German Monist League.* London, 1971.

Gassert, Phillip, and Daniel Mattern, eds. *The Hitler Library: A Bibliography.* Westport, Conn., 2001.

Gay, Peter. *Weimar Culture: The Outsider as Insider.* New York, 1968.

Gentile, Emilio. *Politics as Religion.* Princeton, N.J., 2001.

Genuneit, Jürgen. "Methodische Probleme der quantitativen Analyse früher NSDAP-Mitglieder." In *Die Nationalsozialisten: Analyse faschistischer Bewegungen*, ed. Reinhard Mann. Stuttgart, 1980.

Geyer, Martin. *Verkehrte Welt: Revolution, Inflation und Moderne. München 1914–1924*. Göttingen, 1998.

Geyer, Michael. "Insurrectionary Warfare: The German Debate about a Levee en Masse in October 1918." *JMH* 73 (2001).

Geyer, Michael, and Konrad Jarausch. *Shattered Past: Reconstructing German Histories*. Princeton, N.J., 2003.

Gilbhard, H. *Thule-Gesellschaft: Vom okkulten Mummenschanz zum Hakenkreuz*. Munich, 1994.

Giles, Geoffrey. *Students and National Socialism in Germany*. Princeton, N.J., 1985.

Glaser, Hermann. *The Cultural Roots of National Socialism*. London, 1978.

Godman, Peter. *Hitler and the Vatican*. New York, 2004.

Goldhagen, Daniel. *A Moral Reckoning: The Role of the Catholic Church in the Holocaust and Its Unfulfilled Duty of Repair*. New York, 2002.

Goodrick-Clarke, Nicholas. *Black Sun: Aryan Cults, Esoteric Nazism, and the Politics of Identity*. New York, 2002.

———. *The Occult Roots of Nazism: Secret Aryan Cults and Their Influence on Nazi Ideology*. Wellingborough, England, 1985.

Gordon, Harold. *Hitler and the Beerhall Putsch*. Princeton, N.J., 1972.

Göttler, Norbert. *Die Akte Pater Leonhard Roth*. Dachau, 2004.

Gottwald, Herbert. "Antiultramontaner Reichsverband 1906–1920." In *Die bürgerlichen Parteien in Deutschland*, ed. Dieter Fricke. Vol. 1. Berlin, 1968.

Götz von Olenhusen, Irmtraud. "Die Feminisierung von Religion und Kirche im 19. und 20. Jahrhundert," in *Frauen*, ed. Olenhusen.

Götz von Olenhusen, Irmtraud, ed. *Frauen unter dem Patriarchat der Kirchen: Katholikinnen und Protestantinnen im 19. und 20. Jahrhundert*. Stuttgart, 1995.

———. *Klerus und abweichendes Verhalten: Zur Sozialgeschichte katholischer Priester im 19. Jahrhundert. Die Erzdiözese Freiburg*. Göttingen, 1994.

Graf, Friedrich Wilhelm. *Die Wiederkehr der Götter: Religion in der modernen Kultur*. Munich, 2004.

Grau, Bernhard. *Kurt Eisner 1867–1919: Eine Biographie*. Munich, 2001.

Greiner, George. "Herman Schell and the Reform of the Catholic Church in Germany." *Theological Studies* 54 (1993).

Greive, Hermann. *Theologie und Ideologie: Katholizismus und Judentum in Deutschland und Österreich 1918–1935*. Heidelberg, 1969.

Griech-Polelle, Beth. *Bishop von Galen: German Catholicism and National Socialism*. New Haven, Conn., 2002.

Grieswelle, Detlef. *Propaganda der Friedlosigkeit: Eine Studie zu Hitlers Rhetorik 1920–1933*. Stuttgart, 1972.

Grill, Johnpeter Horst. *The Nazi Movement in Baden, 1920–1945*. Chapel Hill, N.C., 1983.

Gritschneder, Otto. *Bewährungsfrist für den Terroristen Adolf H.: Der Hitler-Putsch und die bayerische Justiz*. Munich, 1990.

Gross, A. *Gehorsame Kirche, ungehorsame Christen im Nationalsozialismus*. Mainz, 2000.

Gross, Michael. *The War against Catholicism: Liberalism and the Anti-Catholic Imagination in Nineteenth-Century Germany*. Ann Arbor, Mich., 2004.

Grunberger, Richard. *Red Rising in Bavaria*. London, 1973.

Gründer, Horst. "Nation und Katholizismus im Kaiserreich." In *Katholizismus, nationaler Gedanke und Europa seit 1800*, ed. Albrecht Langner. Paderborn, 1985.

———. "Rechtskatholizismus im Kaiserreich und in der Weimarer Republik mit besonderer Berücksichtigung der Rheinlande und Westfalens." *Westfälische Zeitschrift* 134 (1984).

Grüttner, Michael. *Studenten im Dritten Reich*. Paderborn, 1995.

Grypa, Dietmar. *Kampfzeit und Machtergreifung der NSDAP in Burghausen*. Burghausen, 2000.

Gurian, Waldemar. *Hitler and the Christians*. London, 1936.

Haag, John. "Students at the University of Vienna in the First World War." *CEH* 17 (1984).

Habermas, Rebekka. "Weibliche Religiosität: oder, Von der Fragilität bürgerliche Identitäten." In *Wege zur Geschichte des Bürgertums*, ed. Klaus Tenfelde and Hans-Ulrich Wehler. Göttingen, 1994.

Hagen, August. *Der Reformkatholizismus in der Diözese Rottenburg 1902–1920*. Stuttgart, 1962.

Hagenlücke, Heinz. *Die Deutsche Vaterlandspartei: Die nationale Rechte am Ende des Kaiserreichs*. Düsseldorf, 1997.

Hamann, Brigitte. *Hitler's Vienna: A Dictator's Apprenticeship*. Oxford, 1999.

Hambrecht, Rainer. *Der Aufstieg der NSDAP in Mittel- und Oberfranken 1925–1933*. Nuremberg, 1976.

Hammond, Phillip. "Religion and the Persistence of Identity." *Journal for the Scientific Study of Religion* 27 (1988).

Hanebrink, Paul. *In Defense of Christian Hungary: Religion, Nationalism, and Antisemitism, 1890–1944*. Ithaca, N.Y., 2006.

Hardtwig, Wolfgang. "Political Religion in Modern Germany." *Bulletin of the German Historical Institute* 28 (2001).

Hartmannsgruber, Friedrich. *Die Bayerische Patriotenpartei 1868–1887*. Munich, 1986.

Hasenfuss, Josef. *Herman Schell als Wegbereiter zum II. Vatikanischen Konzil*. Munich, 1978.

Hastings, Derek. "Fears of a Feminized Church: Catholicism, Clerical Celibacy, and the Crisis of Masculinity in Wilhelmine Germany." *EHQ* 38 (2008).

———. "How 'Catholic' Was the Early Nazi Movement? Religion, Race, and Culture in Munich, 1919–1924." *CEH* 36 (2003).

Hatheway, Jay. "The Pre-1920 Origins of the NSDAP." *JCH* 29 (1994).

Hausberger, Karl. *Herman Schell (1850–1906): Ein Theologenschicksal im Bannkreis der Modernismuskontroverse.* Regensburg, 1999.

Hausfelder, Edmund. "Die Situation der katholischen Kirche in Ingolstadt von 1918 bis 1945." In *Ingolstadt im Nationalsozialismus,* ed. Stadtarchiv Ingolstadt. Ingolstadt, 1995.

Haustein, Jörg. *Liberal-katholische Publizistik im späten Kaiserreich: "Das Neue Jahrhundert" und die Krausgesellschaft.* Göttingen, 2001.

Healy, Roisin. *The Jesuit Specter in Imperial Germany.* Boston, 2003.

Heberle, Rudolf. *Landbevölkerung und Nationalsozialismus.* Stuttgart, 1963.

Heer, F. *Der Glaube des Adolf Hitler: Anatomie einer politischen Religiosität.* Munich, 1968.

———. *Gottes erste Liebe. 2000 Jahre Judentum und Christentum.* Munich, 1967.

Hehl, Ulrich von. *Priester unter Hitlers Terror: Eine biographische und statistische Erhebung.* Mainz, 1984.

Heiber, Helmut. *Adolf Hitler: Eine Biographie.* Berlin, 1960.

Heiden, Konrad. *Der Fuehrer: Hitler's Rise to Power.* Boston, 1944.

Heilbronner, Oded. "The Achilles' Heel of German Catholicism: 'Who Voted for Hitler?' Revisited." *EHQ* 27 (1997).

———. "Catholic Plight in a Rural Area of Germany and the Rise of Hitler." *Social History* 20 (1995).

———. *Catholicism, Political Culture, and the Countryside: A Social History of the Nazi Party in South Germany.* Ann Arbor, Mich., 1998.

———. "The Failure That Succeeded: Nazi Party Activity in a Catholic Region in Germany, 1929–1932." *JCH* 27 (1992).

———. *"Freiheit, Gleichheit, Brüderlichkeit und Dynamit": Populäre Kultur, populärer Liberalismus und Bürgertum im ländlichen Süddeutschland.* Munich, 2007.

Heinacher, Peter. *Der Aufstieg der NSDAP im Stadt- und Landkreis Flensburg 1919–1933.* Flensburg, 1986.

Heinen, Ernst. "Nationale Integration und innere Konflikte des politischen Katholizismus." In *Staatliche Macht und Katholizismus in Deutschland,* ed. E. Heinen. Paderborn, 1979.

Helmreich, Ernst. *The German Churches under Hitler.* Detroit, Mich., 1979.

Hennig, Diethard. *Johannes Hoffmann: Sozialdemokrat und bayerischer Ministerpräsident.* Munich, 1990.

Heschel, Susannah. *The Aryan Jesus: Christian Theologians and the Bible in Nazi Germany.* Princeton, N.J., 2008.

Hesemann, M. *Hitlers Religion: Die fatale Heilslehre des Nationalsozialismus.* Munich, 2004.

Hettler, F. H. *Josef Müller ("Ochsensepp"): Mann des Widerstandes und erster CSU-Vorsitzender.* Munich, 1991.

Hexham, Irving. "A Close Reading of Richard Steigmann-Gall's *Holy Reich.*" *JCH* 42 (2007).

Hillesheim, Elisabeth. *Die Erschaffung eines Märtyrers: Das Bild Albert Leo Schlageters in der deutschen Literatur von 1923 bis 1945.* Frankfurt, 1994.

Hillmayr, Heinrich. "München und die Revolution von 1918/19." in *Umbruch*, ed. Bosl.

———. *Roter und weisser Terror in Bayern nach 1918*. Munich, 1974.

Hochberger, Anton. *Der Bayerische Bauernbund 1893–1914*. Munich, 1991.

Hochhuth, Rolf. *Der Stellvertreter*. Reinbek, 1963.

Hoffmann, Konrad. *Schlaglichter: Belege und Bilder aus dem Kampfe gegen die Kirche*. Freiburg, 1947.

Holzhaider, Hans. "Schwester Pia." *Dachauer Hefte* 10 (1994).

———. "Von allen Teufeln gehetzt: Nazi-Ikone Blutschwester Pia." *SZ* (9 Nov 2007).

Hoover, Arlie. *The Gospel of Nationalism: German Patriotic Preaching from Napoleon to Versailles*. Wiesbaden, 1986.

Horn, Wolfgang. *Führerideologie und Parteiorganisation in der NSDAP*. Düsseldorf, 1972.

Hoser, Paul. "Hitler und die katholische Kirche: Zwei Briefe aus dem Jahr 1927." *VfZ* 42 (1994).

Hüffer, Anton. *Karl Muth als Literaturhistoriker*. Münster, 1959.

Hürten, Heinz. *Deutsche Katholiken 1918–1945*. Paderborn, 1992.

Jablonsky, D. *The Nazi Party in Dissolution: Hitler and the Verbotszeit, 1923–25*. London, 1989.

Jarausch, Konrad. *Students, Society, and Politics in Imperial Germany: The Rise of Academic Illiberalism*. Princeton, N.J., 1982.

Joachimsthaler, Anton. *Hitlers Weg begann in München 1913–1923*. Munich, 2000.

Jochmann, Werner. *Nationalsozialismus und Revolution: Ursprung und Geschichte der NSDAP in Hamburg 1922–1933*. Frankfurt, 1963.

Jones, Larry Eugene. "Catholics on the Right: The Reich Catholic Committee of the German National People's Party, 1920–1933." *HJ* 126 (2006).

———. "The Dying Middle: Weimar Germany and the Fragmentation of Bourgeois Politics." *CEH* 5 (1972).

———. *German Liberalism and the Dissolution of the Weimar Party System, 1918–1933*. Chapel Hill, 1988.

Jones, Nigel. *A Brief History of the Birth of the Nazis: How the Freikorps Blazed a Trail for Hitler*. New York, 1987.

Kane, Paula. *Separatism and Subculture: Boston Catholicism, 1900–1920*. Chapel Hill, N.C., 1994.

Kapfinger, Hans. *Der Eoskreis 1828–1832: Ein Beitrag zur Vorgeschichte des politischen Katholizismus in Deutschland*. Munich, 1928.

Karow, Yvonne. *Deutsches Opfer: Kultische Selbstauslöschung auf den Reichsparteitagen der NSDAP*. Berlin, 1997.

Kater, Michael. *Hitler Youth*. Cambridge, Mass., 2004.

———. *The Nazi Party: A Social Profile of Members and Leaders*. Oxford, 1983.

———. *Studentenschaft und Rechtsradikalismus in Deutschland 1918–1933*. Hamburg, 1975.

———. "Zur Soziographie der frühen NSDAP." *VfZ* 19 (1971).

Katz, Jacob. *From Prejudice to Destruction: Anti-Semitism, 1700–1933.* Cambridge, 1980.

Kellogg, Michael. *The Russian Roots of Nazism: White Emigres and the Making of National Socialism.* Cambridge, 2005.

Kern, Erich. *Adolf Hitler und seine Bewegung.* Göttingen, 1970.

Kershaw, Ian. *Hitler: Hubris, 1889–1936.* New York, 1998.

———. *The Hitler Myth: Image and Reality in the Third Reich.* Oxford, 1987.

Kirmayer, Sieglinde. "Der Miesbacher Anzeiger, Heimat- und Kampfblatt 1847–1950." Ph.D. diss., Munich, 1957.

Kissler, Alexander. *Der deutsche Papst: Benedikt XVI. und seine schwierige Heimat.* Freiburg, 2005.

Klein, Gotthard. *Der Volksverein für das katholische Deutschland 1980–1933.* Paderborn, 1996.

Klöcker, Michael. "Das katholische Milieu: Grundüberlegungen, in besonderer Hinsicht auf das deutsche Kaiserreich." *Zeitschrift für Religions- und Geistesgeschichte* 44 (1992).

Knopp, Guido. *Hitler: Eine Bilanz.* Berlin, 1995.

Knopp, Guido, ed. *Hitler heute: Gespräche über ein deutsches Trauma.* Aschaffenburg, 1979.

Knox, MacGregor. *To the Threshold of Power, 1922/33: Origins and Dynamics of the Fascist and National Socialist Dictatorships.* Cambridge, 2007.

Kohn, Hans. *The Intellectual Roots of National Socialism.* Cambridge, Mass., 1938.

Körling, Martha. "Die literarische Arbeit der Zeitschrift *Hochland* von 1903 bis 1933." Ph.D. diss., Free University of Berlin, 1959.

Kornberg, Jacques. "Ignaz von Döllinger's *Die Juden in Europa:* A Catholic Polemic against Antisemitism." *Zeitschrift für Neuere Theologiegeschichte* 6 (1999).

Koshar, Rudy. *Social Life, Local Politics, and Nazism: Marburg, 1880–1935.* Chapel Hill, N.C., 1986.

Kotowsky, Elke-Vera, and Julius Schoeps, eds. *Der Sexualreformer Magnus Hirschfeld: Ein Leben im Spannungsfeld von Wissenschaft, Politik und Gesellschaft.* Berlin, 2004.

Kotulla, Andreas. *Nach Lourdes! Der französische Marienwallfahrtsort und die Katholiken im Deutschen Kaiserreich.* Munich, 2006.

Kraft, William. *Christ versus Hitler.* New York, 1937.

Krause, T. *Hamburg wird braun: Der Aufstieg der NSDAP von 1921 bis 1933.* Hamburg, 1987.

Krenn, Dorit-Maria. *Die christliche Arbeiterbewegung in Bayern vom Ersten Weltkrieg bis 1933.* Mainz, 1991.

Kreutzer, Heike. *Das Reichskirchenministerium im Gefüge der nationalsozialistischen Herrschaft.* Düsseldorf, 2000.

Krieg, Robert A. *Catholic Theologians in Nazi Germany.* New York, 2004.

———. "German Catholic Views of Jesus and Judaism." In *Antisemitism,* ed. Spicer.

Kuehn, Heinz. *Blutzeugen des Bistums Berlin.* Berlin, 1952.

Kuessner, Dietrich. *Landesbischof Dr. Melmuth Johnsen: Nationaler Luther-aner und Bischof der Mitte in Braunschweig.* Büddenstedt, 1982.

Lachner, Raimund. "Joseph Schnitzer." *BBKL* 9 (1995).

Lane, Barbara Miller. *Architecture and Politics in Germany, 1918–1945.* Cambridge, 1968.

Läpple, Alfred. *Adolf Hitler: Psychogramm einer katholischen Kindheit.* Stein am Rhein, 2001.

Large, David Clay. *The Politics of Law and Order: A History of the Bavarian Einwohnerwehr, 1918–1921.* Philadelphia, 1980.

————. *Where Ghosts Walked: Munich's Road to the Third Reich.* New York, 1997.

Laube, Stefan. *Fest, Religion und Erinnerung: Konfessionelles Gedächtnis in Bayern von 1804–1817.* Munich, 1999.

Laube, Volker. *Fremdarbeiter in kirchlichen Einrichtungen im Erzbistum München und Freising 1939–1945.* Regensburg, 2005.

Layton, Roland. "The *Völkischer Beobachter,* 1920–1933: The Nazi Party Newspaper in the Weimar Era." *CEH* 3 (1970).

Leitzbach, Christian. *Matthias Erzberger: Ein kritischer Beobachter des wil-helminischen Reiches 1895–1918.* Frankfurt, 1998.

Lepier, H. S. *The Church-State Struggle in Germany.* New York, 1933.

Lepsius, M. Rainer. "Parteiensystem und Sozialstruktur: Zum Problem der Demokratisierung der deutschen Gesellschaft." In *Wirtschaft, Geschichte und Wirtschaftsgeschichte,* ed. Wilhelm Abel. Stuttgart, 1966.

Levy, Richard. *The Downfall of the Antisemitic Parties in Imperial Germany.* New Haven, Conn., 1975.

Lewy, Guenter. *The Catholic Church and Nazi Germany.* New York, 1964.

Liebmann, Maximilian. "Ottokar Kernstock, der missbrauchte Dichter." *Zeitschrift des Historischen Vereins für Steiermark* 85 (1994).

Lohalm, Uwe. *Völkischer Radikalismus: Die Geschichte des Deutsch-völkischen Schutz- und Trutzbundes 1918–1923.* Hamburg, 1970.

Löhr, Wolfgang. *Rückbesinnung und Ausblick: KV-Studententum nach 150 Jahren.* Cologne, 2006.

Lönne, Karl-Egon. "Katholizismusforschung." *Geschichte und Gesellschaft* 26 (2000).

Loome, Thomas M. *Liberal Catholicism, Reform Catholicism, Modernism: A Contribution to a New Orientation in Modernist Research.* Mainz, 1979.

Loth, Wilfried, ed. *Deutscher Katholizismus im Umbruch zur Moderne.* Stuttgart, 1991.

————. *Katholiken im Kaiserreich: Der politische Katholizismus in der Krise des wilhelminischen Deutschlands.* Düsseldorf, 1984.

Lutz, Heinrich. *Demokratie im Zwielicht. Der Weg der deutschen Katholiken aus dem Kaiserreich in die Republik 1914–1925.* Munich, 1963.

Lyttleton, Adrian. *The Seizure of Power: Fascism in Italy, 1919–1929.* London, 1973.

Machtan, Lothar. *The Hidden Hitler.* New York, 2001.

Madden, Paul. "Some Social Characteristics of Early Nazi Party Members, 1919–23." *CEH* 15 (1982).

Maier, Hans. "Political Religion: A Concept and Its Limitations." *TMPR* 8 (2007).

Maier, Hans, ed. *Totalitarianism and Political Religions: Concepts for the Comparison of Dictatorships*. New York, 1996.

Manstein, Peter. *Die Mitglieder und Wähler der NSDAP.1919–1933*. Frankfurt, 1988.

Marinoff, Irene. *The Heresy of National Socialism*. New York, 1941.

Maser, Werner. *Frühgeschichte der NSDAP: Hitlers Weg bis 1924*. Frankfurt, 1965.

———. *Hitler: Legende, Mythos, Wirklichkeit*. Munich, 1971.

Massing, Paul. *Rehearsal for Destruction: A Study of Political Antisemitism in Imperial Germany*. New York, 1949.

Mayring, Eva Alexandra. *Bayern nach der französischen Julirevolution: Unruhen, Opposition und antirevolutionäre Regierungspolitik 1830–1833*. Munich, 1990.

Mazura, Uwe. *Zentrumspartei und Judenfrage 1870/71–1933*. Mainz, 1994.

McElligott, Anthony. *Contested City: Municipal Politics and the Rise of Nazism in Altona, 1917–1937*. Ann Arbor, Mich., 1998.

McInerney, Ralph. *The Defamation of Pope Pius XII*. South Bend, Ind., 2001.

McKale, Donald. *The Nazi Party Courts: Hitler's Management of Conflict in His Movement, 1921–1945*. Lawrence, Kans., 1974.

McLeod, Hugh. "Weibliche Frömmigkeit, männlicher Unglaube? Religion und Kirche im bürgerlichen 19. Jahrhundert." In *Bürgerinnen*, ed. Frevert.

Means, P. B. *Things That Are Caesar's: The Genesis of the German Church Conflict*. New York, 1935.

Mennekes, Friedhelm. *Die Republik als Herausforderung: Konservatives Denken in Bayern zwischen Weimarer Republik und antidemokratischer Reaktion 1918–1925*. Berlin, 1972.

Mensing, Björn. "Hitler hat eine göttliche Sendung: Münchens Protestantismus und der Nationalsozialismus." In *Irrlicht*, ed. Prinz and Mensing.

———. "Der Münchener Protestantismus." In *Musenstadt*, ed. Prinz and Krauss.

———. *Pfarrer und Nationalsozialismus: Geschichte einer Verstrickung am Beispiel der Evangelisch-Lutherischen Kirche in Bayern*. Göttingen, 1998.

Mergel, Thomas. "Ultramontanism, Liberalism, Moderation: Political Mentalities and Political Behavior of the German Catholic Bürgertum." *CEH* 29 (1996).

———. *Zwischen Klasse und Konfession: Katholisches Bürgertum im Rheinland 1794–1914*. Göttingen, 1994.

Miesbeck, Peter. *Gründung, Organisation und Mitgliedschaft der Ortsgruppe Rosenheim der NSDAP 1920–1923*. Rosenheim, 2004.

Missalla, H. *"Gott mit uns": Die deutsche katholische Kriegspredigt 1914–1918.* Munich, 1968.

Mitchell, Allan. *Revolution in Bavaria 1918–1919: The Eisner Regime and the Soviet Republic.* Princeton, N.J., 1965.

Möckl, Karl. "Hof und Hofgesellschaft in Bayern in der Prinzregentenzeit." In *Hof, Kultur und Politik im 19. Jahrhundert,* ed. K. F. Werner. Bonn, 1985.

———. *Die Prinzregentenzeit: Gesellschaft und Politik während der Ära des Prinzregenten Luitpold in Bayern.* Munich, 1972.

Möller, Horst, et al., eds. *Nationalsozialismus in der Region.* Munich, 1996.

Mommsen, Hans. "Adolf Hitler und der 9. November 1923." In *Der 9. November: Fünf Essays zur deutschen Geschichte,* ed. Johannes Willms. Munich, 1994.

Moore, Barrington. *The Social Origins of Dictatorship and Democracy.* Boston, 1966.

Morrissey, Michael. *Consciousness and Transcendence: The Theology of Eric Voegelin.* Notre Dame, Ind., 1994.

Morsey, Rudolf. "Die deutschen Katholiken und der Nationalstaat zwischen Kulturkampf und Erstem Weltkrieg." *HJ* 90 (1970).

———. "Die katholische Volksminderheit und der Aufstieg des National-sozialismus." In *Die Katholiken und das Dritte Reich,* ed. K. Gotto and K. Repgen. Mainz, 1983.

Mosse, George. *The Crisis of German Ideology: Intellectual Origins of the Third Reich.* New York, 1961.

———. *Toward the Final Solution: A History of European Racism.* New York, 1978.

Muckermann, Friedrich. *Der deutsche Weg: Aus der Widerstandsbewegung der deutschen Katholiken.* Zurich, 1946.

Mühlberger, Detlef. *Hitler's Voice: The Völkischer Beobachter, 1920–1933.* 2 vols. Bern, 2004.

———. *The Social Bases of Nazis, 1919–1933.* Cambridge, 2003.

Müller, Winfried. "Zwischen Säkularisation und Konkordat: Die Neuord-nung des Verhältnisses von Staat und Kirche 1808–1821." in *Handbuch,* vol. 3, ed. Brandmüller.

Munro, Gregory. *Hitler's Bavarian Antagonist: Georg Moenius and the Allge-meine Rundschau of Munich, 1929–1933.* Lewiston, Maine, 2006.

Muth, Wulfried. *Carl Muth und das Mittelalterbild des Hochland.* Munich, 1974.

Nesner, Hans-Jörg. *Das Erzbistum München und Freising zur Zeit des Erzbischofs und Kardinals Franziskus von Bettingerk 1909–1917.* Munich, 1987.

Neumann, Franz. *Behemoth: The Structure and Practice of National Socialism.* Oxford, 1944.

Nipperdey, Thomas. *Religion im Umbruch: Deutschland 1870–1918.* Munich, 1988.

Noack, Hannelore. *Unbelehrbar? Antijüdische Agitation mit entstellten Talmudzitaten: Antisemitische Aufwiegelung durch Verteufelung der Juden.* Paderborn, 2001.

Noakes, Jeremy. *The Nazi Party in Lower Saxony, 1921–1933.* London, 1971.

Nusser, Horst. *Konservative Wehrverbände in Bayern, Preussen und Österreich 1918–1933: Dokumentenanhang.* Munich, 1973.

O'Meara, Thomas. *Church and Culture: German Catholic Theology, 1860–1914.* Notre Dame, Ind., 1991.

Orlow, Dietrich. *The History of the Nazi Party, 1919–1933.* Pittsburgh, Pa., 1969.

———. "The Organizational History and Structure of the NSDAP. 1919–23." *JMH* 37 (1965).

O'Shea, Paul. *A Cross Too Heavy: Eugenio Pacelli, Politics, and the Jews of Europe, 1917–1943.* Dural, 2009.

Osinski, Jutta. *Katholizismus und deutsche Literatur im 19. Jahrhundert.* Paderborn, 1993.

Padfield, Peter. *Himmler: Reichsführer SS.* London, 1990.

Parsons, Talcott. "Democracy and Social Structure in Pre-Nazi Germany." In Parsons, *Politics and Social Structure.* New York, 1969.

Patschovsky, Alexander. "Der 'Talmudjude': Vom mittelalterlichen Ursprung eines neuzeitlichen Themas." In *Juden in der christlichen Umwelt*, ed. A. Haverkamp. Berlin, 1992.

Pätzold, Kurt, and Manfred Weissbecker. *Adolf Hitler: Eine politische Biographie.* Leipzig, 1995.

Paul, Gerhard. *Die NSDAP des Saargebietes 1920–1935.* Saarbrücken, 1987.

Pauley, Bruce. *From Prejudice to Persecution: A History of Austrian Antisemitism.* Chapel Hill, N.C., 1992.

Pelz, William. *The Spartakusbund and the German Working Class Movement, 1914–1919.* Lewiston, Maine, 1988.

Persch, Martin. "Ernst Thrasolt." *BBKL* 11 (1996).

Peucker, Brigitte. "The Fascist Choreography: Riefenstahl's Tableaux." *Modernism/Modernity* 11 (2004).

Pfister, Peter. *Blutzeugen der Erzdiözese München und Freising: Die Märtyrer des Erzbistums München und Freising in der Zeit des Nationalsozialismus.* Munich, 1999.

Pfister, Peter, Susanne Kornacker, and Volker Laube, eds. *Kardinal Michael von Faulhaber 1869–1952.* Munich, 2002.

Phayer, Michael. *The Catholic Church and the Holocaust, 1930–1945.* Bloomington, Ind., 2000.

———. "The German Catholic Church after the Holocaust." *HGS* 10 (1996).

———. *Pius XII, the Holocaust, and the Cold War.* Bloomington, Ind., 2007.

———. "The Postwar German Catholic Debate Over Holocaust Guilt." *Kirchliche Zeitgeschichte* 8 (1995).

———. *Religion und das gewöhnliche Volk in Bayern in der Zeit von 1750 bis 1850.* Munich, 1970.

Phelps, Reginald. "Anton Drexler, der Gründer der NSDAP." *Deutsche Rundschau* 87 (1961).

———. "Before Hitler Came: Thule Society and Germanenorden." *JMH* 35 (1963).

———. "Hitler and the Deutsche Arbeiterpartei." *AHR* 68 (1961).

Piper, Ernst. *Alfred Rosenberg: Hitlers Chefideologe*. Munich, 2005.

———. *Kurze Geschichte des Nationalsozialismus von 1919 bis heute*. Hamburg, 2007.

Plewnia, M. *Auf dem Weg zu Hitler: Der "völkische" Publizist Dietrich Eckart*. Bremen, 1970.

Poewe, Karla. *New Religions and the Nazis*. New York, 2006.

Pohl, Karl-Heinrich. "Katholische Sozialdemokraten oder sozialdemokratische Katholiken in München: Eine Identitätskonflikt?" In *Religion*, ed. Blaschke and Kuhlemann.

———. *Die Münchener Arbeiterbewegung: Sozialdemokratische Partei, Freie Gewerkschaften, Staat und Gesellschaft in München 1890–1914*. Munich, 1992.

Pois, Robert. *National Socialism and the Religion of Nature*. New York, 1986.

Pörnbacher, Hans. "Katholische Literatur." In *Handbuch*, ed. Brandmüller.

Portmann, Heinrich. *Bischof Galen spricht!* Freiburg, 1946.

Pressel, Wilhelm. *Die Kriegspredigt 1914–1918 in der evangelischen Kirche Deutschlands*. Göttingen, 1967.

Pridham, Geoffrey. *Hitler's Rise to Power: The Nazi Movement in Bavaria, 1923–1933*. London, 1973.

Prinz, Friedrich, and Marita Krauss, eds. *München–Musenstadt mit Hinterhöfen: Die Prinzregentenzeit 1886–1912*. Munich, 1988.

Prinz, Friedrich, and Björn Mensing, eds. *Irrlicht im leuchtenden München: Der Nationalsozialismus in der "Hauptstadt der Bewegung."* Munich, 1991.

Probst, Robert. *Die NSDAP im Bayerischen Landtag 1924–1933*. Munich, 1998.

Proctor, Robert. *Racial Hygiene: Medicine under the Nazis*. Cambridge, Mass., 1988.

Pulzer, Peter. *The Rise of Political Anti-Semitism in Germany and Austria*. New York, 1964.

Puschner, Uwe. *Die völkische Bewegung im wilhelminischen Kaiserreich: Sprache–Rasse–Religion*. Darmstadt, 2001.

Puschner, Uwe, Walter Schmitz, and Justus Ulbricht, eds. *Handbuch zur "Völkischen Bewegung" 1871–1918*. Munich, 1996.

Raab, Heribert. *Joseph Görres (1776–1848): Leben und Werk*. Paderborn, 1985.

———. "Zur Geschichte des Schlagworts 'Ultramontan' im 18. und 19. Jahrhundert." *HJ* 81 (1962).

Redles, David. *Hitler's Millenial Reich: Apocalyptic Belief and the Search for Salvation*. New York, 2005.

Reiche, Eric G. *The Development of the SA in Nürnberg, 1922–1934*. Cambridge, 1986.

Reichel, Peter. *Der schöne Schein des Dritten Reiches: Faszination und Gewalt des Faschismus.* Munich, 1991.

Reinecke, Thomas, "Das Heilige Feuer: Eine katholische Zeitschrift 1913–1931." In *Handbuch*, ed. Puschner et al.

Reuter, Christiane. *Graue Eminenz der bayerischen Politik: Eine politische Biographie Anton Pfeiffers 1888–1957.* Munich, 1987.

Rhodes, James. *The Hitler Movement: A Modern Millenarian Revolution.* Stanford, Calif., 1980.

Richter, Ingrid. *Katholizismus und Eugenik in der Weimarer Republik und im Dritten Reich.* Paderborn, 2001.

Rissmann, Michael. *Hitlers Gott: Vorsehungsglaube und Sendungsbewusstsein des deutschen Diktators.* Zurich, 2001.

Rittner, Carol, and John K. Roth. *Pope Pius XII and the Holocaust.* London, 2002.

Rösch, Matthias. *Die Münchener NSDAP 1925–1933: Eine Untersuchung zur inneren Struktur der NSDAP in der Weimarer Republik.* Munich, 2002.

Rose, Detlev. *Die Thule-Gesellschaft: Legende, Mythos, Wirklichkeit.* Tübingen, 1994.

Rosmus, Anna. *Out of Passau: Leaving a City Hitler Called Home.* Columbia, S.C., 2004.

Ross, Ronald. *Beleaguered Tower: The Dilemma of Political Catholicism in Wilhelmine Germany.* Notre Dame, Ind., 1976.

Ruff, Mark Edward. "The Nazis' *Religionspolitik:* An Assessment of Recent Literature." *CHR* 92 (2006).

Ruppert, Karsten. *Im Dienst am Staat von Weimar: Das Zentrum als regierende Partei in der Weimarer Demokratie 1923–1930.* Düsseldorf, 1992.

Ruster, Thomas. *Die verlorene Nützlichkeit der Religion: Katholizismus und Moderne in der Weimarer Republik.* Paderborn, 1994.

Samuel, Richard, and Paul Kluckhorn, eds. *Novalis Schriften: Die Werke Friedrich von Hardenbergs.* Stuttgart, 1960.

Sauser, Ekkart. "Alban Schachleiter." *BBKL* 21 (2003).

Schärl, Walter. *Die Zusammensetzung der bayerischen Beamtenschaft von 1806 bis 1918.* Kallmünz, 1955.

Schatz, Klaus. *Zwischen Säkularisation und Zweitem Vatikanum: Der Weg des deutschen Katholizismus im 19. und 20. Jahrhundert.* Frankfurt, 1986.

Schieder, Wolfgang. "Die NSDAP vor 1933: Profil einer faschistischen Partei." *GG* 19 (1993).

Schlank, Christoph. *"Kölsch-katholisch": Das katholische Milieu in Köln.* Cologne, 2004.

Schlawe, Fritz. *Literarische Zeitschriften 1885–1910.* Stuttgart, 1961.

Schlossmacher, Norbert. "Antiultramontanismus im Wilhelminischen Deutschland: Ein Versuch." In *Umbruch*, ed. Loth.

Schmidt, Winfried. *" . . . war gegen den Führer äusserst Frech": Der Chefredakteur und nachmalige Tierarzt Hansjörg Maurer.* Würzburg, 1999.

Scholder, Klaus. *Die Kirchen und das Dritte Reich.* Frankfurt, 1977.

Schön, Herbert. *Die Entstehung des Nationalsozialismus in Hessen.* Mannheim, 1972.

Schönhoven, Klaus. *Die Bayerische Volkspartei 1924–1933.* Düsseldorf, 1972.

Schreiber, Gerhard. *Hitler: Interpretationen 1923–1983.* Darmstadt, 1984.

Schreiner, Klaus. "Wann kommt der Retter Deutschlands? Formen und Funktionen von politischem Messianismus in der Weimarer Republik." *Saeculum* 49 (1998).

Schröder, Oskar. *Aufbruch und Missverständnis: Zur Geschichte der reformkatholischen Bewegung.* Graz, 1969.

Schulz, Gerhard. *Aufstieg des Nationalsozialismus.* Frankfurt, 1975.

———. *Von Brüning zu Hitler: Der Wandel des politischen Systems in Deutschland 1930- 1933.* Berlin, 1992.

Schuster, George. *Like a Mighty Army: Hitler versus Established Religion.* New York, 1935.

Schwaiger, Georg, ed. *Aufbruch ins 20. Jahrhundert: Zum Streit um Reformkatholizismus und Modernismus.* Göttingen, 1976.

———, ed. *Das Erzbistum München und Freising im 19. und 20. Jahrhundert.* Munich, 1989.

———, ed. *Das Erzbistum München und Freising in der Zeit der nationalsozialistischen Herrschaft.* 2 vols. Munich, 1984.

———. *Das Herzogliche Georgianum in Ingolstadt, Landshut, München 1494–1994.* Munich, 1994.

———. "Kirche in der Zeitenwende: Die katholische Kirche Bayerns am Beginn des 20. Jahrhunderts." *Münchener Theologische Zeitschrift* 44 (1993).

Schwarz, Jürgen. *Studenten in der Weimarer Republik: Die deutsche Studentenschaft in der Zeit von 1918–1923.* Berlin, 1971.

Schwedt, Hermann. "Vom ultramontanen zum liberalen Döllinger." In *Geschichtlichkeit und Glaube: Zum 100. Todestag Johann Joseph Ignaz von Döllingers 1799–1890,* ed. Georg Denzler and E. L. Grasmück. Munich, 1990.

Schwend, Karl. *Bayern zwischen Monarchie und Diktatur: Beiträger zur bayerischen Frage in der Zeit von 1918 bis 1933.* Munich, 1954.

Seiler, Joachim. "Statistik des Erzbistums München und Freising in der ersten Hälfte des 20. Jahrhunderts." In *Herrschaft,* vol. 1, ed. Schwaiger.

Seipp, Adam. "Scapegoats for a Lost War: Demobiliation, the Kapp Putsch, and the Politics of the Streets in Munich, 1919–1920." *War and Society* 25 (2006).

Senninger, Gerhard. *Glaubenszeugen oder Versager? Katholische Kirche und Nationalsozialismus.* St. Ottilien, 2003.

Sigmund, Anna Maria. *Die Frauen und die Nazis.* Munich, 2004.

Skalnik, Kurt. *Dr. Karl Lueger: Der Mann zwischen den Zeiten.* Vienna, 1954.

Smith, Bradley F. *Heinrich Himmler: A Nazi in the Making.* Stanford, Calif., 1971.

Smith, Bradley F., and Werner Angress. "Diaries of Heinrich Himmler's Early Years." *JMH* 31 (1959).

Smith, Helmut Walser. *German Nationalism and Religious Conflict: Culture, Ideology, Politics, 1870–1914.* Princeton, N.J., 1995.

Sörensen, Christian. *Politische Entwicklung und Aufstieg der NSDAP in den Kreisen Husum und Eiderstedt 1918–1933.* Neumünster, 1995.

Spael, Wilhelm. *Das katholische Deutschland im 20. Jahrhundert.* Würzburg, 1964.

Speckner, Herbert. "Die Ordnungszelle Bayern: Studien zur Politik des bayerischen Bürgertums." Ph.D. diss., University of Erlangen, 1955.

Sperber, Jonathan. *The Kaiser's Voters: Electors and Elections in Imperial Germany.* Cambridge, 1997.

———. *Popular Catholicism in Nineteenth-Century Germany.* Princeton, N.J., 1984.

Spicer, Kevin, ed. *Antisemitism, Christian Ambivalence, and the Holocaust.* Bloomington, Ind., 2007.

———. *Hitler's Priests: Catholic Clergy and National Socialism.* DeKalb, Ill., 2008.

———. *Resisting the Third Reich: The Catholic Clergy in Hitler's Berlin.* DeKalb, Ill., 2004.

Spotts, Frederic. *Hitler and the Power of Aesthetics.* London, 2002.

Stachura, Peter. *Gregor Strasser and the Rise of Nazism.* London, 1983.

Stachura, Peter, ed. *The Shaping of the Nazi State.* London, 1978.

Steger, Bernd. "Der Hitlerprozess und Bayerns Verhältnis zum Reich 1923/24." *VfZ* 25 (1977).

Stehkämper, Hugo. *Konrad Adenauer als Katholikentagspräsident 1922: Form und Grenze politischer Entscheidungsfreiheit im katholischen Raum.* Mainz, 1977.

Steigmann-Gall, Richard. "Christianity and the Nazi Movement: A Response." *JCH* 42 (2007).

———. *The Holy Reich: Nazi Conceptions of Christianity.* Cambridge, 2003.

———. "Nazism and the Revival of Political Religion Theory." *TMPR* 5 (2004).

———. "Was National Socialism a Political Religion or a Religious Politics?" In *Nation und Religion: Beiträge zu einer unbewältigten Geschichte*, ed. Michael Geyer and Hartmut Lehmann. Göttingen, 2004.

Steinberg, Michael. *Sabers and Brown Shirts: The German Students' Path to National Socialism, 1918–1935.* Chicago, 1977.

Steinhoff, Anthony. "Ein zweites konfessionelles Zeitalter? Nachdenken über die Religion im langen 19. Jahrhundert." *GG* 30 (2004).

Steinhoff, Marc. *Widerstand gegen das Dritte Reich im katholischen Raum.* Frankfurt, 1997.

Stern, Fritz. *The Politics of Cultural Despair: A Study in the Rise of the Germanic Ideology.* Berkeley, 1961.

Sternhell, Zeev. *The Birth of Fascist Ideology: From Cultural Rebellion to Political Revolution.* Princeton, N.J., 1994.

———. *Neither Right nor Left: Fascist Ideology in France.* Princeton, N.J., 1996.

Stickler, Matthias. "Zwischen Reich und Republik: Zur Geschichte der studentischen Verbindungen in der Weimarer Republik." In *"Der Burschen Herrlichkeit": Geschichte und Gegenwart des studentischen Korporationswesens*, ed. H. H. Brand and M. Stickler. Würzburg, 1997.

Stitz, Peter. *Der CV.1919–1938: Der hochschulpolitische Weg des Cartellverbandes der katholischen deutschen Studentenverbindungen (CV) vom Ende des 1. Weltkrieges bis zur Vernichtung durch den Nationalsozialismus.* Munich, 1970.

Straub, T. "Adolf Hitler in Ingolstadt." In *Ingolstadt im Nationalsozialismus*, ed. Stadtarchiv Ingolstadt. Ingolstadt, 1995.

Strohm, Harald. *Die Gnosis und der Nationalsozialismus.* Frankfurt, 1997.

Strong, George. *Seedtime for Fascism: The Disintegration of Austrian Political Culture, 1867–1918.* Armonk, N.Y., 1998.

Stümke, Hans-Georg. *Homosexuelle in Deutschland: Eine politisch Geschichte.* Munich, 1989.

Swartout, Lisa. "Dueling Identities: Protestant, Catholic, and Jewish Students in the German Empire, 1890–1914." Ph.D. diss., University of California, Berkeley, 2002.

Tavernaro, Thomas. *Der Verlag Hitlers und der NSDAP: Die Franz Eher Nachfolger GmbH.* Vienna, 2004.

Taylor, Robert. *The World in Stone: The Role of Architecture in National Socialist Ideology.* Berkeley, Calif., 1974.

Thamer, Hans-Ulrich. "Faszination und Manipulation: Die Nürnberger Reichsparteitage der NSDAP." In *Das Fest: Eine Kulturgeschichte von der Antike bis zur Gegenwart*, ed. Uwe Schulz. Munich, 1988.

———. "Politische Rituale und politische Kultur im Europa des 20. Jahrhunderts." *Jahrbuch für Europäische Geschichte* 1 (2000).

Thoma, Emil, and Eugen Weiler, eds. *Die Geistlichen in Dachau.* Mödling, 1971.

Thoss, Bruno. *Der Ludendorff-Kreis 1919–1923: München als Zentrum der mitteleuropäischen Gegenrevolution zwischen Revolution und Hitlerputsch.* Munich, 1978.

Thränhardt, Dietrich. *Wahlen und politische Strukturen in Bayern 1848–1953.* Düsseldorf, 1973.

Tiedemann, Eva-Maria. "Die frühe politische Formierung des Antisemitismus." In *Musenstadt*, ed. Prinz and Krauss.

Toland, John. *Adolf Hitler.* London, 1976.

Trippen, Norbert. *Theologie und Lehramt im Konflikt: Die kirchlichen Massnahmen gegen den Modernismus im Jahre 1907 und ihre Auswirkungen in Deutschland.* Freiburg, 1977.

Tröster, Werner. "Die besondere Eigenart des Herrn Dr. Pieper! Dr. Lorenz Pieper, Priester der Erzdiözese Paderborn, Mitglied der NSDAP Nr. 9740." In *Das Erzbistum Paderborn in der Zeit des Nationalsozialismus*, ed. Ulrich Wagener. Paderborn, 1993.

Turner, Victor. *Image and Pilgrimage in Christian Culture: Anthropological Perspectives.* New York, 1978.

———. "Religious Paradigms and Political Action." In Turner, *Dramas, Fields, and Metaphors: Symbolic Action in Human Society.* Ithaca, N.Y., 1974.

———. *The Ritual Process: Structure and Anti-Structure.* Chicago, 1968.

Tyrell, Albrecht. "Gottfried Feder and the NSDAP." In *Shaping,* ed. Stachura.

———. *Vom Trommler zum Führer: Der Wandel von Hitlers Selbstverständnis zwischen 1919 und 1924.* Munich, 1975.

———. "Wie er der 'Führer' wurde." In *Hitler heute,* ed. Knopp.

Ulbricht, Justus. "'Veni Creator Spiritus' oder 'Wann kehrt Baldur heim'? Deutsche Wiedergeburt als völkisch-religiöses Projekt." In *Politische Religion,* ed. Ferber.

Ullrich, Susanne. "Die Revolutions- und Inflationszeit in Rosenheim." In *Rosenheim in den zwanziger Jahren,* ed. Kulturamt der Stadt Rosenheim. Rosenheim, 1987.

Vanden Heuvel, Jon. *A German Life in the Age of Revolution: Joseph Görres, 1776–1848.* Washington, D.C., 2001.

Verhey, J. *The Spirit of 1914: Militarism, Myth, and Mobilization in Germany.* Cambridge, 2000.

Vieler, Eric. *The Ideological Roots of German National Socialism.* New York, 1999.

Vogel, Wieland. *Katholische Kirche und nationale Kampfverbände in der Weimarer Republik.* Mainz, 1989.

Vondung, Klaus. *The Apocalypse in Germany.* Oxford, 2000.

Vryan, K. D., et al. "Identity." In *Handbook of Symbolic Interactionism,* ed. Larry Reynolds and Nancy Herman-Kinney. Lanham, Md., 2003.

Wagner, Christoph. *Entwicklung, Herrschaft und Untergang der nationalsozialistischen Bewegung in Passau 1920 bis 1945.* Berlin, 2007.

Waite, Robert G. L. *Vanguard of Nazism: The Free Corps Movement in Postwar Germany, 1918–1923.* Cambridge, Mass., 1959.

Webb, Eugene. *Eric Voegelin: Philosopher of History.* Seattle, Wash., 1981.

Weber, Christoph. *"Eine starke, eingeschlossene Phalanx": Der politische Katholizismus in der erste deutsche Reichstagswahl 1871.* Essen, 1992.

———. *Kirchliche Politik zwischen Rom, Berlin und Trier 1876–1888.* Rome, 1970.

———. "Ultramontanismus als katholischer Fundamentalismus," in *Umbruch,* ed. Loth.

Weber, Christoph, ed. *Liberaler Katholizismus: Biographische und kirchenhistorische Essays von Franz Xaver Kraus.* Tübingen, 1983.

Wehler, Hans-Ulrich. *The German Empire, 1871–1918.* Leamington Spa, England, 1985.

Weichlein, Siegfried. *Nation und Region: Integrationsprozesse im Bismarckreich.* Düsseldorf, 2004.

———. *Sozialmilieus und politische Kultur in der Weimarer Republik.* Göttingen, 1996.

Weikart, Richard. *From Darwin to Hitler: Evolutionary Ethics, Eugenics, and Racism in Germany.* New York, 2004.

Weindling, Paul. *Health, Race, and German Politics between National Unification and Nazism, 1870–1945.* New York, 1989.

Weiss, Otto. *Der Modernismus in Deutschland: Ein Beitrag zur Theologiegeschichte.* Regensburg, 1995.

———. *Die Redemptoristen in Bayern 1790–1909: Ein Beitrag zur Geschichte des Ultramontanismus.* St. Ottilien, 1983.

———. "Der Ultramontanismus: Grundlagen, Vorgeschichte, Struktur." *ZBL* 41 (1978).

Wesseling, Klaus-Gunther. "Hugo Koch." *BBKL* 4 (1992).

Whiteside, Andrew. *Austrian National Socialism before 1918.* The Hague, 1962.

———. *The Socialism of Fools: Georg Ritter von Schönerer and Austrian Pan-Germanism.* Berkeley, 1975.

Widdig, Bernd. *Culture and Inflation in Weimar Germany.* Berkeley, Calif., 2001.

Wiggermann, Karl-Friedrich. "Evangelische Katholizität: Leonhard Fendt als Liturg und Liturgiewissenschaftler." Ph.D. diss., University of Erlangen, Nürnberg, 1981.

Wilhelm, Hermann. *Dichter, Denker, Fememörder: Rechtsradikalismus und Antisemitismus in München von der Jahrhundertwende bis 1921.* Berlin, 1989.

Windell, George. *The Catholics and German Unity, 1866–1871.* Minneapolis, Minn., 1954.

Wiwjorra, Ingo. "Die deutsche Vorgeschichtsforschung und ihr Verhältnis zu Nationalismus und Rassismus." In *Handbuch*, ed. Puschner et al.

Wolf, Hubert, ed. *Antimodernismus und Modernismus in der katholischen Kirche: Beiträge zum theologiegeschichtlichen Vorfeld des II. Vatikanums.* Paderborn, 1998.

Wolff, Charlotte. *Magnus Hirschfeld: Portrait of a Pioneer in Sexology.* London, 1986.

Zahn, Gordon. *German Catholics and Hitler's Wars.* New York, 1964.

Zalar, Jeffrey. "Knowledge and Nationalism in Imperial Germany: A Cultural History of the Association of Saint Charles Borromeo." Ph.D. diss., Georgetown University, 2002.

Zipfel, Friedrich. *Kirchenkampf in Deutschland 1933–1945.* Berlin, 1965.

Zoller, Andreas. "Der Landschaftsmaler Edmund Steppes (1873–1968) und seine Vision einer 'Deutschen Malerei.'" Ph.D. diss., Braunschweig, 1999.

Zuccotti, Susan. *Under His Very Windows: The Vatican and the Holocaust in Italy.* New Haven, Conn., 2000.

Zwicker, Stefan. *Nationale Märtyrer, Albert Leo Schlageter und Julius Fucik: Heldenkult, Propaganda und Erinnerungskultur.* Paderborn, 2006.

Index